WHAT IS A DISASTER?

WHAT IS A DISASTER?

New Answers to Old Questions

Ronald W. Perry

E.L. Quarantelli

Editors

Copyright © 2005 by International Research Committee on Disasters.

Library of Congress Number:		2004195094
ISBN :	Hardcover	1-4134-7986-3
	Softcover	1-4134-7985-5

All rights reserved. No part of this book may be reproduced or transmitted in any form or by any means, electronic or mechanical, including photocopying, recording, or by any information storage and retrieval system, without permission in writing from the copyright owner.

This book was printed in the United States of America.

To order additional copies of this book, contact:
Xlibris Corporation
1-888-795-4274
www.Xlibris.com
Orders@Xlibris.com
27509

CONTENTS

Contributors 11
Forward 13
Introduction 19

PART I

1: **An Interpretation Of Disaster In Terms Of Changes In Culture, Society And International Relations**
   David Alexander 25

2: **Are We Asking The Right Question?**
   Susan L. Cutter 39

3: **Disaster: A "Reality" Or Construct"? Perspective From The "East"**
   Rohit Jigyasu 49

4: **What's A Word? Opening Up The Debate**
   Neil R. Britton 60

5: **Not Every Move Is A Step Forward: A Critique Of David Alexander, Susan L. Cutter, Rohit Jigyasu And Neil Britton**
   Wolf R. Dombrowsky 79

6: **The Meaning Of Disaster: A Reply To Wolf Dombrowsky**
   David Alexander 97

7: Pragmatism And Relevance:
A Response To Wolf R. Dombrowsky
Susan L. Cutter 104

8: Defining The Definition For Addressing The "Reality"
Rohit Jigyasu 107

9: Dog Or Demon?
Neil R. Britton 113

PART II

10: Disaster And Collective Stress
Allen H. Barton 125

11: From Crisis To Disaster:
Towards An Integrative Perspective
Arjen Boin 153

12: Disaster: Mandated Definitions,
Local Knowledge And Complexity
Philip Buckle 173

13: In The Eyes Of The Beholder? Making
Sense Of The System(s) Of Disaster(s)
Denis Smith 201

14: Disaster, Crisis, Collective Stress,
And Mass Deprivation
Robert Stallings 237

15: A Response To Robert Stallings: Ideal Type Concepts
And Generalized Analytic Theory
Allen H. Barton 275

16: Back To Nature? A Reply To Stallings
Arjen Boin 280

17: Response To Robert Stallings
    Philip Buckle 286

18: Through A Glass Darkly: A Response To Stallings
    Denis Smith 292

PART III

19: Disasters, Definitions And Theory Construction
    Ronald W. Perry 311

20: A Social Science Research Agenda For The Disasters
    Of The 21st Century: Theoretical, Methodological And
    Empirical Issues And Their Professional Implementation
    E. L. (Henry) Quarantelli 325

Bibliography 397

LIST OF TABLES

Table 1. Globalization, modernity and their
        implications for disaster 207
Table 2. Elements of the crisis timeline 219

LIST OF FIGURES

Figure 1. Disaster: towards an initial construction 209
Figure 2. Elements of disaster research 214
Figure 3. Towards a root definition of disaster 223
Figure 4. Shifting definitions of the disaster
         process in three stages 225
Figure 5. Space-place-time and the development
         of disaster potential 228
Figure 6. Learning and the incubation
         process within disasters 229
Figure 7. Issues for disaster research 235

In memory of
Fred Bates and Ritsuo Akimoto,
Disaster Research Pioneers

CONTRIBUTORS

David Alexander is Scientific Director of the Region of Lombardy School of Civil Protection, based in Milan, Italy. [the.catastrophe@virgin.net]

Allen H. Barton was for many years a Professor of Sociology and Director of the Bureau of Applied Social Research at Columbia University, and has retired to North Carolina at 118 Wolf's Trail, Chapel Hill, NC 27516 USA. [allenbarton@mindspring.com]

Arjen Boin is an Assistant Professor at the Department of Public Administration, Leiden University, The Netherlands. [Boin@fsw.leidenuniv.nl]

Neil R. Britton is Team Leader (International Disaster Reduction Strategies Research) and EqTAP Project Chief Coordinator, at the Earthquake Disaster Mitigation Research Centre, National Research Institute of Earth Sciences and Disaster Prevention, Kobe, Japan. [neil@edm.bosai.go.jp].

Philip Buckle is a Senior Lecturer in the Coventry Centre for Disaster Management, Coventry University, Priory Street, Coventry CV1 5FB United Kingdom. [p.buckle@coventry.ac.uk]

Susan L. Cutter is a Carolina Distinguished Professor and Director of the Hazards Research in the Department of Geography at the University of South Carolina, Columbia, SC 29208 USA. [scutter@sc.edu]

Wolf R. Dombrowsky is Director of the Katastrophenforschungsstelle (KFS) [Disaster Research Unit], Christian-Albrechts-Universität zu Kiel, Olshausenstraße 40, Kiel D-24098, Germany. [wdombro@soziologie.uni-kiel.de]

Rohit Jigyasu is a conservation architect and planner and visiting faculty in the Department of Architectural Conservation, School of Planning and Architecture, New Delhi, India. [rohitjigyasu72@yahoo.com]

Ronald W. Perry is Professor of Public Affairs in the School of Public Affairs, Arizona State University, Tempe, Arizona 85287 USA [ron.perry@asu.edu]

E. L. Quarantelli is Emeritus Professor at the Disaster Research Center, University of Delaware, Newark, Delaware 19716, USA. [elqdrc@udel.edu]

Denis Smith is Professor of Management and Director of the Management School at the University of Liverpool, United Kingdom. [denis.smith@liverpool.ac.uk]

Robert A. Stallings is Professor of Public Policy and Sociology, Program in Public Policy, School of Policy, Planning, and Development, University of Southern California, Los Angeles, California 90089-0626, USA. [rstallin@usc.edu]

FORWARD

T. Joseph Scanlon
Professor Emeritus and Director,
Emergency Communications Research Unit,
Carleton University
Ottawa, Ontario, Canada

On the morning of September 11, 2001, I received a phone call from Canada's public radio system, the CBC, asking me to comment on the terrorist attack on the United States. I said among other things that New York City had enormous resources and that these resources would give it the resilience needed to cope with and recover from the events of that day. My host was to say the least skeptical. Mesmerized by the visuals of the planes hitting the towers and the towers collapsing, she was—at least at that moment—incapable of grasping the concept of resilience or of what Susan Cutter might call an "affordable disaster".

This volume—*What is a Disaster? Perspectives on the Question*—is the fourth volume in our series of books on disaster, the second to tackle the definition of disaster. Reading it, I was struck by how much of the debate was—or so it seemed to me—influenced by awareness of various events and how much of that awareness was media related. That was of course especially true of 9/11, an event which most, but not all of the contributors to this volume, felt compelled to mention, and an event that was not even in the back of our minds when the first volume was published, yet an event that has changed the way many think about disaster. As Neil Britton writes: " . . . the fundamentals of conventional organized emergency management are now about fifty years old. During that period, the practice of emergency management has changed from an essentially reactive and response-focused command-and-control civil defence approach, which grew out of the 1940s World War II and 1950s Korean War eras, phased into a comprehensive and integrated approach during the late 1970s, and from the 1990s started to re-emerge around the twin concepts of risk management and sustainable hazard mitigation." However, recent events connected with highly organized terrorist attacks in different parts of the world, most notably in the USA whereby a strong reaction has resulted in its lead disaster agency being subsumed into a federal homeland security mega-department, might see this latest transformation being short-lived in favour of a replay of earlier cycles.

Ron Perry makes the importance of 9/11 similarly clear: "As we move into the new century, the experience with terrorism has challenged both governments and disaster researchers. In the United States, all levels of government have invested substantial resources in emergency management, with much of that devoted to terrorism consequence management. With the investment of resources, governments expect more from the community of disaster researchers. To answer such questions regarding the need for and implementation of warning systems, appropriate mitigation measures, tactics for response and recovery, researchers need to have a firm grasp on what a disaster is and what it is not."

There is no question 9/11 has become important in our struggle to find an acceptable definition of disaster. Yet reading this book made me reflect not so much on 9/11 and its significance but on the agenda setting role of the mass media in determining what we think about and write about. Everett Rogers and Rahul Sood raised this issue when they discussed the way American media—in fact most of the world's media—ignored the Sahel drought. Phil Buckle touches on it when he mentions the attention given to the heat wave that led to 10,000 deaths in France in 2003. "There is now [Buckle writes] broad acceptance at political and community levels that heat waves are disasters. But heat waves have been with us since time immemorial. So why the change now to move heat wave from a weather condition to a disaster?" The role of media possibly—but this begs the question—why were the media interested? Why is heat wave now a disaster when a year ago it was not? Eric Klinenberg's book *Heat Wave* underlines the importance of this question. Though the heat wave in Chicago costs more lives than the Northridge earthquake, Hurricane Andrew or the bombing at Oklahoma City, there were many debates in Chicago newsrooms about its news value and whether it was truly a disaster. Certainly, Barton makes clear that the absence of media attention explains why some events have not become significant in our attempts to explain how we perceive disaster:

Media coverage of human suffering in countries with authoritarian regimes is subject to government censorship and control of both domestic and outside news media. The outstanding example is the largest famine in modern history in which somewhere around 30,000,000 Chinese died in 1958-61 as a result of Maoist mismanagement. The famine was kept secret within the country and from the outside world, and indeed the highest levels of government refused to accept information on it and continued to demand extraction of food from the starving areas. Other examples of "secret famines" come from the Stalinist dictatorship in the Soviet Union. In the 1930s the government created the Ukraine famine to wipe out peasant resistance to collectivization, and a similar famine right after World War II, in both of which millions died under conditions of secrecy and state terror. The British colonial government imposed wartime censorship on the Bengal famine of 1943 in which over 2,000,000 died, to avoid pressure to divert resources from the war effort. Around 3 million are estimated to have died in the North Korean famines in the 1990s under conditions of secrecy and suppression of information.

Strangely, I also thought of the media when I read Wolf Dombrovsky's story of the old Chinese tale about an Emperor. "One day [the Emperor] asked his court artist, 'What is easy to paint and what is difficult to paint?' The courtier thought hard on this for as long as he knew his master's tolerance would permit and replied, 'Dogs are difficult, but demons are easy.' The courtier explained further to his Emperor that obvious things are hard to get right because everyone knows all about them and hence everyone thinks they know what the essence of a dog is. However, since no one has actually seen a demon then drawing one is easy, because who can say it is not correct."

I once did an examination of reporting textbooks and one thing that became evident was that there is no accepted definition of the term, "news." In fact there was not only massive disagreement among the authors about what the term meant a number simply gave up on the task of definition. At the best they concluded, "News is what an editor says it is," a useful but not very illuminating definition. We are, in short, not alone in struggling to define a seemingly commonplace term. Yet the media seem sometimes to force us into definitions that are adjusted to those events we know or think we know.

All those who read this book will probably notice some references more than others partly because of their own awareness of the world. Just as this book stimulated me to think about the mass media and the problems Journalism scholars have had with definitions, others will think about other concerns. In that way, this book will have achieved its goal—to make us think about disaster. Ron Perry explains why that is important: "The variation observed among researchers permits one to assess the extent and the conceptual dimensions along which the field of study is growing and changing. Second, the discussion of disaster definitions encourages refinement of the concept of disaster. It enables the reader and the authors to reflect on their definitions and trace through the consequences of those definitions for different aspects of the field of disaster study, whether academic or applied. As we sharpen our conception of disaster, we identify the disciplinary niches and their value in a field that is almost inherently interdisciplinary. The extent to which we are able to identify and manage disasters of the future is contingent upon our collective understanding of the meaning and dimensions of the concept."

In a way this book reflects the work of the first and third

generation of scholars in the field of disaster study. I am aware of course that many consider the pioneer to be Samuel Henry Prince with his study of the 1917 Halifax explosion. I am also aware of the recent work Russ Dynes has done on Voltaire and Alexander Pope and others and their appraisals of the significance of the 1775 Lisbon earthquake.

But I think all of us would agree that our field took off roughly 40 years ago with Russell Dynes and Henry Quarantelli and the creation of the Disaster Research Center. One of their students was Bill Anderson and one of his students at Arizona State University was none other than Ron Perry. In fact—and I am relying on the memory of others here—when Ron first became Bill's student he was the only undergraduate allowed into the graduate section of a course on Collective Behavior. [He was also the best in the class.] Historically, that means Ron became the first scholar in our field to have been the student of a student of Russell Dynes and Henry Quarantelli, in short our first third generation scholar. Now he and Quarantelli have teamed up.

I noted the important contribution Henry Quarantelli has made to our field in the foreword to the first version of *What is a Disaster?* and was delighted to do so again at the celebration we had for him and Russell Dynes at the DRC last spring. I have not had the chance until now to say anything in writing about Ron Perry. I first worked with Ron when he was in Seattle shortly after Mount St. Helens but only got to know him well when I was President of the International Research Committee on Disasters and he was editor of the *International Journal of Mass Emergencies and Disasters*. It was a wonderful relationship, one that makes me not the least surprised to note how many scholars he has worked with. Ron maintained his editorial independence and integrity but at the same time was supportive. And when the time came for him to move on we together were fortunate enough to be able to choose a wonderful successor in Bob Stallings. But what most of you will not know if that our relationship was defined not just by mutual respect and goodwill but by a document—a written definition of the role of the editor and the editor's relationship to the President of the IRCD. And that document—this should come as no surprise—was written by none other than Henry Quarantelli. I want to thank both Bob Stallings and Benigno Aguirre for allowing me to stay on as general editor of this series of books because of the opportunity it has given me to say thanks to both Henry and Ron for their contributions to our field of which this book is only the latest example.

INTRODUCTION

This volume represents the second book devoted to the issue of definitions of disasters, and the first to deal with this topic in the International Research Committee on Disasters book series. The first book—*What is a Disaster? Perspectives on the Question*—appeared in 1998 and brought together thirteen contributors and discussants from six countries and nine academic disciplines. The goal for the second book is the same as that for the first: select an interdisciplinary, international collection of disaster researchers and ask them to present their definition of disasters. In both volumes the selection of authors followed a philosophy of gaining wide variation, rather than attempting any sort of random or representative sampling. The principal product of both books is an examination of meaning, as well as the exchange of ideas, with respect to disaster as a phenomenon of study. Ultimately, the purpose of course is to emphasize the exchange, not to promote any particular definition. The exercise of defining and then discussing definitions addresses several important issues in both research and application. First, it enables one to gage the consensus about what disasters are both among researchers and between researchers and practitioners. The authors in this volume go far to differentiating the use of disaster definitions as a basis for government action versus as a basis for identifying a field of study. The variation observed among researchers permits one to assess the extent and the conceptual dimensions along which the field of study is growing and changing. Second, the discussion of disaster definitions encourages refinement of the concept of disaster. It enables the reader and the authors to reflect on their definitions and trace through the consequences of those definitions for different aspects of the field of disaster study, whether academic or applied. As we sharpen our conception of disaster, we identify the disciplinary niches and their value in a field that is almost inherently interdisciplinary. The extent to which we are able to identify and manage disasters of the future is contingent upon our collective understanding of the meaning and dimensions of the concept. Finally, there is a strong policy side to this work. As we move into the new century, the experience with terrorism has challenged both governments and disaster researchers. In the United States, all levels of government have invested substantial resources in emergency management, with much of that devoted to terrorism consequence management. With the investment of resources, governments expect more from the community of disaster researchers. To answer such questions regarding the need for and implementation of warning systems, appropriate mitigation measures, tactics for response and recovery, researchers need to have a firm grasp on what a disaster is and what it is not. This is especially relevant to the issue of comprehensive emergency management and integrated emergency management systems as promoted in the United States. To say that an "in place" system (for mitigation, preparedness, response or recovery) that works for one "disaster" will also work for another requires that one know about the comparability and "types" of disasters.

This volume is structured to follow the first book. Authors were asked to present their definition of disaster and explain it, and in addition to react to the definitions offered by authors in the first volume. The eight contributors were paired with one of two discussants. Wolf Dombrowsky, a German Sociologist by training, was asked to react to the papers created by David Alexander, Susan L. Cutter, Rohit Jigyasu and Neil Britton. David Alexander teaches in England and was trained as a geographer and geologist. Dr. Cutter is an American Geographer, Dr. Jigyasu is an architect and planner, and Dr. Britton is a social scientist with broad applied experience at the national level in disaster management. In Part I, each contributor presents their discussion, followed by Dr.

Dombrosky's critique; the discussion closes with reaction papers to the critique by each author.

Part II of the book presents the definitional statements by four additional authors. Allen Barton is a sociologist and pioneer in the field of disaster studies. Arjen Boin is a professor of public administration, Philip Buckle is professor of disaster management and Denis Smith a professor of management. Robert Stallings, professor of sociology and public policy serves as discussant for this group. This part also closes with reactions from each author to Dr. Stallings' critique.

The book closes with Part III, which contains two papers. Perry reviews the efforts of the contributors and discussants in this book and examines conceptual definitional differences among them and implications for theory construction. Quarantelli's paper is more broad ranging and focuses upon the current state of the field and scenarios for the future. The purpose of this closing paper is to explore the field of disaster research and define an agenda for study in the twenty-first century. He identifies and examines critical questions in the areas of theory, methodology and professional implementation.

Ronald W. Perry
Tempe, Arizona

E. L. (Henry) Quarantelli
Newark, Delaware

PART I

1

AN INTERPRETATION OF DISASTER IN TERMS OF CHANGES IN CULTURE, SOCIETY AND INTERNATIONAL RELATIONS

David Alexander

On average about 220 natural catastrophes, 70 technological disasters and three new armed conflicts occur each year (IFRCRCS 2002). Calamity is thus a recurrent feature of human life. Bearing in mind that the temporal distribution of extreme events of all kinds tends to be irregular, at the world scale, an "average" day would see two or three disasters in their emergency phases, 15-20 in their recovery periods, and about a dozen conflict-based emergencies in progress. Catastrophe is exceptional for the people involved, but at a grander scale it is almost run-of-the-mill, even more so given the recurrent spatial patterns that characterise it. Even at the local scale, extreme events can be routine (see Jeffrey 1981).

Not only is disaster common—and increasingly so—it is an extraordinarily revealing sort of affliction. It can be interpreted in various ways as a window upon the inner workings of society. To begin with, any failure to mitigate hazards is shown up in their impacts. Second, corruption is exposed by bringing its consequences to light, for example in the collapse of a badly-built structure during an earthquake. Third, human relations are made more explicit and conspicuous by the increased levels of socialization that commonly occur in the immediate aftermath of disaster. In this respect, people's attitudes and preferences are revealed (Rogers and Nehnevajsa 1984). Fourth, the spotlight is turned on ways of life that have been threatened or disrupted. As a result, cultural traits may be accentuated and subjected to scrutiny by outsiders (Gherardi 1998).

Models and interpretations of disaster abound, but the phenomenon is so multi-faceted that a general theory of universal explanatory power is unlikely ever to be formulated. Moreover, changes in society and economy (dare one call them evolution?) continually alter the tenets and controlling parameters of disaster. For this reason, it is important periodically to revisit the question "what is disaster?" in the light of current concerns. This chapter will therefore examine various thematic interpretations of calamity—perceptual, symbolic, socio-economic and strategic—in relation to world events and current developments in society. It will seek out the connections between them. First, however, I will begin with a word about definitions.

A DEFINITIONAL MINEFIELD

Some years ago I identified six distinct schools of thought and expertise on disasters (Alexander 1993: 13-14). They can be classed broadly as geography, anthropology, sociology, development studies, health sciences and the geophysical sciences with engineering. Possibly social psychology can be added as a seventh. Not all of these fields have made a serious attempt to define disaster before studying it. Indeed, many researchers have either taken the definitions for granted or have side-stepped the issue.

The explanations and definitions given by Quarantelli and his colleagues in the first symposium and book entitled *What is a Disaster?* (Quarantelli 1998b) are so varied and detailed that they are practically impossible to summarise in brief. All that can be said is that these authors have chosen to define disaster as something that is mostly social in character. Quarantelli himself argued (1998c: 236) that we define disaster intuitively. Gilbert (1998: 11) regarded it, among other things, as the passage to a state of uncertainty. Following Fritz (1961), who interpreted disaster as a state in which the social fabric is disrupted and becomes dysfunctional to a greater or lesser extent, Fischer (2003: 94) suggested that "What *disaster sociologists* actually study is social (structure) change under specialised circumstances" (his italics). Several of the authors in Quarantelli's book seem to bear this out (e.g. Porfiriev 1998: 72), but the definitions are very tentative and mostly rather specific to the sociological perspective on disasters. Would geophysical scientists and engineers accept them?

Perhaps they ought to, as the following comparison suggests. The Sherman landslide in Alaska, a direct consequence of the 1964 earthquake in that state, involved 29 million cubic meters of rock that slid at 180 km/hr into an uninhabited valley (Shreve 1966). Except from the point of view of local flora and fauna, the event was a mere geological curiosity, discovered by accident during a routine aerial photography over flight. In contrast, the Aberfan landslide of 1966 in South Wales was 193 times smaller and moved 25-30 times more slowly, but it killed 144 people, 116 of them small children. It was a major disaster and led to decades of hardship for bereaved survivors (Austin 1967). This implies that physical magnitude is not necessarily very useful to our attempts to develop a general definition of disaster.

Three important questions related to the definition problem are as follows. (1) At what point do routine emergencies pass a quantitative threshold or go through a qualitative change and become disasters? (2) Is a catastrophe a large disaster, and if so, how large? (3) What functional attributes turn an emergency into a disaster? It would be interesting to see whether physical and social scientists have the same answers to these questions. It is pretty clear that the sociologists would look for the solutions in the form, function and mutation of the social system. Most engineers would have at least a rough, intuitive idea of the physical forces (relative to earthquakes, explosions, crashes, etc.) that would be required to cause major disruption to the social system. Their advice is often more central to policy formulation than are those of social scientists who are more able to predict the actual human consequences. But despite the current vogue for examining the societal implications of engineering (Zebrowski 1997), there is little evidence that social and physical scientists are on the same wavelength and would arrive at a common perspective.

Rather than seeking to resolve the definitional problem, in this chapter I will take up a theme discussed by Hewitt (1998) in Quarantelli's book: that of equity in disaster. My aim here is to explore the ways in which our view of the phenomenon should be adapted to accommodate the perspectives of the most severely affected victims, as more than ever before disaster is becoming a question of social equity and manipulation of society (Bankoff 2001).

FIXITY OF PERCEPTION: DISASTER AS MINDSET

Whereas much has been written about the perception of hazard, risk and disaster (Saarinen et al. 1984), little attention has been devoted to disaster as *mindset*, fixity of opinions or states of mind created by events. Regularities in perception are usually considered to be dependent upon consensus (i.e., the mean of individual experiences), which implies a certain freedom of interpretation (Rubonis and Bickman 1991), but what happens when the consensus is manufactured?

The terrorist attacks in the United States on 11 September 2001 ushered in a new era of emergency preparedness in the world's richer countries. It seems logical to assume that the outrages did not change the essence of disaster itself, but perhaps the matter is not quite so simple (Alexander 2002a). The attacks were a watershed in both official and public perception of disaster and they changed the focus of preparedness (Calhoun et al. 2002). The picture that has emerged is that of a large and powerful nation under threat, and a significant number of people, organizations and governments engaged in a gigantic conspiracy to threaten it. Some would even regard it as a clash of civilizations (Huntington 1996). As a strategic reality this generalization may not survive critical analysis, especially as it relies upon maintaining a widespread ignorance of history, both ancient and modern. But for many world leaders it is a convenient fiction, for it endows international relations with a new form of polarity to replace that lost when the Soviet bloc crumbled and the Chinese started to liberalize their economy.

Whether or not it has adopted the right approach towards international relations, the United States of America has shown a genius for organization. The U.S. federal agencies responsible for emergency management have provided a model for the rest of the world (Sylves and Waugh 1996). It is a remarkably progressive model in which the foundations have been laid to tackle one of the great challenges of the 21st century: how to involve ordinary people democratically in preparation for and management of emergency situations, and thus devolve more of the responsibility for public safety to the actual stakeholders (Platt 1999). Thus, civil protection has evolved out of civil defense. Flexible, collaborative forms of the local management of incidents has supplanted monolithic command and control procedures.

However, disaster is not defined by fixed events, or immutable relationships, but by social constructs, and these are liable to change. The new U.S. model that other countries may begin to emulate is, of course, the homeland security one (CSIS 2000). Natural disaster management is once again subsumed into a command-and-control structure in which secrecy and authoritarianism are ever-present risks. At the time of writing, the full implications of homeland security have not yet become clear, but they could easily mean greater rigidity in the approach to extreme events, both conceptually and operationally (Alexander 2002b). At the very least, around the world national priorities seem to have shifted from "neutral" threats, such as earthquakes and floods, to teleological ones, in which deliberate harm is done. This can be judged as mindset if it does not reflect an objective assessment of what is likely to happen.

DISASTER AS SYMBOLISM

Any other collective view of disaster, whether it be a rigid one such as a mindset or a more pluralistic one, is achieved by converting complex events into symbolic ones (Kroll-Smith and Couch 1991). Thus one arrives at models in which phenomena are endowed with meaning. In order to interpret the symbolism of disaster, it is useful to distinguish between individual and collective viewpoints (Dynes and Quarantelli 1976). For the survivor, a catastrophic event is a milestone in his or her life and something that for better or worse will help define the rest of it. Individually, disaster brings people back to the basics of survival, deprivation, injury or bereavement (Erickson 1994). Except perhaps for the chronically imprudent, or for hopelessly disadvantaged people, it graphically demonstrates the apparent arbitrariness of fate. On a more positive note, it may mark a high point of social participation through involvement in the so-called "therapeutic" or "altruistic" community (Barton 1969). Of course, Cuthbertson and Nigg (1987) and Olson and Drury (1997) have questioned the universal applicability of Barton's original concept of the therapeutic community in disaster. For some people, perhaps too few, such social participation represents a direct lesson in the value of hazard and risk mitigation.

With these differences in mind, we may divide the symbolism of disaster into three categories: *functional* (i.e., symbolic of physical or social process), *linguistic* (i.e., a convenient form of notation), and *as an allegory or parable* (i.e., with a tale to tell, possibly of a moral kind). In reality, symbolic views of disaster can be endowed with more than one of these attributes. For example, disaster may be regarded as a punishment, a wake-up call or a betrayal of trust in safety systems (Horlick-Jones 1995), all of which are both functional and allegorical representations. In western societies, there is an increasing tendency to equate disaster with notions of recrimination, scapegoats, negligence and culpability, ideas that have strong moral overtones (Olson 2000). In this process, societies attempt to neutralise fear of disaster through anger and blame. It contrasts with the older, more conventional symbolism in which disaster is seen as a sudden reminder of one's own mortality and the impermanence and precariousness of life:

> And Hell the Shadow of a Soul on fire,
> Cast on the Darkness into which Ourselves,
> So late emerg'd from, shall so soon expire.
>   [*Rubayyat of Omar Khayyam*, LIV,
>   trans. Edward FitzGerald, 1859]

Nothing could be more symbolic than the disaster memorial book, a publication, usually dominated by eye-catching photographs, put together hastily after a particular event and sold mainly in the region affected by the disaster it portrays. Such books are quite common, at least in western societies, and are a perishable record of the events that form their subject matter. A typical example would seek to portray the following aspects of the disaster:\

- the enormity of the event;
- the paradoxical beauty—or at least the visual novelty—of destruction;
- the courage of rescuers;
- humanity reasserted amid terrible physical destruction;
- the pathos of charity and solidarity;
- the triumph of moral purpose over arbitrariness or malevolence;
- the value of determination and staying power;
- the wonder of an indomitable spirit.

As there is seldom much intellectual or analytical depth in such books, they rely heavily on symbolism, which according to the above list uses the functional aspects of disaster to make points that are heavily moral. In the visual images there is often a heavy dose of iconography. Thus in the Florence floods of 1966 the tattered remains of Cimabue's crucifix (circa AD 1284) symbolised the event, especially as that particular work of art was already symbolic of age-old suffering. In New York on September 11, 2001, the jagged screens of lattice-work girders which were all that remained standing of the World Trade Centre towers powerfully symbolised destruction, precariousness and impermanence.

But symbolism changes over time, even with respect to a single event. Symbols thus form markers in the long process of rationalizing a disaster progressively over time, in which the details become hazy and the event gradually loses its grip on people's imagination. The explosions against blue skies that characterised both the May 18, 1980, eruption of Mount St Helens and the attack on the World Trade Centre assume a different significance as they lose their immediacy. They become rather flatter and less suggestive icons, overlain with meanings that accrete during the recovery phase and thereafter (cf. Cross 1990).

Two aspects of symbolism deserve special mention. First, until the 20th century there was very little Darwinism in catastrophe (Alexander 2000: 67). There was little sign of the survival of the fittest building, community, administration, emergency service or infrastructure. To a certain extent, with the endless resurgence of vulnerability, this is still true in the 21st century, as socio-economic inequality continues to grow throughout the world. This implies that good examples of mitigation have had little symbolic value in history (for example, it took 500 years for a short-stubby, earthquake-proof minaret to appear in Turkey, one of the world's most seismic countries). Given the pervasive need to mitigate the recurrent effects of disaster, this is a singular omission, especially as items destroyed have often been heavily endowed with meaning and symbolism.

Rather different is the symbolic value of the victim in modern society (Lifton 1980). Due partly to mass media constructs and partly to the growing culture of blame, victims who survive disaster assume the status of beneficiaries and acquire a degree of moral authority. If they are articulate and well-organized they can become significant players, perhaps even points of reference, in the debates that follow extreme events (Mulwanda 1992). Certainly, in the mass media victims are now often seen as being as authoritative as are technical experts. It is hard to determine whether this shows the democratization of disaster or some kind of inversion of values.

DISASTER AS SPECTACLE

In the modern world the meaning of disaster cannot easily be dissociated from how it is portrayed and interpreted by the mass media (Couch 2000). In the popular culture shaped by and reflected in the media, news is essentially whatever people are interested in. Newsworthiness is defined by people's interest level. Disaster assumes a symbolic value as spectacle, as a story or saga, or as competition, imbued with notions of the breakdown of society, the spread of anarchy, heroic leadership and villainous malevolence. At worst, such crude notions can descend to the level of voyeurism, analogous to watching a spectacular crash at a motor race. Above all, when there is a lack of personal experience to relate it to, an event may become associated with the distillates or stereotypes of popular culture.

Such shallowness is very much in the interests of the main providers of information who are increasingly the same commercial oligarchies that, through intensive lobbying, have done much to shape the political process (Smith 1992). At its most negative, modern journalism reports facts selectively to suit partisan or commercial objectives, seldom explains causes adequately, simplifies events until they are deprived of real meaning, and conflates entertainment values with real-life ones until they become indistinguishable. To obtain an accurate and objective picture of situations requires much reading and comparison between reports. The symbolic aspects of disaster can easily lead one away from real understanding.

Newsworthiness also depends on the systems of values held in common between the purveyors and consumers of news (Goltz 1984). In the western world we see an increasing primacy of the entertainment industry in public communication. News and entertainment are often conflated, or at least given equal weight. Though people are interested in history, current affairs and environment, they seem increasingly willing to accept versions of events that lack depth. In the disasters field, there is no sign of an end to the antagonism of popular culture and academic research. For decades the latter has striven to debunk the model of the breakdown of society in disaster. In this, mass panic and flight occur, chaos and anarchy prevail, antisocial and competitive behaviour proliferate, populations are stunned and made helpless by sudden shock, and authoritarianism is the only means of restoring calm and reason (Mitchell et al. 2000).

The primacy of image in the mass media does little to encourage subtlety of interpretation. The breakdown of society remains extraordinarily persistent in the western public's mind, as this model is continually reinforced by the products of mass entertainment. Conspiracy theorists may argue that this very convenient for the forces that command society, as it prepares the ground for Draconian measures, should homeland security require them to be used. Whether nor not that is so, globalization drives both the diffusion of media stereotypes of disaster and the real patterns of change in the impacts of extreme phenomena.

DISASTER AS A CONSEQUENCE OF GLOBALIZATION

More than ever before, natural, technological and social disasters are becoming internationalised. They are intertwined with the course of human affairs in ways that were unimaginable decades ago. The rapid global movement of capital and standardization of information, the importance of disaster to geo-strategic policies, and the multinational growth of poverty and marginalization all have a bearing on our interpretation of calamity in the modern world (Dembo et al. 1990). Disaster occurs against the background of three separate worldwide tendencies:

- the onset of global change, which for the present purposes means the possibility of more frequent or higher magnitude natural hazard events;

- the rise of globalization, which could signify mo[re] frequent or higher magnitude exploitation, given [its] tendency to concentrate power and wealth in the ha[nds] of international corporations and oligarchies;
- the emergence of global consciousness in the form of a collective, international attempt to fight injustice.

Although the alignments that prevailed during the Cold War (1948-89) have changed, it appears that it may take 15 years or more to shape the new pattern of global strategic alliances. Currently it is not clear what the final balance of power and interests will be. Capital has scored many victories over labor (hence the second point, above), but there are signs of a resurgence in popular consciousness in response to the excesses of capitalistic exploitation (hence the third).

I suggested above that the contemporary challenge is to democratize society's responses to risk and disaster. However, there are two kinds of democracy, not one. In the present day we have become used to the idea that democracy should take its representative form by allowing people to choose and vote periodically for candidates at elections. This idea has been vigorously fostered in western society by the mass media and has proved convenient to the ruling oligarchies in that many people tend to demonstrate innate conservatism in their choice of candidates and political ideologies. It is wrongly supposed that representative democracy is part of a tradition invented in the city-states of Greece more than 2500 years ago. In fact, democracy was born in its participatory form, which is now regarded by the rich and powerful as "subversive," because it involves direct collective action.

If, for the purposes of argument, we consider representative democracy to be "top-down" in its organization and participatory democracy to be "bottom-up" or grass-roots based, then there is clearly a need for more of the latter in disaster mitigation and management throughout the world, for risks and emergencies cannot be tackled effectively without robust local organization.

In fact, the Western mass media have put about the idea that participatory democracy is inimical to representative democracy, which it undermines. In reality, the two are complementary: democracy cannot be healthy unless it is both participatory and representative. Three aspects of modern western presidential and parliamentary democracies suggest that they have become insalubrious: first, people have become disaffected and, in many cases, disinclined to vote; secondly, corruption in high places has become very hard to stem, which points to a lack of accountability; and thirdly, industrial and commercial lobbies seem to have gained as much power as the voters have. Therefore it is hardly surprising that resilience to disaster has only increased, where it has increased at all, painfully slowly: in many places it lacks the essential democratic base.

It is axiomatic that socio-economic stability is a pre-condition for resilience against disaster. Instead, increased militarization has had the effect of fragmenting and factionalizing peoples, as in Colombia, Liberia, Somalia and Angola. A divide and rule strategy has preserved the West's global hegemony. But this is beginning to look fragile. It is possible that people of entirely different persuasions who are disaffected with the course of globalization will eventually find common cause.

Clausewitz wrote that war is politics carried on by other means. Others have since suggested that economics, more than politics, are at the root (Atmore 2001). If this is true, then global polarization is a response to economic forces which create and maintain the forms of deprivation that foster ideological struggle. Globalization has resulted in increasingly vast expenditures on defending particular interests, especially the main sources of crude oil exported to North America and Europe. The Persian Gulf War of 1991, for example, is reputed to have cost $692 billion (1992 dollars) in short term expenditures on military action (Hillel 1994). Policies leading to containment or regime change in Iraq have, at the time of writing, met with only limited success but have been extremely expensive.

There seems to be no better example of lack of resilience to disaster than that of Afghanistan. The rural and provincial areas of the country, perhaps Kabul too, appear to be stuck at the lowest level of mitigation and highest level of vulnerability. With regard to one of the country's most frequent kinds of natural disaster, the earthquake, for the overwhelming majority of the population all the achievements in seismic engineering and civil protection of the last hundred years might as well never have happened. There is no sign that progress has been made in protecting the population since the magnitude 8.1 earthquake of 1907 that killed 12,000 Afghanis. Over most of the twentieth century lethal earthquakes have occurred in the Hindu Kush at the rate of one every nine years, but in the period 1993-2002 there were nearly 10,000 deaths in five events—once every two years. The trend is towards larger, more lethal seismic disasters: the average magnitude is 6.3, but twice as many people are killed as are significantly injured, a clear sign of the severity of disasters or the heightened nature of vulnerability in Afghanistan. The country is populated by an inter-ethnic society. It slides towards the contemporary model of "war lordism" by a process of vicious circles within vicious circles: internal factions thrive because of the existence of external divisions between the forces that have intervened in Afghanistan (Atmore 2001). This, of course, is a disaster in its own right, and it adds up to the complete stagnation of measures to reduce the impact of other prevalent forms of disaster, such as earthquake and landslide.

Many traditional societies still face up to the scourge of disaster with religiously-inspired fatalism (Sims and Baumann 1972). Catastrophe is once again an "Act of God", a punishment for sins committed, part of an inscrutable higher plan. Are we to call this retrograde, a sign of cultural underdevelopment? Such means of rationalizing disaster are coping mechanisms and we might judge whether or not they are effective ones. Certainly the symbolism involved is no worse than that constructed by the western media (Vitaliano 1973, frontispiece).

CONCLUSION

Disasters are rationalized or interpreted according to the canons and preoccupations of the contemporary period. Modern interpretations are increasingly dominated by the new forms of symbolism constructed by the mass communication industry (Lombardi 1997). These encourage a shallow view of history and strategic relationships, and thus a superficial approach to causality. Instead, one needs to search for the explanations of disaster in the global changes that are currently altering the scope and tenor of international relations (Anderson 1997). On aggregate, vulnerability to disaster is set to rise with the increasing polarization of a world in which two billion people have practically no access to modern technology and 800 million live in conditions of misery. As yet they have little collective voice, but that cannot be true forever, as present trends are unsustainable.

The foregoing discussion implies very strongly that disasters in the modern world are an artifact of two forces: commercialism and strategic hegemonies inherent in globalization. At the broadest scale that may be true, though it does not preclude more traditional interpretations based on primary vulnerability (Blaikie et al. 1994), or more optimistic ones based on globalism (Kelman and Koukis 2000). Perhaps one reason why "disaster" will probably never be completely, immutably defined is because the definition depends on shifting portrayals and perceptions of what is significant about the phenomenon. I would argue that it must be interpreted, and continually reinterpreted in the context of contemporary issues.

NOTES

[1] "Der Krieg ist nichts als eine Fortsetzung des politischen Verkehrs mit Einmischung anderer Mittel." War is nothing but a continuation of politics with the admixture of other means. Karl von Clausewitz (1780-1831) Vom Kriege (1832-4) book. 8, chapter 6, section B.

2

ARE WE ASKING THE RIGHT QUESTION?

Susan L. Cutter

In his landmark volume, *What is a Disaster?*, Quarantelli (1998b) lamented the state of theory building and conceptual development the disasters field. In his imperturbable manner, Quarantelli challenged the community to come to some conceptual closure regarding the nature of a disaster—was it fundamentally a social construction, some physical event, or a combination of the two? As he stated, " . . . unless we clarify and obtain minimum consensus on the defining features per se, we will continue to talk past one another on the characteristics, conditions and consequences of disasters (Quarantelli 1998b:4)."

I submit that disasters studies (as recognized in the 1998 volume) are spending too much time and intellectual capital in defining the phenomena under study, rather than in researching more important and fundamental concerns of the field. The question is not what is a disaster, but what is our vulnerability (and resiliency) to environmental threats and extreme events? In other words, what makes human and environmental systems vulnerable and more or less resilient to threats and extreme events? As conceptual frameworks, vulnerability and resiliency imply an examination of human systems, natural (or environmental) and technological systems, and the interconnectedness between them. It is, in fact, the linkages and interdependencies between these three systems and the built environment that amplify or attenuate vulnerability. While each component can be studied independently, it is the interaction that becomes most important in understanding vulnerability, resiliency, and their correlates. To use the old adage, the whole (vulnerability) is greater than the sum of its parts (human systems, the built environment, technological systems, natural systems).

TALKING PAST EACH OTHER

It has always been a source of professional frustration that as the risk, hazards, and disasters communities evolved along parallel paths, there was little intersection and integration of knowledge between them (Cutter 2001a). White (1988) noted this communication and intellectual divide more than a decade ago, when he opined that the risk analysis field failed to include the social context within which risks occurred, a fundamentally important element for social scientists. With a few rare exceptions, there is very little crossover in literature, concepts, and methodologies among these three communities who study disasters (Kunreuther and Slovic 1996). Simply put, we rarely read each other's work unless it is in our own academic discipline (e.g. geography, sociology, planning) or in our own hazard specialty domain (e.g. earthquakes, floods, hazardous technologies). Why is this?

The segregation of the research community is due to a number of factors, among them differences in the type of event examined (natural hazards, technological risks, industrial failures); methods employed (qualitative versus quantitative analyses, computer modeling and simulations versus survey interviews); and outlets for research findings (*Risk Analysis, International Journal of Mass Emergencies and Disasters, Natural Hazards Review, Environmental Hazards, Disasters*). In many ways, the risk, hazards, and disasters communities could not (and still do not) fully understand each other's "science". How are we ever going to advance social science perspectives on risk, hazards, and disasters if we are unaware of the totality of social science perspectives that can be brought to bear? There are many critical challenges that confront the disaster research and practitioner communities. How we approach them will dictate the relevance of disaster studies in the future. Will the field be mired in the depths of ontological debates on the meaning of disaster, risk, hazards, and vulnerability? Or, will the field forge ahead with new understandings of how these phenomenon affect the human condition, how human agency increases or decreases their temporal and spatial distribution, and how individuals, social groups, and society at large perceives of and responds to external threats, regardless of their origin?

REFLEXIVE SOCIETIES AND ADAPTIVE THREATS

The centrality of risk in modern society pervades everyday life—from the food that we eat, to the water we drink, to the air we breathe, to where we live and work. We live in a global risk society (Beck 1992; Adam, Beck and Van Loon 2000), one that is influenced by a myriad of global processes, many of which interact to produce unforeseen dangers and an endless array of risks. The range and diversity of threats that face modern society are too numerous to catalog and they constantly change. Some arise from the intersection of human use and natural systems, which in turn are exacerbated by social practices such as construction in known floodplains or along coastal margins (Heinz Center 2002). Others are seemingly random events, by-products of locational choices, decisions often constrained by class (Davis 1998), privilege (Pulido 2000), and gender (Fothergill 1996, Enarson and Morrow 1998). Some threats are perpetuated over time and across space creating a disaster culture replete with unsustainable practices. Others like human-induced threats, such as terrorism, are equally complex, yet they entail even greater challenges in detection, warning, and response because of their adaptive nature. There is little constancy to the threat, which is highly responsive to changing conditions and opportunities in both targets and methods. If detected, the terrorist simply changes the preferred target, location, method of delivery, or scale of the attack. Under these conditions, it is very difficult to assess all the known points of vulnerability within modern systems, systems that in turn give rise to and ultimately produce the global risk society.

The global extent of risks (and disasters and hazards) does not imply that they are equally distributed among all places or among all social groups. Often, they are also influenced by societal needs and wants, which are quite variable as well. The reflexive nature of the risk society (influences risk production and is influenced by risks) suggests a need to move away from analyses (and control strategies) based on singular events with proximate causes (somewhat akin to a simple cause and effect model) toward a more dynamical understanding of the global interdependence of human, natural, and technological systems. The interaction of these systems in untold ways produces risks, hazards, and disasters, or what some term, complex emergencies. Some are controllable, others are unintended; some have spatial-temporal limits, while others are simply accepted by those affected. The scare of the week or hazard *de jour* approach to the disasters field is rapidly becoming passé. In its place, we see a more complicated and nuanced set of explanations that help us to understand how, where and why human intervention 1) changes the way in which individuals and societies cognize and detect threats, 2) reduces the initiating sources and root causes of threats, 3) mediates vulnerability to threats, and 4) improves resiliency and responses to threats.

POST-SEPTEMBER 11th

The world was significantly altered by the events of September 11, 2001 in both incalculable and measurable ways. The trio of events on that day—airline crash in Pennsylvania, airline projectile into the Pentagon, and the collapse of the World Trade Center in New York City—were clearly disasters. There is no debate about that. Disaster researchers were mobilized and dispatched into the field to examine a wide range of post disaster event responses (Natural Hazards Research and Applications Information Center 2003). These field studies included an examination of student responses in New York City (Peek 2002); the development of emergent organizations in the crisis response (Tierney 2002), mental health impacts (Sattler 2002), institutional warnings and response (Grant et al. 2002; Rubin and Renda-Tenali 2001); and the role of geographic information technologies and digital disaster assistance in the rescue and relief efforts (Thomas et al. 2002; Michaels 2001). This is what the community does extremely well—applications of our social science in understanding the immediate disaster situation and assisting in recovery operations. What we don't do as well or as consistently is examining the historical antecedents (Alexander 2002), or underlying conditions (or root causes) that produced such an unexpected event in the first place (Blaikie et al. 1994).

Why didn't we foresee the events of 9/11 occurring? How did we become so vulnerable in the first place? How can we reduce our vulnerability and make society, the built environment, and the natural world more resilient in the face of unanticipated, unexpected, and unknown threats? How do we move beyond the singular disaster or disaster situation to a more robust understanding of local conditions and the geography of the everyday that gives rise to crises in the first place? What conceptual frameworks and organizational structures are required to anticipate and respond to human-induced deliberate threats? Can we build a more secure homeland with increasing security without reductions in privacy, civil liberties, and trust in democratic institutions?

I have intentionally conflated the terms to make the point. Disasters research, thus far, has failed in responding to many of these questions, but this is precisely how a shift in our orientation towards vulnerability science can assist and advance our thinking. So where do we begin? How do we identify non-structural vulnerabilities in society? How do we understand our vulnerability to the unknown? What theoretical constructs are required to address vulnerability from a social science perspective?

A PARADIGM SHIFT

A number of researchers have commented on the need for a redirection of risk, hazards, and disasters research into understanding vulnerability and reorienting disaster policy (Comfort et al. 1999; Cutter 2001b, 2003). Science, as a 20th century construct has lost some of its explanatory power in anticipating and understanding unexpected events. Questions surrounding applied versus basic science (Stokes 1997), science as a driver for technological change, and science in support of public policy have increased science's own vulnerability as the dominant explanatory paradigm. This has lead some to question whether we've reached the limits of scientific explanation (Horgan 1996). For example, one of the most powerful weapons in the terrorist arsenal is fear. How do we understand the social consequences of fear in modern society and what does this tell us about individual and collective willingness to respond to and recover from disasters? One of the conclusions of the National Research Council's (2002) post-September 11th study, *Making the Nation Safer*, was a need for better understanding of human systems—how people respond to crises and threats; how they reduce their vulnerability to them; what social conditions give rise to terrorist threats in the first place. Yet, the contributions from the disasters research community are conspicuous by their absence or unknowing misinterpretation.

In responding to the events of 9/11, the geographical community developed a research agenda on the geographical dimensions of terrorism (Cutter et al. 2003) and highlighted a number of research themes focusing on variability in the root causes, geo-spatial technologies, and hazards research including vulnerability. Many of the research questions that were identified transcend disciplinary boundaries and thus form a core set of topics that warrant further investigation by the research community interested in risk, hazards, and disasters as well as vulnerability science (Cutter 2001b, 2003). These broad domains are listed below:

> *Root causes/driving forces*—Identification of the root causes, underlying conditions, and driving forces that amplify or attenuate vulnerability across social groups, over time, and through space.
> *Risk transference*—Role of current policies and practices in transferring threat burdens from one social group to

another or from one institution to another, transfer[e] of threat burdens from one generation to ano[ther] (generational inequity), and risk relocation (sp[atial] transference from one region or place to another).

Dynamic models—Advancements in risk, hazards exposure, and consequences modeling that link events to impacts (biophysical and social) and to causal factors in dynamic ways.

Vulnerability/resiliency indicators—Development of relative indicators of vulnerability to enable comparisons among social groups and/or places.

Decision making under uncertainty—Enhanced understanding of individual and collective decision making processes, especially those decisions made under high levels of uncertainty.

Perception-behavioral linkages—Role of fear, emotions, trust, personal responsibility, and altruism in risk perception, risk sharing, and disaster response.

Capturing surprise—Incorporate surprise, uncertainty, and adaptability into models of understanding human responses to disasters and unexpected events.

Emergence and convergence—Role of emergent technologies, organizations, social groups in anticipatory planning for and response to disasters, role of convergence in response, and conditions that support adaptive behaviors during crises.

Universality and replication—Movement beyond localized case studies and after-event analyses to broader generalizations of human responses to environmental threats and unexpected events utilizing both qualitative and quantitative analytical techniques.

AFFORDABLE DISASTERS?

Disaster research was conceived as an applied subject—an effort to engage the sociological community in responding to an external threat, initially viewed as warfare and then later expanded into disaster studies (Gilbert 1998; Quarantelli 1988b). This public policy orientation is one of the great strengths of the field and is as important today as it was fifty years ago, perhaps more so.

The United States has a set of policy constructs that enable the federal government to assist state and local communities in the aftermath of a natural hazard or unexpected event. Largely codified and implemented under the auspices of the Robert T. Stafford Disaster Relief and Emergency Assistance Act (commonly known as the Stafford Act) disaster policy in the U.S. essentially begs the question of what is a disaster? As defined in the legislation, a major disaster

> . . . means any natural catastrophe (including hurricane, tornado, storm, high water, wind driven water, tidal wave, tsunami, earthquake, volcanic eruption, landslide, mudslide, snowstorm, or drought), or, regardless of cause, any fire, flood, or explosion, in any part of the United States, which in the determination of the President causes damage of sufficient severity and magnitude to warrant major disaster assistance under this chapter to supplement the efforts and available resources of States, local governments, and disaster relief organizations in alleviating the damage, loss, hardship, or suffering caused thereby (FEMA 2003).

As many have suggested (Platt 1999; Downton and Pielke 2001), the mechanism for declaring Presidential disasters (and thus determining what is a major disaster) is essentially a political process, not a determination based on a consistent definition or clear-cut criteria. Are disasters the same for all places? How do we know whether they are or are not?

Some communities are more resilient to environmental hazards and unexpected events than others. This resiliency is derived, in part, from individual wealth and financial health; human resources and social networks; infrastructure age and density; adequate planning, mitigation, and preparedness; local governance; and the site and situation (absolute and relative location) of communities. A million dollar loss in Miami-Dade County, Florida, for example, might be expensive and devastating to the individuals who incurred the loss, but in fact might be quite "absorbable" within the existing financial setting of the county. It might even spur a rise in economic growth given the need to rebuild and recover. If this same million-dollar loss was to occur in eastern North Carolina, say in Edgecombe County (where Princeville, a historic African American community hard hit by Hurricane Floyd is located), it could prove devastating to the community. Edgecombe County had a local economy based on slave labor and plantation agriculture (cotton and tobacco). The declining agricultural base, the county's rural nature devoid of any industrial development, the above average levels of poverty, and the below average levels of educational attainment all contribute to Edgecombe's vulnerability and weaken its ability to respond in the aftermath of a disaster such as Hurricane Floyd. At what point does an event overwhelm local capacity to respond and recover? Is this point the same for all communities and all states? Should there be a minimum threshold of disruption, lives lost, property damage to even qualify as a disaster, regardless of where you are? Similarly, are some disasters affordable while others are not, and if so, according to whom? How might the concept of an "affordable disaster" be manifested socially, economically, politically, temporally, and spatially?

These questions require sound social scientific responses to help us understand the socioeconomic and demographic differences among communities and how this influences their vulnerability and resiliency to environmental threats. Perhaps a differential system of qualification (with minimum thresholds, and triaged based on local capacities) for Presidential disaster declarations might be warranted rather than a one-size-fits-all model, which is subject to political whim and favoritism, and the continued irresponsibility of state and local governments. Disaster studies and broader-based social science perspectives will be important in helping to reformulate disaster policy in the U.S. This type of research is what the community should be pursuing, not examining semantic differences in our terminology.

CONCLUSIONS

While it is important to advance conceptual and theoretical understanding of the field, we also must be vigilant to apply this knowledge in the solution of real-world concerns and every day issues. The prescriptive agenda suggested here will position the field to undertake the requisite research on the "big unanswered" questions in disaster studies, while at the same time enhancing our capabilities to inform policy makers and local responders on the human dimensions of disasters and emergency response. It is difficult to do one without the other.

We are facing a future full of pessimism. The events of September 11, 2001, as tragic as they were, provided a newly found respect for the social sciences, especially those engaged in risk, hazards, and disasters research. We must capitalize on this and turn our knowledge base and practical experience into addressing some of the most vexing issues in the next decade. The motivating question for this new paradigm is not *what is a disaster*, but rather *what makes people and places vulnerable (and resilient) to environmental threats and unexpected events?*

3

DISASTER: A "REALITY" OR CONSTRUCT"? PERSPECTIVE FROM THE "EAST"

Rohit Jigyasu

Disaster is a term, which has been defined, understood and packaged by the so-called "experts" to an extent that disaster reduction has become merely a problem solving exercise. The definers declare what they perceive as a problem and how they intend to solve it (Dombrowsky 1998: 19). Gilbert (1998: 11) has classified numerous theoretical approaches to disasters into three main paradigms:

The first is disaster as a duplication of war (catastrophe can be imputed to an external agent; human communities are entities that react globally against aggression). The second is disaster as an expression of social vulnerabilities (disaster is the result of underlying community logic, of an inward and social process). The third is disaster as an entrance into a state of uncertainty (disaster is tightly tied into the impossibility of defining real or supposed, especially after the upsetting of the mental frameworks we use to know and understand reality).

Disaster has been viewed in its extended scope and definition by taking into account all these perspectives and together these form the basis on which disaster vulnerability is understood and defined. The bottom line of all these paradigms is that disaster is

49

supposed to represent total or near total breakdown of local systems. Ironically, the dilemma with all these paradigms is that while on one hand they define disaster as an objective reality, on the other hand measures to reduce disaster seem to be so far from reality, that in most cases one finds that disaster vulnerability is increasing at very fast pace. Dombrowsky (1998:19) rightly states that emancipation of the field from everyday knowledge and from the practical needs of disaster management has been neglected during the phase of its establishment.

This leads us to ask several questions. Has disaster lost touch with the reality? If yes, why this is so? What is this reality, after all? Is there anything that we can say is universally "real" or reality itself is a construct, specific to shared values, thinking processes and visions of the groups of people—which we call communities. Many or rather most of the times, these values, thinking processes and visions are consciously or sub-consciously shaped by religious philosophies, which have broadly or rather vaguely been categorized as "western" and "eastern". The latter is primarily based on Hinduism and Buddhism, two great religions that originated in South Asian subcontinent. In this chapter, I will make an attempt at understanding the "reality" of disaster from "eastern" perspective.

Let us begin by discussing the main aspects, which help us define the scope and extent of the "reality" of disaster. Dombrowsky (1998) sees disaster as the outcome of a scientific tradition that is "concentrated in time and space", implying that disaster has mainly two types of "reality;" the spatial and the temporal. In the following sections, I will discuss each of these in detail with respect to spatial and temporal connotations in "eastern" way of thought

DISASTER: A "SPATIAL" REALITY

Disaster has clear geographical connotations with defined extent and boundaries. In fact space characterizes key local factors that trigger disasters. These include natural hazards such as earthquakes that a particular space is exposed to. Also it is characterised by local vulnerability processes at a particular point of time. to say, space is also defined by the natural resources ava not to forget the people who inhabit that particular intervene over time to create a distinct cultural landscape. Disaster adversely affects the natural and human resources characterising the space and creates sudden disruption in the local processes defining human environment relationships in that particular space. All these aspects help us to spatially delimit disasters.

Now let us understand how space is understood and defined in an "eastern" way of thought. The physical manifestation remains the same, as this is the reality which human senses can perceive, irrespective of social, cultural or religious background. However, in eastern thought, such a physical manifestation gets directly linked to the understanding at sub-conscious level, which give shape and deeper meaning to the landscape. Such a landscape is constructed through symbolic representations, sometimes even representing the whole cosmos at the micro level (Galtung 1979; Vatsayan 1994). This has clear philosophical connotations, which I would not pursue in detail. However, the main point is that space—its elements and processes—is no longer "real", but in fact a "construction" at one or more levels of consciousness, which we will discuss later in detail.

This forces us to go beyond our traditional understanding of disaster as a spatial reality and view it as a phenomenon, which has impact deeper than visual. Its comprehension goes deeper for its effect on human perceptions. Disaster is no longer bounded by the physical boundaries; rather it extends deeper into human consciousness, extending much beyond physically perceived boundaries. The psychological impact of this is very deep. It is much deeper than one can expect, not only shaping the way people perceive the cause of disasters but also the way they respond to it. Interestingly, similar kinds of symbolical associations shape the perceptions and response actions as the ones, which give meaning to the space in the first place. However, there is always a limit to what our senses and the tools available can measure and these in fact pose a limit to individual ability of comprehension.

DISASTER: A "TEMPORAL" REALITY

Our understanding of disasters is also linked to temporal dimensions. In fact the changing theoretical paradigms of disaster mentioned before are very much linked to the notion of time. The perception of disaster as an "event" implies that disaster has a point of beginning and an end. Therefore we categorize disaster situations with reference to the event in focus; before, during and after disasters. This also determines disaster management actions as prevention or mitigation (before), emergency response (during) and long term rehabilitation and development (after), which together form part of disaster management cycle. When viewed this way, disaster has periods of onset, development and finally an end One wonders, if it begins at a moment in time and stops at another moment; the moment being the smallest possible unit in time scale, which our senses or available tools can visualise. While considering disaster this way, we view time in a linear scale. (Jigyasu 2002)

However the "eastern" notion of time is cyclic; an endless cycle of birth and death, creation and destruction, implying that there is no beginning or an end (Galtung, 1979; Vatsayan, 1994). When seen from this perspective, disasters repeat themselves as part of this endless cycle of creation and destruction. Although, this seems to be compatible with widely accepted disaster management cycle, the division of cycle into clearly demarcated phases, is very much part of the "reality" that we construct for the sake of comprehension. However, when we dissolve these thresholds which distinguish one phase from another, disaster is a continuum; a part of the continuous complex process, which cannot be clearly distinguished.

Another interesting aspect of this continuum is that the cyclic process is not really a cycle, as we do not return to the point from where we begin. This is because nothing is permanent. All things change. One has to work hard to reach salvation (Buddha, 543BC). Our actions and thinking processes can change the point of return in a way that we return but not exactly at the same point. It is part of our evolution process in a cyclic loop (and not a cycle). So we discover that even the "reality" of time is what we "construct" for the sake of comprehension.

THE "EXPERIENTIAL" DIMENSION

Now that we are breaking boundaries between "reality" and "construct", I would like to bring in the third dimension, which is crucial in our understanding of disaster but has often been overlooked. This is "experiential" dimension, which is inherently linked to our cognition levels determined by three modes of comprehension, namely conscious (visible), sub-conscious (hidden) and unconscious (invisible) modes. In fact, the "spatial" and "temporal" constructs that we discussed before get their enlarged meanings when we adopt a holistic view combining these three modes, each of which I will discuss briefly.

The visible *pratakshya* refers to the tangible aspect, which is mostly physical. The world itself is an illusion and its material content is completely destructible. The illusion is created to confuse oneself from the right path of God. The *Maya* or illusion seduces one into the "worldly materialist aspects away from God and the real experience and thus all tangible aspects are of no or very little importance (Gupta 2003). This mode of comprehension is most easily and clearly measured by our senses.

The hidden, covered, *adrishya* is the second level where one starts recognizing the illusion and making the effort of "discovering" (trying finding the truth and the meanings). This aspect is represented in nature, as it is believed that whatever God "created" (even illusionary) is greater than man-made, so sacred gets associated with nature. The divine aspect of trees, mountains, rivers, water bodies, forests, stones etc. may not be apparent but needs discovery and creativity in this mode of comprehension (Gupta 2003). The "visible" manifestation of this hidden aspect is in the form of rituals and practices.

The invisible, intangible, *apratakshya* can never be seen by "human eye" and can only be accessed through a pure heart. However, it can be experienced. This is considered as the "true" landscape where all tangible and intangible, visible and hidden aspects become meaningless. The quality is only experiential without any physical attributes. It is something, which is a perfection of divinity and even difficult to define (ibid.)

One of the important aspects which come forth in the last mode of comprehension is that human being is inseparable part of these "constructs". After all, these are "constructed" within his "self", which is defined metaphorically but experienced spiritually. Importantly, "experience" is different from "perception". The latter determines opinion and not comprehension.

Now I return to our discussion on disasters. "Experiencing" a disaster may be part of survival strategy; a source of continuity of existence, by accepting disaster as part of the endless cycle of birth and death. Within experiential mode, disaster is not an event to fight with; it is part of existence to live with. In a way, this seems to point to a tendency to turn people passive and not take actions they are supposed to take. Clearly this might be the case, but on the other hand, this also turns out to be an effective psychological coping mechanism that helps communities to live with disasters.

THE UNDERLYING REASON: INTERNAL CHAOS?

I shall like to extend the discussion from the core question "What is a disaster? to finding out the underlying causes of disaster in the first place and also probing the reasons for its increasing frequency and intensity. This will again require an understanding much beyond the tangible level of comprehension. In the present age, we are changing at a fast pace, faster than ever before. We have reached a point where science and technology has completely over-dominated our lives. From a tool, it has become a weapon, which is turning back on us; from masters of technology; we have become its slaves.

This has a direct implication on our conception of space and time. At spatial level, world has become much smaller due to increasing mobility and powerful media images, which was unthinkable proposition before. However, contrary to these achievements, it is getting larger in our subconscious mind. We tend to see it physically so small, but perceive many more distinctions within it. Similar changes are happening at temporal level. We have been able to beat time through sophisticated technology but now we have reached a stage, where time is beating us. We are no longer able to get hold of it, rather always running after it. Undoubtedly, our ability to grasp time and space are being severely delimited, if not at the physical level, at the experiential and metaphysical level.

We, the humans (I would say, humans will be more appropriate term than human beings as many times, we cease to exist as beings; forget what is "to be") are finding ourselves in the midst of deep metaphorically divisions. We have become "educated" and supposedly "expert" with tonnes of information loads and not necessarily knowledge (to know one needs to develop cognitive thinking abilities). We make notions of "development", which are primarily visible in nature and overlook other dimensions. On the other hand, the local "illiterate" people (I will call them illiterate and not ignorant as they may have their cognitive abilities but may not be formally able to read and write) may have the hidden and invisible dimensions intact but fail to link these to the visible reality. To substantiate this, I will cite an example from my own "eastern" context.

River Ganga and Yamuna are the holiest rivers for Hindus. The spiritual association with these rivers has been so strong that it has led to the evolution of one of the greatest civilizations in the world. In fact religious landscapes like Braj, in which the story of Lord Krishna"s childhood is interwoven with the natural landscape, have evolved around these rivers. Undoubtedly, the visible qualities of these human interventions were (and remain) of extraordinary architectural and ecological merit. For generations these have been maintained without much or rather any help from the so called "experts;" the distinct elitist category of engineers, architects, disaster managers, sociologists, that we, the users of this book, identify ourselves with.

To get to the issue lets look at the present status. Most of the rituals and beliefs remain as strong as ever (in fact, many of them have become more intense for better or for worse). So the hidden and invisible dimensions are intact to a great extent. But what about their "visible" condition?

The rivers are polluted to dangerous proportions. In fact these have become dumping grounds for throwing all kinds of waste. There is a clear indifference towards cultural heritage, which in more tangible aspects continuous to be replaced by poor and ugly "modern" construction. So most of the times, even new creation is not visibly pleasing. True, these are directly linked to increasing poverty, urbanisation and population growth. But on close inspection, one can easily see that much of the threats to visible aspects of cultural heritage are due to indifference and neglect. It seems that heritage is slowly but consistently being disowned by its own bearers. It is like separating body from the soul.

Now let us look at the way, we "the experts" handle the problems. To get rid of pollution in these "holy" rivers, an action plan was drafted in early 90s spending millions of dollars from international aid. Most of this money was used to install sewage treatment plants to clean the water. Nearly every town along these rivers established these plants, including the holy cities of Mathura and Vrindavan, which were part of sacred landscape that I mentioned before. So the entire urban sewage in these towns was collected through electrically driven motors. These were installed in a direction opposite to the natural slope to prevent the sewage to flow towards the river. The entire system was heavily dependent on technology. Also it required regular maintenance. Contrary to this, the traditional system worked obeying the natural landform. Not to mention, there also existed some local ecological ways and means to dispose the sewage. People had a certain sense of responsibility towards the river, which deliberately prevented them from doing those things, which polluted the river. Now, this I would not say was a perfect system, but nevertheless it worked to an extent that we read such beautiful accounts of pleasant experiences of the pilgrims and travellers.

But what is the status of these plants now? Most of them are not working at all or working half of their original capacity. This is because there is not enough electricity to keep them running all the time and once power fails, the entire sewage system gets clogged and pollutes the river (remember it is in a direction opposite to natural topography). And the "visible" results are devastating. Most people do not take the initiative as they think, technology is meant to do the job. So here is what we end up with solely techno-centric way of thinking.

Here one can see clear dilemma and conflict at two levels. First, increasing gap between visible, hidden and invisible dimensions. Second, between the perceptions of "experts" and local people. No longer are we able to make the link between the three levels of cognition. We need to ask ourselves, why this is so? Are these a result of some deeper struggle that we are entangled within ourselves, at this stage of our super technological advancement? (Malik, 1990, 1995). I believe that this internal chaos is the underlying cause of the slow onset of disaster situation; the central subject of our discussion.

CONCLUSION

We are now at the "crossroads" where we suffer from this internal chaos and all this is getting reflected in what we call "a disaster". Although it is triggered by an extreme natural hazard, it is a slow onset process, which is making us, the humans, not just physically but mentally more vulnerable than ever before. We are living in an age of "lost" generations, which are neither able to reap benefits of what we call as "modern", nor able to make use of traditional systems developed over time through trial and error, which seem to have become outdated.

According to me, the main reason for all these contradictions is that we no longer live on our own terms; by this I mean those conditions which are collectively defined by particular group of people with shared values and visions. Although our perception of world has drastically changed, thanks to technological advancement, our humanness (that we can not deny even if we want) enables us to relate best to other humans through these shared values and visions. No matter how much these values and visions change, they still exist in various forms.

There is a deep division between our perceptions of what is "modern" and what is "traditional". The former carries with itself the notions of development of "backward" traditional communities; while latter either implies outdated knowledge or nostalgic images to be romanticised. Our perceptions have taken over our ability of comprehension at various levels. We no longer look deep inwards but tend to look outwards, denying "internal" contradictions as well as capacities. All this clearly influences the actions that we take to reduce the impact of disaster.

I shall like to exemplify this on a more tangible level by citing the case of post earthquake reconstruction process following 1993 earthquake in Marathwada region in India. The reconstructed villages had "city-like" plan with wide streets forming grid-.iron pattern and row housing. The designers in the local town planning office perceived that such a "modern" planning would ensure "development" of "backward" local communities. Ironically many local people also shared this perception. Interestingly however, several years after the quake, the villagers themselves have initiated drastic changes in these tailor-made designs to suit their way of life. Moreover, "earthquake resistant" technology, which was imported as rigid design packages has failed to take roots with local communities, owing to the fact that these were found to be unsuited to local climate, affordability and identity. Besides in the absence of proper workmanship, these in fact have resulted in poor constructions, which ironically are even poorer than traditional technology that they have replaced (Jigyasu 2001). Such examples are not uncommon. In fact, we continue to see the same phenomenon and repeat the same mistakes, over and over again, irrespective of geographical context. Again, I would emphasis that this should force us to look for deeper reasons behind which I have mentioned before.

I would like to conclude this discussion by stressing on the fact that "disaster" is not just about spatial and temporal reality that has to be resisted. Disaster is as much rooted in consciousness of "the self", which makes and breaks these spatial and temporal boundaries. This rediscovering of "the self" places ethics and responsibility on each human being. In this experiential realm, we start from "the self", move on to the community (with whom we share values and visions by choice and not compulsion) and to other levels, even extending to the cosmos (the most perceivable entity). But at the end, we must return and get connected to "the self".

This implies that our understanding of disaster needs to be turned inside out and not the other way around, as it tends to become, thanks to the "expert" notions of what is a disaster. There needs to be a strong interface between "reality" of disaster constructed by us "the experts" and the one created by the victims, based on their worldviews. After all, "reality" is nothing but a "construct;" it is about rediscovering "the self." Only "the self" is real in the sense that it is insurmountable truth of our existence; omnipresent in visible, hidden and invisible realms of consciousness.

Rather than wasting all our time and efforts in finding out ways to fight the disaster as an external objective reality, we need to live with disaster, not as passive recipients but as proactive participants. This essentially requires moving from "perceptual" mode of thinking (that unfortunately we have got entangled at present) to an "experiential" mode of comprehension. To this end, I would even deny the very understanding and divisions of so called "east" and "west" that we construct as part of perceptual reality. The perspective on disaster that I have brought forward through this discussion is not "eastern"; it is rather "human".

4

WHAT'S A WORD? OPENING UP THE DEBATE

Neil R. Britton

Definitions are meant to be clarifying statements that assist to distinguish a specific phenomenon from others in a way that highlights any unique attribute or set of differentiating features so that all potential social actors, operating in similar social time and social space, can extract the same, or similar, meaning and/or application from the term. However, to achieve this there needs at the very least, to be consensus about what the distinguishing features are. This might be achieved by comparing phenomena that have some level of commonality but when put side by side, the uniqueness of each is made clearer: this is what I tried to do, primarily for my own benefit, in an early attempt to understand what a disaster was (Britton 1986). Since many terms are dependent on others, for example the concept of masculine is dependent in explanation as well as in social action on the reciprocal concept of feminine this approach has some sense. However, defining phenomenon by comparison only will not by itself provide a full explanation. A concept should stand in its own right; its uniqueness should be expressed. If this is not possible then perhaps it is not a unique phenomenon and is dependent on reciprocal relationships. Hence a relative distinction may be all that is required for social actors in social time and social space to develop a mutual acknowledgement of what "it" is. This last point is significant because, at the end of the day, if different groups of social actors cannot agree on what "it" is in terms of distinguishing features or, more importantly, about how to explain the phenomenon then successful social action based on mutual understanding will be difficult to achieve. For a notion like "disaster" with its connotation that specific social action is an associative factor, this is an important consideration.

Is it important that disaster has a "pure" definition or is a relational explanation acceptable? I don't know the answer, although in many ways this seems to be where we are in the current debate. We appear to be having problems reaching agreement on what we are dealing with in a pure sense even though we all seem to agree on, and are comfortable with, the parameters that distinguish disaster from other relative terms. Is there anything really wrong then, working with a concept that portrays "family resemblance", as Tony Oliver-Smith (1999: 21) aptly puts it? I acknowledge that for some, such as most of those who contributed to the 1998 text (which includes Oliver-Smith), and its precursor, the 1995 special volume of the *International Journal of Mass Emergencies and Disasters*, that developing a precise definition for "disaster" is an intellectual challenge worth the effort; even if this is undertaken by a comparatively homogeneous group of social actors (that is, scholars), albeit from a range of disciplines that have very different start and end points. There is no doubt that scholars have been a major contributing force in helping wider society recognize that disaster, as a specific phenomenon, has distinct characteristics and that these need to be taken into account in terms of social organization. Moreover, many of these same scholars have turned their attention to implementation strategies that has enabled a generation of practitioners to more readily utilize the results of research. This contribution has been outstanding and it is a legacy that these researchers should be especially proud.

My suggestion, however, and hence the point of this essay, is to bring into the debate the perspective of emergency management ers. The fact that researchers and practitioners have distinct institutional constraints and rewards, linkages and interaction needs (Fothergill 2000:93) would add strength to any definition produced. To be fair, scholars who study disasters have never claimed sovereignty over this field, and I am not asserting otherwise. In fact, most of the contributors to *What is a Disaster?* mention in some way or another that other actors have and need working definitions. Equally, the current group of disaster scholars exploring issues of definition are themselves an eclectic lot covering several disciplines, mostly from the social sciences. I suspect that this is also one of the reasons why the debate is still open-ended currently, since different disciplines naturally have different construct parameters and focus on different attributes. This is the strength of inter-disciplinary and cross-cultural research and is one of the many reasons why disaster research is such an exciting field to be part of. To be fairer still, there are ample opportunities for scholars and practitioners to come together to discuss, debate, refine and reflect on issues of definitions and their implications, and many of these opportunities are regularly taken up. In recent years this has been made easier because of increasing professionalism within emergency management and in particular the development of university-level degree courses now being offered in disasters. This latter point is important because degree courses provide researcher and practitioner with common platforms. Nevertheless, it is the emergency manager who has to interpret definitions, circumstances and information from which to develop disaster pertinent strategies, policies, procedures and practices. It is also the emergency manager who has to negotiate, mobilize and maintain resources from which to create appropriate public safety programs. How emergency managers view the world and how they define disaster is therefore highly relevant. So, why not bring disaster researcher and emergency practitioner together to work on the matter of "what is a disaster?"

I acknowledge this would not be an easy task. For one thing, such an activity necessitates a definition of emergency management: and here I agree with Waugh's (2000) observation that a major problem in defining emergency management today is finding the boundaries of the field; and the field is as broad as the risks that society faces. Similarly, many practitioners would dismiss such an exercise as too esoteric, and no doubt some academics would dismiss the idea as being mundane, although I suspect that these views are not as prevalent now as they were even a few years ago. There are nonetheless some helpful signs. For example, the evolution of emergency management practice closely follows advances in disaster research, especially within the social sciences (Drabek 1991; Lindell and Perry 1992; Lindell and Perry 2004). Likewise, as Anderson and Mattingly (1991) observed over a decade ago, a symbiotic relationship exists between the disaster researcher and the emergency manager. Indeed, since an explicit public policy component to hazard and disaster research exists in several countries, many scholars have an interest in, and concern about knowledge transfer (Fothergill 2000). More significantly, researchers and practitioners are together developing a sustainable hazard mitigation approach to disaster reduction (Mileti 2002). There is also the fact that universities in many countries are increasingly recognizing the benefits of providing outreach or service work programs to the community, and fields such as disaster research serve this purpose well.

I want to build on my conviction that the professional emergency manager can assist to deepen levels of understanding about disaster, which may lead to the creation of a definition that will reduce the current level of discontent. Not every emergency manager will be helpful in this exercise, certainly, as is the case with disaster researchers: there is wide variation in terms of competence and credibility in both groups. My purpose is not to offer a definition of disaster (although I will express a view about what I believe some essential attributes are in the latter part of this discussion) but rather to request an opening up of the debate in a collaborative manner beyond the current cadre of interested spectators.

To initiate this process, I set out below some brief comments that illustrate the major shifts within emergency management practice as well as developments in the professionalization of emergency managers that give reason for their ability to participate in developing definitions of what a disaster might be. I then justify my conviction for a pluralist approach to definition setting by employing four triggers, three of which are offered up by contributors to *What is a Disaster?* The first is predicated on one of sociology's basic concepts, the definition of the situation. The second originates from two comments by Ron Perry in *What is a Disaster?* In the first he states that "many people and groups both define and need definitions of disaster" and in the second he reminds us that "each group or individual creates a definition with different ends in mind" (1998: 214). The third trigger is Ken Hewitt's observation, in the same text, that "the question behind the question seems to be: How do we characterize disaster as a social problem for centralized organizations and professional management?" (1998: 88). The final entry is a proclamation by Henry Quarantelli, also in *What is a Disaster?*, wherein he seems worried that "our continuing dependence on the jargon inherent in everyday or popular speech continues to blind us to other more useful ways of looking at "disasters" (1998c: 246). To set the context to the discussion, however, an overview of emergency management as a research area and a practice field is useful.

DISASTER RESEARCH AND EMERGENCY MANAGEMENT

Modern disaster research in the western world has its origins in Samuel Prince's 1917 doctoral study of the Halifax, Canada, munitions ship explosion and its impact on the local community (Prince 1920). In the ensuing 85 years the field has evolved into a well-established and eclectic area of research conducted primarily by university-based academics who, in the past decade especially, have increasingly learned to work and communicate with policymakers and practitioners. Disaster academics have also learnt to cohabit with researchers outside their own discipline to the point where inter-disciplinary and applied approaches to research have given birth to a "hazards community;" people from many fields and agencies who address the myriad of aspects of natural disasters" (Mileti 1999a: 1-2). The most recent manifestation of this endeavor is the sustainable hazard mitigation approach (Mileti 1997, 1999a, 1999b, 1999c; Beavers et al. 2000) which, since losses from hazards have now been shown to be predictable, has given rise to the call for a reconsideration of the relationship between the natural environment and human use. This approach recommends the need to think about the long-term effectiveness of various types of mitigation efforts and the adoption of a framework for sustainable development practices and. The approach, however, is not without concern being expressed (see for instance, Aguirre 2002; Sachs 1999).

With specific interest on group and organizational aspects, many disaster researchers also directed their attention to emergency management aspects. During the late 1970s and early 1980s in particular, US social scientists raised some serious questions about the practice of emergency management. Picking up on the research output of groups such as the Disaster Research Center, the USA's National Governors' Association (1979), for instance, expressed concern about a lack of comprehensive management at both policy and operational levels; about the lack of understanding of the relationship between preparedness and response on the one hand and recovery and mitigation on the other; about the limited talent pool available to manage all four phases; and about the narrow focus on quick-onset natural hazards and the concomitant lack of planning for technological hazards, energy and material shortages, and long-onset natural disasters. Perry (1982) raised issues about the appropriateness of the "dual use" policy connecting civil defense and emergency management. Dynes (1983) queried the relevance of the dominant "command and control" practice model. Other issues ranged from the narrow frame of reference within which hazards and disasters were viewed (Hewitt, 1983); to emergency management's tenuous links with hazard management (Burton et al. 1978; White 1974), planning practices (Kartez 1984); and the relative lack of understanding within the emergency management community of mental health issues in the disaster context (Parad et al. 1976; Raphael 1986). With the expansion of academic interest beyond these areas in the past two decades there has been a corresponding increase in attention about their theoretical implications for emergency management. This has resulted in the study of disaster research, sustainable hazard mitigation and emergency management starting to blend as well as to burgeon.

Emergency management has followed a similar pattern and the fundamentals of conventional organized emergency management are now about fifty years old. During that period, the practice of emergency management has changed from an essentially reactive and response-focused command-and-control civil defense approach, which grew out of the 1940s World War II and 1950s Korean War eras, phased into a comprehensive and integrated approach during the late 1970s, and from the 1990s started to re-emerge around the twin concepts of risk management and sustainable hazard mitigation. However, recent events connected with highly organized terrorist attacks in different parts of the world, most notably in the USA whereby a strong reaction has resulted in its lead disaster agency being subsumed into a federal homeland security mega-department, might see this latest transformation being short-lived in favor of a replay of earlier cycles.

Attempts to bring practice into line produced the Comprehensive Emergency Management (CEM) approach. CEM referred to the responsibility and capability of a political unit (nation, state, local area) to manage all types of emergencies and disasters by coordinating the actions of all players involved. The "comprehensive" aspect was based on the idea that there are generic processes for addressing most kinds of hazards and disasters. The model included four phases of an emergency activity: mitigation, preparedness, response and recovery. While this may have been somewhat simplistic in terms of disaster authenticity, it greatly assisted bureaucratic agencies to develop more realistic administrative and human resource capacities. One of these initiatives was the bringing forth of the "emergency manager" as a specific administrator/practitioner. Also stemming from this approach was the Integrated Emergency Management System

(IEMS), which would help form partnerships between different levels of resource owners, both vertically (between levels of government) and horizontally (between different agencies and the public-private sector). Basically a process model, Integrated Emergency Management Systems, focused attention on hazard analysis, capability assessment, disaster planning, capacity maintenance, and disaster response/recovery requirements. In this way CEM/IEMS dominated emergency management thinking for the subsequent two decades.

The 1990s and the early twenty-first century witnessed a different set of imperatives on the role and direction of emergency management. Two unambiguous influences are sustainable development and the heightened public demand for increased safety. In this respect, disasters, now more broadly considered than ever before, have started to become a policy problem of global proportion because of the growing realization that what humans do in the normal course of their lives can magnify the vulnerability of their community. With this understanding starting to take root emergency management is incorporating its activities into a wider risk management framework. This approach places emergency management in the overall context of a community's economic and social activities. Steps taken to manage risks of extreme events can be justified to the extent that they deliver a net benefit to society. Attempts to manage risks, however, will invariably impose costs as well as benefits. Hence, the social function of emergency management is shifting from one that only minimizes losses (for example, reducing loss of life or property damage), but also maximizes gains (such as supporting sound investment decision-making, and general community well being). A key factor in this new thinking is the concentration on the "management" component rather than the "emergency". This has widened the focus of emergency management from being highly task-specific (that is planning and responding to particular categories of events by engaging dedicated skilled personnel and resources) to a more generic social function looking at socially disruptive episodes from a holistic perspective. This, in turn, directs attention to integration as a central concept. Possible implications have been outlined elsewhere for emergency management (Britton 2002) and emergency managers (Britton 1999a). However, the inference that emergency management trends have on research does not appear to have been reciprocally and systematically explored.

WHOSE DEFINITION OF THE SITUATION SHOULD BE CONSIDERED?

I want to return to the assertion I made at the outset of this essay, that the supply side for current definitions of disaster is too narrow, and turn attention to the four triggers I mentioned earlier that, in my view help justify why an expansion of intellectual input is required. One of the basic postulates of sociology is that each person acts on the basis of his or her definition of the situation (Thomas 1918). Human beings do not passively respond to environmental stimuli, but rather we constantly interpret what we perceive. It is difficult to account for the social action of others except in terms of how those actors define the situation they find themselves in. The way people define a situation is the reality for them and they fashion attitudes, behavior and action accordingly. Even if others regard them as misguided, if scientists or any other social group might prove them wrong through social facts, or the initial idea turns out to be inappropriate or false they nevertheless during the time that they are salient have consequences for action. Perhaps a more contemporary and non-sociological way of articulating this might be, "where you stand on an issue depends on where you sit"; or to put it another way, "how a person/group interprets something depends on what they are required to do about it". These expressions resonate with Dombrowsky's comment that definitions provide a justification of positions (1998: 20). One important implication of this principle is that people, especially if they are drawn from dissimilar backgrounds, may define an identical situation quite differently and for valid reasons.

Placing this into the context at hand, Aguirre sums it up superbly when he states, "disasters are what communities define as disasters, and are thus the outcome of social constructions" 114). If this is the case, then bringing practitioner persp into definition deliberations will be useful. Governments a theoretical in orientation, but empirical. They form positions and policies on the basis of reflection—and reaction—to occasions that impact on the lives of citizens they (the government) are obliged, both legally and morally, to protect. Disasters, as social disruptions, are one such category of occasion that requires governmental attention, although it must be said that low probability events tend not to carry much weight in policymaking unless, of course, the consequences are so great they cannot be ignored. Be this as it may, how government defines disaster is important because this starts the process of policy development that leads to the domain, tasks, resources and activities mix described by Kreps (1998), the combination of which frames social action in disaster. Moreover, practitioners tend to operate within action frameworks that are handed down by governments through legislation, and which they have helped shape. Hence, practitioner explanations tend to include statements outlining general directions and commitment of resources. These elements give focus to specific dimensions that may be important for clarifying what a disaster is. Two non-USA examples will suffice.

Probably the most recent emergency management legislation comes from New Zealand, when in December 2002 the Civil Defence Emergency Management Act came into force, replacing earlier legislation originally enacted in 1967. The Act redefines the duties of central and local governments, and also directly brings the private sector, specifically utilities, into both emergency management strategic decision-making and operational contexts. In particular, the Act promotes sustainable management of hazards and risks in a way that contributes to the well-being and safety of the public and property. This Act states "emergency" to mean a situation that:

1. is the result of any happening, whether natural or otherwise, including without limitation, any explosion, earthquake,

eruption, tsunami, land movement, flood, storm, tornado, cyclone, serious fire, leakage or spillage of any dangerous gas or substance, technological failure, infestation, plague, epidemic, failure or disruption to an emergency service or lifeline utility, or actual or imminent attack or warlike act; and

2. causes or may cause loss of life or injury or illness or distress or in any way endangers the safety of the public or property in New Zealand or any part of New Zealand; and
3. cannot be dealt with by emergency services, or otherwise requires a significant co-ordinated response under this Act. (New Zealand Government, 2002: Section 4)

The link between disaster, sustainable hazard mitigation and sustainable development proposed by Mileti and his contemporaries are evidenced in the new legislation. This orientation helps to distance the approach from the traditional "preoccupation" (to use Rosenthal's word, 1998: 148) of a prompt return to normalcy. Instead of this, the New Zealand approach is very much an attempt toward moving to a higher state of resilience. Moreover, the concerns Kroll-Smith and Gunter (1998) raise in *What is a Disaster?* about overly restrictive legislated definitions hamstringing local needs and efforts are overcome in the New Zealand context through the legislation being explicitly directed to encouraging innovation and providing empowerment at local levels so long as these actions are not inconsistent with national requirements. To ensure overall consistency, the Act requires the national administering agency to develop a national emergency management strategy that sets out goals, objectives and measurable targets, and which has to be publicly notified. The framework for the national strategy is based on a risk management approach developed by Standards Australia and Standards New Zealand. This non-mandatory Standard defines risk management as "the culture, practices, processes and structures that come together to optimise the management of potential opportunities and adverse effects" (Standards Australia 1999: 4). Together with a risk management approach for local governments (Standards New Zealand 2000), the Standard is being promoted as the basis for developing a risk management approach to emergency management and for communicating the concepts of risk management to all groups and individuals with emergency management responsibilities.

The New Zealand Act also provides an explanation about what is expected from emergency management when it explains the concept as being:

1. the application of knowledge, measures and practices that are necessary or desirable for the safety of the public or property; and are designed to guard against, prevent, reduce, or overcome any hazard or harm or loss that may be associated with an emergency; and
2. includes, without limitation, the planning, organisation, co-ordination, and implementation of measures, knowledge, and practices (New Zealand Government, 2002: Section 4).

Similarly, Emergency Management Australia suggests "disaster" is,

> A serious disruption to community life which threatens or causes death or injury in that community and/or damage to property which is beyond the day-to-day capacity of the prescribed statutory authorities and which requires special mobilization and organisation of resources other than those normally available to those authorities. See also *accident, emergency* and *incident* (Emergency Management Australia, 1998: 33).

By inviting the reader to also look at the explanations offered for other disruptive situations, Emergency Management Australia infers that "disaster" is a relative state and its meaning made clearer through contrast.

As sensitizing concepts (Kreps 1998: 34), these working characterizations bring forth all the components discussed by the contributors in *What is a Disaster?* They are socially defined requiring social action by social actors in social space; they identify triggers; they imply a collapse of cultural protection and convey the notion of harm to the physical and social environment entailing a state or condition that is destabilizing; they require exception routines and extraordinary countermeasures. While the expression and approach between the researcher and practitioner is different, the result is similar. Few practitioners (or researchers, I suspect) would disagree with Stallings when he states that disasters are fundamentally disruptions of routines (1998: 129). Since researchers and practitioners emphasize different attributes that have been extracted from the understood agreed common pool of components, the perspectives of each can be explored and hopefully enhanced.

SHOULD RESEARCHER PERCEPTIONS BE PARAMOUNT?

Ron Perry's comments that "many people and groups both define and need definitions of disaster" (1998:214) and that "each group or individual creates a definition with different ends in mind" raises an issue about why the researchers' notion of a definition should be the one to prevail, particularly when such definitions tend to be restricted to academic publications that even researchers themselves agree are not good vehicles for dissemination (Fothergill 2000). Once they have been extricated from these constraining devices, however, which takes a lot of time and effort, academic definitions can be very influential in directing, and re-directing, the focus of official orientations (a trawl through relevant archives gives a fascinating insight into how word changes in official documents has followed changes in academic thinking, although the lag time is often considerable and the two never quite seem to catch up). In particular, academic input has helped practitioners to at least get some thinking straight and develop a pattern of the type urged by Quarantelli when he stated that we should stop confusing antecedent conditions and subsequent consequences with the characteristics of disaster (1987a: 7).

Examples of how close collaboration can have positive effects are becoming more frequent and the results promising: New Zealand's emergency management legislation that is explicitly built upon risk management principles rather than the more typical disaster preparedness and response duo is a case in point. Another observation about New Zealand's legislation is that its purposeful updating and refinement of the duties of officials and citizens took place without a major disaster portraying the gaps and omissions in existing systems and hence changes being demanded. It is a nice example of a proactive output resulting from systematic consultation with all social groups, which also involved national and international academics. This is not an isolated example, but it is a case in point of how things can be done, and in particular it is a case in point that shows how significant progress can be achieved when different sectors work together on a single issue. To quote Alice Fothergill again, "working in separate cultures does not mean that there cannot be communication and respect" (2000: 97). Hence, Perry's observation is useful, in that while different groups inevitably have different ends in mind, it does not follow that those ends are incompatible or unable to be linked. In the context of definition creation, differing ends may well be a key to establishing a better explanation of the whole.

QUESTIONS WITHIN QUESTIONS

Ken Hewitt's point that the question *What is a Disaster?* has more to do with how disaster is characterized for centralized organizations and professional management (Hewitt 1998: 88) is, to me, important. For decades government and non-government agencies accepted notions implicit in the definitions at the time that the real tasks about organizing for disaster was to concentrate on preparedness and response. This approach seriously hampered addressing underlying causal issues, and it weakened hazard mitigation efforts. Even now, practitioners tend to focus on the consequences of disasters, but many do so in a way that has shifted their thinking from a response-focused to a consequence-based analysis. In this respect, their thinking reflected a definitional shift that incorporates political, economic and cultural ecological perspectives. Emergency managers are now more likely to ask themselves "what will the overall societal effects of impact be?" The sustainable hazard mitigation approach will consolidate this thinking: emergency managers in some countries have spent a great deal of effort thinking about disaster resilience and what it means for social stability. This thinking and the practical applications derived from it give another dimension to the issue of how disaster can be defined. Over time, the sustainable hazard mitigation approach will also move thinking on, but whatever direction it takes it is unlikely to only involve academics. Emergency managers and many of their political masters are, now, too interested in these fundamental issues.

ARE WE BLINDED BY EVERYDAY LANGUAGE?

Four years ago I attended a workshop sponsored by the Federal Emergency Management Agency's teaching arm, the Emergency Management Institute, in Emmitsburg, Maryland. The workshop comprised full-time academics from throughout the US who were currently providing emergency management courses or who were interested in teaching emergency management courses. Some were old hands, others new. They came from a variety of disciplines and facilitation was provided by an equally diverse group of academic hazard and disaster specialists. The workshop highlighted several positive aspects; such as how far and how fast practitioners are moving to incorporate theory and empirically based knowledge into their practice ideology, the close relationships between academic and practitioner, and how quickly the academic community was responding to the needs of practitioners. Perhaps too quickly, because the workshop illustrated another, more worrying, quality. Many of the academics at the workshop were struggling to comprehend the basics of what they were being told. The questions they asked about hazards, disasters and emergency management appeared naïve and the responses given by the facilitators seemed not to resonate. Much of the difficulty centered on the precise academic language and definitions used to describe the characteristics and components of disaster-relevant findings, and a lot of time was spent having to "translate" definitions so they could be better understood.

Quarantelli (1993a) has argued that scientific jargon actually makes for precise and clear communication *within* a discipline, and that to lose the jargon would signify a loss of precision and clarity of that discipline. In *What is a Disaster?* he extends this line of argument by stating, "our continuing dependence on the jargon inherent in everyday or popular speech continues to blind us to other more useful ways of looking at disaster (1998c: 246). That may be the case, but if it is then it is not without penalty. I have emphasized the word "within" in the first reference to Quarantelli above because we are not actually dealing with a single disciplinary issue when it comes to disaster research. Progress in the field of disaster research, especially over recent decades, has been the result of *inter*-disciplinary activity. What this suggests to me is that a single disciplinary perspective in terms of a definition of the field is now incongruous. Disciplinary specific explanations couched in jargon are not going to win the day, even for academics with an interest in the field, as the example of the FEMA workshop illustrates.

What is the implication of this for emergency management practice, especially at a time when other sectors of the community, such as lawmakers and parliamentary legislation writers are turning more and more to "everyday language" in an attempt to make important documents accessible to as many as possible? My own experience tells me that if the intention is to inform and elucidate then there is an inherent problem with academic definitions. Lawmakers, decision-makers, teachers, practitioners and publics don't want to spend time being tripped up by unfamiliar words that are strung together in an odd manner. They want to know what the words actually mean. Surely definitions can be written to convey unambiguous meaning while at the same time using familiar language. This act alone would go a long way to bridge the "town-gown" gap that currently exists. Since so much time has to be given to "translating" definitions so they can be understood (and not only for non-academics!), and since so much antagonism and apprehension is created by having to do this, why don't disaster researchers adopt a user-friendly approach to their explanations? This makes a lot of sense since much current disaster literature tends to be a combination of scientific and engineering technical reports and social science analyses, much of which is synthesized and translated into plain English so that emergency managers, policymakers and other researchers can understand their policy implications (Waugh, 2000: 16). Such an approach would not demean the scientific input. Although research sometimes seems theoretical, jargon-laden and impractical (Quarantelli 1993b), this research nevertheless has an important practical value even if it does not give specific answers to specific questions. However, by working alongside emergency managers, issues relating to translation and the link with practicality could be ameliorated.

A CONCLUDING COMMENT

So, what is a disaster? It seems to me that it is something to do about a set of circumstances wherein risk is realized and collective expectations about societal safety is acknowledged to be inadequate. Risk is realized in the form of either/or manifest and latent threats and opportunities, and can be due to a social system's geographical proximity to biological, environmental, socio-political or technological attributes that have not been sufficiently incorporated into planning regimes of one kind or another (land-use planning, technical systems management, public security measures, and so forth). Collective expectations about safety are inadequate because institutionalized beliefs, experiences and perspectives are somehow not matched with the risk reality. These "sets of circumstances" necessitates social redefinition and requires changes in social action, particularly about understanding the implications of both context and consequence with respect to mitigation as well as remediation.

I should point out that this is not a definition of disaster: I stand by my original assertion that developing an acceptable definition is more likely to be achieved if it is derived from a broad base. I don't think single discipline specialist definitions are advantageous. This is where the four starting points outlined above come in. They each provide justification for broadening the inputs with respect to different social actors who can make a valuable contribution to defining disaster.

Academic researchers have provided, and will continue to provide, invaluable insights into the phenomenon of disaster. There is no question about this. The systematic and objective approach that typifies much (unfortunately not all) of disaster research provides an essential framework for the wealth of rich descriptions about how nature, technology or fellow humans have disrupted social systems, much of which comes from practitioner and other official sources. The analytic approach that most researchers display has provided us with a detailed understanding about what the key components of disaster might be, and this in turn has produced a of definitions that is getting closer and closer to what disaster might actually be in both "pure" and relative terms. Whether disaster researchers alone can—or should—take this burden on their shoulders exclusively is the question that I have posed. My answer is "no", I don't think it is possible or desirable. When it comes to the context and consequences of the set of circumstances I outlined above, disaster managers are more likely to be attuned to many of the relevant nuances. Current practitioner definitions, reflected in recent legislation as well as in practice ideology, now reflect academic thinking; the result of collaboration between the two groups. Since practitioner definitions reflect the current status, there is every reason to believe that this new breed of practitioners can also project their reality into the definition debate and help work through this important activity.

Outlining the role anthropology can play in disaster research and in developing disaster theory, Tony Oliver-Smith (2002) concluded by encouraging more of his fellow anthropologists to become engaged. He said that "in grappling with the problematics of disasters, anthropologists . . . can clarify the important distinction between symptoms, the disaster events and processes themselves, and their underlying and largely systemic causes, (2002: 46). While he did not explicitly state it, I have a suspicion that he was also reminding the current doyens of disaster research, who are mainly sociologists, of this matter and to let them in. Far less eloquently than he, but with the same conviction, I am also asking disaster researchers to open up and let others in. I am certain that the new breed of emergency managers, as practitioners who are becoming more capable and more willing to conceptualize the issues they confront in their profession of choice, can make a valuable contribution. And once the notion that other sectors can—and should—contribute to this exercise, there is another group that needs to be seriously considered: those involved in development research and practice. As Quarantelli reminds us, "we can all learn from one another if we but listen" (1993: 37).

5

NOT EVERY MOVE IS A STEP FORWARD: A CRITIQUE OF DAVID ALEXANDER, SUSAN L. CUTTER, ROHIT JIGYASU AND NEIL BRITTON

Wolf R. Dombrowsky

One of the founders and doyens of disaster sociology initiated the debate on the question "what is a disaster?" but in doing so E.L. Quarantelli (1998b) probably did not intend to reflect on disasters in epic breadth. After decades of contributions in research, teaching and—most important, contributing inspiration and incentive to others all over the world—he may have desired to share the *results* of his assessment of his sociological specialization. Normally, the idea of a specialization needs clarification: What is the specialty like? In sociology, this question has historically been, and remains, difficult to answer. Students will find dozens of books on the question "What is sociology?" (Elias 1981). The struggle for sociology to be recognized as legitimate science took generations. In dispute was the subject matter of sociology, its "field" (Reiss 1972: 10f.). For the "sub-science" of "disaster-sociology", which emerged far later and which carries the field of sociology in its name, one should expect an understanding of what "disaster" means;

in sociological terms above all. However, decades after establishing sociological disaster research as a uniquely sociological conceptualization of the core matter is still lacking. This appears to be one of histories ironies—particularly for Quarantelli—that the definition of the science to which he devoted his work has to be argued out well after the original founding.

In fact, there is only a little sociology in "disaster," but there are a lot of other concepts derived from other sciences and from the practitioners (see Britton's arguments). The practitioners, of course, strive for applicability. They prefer theoretical models that are highly congruent with their operational needs and experiences. However, the proximity of phase or stage models of disaster to the demands on scene (i.e. to sequence the chaos into manageable portions) makes them excessively attractive but not very revealing. In the end, the sequence of phases models describe an ideal succession, but never the social configurations of the disaster events themselves. To some degree the description of disaster as a sequence of phases (or stages) is in itself ideological. It is the modelled order of succession that persuades into thinking that relief work and reality proceed not only in the same sequence but more than that in an orderly manner, which suggests coping will be successful and action controlled.

Much more difficult to reconcile with the disaster proper are so-called disaster theories that adopt fragments of models and theories from other disciplines. Barry A. Turner (1978) adopted a central category from physics when he defined disaster as wrong amount of energy in the wrong place at the wrong time. To argue consistently, the theoretical loan from physics would need to apply the matching categorical apparatus *and* its appropriate transformation into sociology, otherwise it will be nothing more than a nice analogy without significant sociological explanatory power. The same is true for other adoptions from other disciplines. To define disaster as an event concentrated in time and space combines quantity with spatial dimensions and has its roots in geographical concepts; Jigyasu reflects on that issue. Resource related definitions (i.e. a "lack" of something) basically stem from economics and primarily transform the concept of disaster into a miscalculated supply and demand ratio. In the end every shortage could be disastrous and, consequently, turns "disaster" into an empty term that includes many diverse, unrelated events.

It is important not to be misunderstood on the issue of borrowing concepts and vision from other sciences and social sciences. There is no reason to avoid the use of concepts from other disciplines or different paradigmatic orientations. In this point I agree with Cutter's remark on the "segregation" of the research communities and their mutual ignorance. However, ignorance is something different than a special, disciplinary quality. Sociological disaster research should have the ability and scientific power to mark its disciplinary originality, not in special self-references (or even worse as jargon), but as evidence that sociology provides concepts and frameworks to solve societal problems (and here again I agree with Cutter). This notion captures the core point of my argument and the foundation of my critique of the contributions of David Alexander, Susan L. Cutter, Rohit Jigyasuand Neil Britton. I simply do not believe that conceptualizations like those cited in the two paragraphs above will achieve explanation, particularly not in a sociological way, of the target social phenomena. I shall use this yardstick to measure their contributions. The adoption of paradigmatic or conceptual bits and pieces will, from my point of view, quickly lead to a theoretically fragmented perspective that will not serve as an effective foundation for sociological explanation.

David Alexander's contribution confronts the reader with a mix of theoretical imagery from multiple paradigms. I do not contend that Alexander is inappropriately borrowing. Instead, he is doing what his title says: providing an interpretation. I recall Marx' eleven theses on Feuerbach. The philosophers only have interpreted the world differently, however, the important thing is to change it. This is very close to what I find here. Alexander delivers another interpretation of disaster; the important thing, however, is to understand it.

Alexander himself has done much research and published well-known books; the most prominent in Germany is "Natural

Disasters" (1993). These are good reasons to find substance in his contribution to the question "what is a disaster". However, Alexander did not proceed beyond interpretation. His approach combines many things together: disaster, catastrophe, calamity, corruption, terrorism, and war, at least generalized into "affliction". In affliction—these so-called "phenomena"—are included the ways to analyse them, methods, paradigms, and epistemology in the widest sense. Alexander does not advance a notion of what "disaster" could be in reality nor in scientific terms, because to him "the definition depends on shifting portrayals and perceptions of what is significant about the phenomenon." And the phenomenon, he argues, is "so multi-faceted that a general theory of universal explanatory power is unlikely ever to be formulated", which is "the reason why 'disaster' will probably never be completely, immutably defined."

Leaving aside that general theories (as well as their operational distinctive marks) are always subject to falsification, the quest never was for a "general theory" or for "complete, immutable" definitions, but simply for a scientifically solid concept, a *precise* definition at least. That, of course, has nothing to do with ones disciplinary affiliation. Alexander, as a geographer, is not expected to clarify the specifically sociological aspects of the question. But of what fabric is *his* answer? I have neither found an answer nor could I identify the "fabric" of his multi-facetted presentation. At first I had the impression that Alexander does not differentiate between *definiens* and *definiendum*. Sentences like "disasters in the modern world are an artifact of two forces: commercialism and strategic hegemonies inherent in globalization", disaster is "an extraordinarily revealing sort of affliction", and "disaster is not defined by fixed events, or immutable relationships, but by social constructs, and these are liable to change" are indeed asking for "the tenets and controlling parameters of disaster." Thus, one is eager to learn how the geographer operationalizes "artifact", "affliction", "social constructs" or "change," and all of the other "parameters" he is mentioning.

My examination of Alexander's work also revealed what I see as inconsistency. Alexander surprises the reader with the introduction of the concept of "mindset", to which, in the author's words, "little attention has been devoted". However, neither an elaboration of "mindset" nor a thorough application to disaster is presented. Very briefly Alexander defines *mindset* as "fixity of opinions or states of mind created by events" which stems from cognitive psychology and learning theory and is contradictory to his expression that "disaster is not defined by fixed events" (and, conclusively, will not create a corresponding mindset). In fact, Alexander does not aim at real phenomena (in the sense of hermeneutics; see Dilthey 1972 and Habermas 1973) or of phenomenology (see Schütz 1974). Instead, he focuses upon perception and further on "new forms of symbolism constructed by the mass communication industry", which originate from various possible approaches (see, for example, Cassirer 1958; Schütz 1967; Marcuse 1964) that Alexander again does not cite. There is some evidence, however, that Alexander favors some sort of symbolic constructivism with an emphasis on psychological approaches combined with some sort of contemporary ideology critique. Perhaps this view allows too much influence of ideology upon science as evidenced when we consider his judgements on poverty and globalization, or more clearly, his comparison between modern and traditional societies and their matching symbolic constructs. Alexander describes these as historically— more or less—appropriate "coping mechanisms", and "means of rationalizing disaster". From such a perspective of a vernacular "Anything-Goes Constructivism" (see Feyerabend 1979), even going back to declare a disaster as an "Act of God" appears (politically or ideologically) as equal rights. This perspective leaves Alexander asking rhetorically: "Are we to call this retrograde, a sign of cultural underdevelopment?"

Coincidentally, Eric Arthur Blair, born in 1903, created under the name George Orwell the term "New Speak" in his famous novel "1984". One hundred years later, David Alexander uses the new speak principle to interpret disaster as continuous interpretation, which has to be interpreted and reinterpreted as often as interpretation appears contemporarily appropriate.

This disintegration of social science into interpretive discretion appears to capture the consequences of Alexander's admonition to abstain from "general theory". In his case it is more (and worse) than a subtle subversion of the ideologically loaded controversy on "grand theory" (see Mills 1963). It challenges the traditional principles and practice of scientific craft. Within an approach of continuous interpretation, precise definitions and consistent theorizing appear to hinder the bulwarks of scrutiny and understanding. Alexander's characterization of science as "universal explanatory power" and of defining toward *completion* and *immutability* appears entirely dismissive scientific craft and reasoning (see Chalmers 1982).

Susan L. Cutter advances another strategy. She simply redefines the question: "The question is not what is a disaster, but what is our vulnerability (and resiliency) to environmental threats and extreme events?" That reminds me of the innocent question: "what is a car?". The reply is: "the question is not what is a car, but what is your danger of an accident and of the vehicles pollution potential and extreme speed?" In science, it is important to avoid answering questions by deflecting them and redirect our attention to the original question.

Redefined that way, Cutter becomes systematic: "What makes human and environmental systems vulnerable and more or less resilient to threats and extreme events?" In elaborating conceptual frameworks, she posits that "vulnerability and resiliency imply an examination of human systems, natural (or environmental) and technological systems, and the interconnectedness between them ... it is, in fact, the linkages and interdependencies between these three systems and the built environment that amplify or attenuate vulnerability." Cutter elaborates this "four systems" approach, but does not elaborate on the question of which "systems theory" paradigm she really has in mind. Parenthetically, to reveal ones paradigmatic background is, in my point of view, the *conditio sine qua non* of mutual understanding.

I embrace Cutter's cautions regarding the segregation of research communities, their mutually unperceived publications, their different methods, and the "differences in the type of event examined," exemplified by "natural hazards, technological risks, industrial failures". This enumeration is revealing, because "hazard" is not "risk" and "risk" is not "failure" and "failure" is not "disaster". Above all, "disaster" is not "vulnerability". In fact, and in that I completely agree with Cutter, "the risk, hazards, and disasters communities could not (and still do not) fully understand each other's 'science'." Cutter's conclusion, however, I do not understand. For her, the mutual ignorance of the different communities makes each "unaware of the totality of social science perspectives" and thus of their progressive capacities for future advance. (May be that the reason for quotation marks around science?) But instead of forging ahead with new understandings reflected in distinctions among these phenomena (such as disaster, risk, hazards and vulnerability), Cutter argues, the field "will mire in the depths of ontological debates" about their meaning. Cutter's vision of ontological debate as problematic reveals her apparent suspicious view of philosophy of science. In its neo-positivist interpretation (which predominates in Anglo-American science in contrast to Husserl's idealistic restoration together with Heidegger in Old Europe) "ontology" focuses on the relation between "word" and "phenomenon", or more precisely, on "term" or "idea" and "thing" or "object". In the German language, the play on words with "Begriff" (term) and "Begreifen" (understand, but also touch, grasp) was invoked by Dieter Claessens (1980) to clarify that hand and brain have to work together to understand the world and that this understanding is impossible without appropriate terms ("abstract thinking"). The terms (concepts) in mind represent (conceptualize) the world's reality. Thus, without correct words there will be no correct practice. In this sense, Popper's dictum: "Words don't matter, let's look for the problems" was a joke, because without words we would be unable to solve any problem, much less to recognize it. This appears to be what Cutter has in mind: To proceed to better practice while leaving the fruitless hair-splitting aside.

In the light of the interdependence of concept and conceptualising, Cutter's central question, her "telos" perhaps, appears at once well-meaning but without appreciation of philosophy of science. She asks "... will the field forge ahead with new understandings of how these phenomenon affect the human condition, how human agency increases or decreases their temporal and spatial distribution, and how individuals, social groups, and society at large perceives of and responds to external threats, *regardless of their origin?*" (emphasis added).

Regardless of their origin? Obviously, the 11th September attack has focused the theorizing of both Cutter and Alexander upon catastrophic terrorism and motivated them to do something about the shocking brutality of international terrorism. As their first step, they combine the incompatible together: vulnerability, disaster, danger, failure, hazards, threat, risk, emergency, terrorism, and war. *Because* they do not appreciate the origins and advances in science, "new understandings", *can not* take place.

Taking up the findings of the different communities, four rough categories can be built, leading toward a four pattern scheme: The 1) potential and 2) manifest phenomenon, the 3) intended and planned and the 4) unintended and unplanned. In contrast to failures, disasters, terrorism and war, hazards, threats, dangers and risks have not occurred yet, "vulnerability" has to be counted for potentiality, as a result of preventive (risk and/or danger) reduction measures. In contrast to war and terrorism, which are both intended and planned action, normally nobody intends and plans to produce failure, accident or disaster. Of course, there are always, exceptions. On 1 October 1944 General Dwight D. Eisenhower approved the decision to flood Walcheren Island, the Netherlands, by bombing the dikes. This attempt to isolate German forces on the island has often, incorrectly, been attributed to the defensive efforts of the German army. On 3 October 1944 dykes around Walcheren Island were bombed and breached by the RAF. There are also many deliberate violations of laws, standards and regulations—in work, health and environmental safety, in constructional engineering and building codes—but nowhere are illness, pollution or collapses, or disasters intended. Instead, what is sought often are profits or other immediate advantages. The same is true for intended accidents as insurance fraud.

The heuristic four-pattern scheme may be shown as a table.

	POTENTIAL	MANIFEST
INTENDED & PLANNED	Risk Danger Threat Vulnerability	War Terrorism
UNINTENDED & UNPLANNED	Stupidity: failure to recognize and prepare	Failure Accident Disaster

When we try to fill the "unintended/unplanned-potential" cell, we may realize that Cutter's borrowed terminology from systems theory remains very cursory. Each of her "human systems", sometimes "individuals" and "social action", in untold ways produces risks, hazards, and disasters, or what some refer to as complex emergencies. Some are controllable, others are unintended; some have spatial-temporal limits, while others are simply accepted by those affected. I agree with this contention in general, but I have not found the "more complicated and nuanced set of explanations" that may help us "to understand how, where and why human intervention 1) changes the way in which individuals and societies conceptualize and detect threats, 2) reduces the initiating sources and root causes of threats, 3) mediates vulnerability to threats, and 4) improves resiliency and responses to threats." What we find, as an empirical outcome of existing research, is in contrast to Cutter's observation some sort of social disintegration, a loss of coherence and mutual commitment. We find an increase in carelessness, inattentiveness, thoughtlessness, inconsiderateness, indifference, irresponsibility, or "to-hell-with-it" attitude. But how do we conceptualize that? Has it to do with "will" and "decision", or is it a (self-referential) systemic outcome? I would choose, for heuristic purposes, "stupidity" for the "unintended/unplanned-potential" cell; in such events there was a failure to recognize coupled with an unplanned outcome. All the other attributes, particularly the "to-the-hell-with-it" attitude, should go into the "intended/planned-potential" cell, because alternative behaviors are possible but shunned. Sennet (1998), for example, has described this development as loss of interpersonal narratives, which tends toward the loss of ones own history and, consequently, toward the loss of identity and sociability. Cutter's contingency "regardless of their origin . . ." makes a system (but no systems theory) of this loss, and, unknowingly or not, undermines the precepts of science.

When we regard the origins, then the differences between hazard, threat, danger and risk reveal significant cultural differentiation and conclusively, insight into the cultural evolution of the fabric of the perception of our world. This is close to Alexander's notion of the historical "coping mechanisms" every culture has invented as "means of rationalizing" disasters. But in contrast to his context of political correctness, the historical reassurance of the development of concepts should enable a reflexivity of our own conceptualization. Thus the disaster-researcher should appreciate that *des astro*, the evil star, derives from astrology and astronomy and inherits completely different traditions of viewing the world. This is distinct from *catastrophe*, with its strong and influential connotations stemming from Jewish-Christian apocalyptic traditions (see Cohn 1993). The geographer might recognize that *hazard* stems from Indian-Arabic roots of fortune-telling (throwing bones, engraved stones, coins or dice). Then, and most important to me, other sciences will recognize that sociologists are not simply espousing an argot by do not mixing concepts into an indefinable whole with little explanatory power.

Only a few scholars in the field have paid attention to the historical influences on our present (scientific) concepts. Barkun (1979) did, also Dynes (2000), some others too. I (1989) have spent some years on studying these others, finding that our modes of perceiving, coping with and learning from failures are completely determined by these historio-cultural but hidden, "underground insinuating" heritages.

Looking closer, we will find how these heritages work to shape our scientific thinking. The transformation of a religious mode of "prediction" into a secular dice game called *az-zahr*, where money was put into molds, expresses a far-reaching social change over centuries. Its most momentous aspect was the capability to dissect and analyse the seemingly uniform and consistent. The game *az-zahr* dissected decision and result. As long as the dice turn, the effect of a past decision remains its future. Time enough to think about and to analyse how *fortuna* could be charmed. In the end, gambling and its accompanying desire to influence ones luck and to find regularities, has led to our theories of the distribution of numbers, of randomness, and statistics, but also to social strategies of assurance and economical insurance (Bernstein 1996). Risk-taking in the sense of *riscare*, (Latin-Italian for circumnavigate) and *risco* (cliff, rock) originate from ancient shipping and have nothing in common with our present concept of risk, which is a mere statistical calculus which depends on a certain amount of comparable cases and a certain time period of observation. Historically the more appropriate term would be *venture*, which literally dared the devil if it was not considered together with those who were potentially affected. The so called "Philosophical Probabilism" of Bartholomé de Medina (1577; see Gigerenzer et al. 1989), a catholic moralist, formulated an ethical procedure with which ventures had jointly to weigh up the pros and cons until so called "probable reasons" could be defined. Before God, only the well-considered, probably best solution was pleasant, whereas the ill-considered, "daredevil" venture was an *adventure* and a sin.

In contemporary terms, this process of consideration could be defined as "risk-communication". Alexander is discussing the problem when he considers "how to involve ordinary people democratically in preparation for and management of emergency situations". Our ancestors have had an appropriate answer, although it does not originate from the field of politics. From there stemmed the principle of majority rule that was never accepted within the private and economic sphere. There the principle of (unanimous) consensus rule predominated, because the "whole house" (*dominium*), life, life-stock and property was "at risk" when a venture failed. Therefore, regarding the origins, one would never mix political decision-making and the modes of democratic participation with risk-taking and the modes of sharing losses and profits or disadvantages and advantages.

A similar etiology holds for the concepts of "danger" and "threat". By exploring the origins, one realizes that incompatible social relations and interaction patterns are lying underneath. "Danger" stems from the Latin words *dominium/dominus* and *damnum*. The first meant a very specific relationship, the ownership of a thing (slave) or a person (woman, children); the second meant a very delicate juridical and economical relation, a flaw that could be directly executed and, historically later, sued before a judge. On slave markets or before marriages transfers to reserve have been common to change the contracted prizes (or the contract itself) or to refund in case of hidden flaws (complaint, ailment, etc.). In addition to the right to claim for the *damnum* in case of a flaw, initially the proprietor also owed the right to "damage" his possession when he discovered a flaw, or other cases of diminished value. Unsurprisingly, "danger" was closely connected with modesty and haughtiness on the side of the possessed (be with or without flaw) and with "pity" at the side of those who were imperfect and with "mercy" at the side of the proprietor who could graciously overlook imperfection. Our whole Christian behavior codex roots back to this until today: "nobody is perfect".

Therefore a nonchalant (regardless of origin) translation of "danger" into the German word "Gefahr" would radically miss the subject. Etymologically, "Gefahr" stems from drive, travel, lead, cart, ford and companion (fahren, führen, Fuhre, Furt, Gefährte) and connotes to the venture to go on unknown or rough terrain, virtually impassible routes or fords. On the way, only two sorts of adversities posed peril: insurmountable natural conditions and encroachments, mostly assaults, ambush, hold-ups. "Threat" derives from the latter context. The Indo-European word *treud* as well as the old-german *thrustjan* meant squeeze, press, oppression, use force.

Both are related with the Latin word trudere, which is found in obtrude, protrude, abstruse (originally: push from the hidden!). Threat also meant troop, crowd and trouble, which altogether points at the relation with weaponry and military force (knights or warriors). Our present meaning of threat as an intention to inflict pain, injury, evil, or punishment, as an indication of impending or possible harm or menace, eludes the violent, destructive aspects, the intentional, deliberate brutality of its origin. Therefore, the use of the word *threat* in the context with nature is a mere misconception or, to cite Alexander, "a retrograde" toward a state of belief where an animated, intentionally acting nature "strikes back" and "takes revenge". This is even more true for the term "hazard" because gambling, not the game, is hazardous. The notion "natural hazard" distorts subject and object in the same way. Nature is nature is nature, regardless of its form: air movement, for example. As a mild summer wind, we love "mother nature", as an unruly, "destructive" tornado we blame her destructiveness.

Rohit Jigyasu's contribution was not easy to critique: both because of his closeness to my own ways of thinking and because his subject matter is not familiar to me. I have never before studied "eastern" philosophy, apart from general education (based on Boorstin 1992). Jigyasu's work was a pleasing expansion of my knowledge, but simultaneously disturbing because of his central issue: "Has disaster lost touch with the reality? If yes, why this is so? What is this reality, after all?" As typical "Westerner" I immediately thought of Paul Watzlawick's question: "How real is reality?" (1976) and the constructivist debate (see v. Foerster 1985; Putnam 1975, 1985). Then I realized that Jigyasu referred to the religious sources of worldview and the contemplative aspects of "being in the world", as Heidegger would say. The disturbing aspect was that Jigyasu did not answer his own question. This contrasts with the work by Alexander and Cutter that implies that the human perceptive faculty lost touch with disaster than that disaster loses touch with reality.

From the long pathway from Plato's parable of the cave (Politeia), Kant and Hegel, the Marxist theory of reflection (see Bloch 1977) through radical constructivism, the core question always was the relation between idea and the world beyond perception. Insofar as these philosophical issues are concerned, Jigyasu's expression that disaster "is no longer bounded by the physical boundaries" fell short. Disaster is not and never was a reality, it is a word that describes something (damage, destruction, harm, and so on) we perceive within the space and time we observe. More important, disaster takes its "boundaries" from long lasting heritages. Sometimes, the heritages are more meaningful (and thus binding) than the present phenomena we want to describe. When we talk in tongues, the mindsets are light years apart from present reality. (Which is reason enough to flee such contaminated words or to define them as precisely as possible!) Jigyasu forces us to leave the security of our western abstract thinking. The problem of abstract thinking, however, is the same everywhere and that is why Jigyasu concluded that it is rather 'human'. "Yeah! Thank God!", I thought, reinforced in my believe that science in the first place has to sharpen the instruments, which, for sociologists, always are words.

Neil R. Britton has chosen that as a title: "what's in a word". He is asking and reopening E.L. Quarantelli's and his own conceptual debate (Britton 1986). Britton is the only one of the four contributors to explore "ontology" and makes a serious attempt to come to terms with the term "disaster". A concept, Britton argues, should be more than "a set of differentiating features", it "should stand in its own right; its uniqueness should be expressed." But what if that fails? Britton offers *two* answers: "If this is not possible then perhaps it is not a unique phenomenon and is dependent on reciprocal relationships."

Both answers are touching the core of our debate, although it is not clear whether Britton really distinguishes between "phenomenon" and "concept", between *definiens* and *definiendum*. Be that as it may, I will not allege that "unique phenomenon" was meant as real. To do so would place Britton in the same category as Alexander who looks at infinite changing facets of something one always calls disaster (as the "real" phenomenon) no matter which facets anew and anew will become selected. Taking Britton's argument epistemologically, the uniqueness of a concept will only emerge when it is expressed "uniquely," which is means "scientifically" which is tantamount to the "uniqueness" of sociology (or another science) as discipline, not as collection of paradigmatic "facets". Seen that way, Britton is pointing at our proper problem. The notion "in its own right" is only meaningful in the sense of "expressed in sociological (or any disciplinary word) originality". Conclusively, Britton's answer should read: If this is not possible then perhaps it is not a unique science and is dependent on more settled or accepted sciences. (Which explains why sociology still applies definitions from other disciplines, from geography for example, or from biology that defines disaster as infection or disease.)

The second part of Britton's answer, his emphasis on "consensus", corresponds with the peculiar self-image of sociologists. No physicist would accept a definition of "light" other than an electromagnetic phenomenon within the current "corpuscle-wave" paradigm. Sociologists, however, seem to accept every "interpretation" of disaster, the main criterion being that it is consensual. But is "truth" a variable of consensus and scientific precision a variable of majority? Britton's line of argument is a little bit different, of course. I have carried my own argument too far. Hence, Britton's distinction between "a 'pure' definition" and "a relational explanation" is again not far from Alexander's argument. Britton prefers "relational" explanations as a temporary accepted "mutual acknowledgement" of the needs of "social actors in social time and social space". Thus, "disaster" is what we think it is the moment we deal with it. That is very close to the idea of truth as the handy; and finally to Mao's interpretative misshapen figure that the truth comes out of barrels. Such a conclusion is rude and surely never intended by Britton, although internally logical.

The problem with Britton's contribution is that his description of practitioners and their fruitful exchange with science makes any critique twice difficult. First, because practitioners are "the good ones" (the global volunteer helpers) which may bias our scientific view a little bit, and second because they are our most important first hand engagers of disasters (the hand we should not bite because it feeds us). Britton knows this, because he calls it a "symbiotic relationship" and gives many convincing examples of successful symbioses. Sir Karl Popper however taught us that successes are no real proof. And to carry my argument once more too far, the successful symbioses are at the least an indication for successful scientific scholarship. In the worst case, particularly the symbioses could be an indication for being an accomplice with a reality far from optimum; if not studied appropriately.

The International Decade for the Reduction of Natural Disasters (IDNDR), for example, literally needed a decade to overcome the ideology of "natural" disasters. The conceptual changes from the initial UN Declaration toward the final "Yokohama-Protocol" testify impressively to the negative effects of too successful symbioses (Plate/Merz 2001). Thomas S. Kuhn (1962) has shown that in most cases scientific progress was thwarted by so called "consensus", which very often is nothing else than the stubborn sticking to ingrained concepts. What might the IDNDR outcome have been like if the decade started with its final conceptual approach to disaster? This is exactly my question for Britton: Where might the practitioners stay if disaster sociology would provide them with "pure", "unique" concepts (instead of reflecting their every-day-concepts)?

This is, of course, a heuristic question. In reverse, we know that wrong concepts result in wrong practice. Even today, disaster sociology has not yet developed indicators that measure the success of disaster management. We still have no standardized benchmark, no exact criterion to identify any valid relation between "severity" of a disaster and the "efficacy" of disaster management. That is the reason why each person defines disaster idiosyncratically and why the fashionable trends rotate faster and faster. That is also the reason why "modern" approaches focus more on management than on emergency, as Britton reports, because "emergency" since long has disappeared in the indefinable mush of all-is-all-terminology. Even the legislation Britton cites as exemplary is far distant from understandable, measurable criteria. It is more a "programmatic declaration" of those who are in charge for emergency management but not a scientifically appropriate definition.

I completely agree with Britton that definitions about which only researchers themselves agree are of marginal value. On the other hand, definitions are not only the tools of our thinking, which also includes mental and emotional orientations, models for meaning, and worldview. Britton is absolutely right when he points at the influence of definitions for Government Organizations (GOs) and Nongovernmental Organizations (NGOs), governmental politics and policies and international aid concepts. Supposing that the practitioners all over the world base their practice on inappropriate concepts, and disaster sociology reproduces these concepts because they are consensual in practice. What then is our science worth?

That has nothing to do with jargon and Britton's attack against unintelligibility. To communicate scientific findings in a manner laypersons can grasp is no argument against (internal) scientific draft (including conceptual precision). More elucidating is Britton's reference to the FEMA workshop and the scientists who hadn't the faintest idea of the empirical reality of their field. Empirically oriented researchers can tell you a thing or two about the incongruence of the factual dealing with disaster, the after-action reports and the different "narratives" along the levels of action, how "emergency management" was taught and trained and the so called "programmatic declarations" forming legislation. Scientific precision cannot be achieved if scientists simply parrot one or another of these "every-day-concepts". They should decipher the underlying "truth" and develop a concept of "disaster" as a measurable test criterion beyond the appeasing, easing, and whitewashing telling that dominates in practice.

That, again, has nothing to do with disciplinary narrow-mindedness or with intellectual imperialism. Each science has to have a unique intellectual discipline, which is in the first place, conceptual precision. Otherwise mutual understanding across disciplines at least, will remain impossible. To me, Britton is wrong in setting the broadness and intellectual richness of all sciences into an irreconcilable contradiction with the "iron discipline", as Max Weber has put it, of the internal disciplinary reasoning. Without such an iron discipline sciences in general and disaster sociology in particular will not survive as specialized fields. Britton's statement that "disaster managers are more likely to be attuned to many of the relevant nuances" sounds alarming. What might happen to all contributing sciences, when their field can create only disciplinary instruments that miss real nuances? In that case we have to ask ourselves what our discipline is useful for; certainly not explanation.

What can I conclude? I read four interesting, stimulating, thoughtful articles that seemed to be entirely individual in the positive sense of "headstrong" but which turned out to be very similar, almost corresponding in their disregard of terminological accuracy and scientific efficiency and efficacy. I was alarmed that none of the authors seemed to embrace science, at least "western" science, and that a strange "liberalism" comes to the fore which makes everything equal, or at least indifferent. No wonder that the emergency managers become the real sentinels among the intermissions between the endless "run-of-the-mill" of their failures.

6

THE MEANING OF DISASTER:
A REPLY TO WOLF DOMBROWSKY

David Alexander

"Tell me, my man, which is the quickest way to Dublin?"
"Well, Sir, to begin with, I wouldn't start from here."

In this essay, I shall reflect on both Dombrowsky's critique of my chapter in this book and the wider issue he raises: namely, the role of science and academic disciplines in conditioning the theoretical study and practical management of disaster. With particular reference to disaster, I shall consider how the agendas of scientific and academic organization may have influenced the ways in which we define the phenomena we study. The paradox of modern intellectual activity is that we strive for objectivity but, in the Kantian manner, construct knowledge out of our own rather fragile sensory impressions guided by universal concepts and received wisdom. If this makes for incomplete theories and fluid interpretations, then perhaps that is all to the good, as they are the raw material of healthy debate. Science is a record of incomplete progress, rather than a path to ultimate enlightenment (Davies 1989) and hence none of us should presume to have all the answers.

Throughout the 1950s and 1960s geographers conducted a long and introspective debate on the meaning of their subject.

They were concerned that its breadth and division into human and physical branches allowed very little common ground. The only lasting consensus to be achieved was that, in the words of Peter Haggett's famous phrase, "geography is what geographers do." Fortunately, the diversity of the subject is its principal strength and so geography has survived, the science of the spatial view of everything and anything (Holt-Jensen 1988). Geographers have grown accustomed to the diffuseness of their collective aims, and I would hope that sociologists and other students of disaster have as well, for diversity is strength in this field too.

Although I have great sympathy for sociologists in their struggle to gain as much acceptance as physical scientists and engineers, I am not concerned about how much sociology there is in disaster. Let there be no doctrine or dogma in studies of catastrophe: I believe such works should be adisciplinary, based on the demands of the problem, not the strictures of academic disciplines (Alexander 1991), though the expertise of sociologists is obviously fundamental to such endeavours.

I do, however, believe that we should look at disaster from different perspectives and then try to integrate them. The whole is very definitely the sum of the parts, but, in certain cases, lack of adequate knowledge and understanding may make integration impossible: that is one reason why more research is needed in order to bring subtle connections to light. In this respect, it is not clear to me why Dombrowsky thinks that the economic interpretation of disaster "turns [it] into an empty term that includes many diverse, unrelated events." Disaster *does* involve imbalance between supply and demand, but no one is suggesting that this is our key to the deepest level of understanding. It is nevertheless a factor that influences attitudes and in some cases the ability to survive. Hence the relationships do exist. For a detailed demonstration of this, I recommend Eric Jones's chapter on disaster in his brilliant treatise on European and Asian economic history (Jones 1987).

Whether in economics, sociology, geography or another discipline, concentrating on a sectoral interpretation of disaster fails to gain us a holistic perspective—that was supposed to be the message of my chapter. Trying to gauge how closely or not my contribution sticks to disciplinary norms therefore misses the point. I believe instead that we should seek holistic perspectives even if progress in creating them is slow and arduous—*ad astra per aspera*. Contrary to Dombrowsky's interpretation of my chapter, I do not "admonish" the reader to "abstain from general theory". On the contrary, I have been struggling for years to construct one (see Alexander 2000: 238-247). If my perspective tends to shift as I write, besides any failings on my part, this is because of the need to view the phenomenon of disaster from different angles in order to get at the truth. This, *pace* may involve taking an epic approach in order to search for the overall picture and at more modest levels it may involve seeking connections between, as Dombrowsky puts it, "diverse, unrelated events". I fear that the links may take many more years to establish fully.

Like Dombrowsky, I have studied the antecedents of modern science (e.g. Alexander 1982, 1989) and found modern practitioners to be strongly influenced by them. Science has developed a long and honourable tradition of objective research, but it has also developed under the shadow of various questionable ideologies (see critiques by Meyer-Abich 1997 and Ehrlich and Ehrlich 1996). Anderson (1997) argued that this is equally true for sociology, whose emergence as a discipline in the nineteenth century reflected the need for systematic control of the industrial proletariat. I am not qualified to comment on the rightness of wrongness of that interpretation, but I do think that, even if Dombrowsky complains about it, we should "challenge the principles and practices of scientific craft": after all, they were brought to you by the folks who gave you, not only cures for major diseases, but also weapons of mass destruction. Hence, I have tried to lend support to the process of breaking out from scientific orthodoxy and academic territoriality. At the very least we should ask ourselves whose interests science is meant to serve.

Dombrowsky seems preoccupied with the terminology of definitions (and also with the process of defining things—*circulus in definiendo*), but let us not follow his example. Whether what I say is symbolic constructivism[1] as he argues, or not matters very little: it is all part of the struggle to understand disaster, and preferably without loading it with too much cumbersome intellectual baggage. I agree with Dombrowsky that the "sequence of phases" model of disaster (the "disaster cycle") has its faults, but I am not sure that students of disaster regard the phases as necessarily consecutive (Drabek 1985). Like all models, it is a convenient simplification and we fully appreciate that the fit with reality is somewhat awkward (Neal 1997).

Rather than being a politically correct acolyte of liberalism, I believe the current era is similar to the Baroque period, in that interpretations of reality are increasingly dominated by the tension of opposites (Maravall 1979). Far from "mixing the incompatible together", it is my intention to differentiate them by looking at the relationships between them (see Alexander 2000, 244-247). To give due weight to the role of different types of coping mechanism in reducing the impact of disasters is not "political correctness". Instead, it shows due respect for different ways of viewing disasters and surviving their impacts. In this, it is well known that modern institutional science does not have all the answers. For instance, the original, mid-1980s version of the Bangladesh Flood Action Plan (FAP) would have canalised the Brahmaputra River in order to reduce its contingent flood propensity (Dempster and Brammer 1992). Some riparian rice-farmers in Bangladesh have developed as many as 75 ways of coping with seasonal and contingent flooding. Most of these would have been no use after the restricted drainage and inadequate flood protection that massive levee building would have imposed (Westcoat *et al.* 1992). Fortunately, significant pressure from knowledgeable academics and others forced the transformation of the FAP into a series of smaller projects that are more hospitable to local expertise, though unfortunately, the mindset of provincial administrators in Bangladesh quelled most of the nascent democratisation of flood prevention (Warner 2003).

Dombrowsky argues that I contradict myself in saying that disasters are not defined by fixed events but mindset is. This is not so. I regard the definition of disaster to be fluid, but I see fixed attitudes to it developing in some quarters. Regarding the situation in which perceptions and opinions are manufactured by the controllers of mass communication, mindset is perhaps more of a convenience term than a descriptive one. Nevertheless, Thomas Love Peacock satirised the process very elegantly in his novel *Crochet Castle* (1831):

> He [Crochet of Crochet] found it essential to his dignity to furnish himself with a coat of arms, which, after the proper ceremonies (payment being the principal), he obtained, *vide-licet*: Crest, a crochet rampant, in A sharp: Arms, three empty bladders, turgescent, to show how opinions are formed; three bags of gold, pendant, so show how they are maintained; three naked swords, tranchant, to show how they are administered; and three barbers' blocks, gaspant, to show how they are swallowed.

How very appropriate this seems in the modern world of mass-media empires!

While on the subject of public opinion-mongering, Dombrowsky appears to have misinterpreted *Newspeak*, from Orwell's *Nineteen Eighty-Four* (first published in 1949), which was an attempt to reduce concepts to a simple, black-and-white juxtaposition of opposites (in the form of single words), and then to satirise them, *reductio ad absurdum*, in order to stop people thinking deeply. That was not my intention and I hope very much that it was not the outcome of my chapter. I do not see why the interpretation of disaster in contemporary terms is a form of *Newspeak*. Instead, it is something that has always taken place. Mere tradition may not be a good argument for its continuation, but as people perceive disaster and deal with it in the context of the realities of their times, so it deserves to be interpreted in that light. Hence, we will probably never achieve a *telos*, or masterful completion to our studies of disaster, so let us return to Omar Khayyam and reconcile ourselves to transiency:

> With them the Seed of Wisdom did I sow,
> And with my own hand labour'd it to grow:
> And this was all the Harvest that I reap'd—
> "I came like Water and like Wind I go."
> (*Rubayyat*, XXX, trans. Edward Fitzgerald, 1859)

I do agree with Orwell that we are creating a dystopia (a society which is considered undesirable), but that is as far as it goes. With respect to Orwell's times, the world has changed, the context is different, and the root causes of dystopia are now based on different patterns of inequality and power imbalances.

In his essay Dombrowsky has mounted a spirited defence of science against "liberalism". I agree with that stance, in so far as neo-liberalism has done so much to subvert the aims and choices inherent in modern scientific activity. However, that should not be a reason for ignoring the role of science, hand-in-hand with neo-liberalism, in the creation of both vulnerability and disaster, as well as a set of public attitudes and perceptions connected with technocentrism and fuelled by lucrocentrism (yes, I did coin that term—see Alexander 2000: 244). Indigenous coping mechanisms are thus increasingly a defence against both disasters and the depredations wrought by the modern world's power structures.

It is not political correctness to discuss coping mechanisms as a means of rationalising disaster (though in reality they are a means of coping with it). The message from fieldwork is that indigenous coping mechanisms are not to be swept aside and replaced with imported ones without very good justification (for a good example of this, see Schware 1982). However, it is becoming increasingly clear that the way to involve people in managing their own security is to resort to participatory rather than representative democracy. The latter has proved inadequate on numerous occasions, as Wisner (2003) has chronicled (Dombrowsky should see this excellent article for the details he is seeking of how geographers operationally define the concepts "artifact", "affliction", "social construct" and "change").

Finally, if emergency managers are the real custodians of truth about disasters, as Dombrowsky seems to be saying, this is because of the failure of academics to communicate in simple language to a wider audience than people of their own kind. Disaster studies are very distinctive in that they rely on a mixture of theoretical constructions by scholars and reports from the field by practitioners. It is a major task to get the two groups to communicate with one another, but a vitally important one.

I trust I have not been too idiosyncratic in my definition of disaster, and have not preferred convenient fictions to awkward truths. Scientific (or more precisely social scientific) orthodoxy is not necessarily efficient or efficacious in getting at the latter. Instead, it is time to strike out and look for radical new interpretations of disaster, and that will also help keep the debate fresh and vigorous.

NOTES

[1] "Symbolic constructivism" seems to be a neologism and hence its meaning is unclear. The more common term in the social sciences is "symbolic interactionism", in which the individual's concept of self is regarded as an internalisation of social processes (Charron 2000). "Constructivism" was originally the movement through which art was "constructed" to be functional in some manner. The term has since been applied to the way that images are created by publicity (Ploughman 1995). I am not aware that this notion has yet been merged with symbolic interactionism, though presumably it could be.

7

PRAGMATISM AND RELEVANCE: A RESPONSE TO WOLF R. DOMBROWSKY

Susan L. Cutter

I read Dombrowsky's critique of the set of papers with great interest. His critique was often difficult to follow especially the logic of his argument, but the paper did present some interesting points worth considering.

First, I do not hold a "suspicious view of philosophy of science". Rather, I acknowledge that there are competing views of science and scientific explanation (Snow 1993). From my perspective, science (and scientific practice) is socially constructed, a position that is viewed as membership in relativist school of thought within the "science wars" (Gould 2000). Science is but one set of beliefs that help us to understanding the intrinsic order of nature. Scientific "truth" or the universality of the findings are not absolute, but are in fact socially conditioned. The production of knowledge itself is partially determined by human agency and influenced by gender, race, social, and cultural differences (Harding 1991). Thus, the choice of scientific problems and hypotheses are not based on some objective truth in as much as they can be defined and structured differently depending on one's personal agenda and perspective.

Second, I am skeptical of the continuing definitional debates and arguments regarding the terminology that is used in our discourse involving hazards, risks, disasters, and vulnerability. Instead of being mired in these definitional concerns about what is a disaster, we should simply state our usage of the term and move forward to solve some of the pressing research and applications questions. In that spirit, I use the following definitions: risk is the likelihood or the probability of occurrence of an event; hazards are the potential threats to people and the things they value as well as the impact of an event on society and the environment; vulnerability is the potential for loss or the capacity to suffer harm from a hazard; and disasters are singular (or interactive) events that have a profound impact on local people or places in terms of injuries, deaths, property damages or environmental impacts. I contended in the paper, and re-iterate here, that this line of scholarly inquiry into semantics (or ontological debates) is counter-productive at this point in the intellectual development of the field. We need to move on to more important questions. Dombrowsky suggests one himself: "We still have no standardized benchmark, no exact criterion to identify any valid relation between 'severity' of a disaster and the 'efficacy' of disaster management". This is an important consideration that the social sciences can and should address. The academic practice of navel staring is fine for some scholars and disciplines, but disaster research is a relevant and pragmatic endeavor; one that uncovers new knowledge and then applies it to reduce the impacts of disasters on society. We must not forget that.

Third, I would like the research community to read more widely than we do at present and develop more intellectual synergism in our range of perspectives and methodologies that impinge on disaster research. Ignorance of the contributions of allied disciplines is inexcusable especially when they can inform and advance multidisciplinary understanding of disasters and their consequences on society. On this point, Dombrowsky and I concur.

Fourth, I think Dombrowsky misunderstood the meaning of my phrasing "regardless of origin". Until very recently, research and practice in the disasters field was segmented into specific hazard domains; earthquake response, hurricane preparedness and so on.

Now the dominant approach by state and local governments in the U.S. is increasingly oriented towards an "all hazards" perspective. There is a set of generic understandings about hazards assessment and response, which are then customized based on the source of the threat (e.g. flooding, terrorist act). In contrast to this more integrative perspective, the research community still generally practices its science based on specific hazard etiologies and is not examining the commonalities in how society responds to, learns from, and mitigates environmental threats. This is not to suggest that all hazards are equal in their characteristics, impact, or importance, however. Dombrowsky does make a good point about the intent heuristic (or what many call adaptive threats or social hazards) as a distinguishing attribute of hazards. I would also include the voluntary/involuntary nature of the hazard exposure and the geographic scale as other key heuristics in differentiating among different hazards. However, we don't need to reinvent a typology of hazards or taxonomies of causal agents for disasters—work that was done decades ago (Hohenemser, Kates and Slovic 1985; Burton, Kates, and White, 1993).

Finally, I remain steadfast in my opinion that social science perspectives on disasters will assume increasing importance and relevance in the next decade. There are serious concerns about the role of human agency in threat perception, hazard production, vulnerability mediation, and response. Are disasters the same everywhere and do they have similar effects? How are risks transferred over space and through time? What conditions cause adaptive or maladaptive responses to crises? In what ways do disasters threaten the environmental security of nations? How have the processes of urbanization and globalization increased societal vulnerability to hazards? How do individuals and communities respond to unexpected events? Are our organizational structures and institutions adequately prepared to respond to unanticipated and unexpected events? We need to shift our focus away from semantic debates on what is a disaster to a more focused research endeavor that is theoretically robust, methodologically challenging, and above all, responsive to the informational needs of the hazard and disaster practitioner communities.

8

DEFINING THE DEFINITION FOR ADDRESSING THE "REALITY"

Rohit Jigyasu

Dombrowsky's response to the four approach papers is very articulate and he manages to raise some very basic issues concerning the theme of our discussion of "What is a disaster?". I think one of his main achievements has been to pull together various papers (even those which manage to drift away) and bring them back to the central point of our discussion.

My response to Dombrowsky and also to other approach papers will be an elaboration of some central points raised by the authors. I will be touching on two aspects; firstly regarding the scope, limits and purpose behind the definition of "disaster" and secondly, I shall attempt to answer the apt question put forward by Dombrowsky: "How real is the reality of disaster?"

DEFINING THE DEFINITION

I shall begin by bringing forth Perry's (1998) view that many people and groups both define and need definitions of disaster and that each group or individual creates a definition with different ends in mind. In the words of Britton, definitions are not only the tools of our thinking, but also mental and emotional orientations, models for meaning and world-views. In my opinion, the question of definitions with respect to important terms such as disaster in our case is paramount but the strive towards defining commonly acceptable definitions should be open and flexible. There may be multiple definitions of a single term, based on what we put in the center, whether viewed purely from a sociological view or taking into consideration multiple disciplinary views. Even one discipline may take an ideological view based on the undercurrents of political standpoint and this is all the more evident in the case of sociology, which forms diverse views on how the researcher views the society and its interrelationships.

While the definitions are crucial for deciding the limits of any particular discipline they should also form a blueprint where flexible relationships with other disciplines can be developed leading to gradual advance and extending the scope of the discipline. The ultimate point of a field is not to become isolated shell, something that is complete within itself, rather any advancement in the field should ultimately contribute towards larger goals for the betterment of humanity. Therefore it is good to have multiple definitions of a concept. What is also needed is a debate on inherent similarities and differences between these multiple definitions so as to be able to create a symbiosis on the concept, thereby giving it totality of meaning.

"RESEARCHER" VERSUS "PRACTITIONER"

Britton, in his approach paper also stresses on the need as well as existing opportunities to bring together scholars and practitioners to discuss, debate, refine and reflect on the issues of definitions of disasters and their implications. He emphasizes the need of providing researcher and practitioner with common platforms. As a practitioner, the emergency manager plays an important role in developing procedures in disaster situations. Britton agrees with Waugh's observation that a major problem in defining emergency management today is finding the boundaries of the field; and the field is as broad as the risks that society faces. He raises the issue of both researchers and practitioners dismissing each other.

While common platforms for researcher and practiti
indeed be useful in order that both can draw from the ex
of each other. The question is whether the boundaries
emergency manager (basically a practitioner) and a disaster
researcher should be merged. I am very skeptical to this idea as
both have different, although closely related roles to perform. While
a "research" (literally meaning "to search again") by its very
definition is a backward looking activity, a practice is based on a
vision, which is drawn on past knowledge or experience. A researcher
can put on the hat of a practitioner and vice versa but a researcher
cannot be in the same mode of thinking as a practitioner at the
same time.

Actually a researcher and a practitioner can work hand in hand, learning from each other. While a practitioner can try testing some theoretical construct in practice, the researcher can generate significant knowledge on the basis of the experience gathered by the practitioner and in many cases can even decide on the question of his or her research based on the hole in the knowledge that he will be able to figure out only by gathering flaws in existing practice. How emergency managers view the world and how they define disaster is therefore highly relevant. But I feel that the task of defining a disaster should be left mainly on to disaster researcher, who may generate significant knowledge from the results in practice and use that very knowledge to improve the definition of disaster. We may define disasters for the sake of research or practice but our crucial search here is about the meanings and characteristics of the term itself.

To conclude however, the fundamental question is whether we are addressing, "disaster research" or "disaster (emergency) management". Both these terms are quite different but may ultimately contribute towards the definition of the disaster. As part of disaster research, one may research on existing emergency management systems as part of exploring the successes and failures in dealing with disasters. Disaster Research may ultimately mean research on disaster, research in disaster or research on disaster management. To put it in other words, disaster researcher may call for reflecting in the action, on the action or on the phenomena itself that leads to or calls for action. Each of this type of distinct research activity will contribute towards definition of disasters.

THEORY AS "PRODUCT" AND "GENERATOR" OF DEFINITION

In order to take this discussion further, I wish to bring in the importance of theory in the definition of disaster. Needless to say, in the pursuit towards defining disaster, one needs a strong theoretical basis. While I do not wish to deny the importance of developing the theory itself, I am quite critical to the process in which theory is constructed and packaged in many cases. Disaster research can significantly aid towards construction of theory, which will aid in refining the definition of disaster. However at the same time, we need to find out why theory is not influencing results and based on our results modify the theory. A theory might well be the starting point of research (theory as generator) or it might be the result of practical experience in the field (theory as product).

I agree with Dombrowsky's criticism of Cutter that while the relationship between disaster and vulnerability are paramount, these cannot be lumped together. One needs to separate normative aspects from the phenomenon itself. Underlying or root causes of vulnerability are important in order to be able to reduce vulnerability.

FROM PERCEPTION TO COMPREHENSION FOR THE SAKE OF "REALITY"

Britton refers to Thomas (1918) while talking about the basic postulates of sociology that each person acts on the basis of his or definition of the situation. According to him, human beings do not passively respond to environmental stimuli, but rather we constantly interpret what we perceive. It is difficult to account for the social action of others except in terms of how those actors define the situation they find themselves in. This issue of perception is again raised by Dombrowsky when he raises a critique question on the "reality" of the disaster. I agree with his vie disaster is not and never was a reality and that it is a wor describes something we perceive within the space and time we observe. However, the critical question is whose perception are we talking about. The moment we bring in perception, the "object" which could be "described" turns into a "subject" which is colored by the images, which in most societies are result of religious or other belief systems.

In my paper, I have taken this debate further by stressing that we need to move beyond perception. Very much the way Dombrowsky states, the core question always was and still is the relation between idea and the world beyond perception. In my opinion, the world beyond perceptions is not about constructivism but about comprehension in physical and mental space and time. Although as geographers we describe disaster in space and time, it is the mental description (collective as well as individual), that constructs disaster in human conscience. Therefore disaster no matter how we describe it in constructivist tradition (image formation) is ultimately a reality, which is constructed in cognitive mind of those who experience and also those who address disasters.

Another important point, which Dombrowsky touches upon while giving a critique on my paper is about the problem of "abstract thinking". However I believe that thinking or rather thought process is not abstract, it is always based on some underlying assumptions and belief systems. Rather, it is only human behavior, which is abstract in more than one ways. I am in fact glad to learn that my paper reinforced his belief in sharpening instruments of science, so that they are able to recognize the recognizable human behavior and brings them into a mode of indicators, which gives us the ability to "construct" the reality of the disaster in a scientific manner.

It is important to move beyond western world views on which our notions of "reality" have been well-founded and take into consideration multiple world views from various cultures, not only to emphasize what is different, but rather more importantly to recognize the basic similarities which form the crux of human

behavior in the times of "disasters" as is understand by us and them. On the other hand, I very much agree with Thomas Kuhn's (1962) viewpoint mentioned by Dombrwosky that in most cases, scientific progress was thwarted by so called "consensus". For advance of the field , it is equally important to make the differences explicit and base our definitions on the premises of recognizing these subtle or sharp differences in "comprehensions" and not mere "perceptions" of a phenomena described as "disaster".

9

DOG OR DEMON?

Neil R. Britton

Wolf Dombrowsky's comments remind me of an old Chinese tale about an Emperor who one day asked his court artist, "What is easy to paint and what is difficult to paint?" The courtier thought hard on this for as long as he knew his master's tolerance would permit and replied, "Dogs are difficult, but demons are easy." The courtier explained further to his Emperor that obvious things are hard to get right because everyone knows all about them and hence everyone thinks they know what the essence of a dog is. However, since no one has actually seen a demon then drawing one is easy, because who can say it is not correct.

To me, this ancient tale strikes at the heart of the debate about 'What is a Disaster?' Is disaster a dog because when one occurs it is "obvious", or is it a demon because, up to now at least, no-one really knows what it is? Even though both scientist and citizen have trouble reaching agreement about what the precise factors are, it seems that most are certain when one has occurred. While there are major policy and practice, let alone theoretical, implications in having disaster as dog, it must surely be better than having disaster as demon. In fact, we have already been down the latter track and thankfully got off it, although it took a concerted effort to overcome the comfort that disaster as an "act of god" provided. It was no doubt comforting for policy—and decision-makers to regard disaster as an event beyond their control. Old-time disaster practitioners certainly benefited; all they needed to be seen to do was to play games and everyone was happy. The reason why we overcame that particular superstition and silliness was because academics—sociologists in particular—were able to set the stage by identifying, qualifying and documenting disaster's key parameters and over time to associate many of the causal factors to human activity rather than other-world demons. Although some influential segments of society have not lost the need to conjure up demons or insist on demon definitions, and here I am thinking particularly of the current US Administration and its bizarre rhetoric in its so-called war against terrorism, it is pleasing to know that such a fundamentalist attitude does not appear to be in the ascendance. The real dilemma about this specific situation is that after all the events that the modern world has gone through, why can such a view be tolerated at all as we move on through the twenty-first century?

The question that I posed in my initial contribution centers on these issues. Namely, if disaster is a social action that everyone as a social actor has the potential to experience, but at the same there is a gap between groups of actors about what the said activity is, then one way to bridge this disparity is to release the definitional debate from its customary keepers (the academics) and allow other groups at least to contribute as of right. This should not be regarded as an heretical recommendation, especially given today's reality that there are many social groups now who have the credentials as well as the inclination to worry about definitions and generate theories apart from the professional academic-as-scientist-or-researcher, who at one stage were society's paid elite thinkers, but now are experiencing competition from many sources outside the university or research agency. Today there are tens of thousands of highly trained practitioners many of whom hold doctoral degrees, who have received higher education that permits them to be systematic in their thinking and to have excellent analytical capabilities. Moreover, this non-academic group is able to offer different perspectives from which to view disaster. Disaster after all, as Quarantelli and Dynes reminded us many years ago, is a social occasion. To take this one step further, defining disaster should also be a social occasion in the sense that those groups who have a declared interest in it should be able to contribute to its definition. If this was done as an open process, then it might be possible to overcome the perennial issue of not being able to agree on what "it" is. Of course, social scientists will be amongst those who will put up their hands to indicate they have a vested interest; and so they should. Social science and sociology in particular has contributed immensely to the de-mystification of disaster. One of the many contributions sociology makes is that it helps to explain the obvious, the everyday as well as the unintended and unanticipated implications of social action. In this respect, the courtier's "dog or demon" distinction is just as relevant for sociology as it is for disaster:

1. Sociology as dog provides explanation of the 'obvious' factors pertaining to social interaction, social systems, social processes, social structure, interpretation of social life and so on;
2. Disaster as dog; sociology provides explanation of the obvious pertaining to social sequelae of threat and/or impact;
3. Sociology as demon; provides explanation of the latent, unintended, hidden, and masked;
4. Disaster as demon; sociology provides explanation of latent, unintended, hidden, and masked effects surrounding non-routine events.

In my view, sociology will contribute more in the future, particularly after sociologists specializing in disaster willingly and systematically assess their own contribution within a wider definitional field, which would include other disciplines as well as practitioners from backgrounds as diverse as emergency management, development, environment, health, welfare and justice, and also the public administration and policy-oriented sector. If this were to occur, it is likely to spark some interesting synthesis. I don't believe it will be to the detriment of any specific discipline, certainly not sociology, in fact it might be the light that flames a truly multi-disciplinary fusion. It will definitely be to the betterment of understanding what disaster is. In this respect, everyone will win.

Moving on to Dombrowsky's central comment about my initial paper, my sense is that he over-read my statements or else I failed to make the point clear that contemporary practitioners who have academic training, and who contribute significantly in academic settings (for example as adjunct professors, special advisers, contributors to journals, journal editors, academic text writers, specialist presenters to academic conferences) are now very capable of making a contribution to theory, which is an area that academics have traditionally considered to be their turf. One aspect I failed to mention in my initial paper is that my view on the significance of practitioners to academic activities was formed in large part after I had spent a few years pursuing a second career away from universities, to realize what relatively little impact academics had on framing and explaining some vexed issues confronting government policy—and decision-makers. As a manager specializing in disaster management in both local and central government settings, and later in the international arena, one of my frustrations was dealing with the reluctance of academics to come to grips with the reality of actual situations that disaster managers were dealing with. More recently, this frustration has been compounded by the realization that academic researchers in some non-western societies, including social scientists, are reluctant to acknowledge practitioners as legitimate stakeholders worth engaging. In a way, academics need to "unlearn" in order to learn what the issues are, how the issues are perceived and dealt with by other sectors, and how they could contribute to a process of issue solution. Of course, this is a generalization. There are some extremely competent academics who intuitively know how to convert their specialized knowledge into meaningful and practical outputs. However, they seem to be in the minority. Whether overall this is a good thing or not, I am not in a position to answer, but I do believe this situation is socially unbeneficial. What my experience has taught me is that these days I am more ready to call upon a practitioner with academic training to help me out rather than a professional academic. The specialized disciplinary approach that comes with most academics seems to somehow get in the way.

I presented this line of argument to Dombrowsky during the course of one of our email exchanges following his review of the first set of contributions, and he agrees that he may have over-emphasized the impression I placed on practitioners. However, he did it for a reason (Wolf never does anything without having a reason!), and that was to express a concern about what he detects as an increasing undertone against sociology and a growing over-estimation of what practitioners are capable of doing. In this respect, Dombrowsky is concerned that some new myths are being created.

I do not dispute Dombrowsky's concern. In fact I sense he is correct in his suggestion that academics are currently afflicted by a relative decline in favor, and that perhaps the pendulum is currently swinging away from them. This, however, is a separate issue from that to which the current focus is directed. On this point, however, let me simply state that I am not happy with the apparent anti-intellectual sentiment that often surfaces, although it does not really surprise me. What does surprise me is how well academia has been able to avoid, in relative terms, close scrutiny of much of its activities, especially at a time when other sectors of society are witnessing often nasty attacks from above and below. Nevertheless, I would not like the comments I made in the initial paper, or in this reply, to be regarded as an attack on academics even though I do think there are issues pertaining to academic competence, performance and in some cases relevance that need to be dealt with as a matter of some urgency. Bringing this back to the matter at hand, my reply to Dombrowsky is that it should not be regarded as one group *against* another; it should be groups *complementing* other groups. The matter at hand is how to *combine* the efforts of all groups so that the insights and potential of all can be brought together. This seems like an appropriate sociological exercise to me.

ombrowsky further states the problem with my contribution : my eulogy (sic) on practitioners and their fruitful exchange with science makes any critique twice difficult: because the practitioners are "the good ones". In response, I don't think in terms of good or bad ones. I certainly do not believe for a moment that practitioners are capable of providing the conceptual answers *on their own*. This is not the point I was trying to make. Let me repeat my original position: thinking that one group alone can provide an acceptable definition for something as eclectic and far-reaching as disaster is naïve. The real world is not a disaggregated or disassembled, mass; this is the creation of academic compartmentalization. Rather, it is a coherent, connected, consolidated and continuous series of inter-linked phenomena (what academia has not solved, however, is how to re-assemble the world they have so carefully separated into different disciplinary components). Practitioners do not have the luxury of working like this, not when they have to deal within the political reality of multiple jurisdictions, different and diverse publics, multiple task masters, a plethora of organizations and agencies, unequal resource distribution, competing tasks, and so on.

Dombrowsky is also concerned with my comment that "disaster managers are more likely to be attuned to many of the relevant nuances". He thinks this is "alarming". I think this is the reality. I am not quite sure why he thinks that the group that does the managing, and who know the most empirically (even if the majority do not always have frameworks in their heads or on their shelves), would not be attuned to the nuances. How many disaster researchers get to routinely meet with government ministers or city mayors to discuss the politically feasibility of a possible activity that has city-wide, regional or national implications? Or how many can deal with local or national constituencies to hear their voice, or sit in inter-agency meetings to discuss joint planning programs that have significant long-term economic and development implications? Or how many can deliberate on the implementation a contingency plan that has the potential to re-shape the direction or look of an entire community; or make choices that can have life-

or-death consequences? These are the everyday matters of disaster practitioners. They are the things disaster researchers' dream of. In a field like disaster, policy development for appropriate operational planning and practice, on the one hand, and theory development, on the other, are closely entwined; or they should be. If they are not, then one or the other is seriously out of alignment with the real world. By forging closer alliances between practitioner and researcher, the more likely the reality of disaster will be explored, explained, codified, understood—and acted upon. Isn't this what we all want?

Disaster research cannot afford to have a situation where, for all practical purposes, researchers and practitioners belong to two different cultures, or think they do. This was the situation described by C.P. Snow who by training was a scientist and by vocation a writer. To maintain his interests he felt obliged to live in two different worlds; or 'two cultures' as he described it. His description about the gulf between these two sectors and how it barred inter-linkages that should have been natural concomitants should give pause:

> There have been plenty of days when I have spent the working hours with scientists and then gone off at night with some literary colleagues. I mean that literally. I have had, of course, intimate friends among both scientists and writers. It was through living among these groups and much more, I think, through moving regularly from one to the other and back again that I got occupied with the problem of what, long before I put it on paper, I christened to myself as the 'two cultures'. For constantly I felt I was moving among two groups—comparable in intelligence, identical in race, not grossly different in social origin, earning about the same incomes, who had almost ceased to communicate at all, who in intellectual, moral and psychological climate had so little in common that instead of going from Burlington House or South Kensington to Chelsea, one might have crossed an ocean (Snow 1969: 2).

While sociology teaches us about the process of secondary (or adult) socialization as we enter the workforce and which molds us so we can function with a minimum of discomfort within the workplace and identify with a new set of peers (called workmates), this process should not close us off to other groups whose activities are reciprocal. There is a serious need to minimize any thinking gaps that exist between academic and practitioner. This is why I am ambivalent about trying to preserve the uniqueness of the sociological enterprise to disaster research if, by doing so, it blinkers sociologists. The unique approach of sociology, especially to go behind the veneer of society and see what is lurking underneath (I think this was C.W. Mills phrase), is a tremendous asset. I have always liked the legitimating feel this has given to poke, prod and expose aspects of society that need to be revealed. For my part, I am more interested in trying to get a better understanding of what disaster is in all its manifestations and not just what sociology thinks it is. This can best be achieved by merging all perspectives (something like this was attempted many years ago, if I recall correctly, by some of the early NORC researchers, but I have not seen any recent replication), by looking at the issue full on, by directing attention to finding out 'what is a disaster?', rather than what do sociologists think, or what do anthropologists think, or economists, engineers, earth scientists, or political scientists think. The sociological perspective is, after all, only one way to look at an issue. What is needed is recognition of the complexity, uncertainty and ambiguity that is inherent in disaster *qua* disaster and to approach the process of understanding it in a way that values and includes the contributions provided by a wide range of observers from academia and practice. And it should be remembered that the practice line of work is as diverse as academia in terms of its specializations and sub-specializations).

This line of argument reminds me of a paper I read a while ago by Russell Blong, an Australian hazards geographer who, amongst his many other credentials, acquired a degree in engineering and almost also got an MBA before he saw the light (his words!). He has spent much of his professional academic life working with the insurance sector, which is why he titled the paper I am referring to as, "a geography of natural perils". One part of his paper reflects on a period of geography during the 1960s when it was struggling for respectability (I wonder if every discipline goes through a stage like this?). The issue seemed to resolve itself, at least for one geographical school of thought, when one of its advocates, Ron Johnston (my former geography professor) declared that 'geography is what geographers do' (Johnston 1987: 47). What a pragmatic and, I believe, a mature position to take. In essence it says, let's get on with things and stop messing around with the small stuff that no one (apart from a few geographers) seems concerned with. While the few were worrying themselves about definitional purity others linked to the geographical enterprise went on to develop useful tools such as GIS and contributed to new approaches like environmental engineering. Setting aside the question of defining the field hasn't affected the credibility or output of the discipline of geography, and if anything this pragmatism has helped it to develop into a more useful area of study. I wonder when sociology might do likewise. I get the feeling this is what Aguirre (2002) might like us to do, even though in many ways he is the quintessential sociology disaster academic.

PART II

10

DISASTER AND COLLECTIVE STRESS

Allen H. Barton

ORIGINS OF CONTEMPORARY DISASTER RESEARCH

In 1961 I was asked to prepare a sociological review of existing research on disasters for the Disaster Research Group of the Division of Anthropology and Psychology of the National Academy of Sciences and National Research Council. Note the absence of Sociology from the National Academy division; Anthropology and Psychology were sciences recognized by the government, but Sociology was not. The study was intended to show how sociology was relevant to policy advice and help get sociology into that establishment.

The Disaster Research Group had been established in 1952 as the result of a request from the Surgeons General of the Army, Navy and Air Force that the NAS-NRC "conduct a survey and study in the fields of scientific research and development applicable to problems which might result from disasters by enemy action—other words to examine how research on disasters could be applied to civil defense in a nuclear war (Committee on Disaster Studies 1956). After US-Soviet relations became more stabilized and the grim interest in "thinking about the unthinkable" lost priority, the Disaster Research Group and its successor programs turned more toward trying to improve response to "normal disasters," but in the early 1960s civil defense against nuclear war was the overriding concern, and it has continued to be one reason for governmental interest.

At that time disaster research consisted of a few dozen field studies of natural and accidental disasters, along with some studies of wartime bombing including the great fire raids on Hamburg, Dresden and Tokyo and the final paroxysms of Hiroshima and Nagasaki. The studies were mostly observational or based on informant stories, accompanied by such aggregate statistics on damage and loss as were available; a handful had quantitative sample-survey data on behavior of individuals and organizations. It should be noted that in the 1960s I tried to codify results from less than 100 studies. By 1986 when Thomas Drabek created his encyclopedic *Human Response to Disaster: An Inventory of Sociological Findings*, he worked with 1000 studies. How many are there now?

RECONCEPTUALIZING DISASTER AS A FORM OF COLLECTIVE STRESS

In examining the disaster literature available in the 1960s I confronted the vast discrepancy between the small scale of most of the disasters actually studied—tornadoes, explosions, impact of a flood or hurricane in one community or at most a number of communities within a region of a nation—and the apocalyptic scale of a nuclear war on a whole nation. I was forced to come up with a much broader concept than the usual one of disaster, to avoid the folly of extrapolating from how communities and nations dealt with localized stresses to the problems of the nationwide impact of nuclear war, and thus encouraging the idea that nuclear war was a workable national strategy. My overall concept was "collective stress" (Barton 1963, 1969).

I defined collective stress situations as those in which "many members of a social system fail to receive expected conditions of life from the system." This brought in comparisons with larger and less sudden stresses such as wartime bombing, genocide, crop failures and famines, depressions, epidemics, and environmental decay, as well as chronic conditions like poverty, slums, racial oppression, and endemic disease. All of these prevent large numbers of members of a society from living under conditions socially defined as normal or adequate in terms of human needs.

Defining collective stress as arising from large-scale deprivation of conditions of a socially defined normal way of life means that there may be disagreement on whether conditions are normal or create undue stress and require a remedy. The immediate victims suffer stress, but the extent to which the rest of society and its leadership are under stress depends on their sympathetic identification with the victims and whether they feel psychological or social pressure to do anything about the situation. In particular there is often disagreement between social and economic elites and the underlying population, and between those who define themselves as superior in race or caste or achievement and those they consider inferior.

Recent cross-national research on social conditions has tried to avoid conflict with socially constructed definitions of "deprivation" by using objective physiological indicators. United Nations and World Bank sponsored research on "human development" in different countries has used such indicators as life expectancy, infant mortality, maternal mortality, health statistics and dietary standards. Such research finds for example that the survival rate of men in Harlem is lower than in Bangladesh (Sen 1993), and that life expectancy fell by ten years in Russia after the "big bang" replacement of a "stagnant" socialism with a chaotic parody of capitalism (Stiglitz 2002).

These physiological measures are powerful and convincing evidence of extremes of deprivation, but defining "human needs" in terms of physical survival or physiological functioning omits a great deal which we may want to consider in making social policy. There are psychological stresses for otherwise healthy survivors who have lost family members, for people defined as "inferior races" or "inferior castes", people fired from long-time jobs in the "creative destruction" of laissez-faire market economies, or the working poor in such economies who experience relative deprivation. It seems best to use a concept of deprivation relative to the standards of a given society and historical period, and recognize that there is often a lack of consensus between victims and non-victims, or between sympathetic reformers and ideological conservatives. This avoids the problem of defining even the aristocracy of medieval Europe as "deprived" because their health was not as good as that of 20th century populations, or arguments that because the American poor have much higher per capita income than Namibian desert tribesmen they are not "really deprived." It allows for considering the social stress created when there is a "revolution of rising expectations", or a redefinition of human needs. On the other hand it does leave us with the problem of how to regard the situation of those who seem resigned to loss, poverty, or enslavement, whose aspirations have shrunk to what experience tells them is their lot. The degree of consensus becomes a variable highly important in understanding response or lack of response to given situations.

Some research on "development" of nations uses level of expenditures on various public services as a measure of quality of life; for example health or education expenditures. However as an engineer put it when told that his local schools were excellent because they spent so many dollars per pupil, "In my field we put the cost in the denominator, not the numerator." By this he meant that quality of services should be measured by the social output, not the economic input; education by what the students learn; health services by how much they improve health; and so on. Considering both output and cost gives a measure of efficiency of the service, but the output cannot be assumed to be measured by the cost.

AN ATTRIBUTE-SPACE FOR COLLECTIVE STRESS SITUATIONS

In my 1963 monograph for the National Academy and my 1969 book *Communities in Disaster*, I developed a typology of collective stress situations based on the spatial and temporal dimensions of deprivation:

Societal scope: national, regional, community, or a social category. The addition of "social category" to the otherwise geographical levels of this dimension allows inclusion of stress impacting a large number of people who are geographically scattered but members of an identifiable social group.

—*Concentration in time*: sudden, gradual, chronic.

Combining the two of these gives a typology with twelve categories of collective stress situations, in which sudden physical impacts at the local or regional level, most often studied by disaster research, are only two of many types of collective stress.

A TYPOLOGY OF COLLECTIVE STRESS SITUATIONS				
	NATIONAL	REGIONAL	SEGMENTAL	LOCAL
SUDDEN	Nuclear war Invasion Economic crash Rebellion	Earthquake Major flood Nuclear plant meltdown Hurricane	Ethnic massacre Corporate layoff Expropriation of a class	Tornado Explosion Ghetto riot Plant closing by main employer
GRADUAL	Depression Epidemic Environment decay Government breakdown	Famine Drought Price collapse of main crop Land exhaustion	Aborigines dying off Obsolete occupation Rise of group discrimination Addictions to harmful substances	Decline of main industry Environmental pollution Land sinking Coal seam fire
CHRONIC	Poverty Endemic disease Wartime bombing Colonialism	Backward regions Endemic disease Internal colonialism	Enslavement Race or Class discrimination, persecution Political persecution Gender or sexual orientation discrimination	Slum, ghetto, rural slum Pockets of joblessness High crime areas

QUESTIONS RAISED BY THE COLLECTIVE STRESS CONCEPT

Comparing the results of disaster studies with research on other types of collective stress situations, I found several main sociological questions:

> *Question 1*: Why are the public, the government, and organizational elites so *responsive to the needs of victims* in some situations of collective deprivation (particularly physical disasters) and not to the deprived in other situations?

This question is particularly raised by those such as Charles Fritz (1961) who find that disasters create a "therapeutic community," or in Wolfenstein's (1957) term, a "post-disaster Utopia," dominated by altruistic behavior and social solidarity, while other forms of mass deprivation go unnoticed and unchallenged by both public and leadership.

> *Question 2*: What determines whether the immediate victims of collective stress *respond rationally and capably*, or conversely are passive, ineffective, or demoralized?

One of the first findings of research on physical disasters in modern Western societies was that victims typically engage in active and reasonably competent self-help. Other situations of mass deprivation seem to generate fatalism, lack of active self-help, self-blame, or irrational scapegoating. Some victims of collective stress develop organization and win political influence, while others are passive and unorganized. Comparative studies have found areas in which the experience of centuries of oppression has generated a culture of "amoral familism" which rejects community action (Banfield 1958). In such societies natural disasters do not result in restoration but neglect or the theft of relief funds by a corrupt elite.

Question 3: What determines the *effectiveness* of responses to mass deprivations of various sorts, and how can societies learn to improve that effectiveness?

This question arises from comparison of effective with ineffective responses to particular types of collective stress in different communities, societies and historical periods, as well as from comparison of effectiveness in dealing with different types of collective stress (e.g. chronic vs. sudden, recurrent vs. infrequent, originating in "natural hazards" vs. social conflict.) The sources of effectiveness lie at the individual level (motivation, skill), at the group and organizational level (cooperation, leadership, resources), at the community level (inter-organizational coordination, technical and social skill of leadership, capacity to mobilize resources), and social leadership at higher levels (in state and national government, in large corporations, in large voluntary organizations, in professional and intellectual communities providing knowledge to guide policies.) At each level there can be activity or passivity, cooperation or non-cooperation, knowledge or ignorance, and ability or inability to bring resources to the problem. The research I reviewed also shows that coordination between levels—mass individual responses and organizational responses, governmental and non-governmental organizations, and levels of government— is a general problem.

The research reviewed also showed a problem in the transition from immediate spontaneous and emergency-organization response to the phase of reconstruction of a "normal" situation. Many of the variables which stimulate the first response fade out or run into competition with other values and interests in the restoration phase.

Question 4: Why do some collective stresses lead to major *efforts to minimize future vulnerability* and to make preparations to reduce losses in the future, while others are allowed to recur with little effort at avoidance or mitigation?

Some societies historically have invested great efforts in flood control, in water control systems to counter periodic drought, in defense against hostile invaders, in organizations to help those in need. Others have gone on for centuries accepting housing which guarantees mass casualties in earthquakes, settling lowlands prone to catastrophic flooding, failing to provide food reserves for periods of crop failure, or allowing victims of accident or illness and their families to be reduced to beggary or starvation. One criticism of "modern" societies is their failure to consider the long-term environmental impacts to their economic and population growth, or of the catastrophic potential of complex systems in the realm of energy production, transportation, and urban structures. On the other hand some modern societies have created "welfare states" which protect their populations from the worst effects of business cycles, structural unemployment, normal accidents and illnesses, and the economic problems of aging better than those practicing purer laissez-faire.

My 1960s work covered the first three questions in some detail based on the existing research on physical disasters and comparisons with studies of other forms of collective stress. It did not however look into the problem of reducing vulnerability to physical disaster or collective stress generally. Since the 1960s a large literature has grown up on problems of vulnerability to natural hazards and its reduction.

On the first question, a propositional model was developed including variables at both the individual and collective level, to explain why some situations of mass suffering evoke quick and massive social response while others do not. The variables in the model included both characteristics of the "stressor" and characteristics of the social structure, culture, and ideology of the community and society.

This paper re-examines that model of what determines differences in response to collective stress, in the light of developments of the last half century, the changes in social organization to cope with large-scale stresses, and developments in the theory of response to collective stress. Developments in social organization include greatly expanded national and international organization for disaster response, social movements aimed at advancing "social rights" of deprived people, extension and withdrawal of "welfare state" programs, and expansion or denial of various "human rights." It does not however try to systematically review the vast body of research on physical disasters or other collective stresses since the original model was created.

THE POPULATION OF COLLECTIVE STRESS SITUATIONS IN THE 20TH CENTURY.

It must be realized that of the largest sources of "unusual loss of life" over the last century, the major famines take precedence. Famines have killed about 75 million people in the last century, over ten times more people than competing sources like earthquakes, cyclonic storms, and floods combined, and about half of these in the last 50 years (Devereaux 2000). Cyclonic storms and storm-induced flooding have killed hundreds of thousands of people at a time in the most extreme cases, but probably less than a million altogether in the last century. Earthquakes have produced deaths also running above 100,000 in the worst case, with perhaps again under a million in total for the 20th century (NEIC 1999). The greatest toll from famines, storms and floods is in heavily populated poor countries. On the other hand highly developed countries like Germany and the Soviet Union produced deaths of many millions in death camps and state-organized famines.

The last 35 years have also highlighted a huge toll taken by violent internal conflict. The concept of "Complex Humanitarian Emergencies" has been created to apply to those cases in which civil war and inter-ethnic violence exacerbates natural forces like drought and flood and economic problems like backward production systems and overpopulation in relation to resources (Weiss and Collins 2000; Natsios 1997).

Disaster research within the United States is limited by an advanced agriculture which avoids famines, the more limited danger of earthquakes due to our geological underpinning and less vulnerable housing, and a geography which lacks the extreme vulnerability to oceanic storms and river floods found in some parts of the world. On the other hand the United States has historically been a country of slavery and racial oppression, of genocidal treatment of the Native Americans, and of periodic poverty and unemployment, so that its history is not free from examples of large-scale collective stress. Comparison of U.S. history on these matters with contemporary "complex humanitarian emergencies" should help clarify the limitations of a formally democratic political structure as a means of preventing mass emergencies or chronic situations of oppression.

THE ALTRUISTIC COMMUNITY MODEL REVISITED

The model laid out in *Communities in Disaster* operated at the level of a local community, and was mainly based on research in the United States, although there was reference to the Irish famine of the 1840s and the World War II bombings. It elaborated on Charles Fritz's central idea of the "therapeutic community of sufferers." It tried to develop a model of response not only to sudden natural disasters but to situations of large-scale deprivation generally, including chronic poverty and institutionalized oppression. However the model needs to be extended to explicitly cover the levels of national and global response to disasters, and to consider types of disasters found in other parts of the world. I will review the model, and for each segment suggest how future research on collective stress might respond to world developments since the 1960s.

The model was built up from several clusters of propositions organized around the social "mechanisms" through which helping behavior is produced. It included 71 propositions: 39 relating individual-level variables to one another, 23 "contextual" relationships in which an aggregate or global variable influences an individual level variable or relationship, and nine collective-level relationships. Seven "global" variables characterized the overall impact and community institutional structure.

Symbol	Variable
Q	Suddenness of deprivation
P	Severity of Impact
R	Randomness of deprivation
S	Vested interests in causes of deprivation
U	Control of media by vested interests
Md	Media Coverage of victim deprivation
Mf	Media content blaming victims

There were 13 individual-level variables, 6 matching aggregate variables, and 3 individual perceptions of these aggregate numbers.

INDIVIDUAL LEVEL	AGGREGATE LEVEL
a. Helping victims Perc. Na. Perceived number helping	Na. Number helping victims
b. Sympathetic identification with victims	
c. Personal moral standard requiring help Perc.Nc. Perceived number holding standard	Nc. Number holding standard
d. Objective deprivation of individual Perc. Nd. Perceived number of victims	Nd. Number of victims
e. Subjective deprivation	
f. Blaming victims	Nf. Number blaming victims
g. Altruistic values and ideology	
h. Personal contact with victims	
i. Number of primary group ties	
j. Discussing own deprivation	Nj. Number discussing own deprivation
k. Discussing victims deprivation	Nk. Number discussing others deprivation
t. Proximity to deprivation	
v. Heterogeneity of social ties	

The propositions were organized around several social processes and sub-processes: determinants of communication and knowledge of mass deprivation, determinants of individual motivation to help victims, and some factors involved in effectively implementing individual and collective help.

DETERMINANTS OF COMMUNICATION AND KNOWLEDGE

Interpersonal Communication About Mass Deprivation

For members of the *community* in which the mass deprivation occurs, interpersonal discussion is a major source of their knowledge of the situation, and this is influenced by the overall dimensions of the deprivation and the social ties of the individual. (Numbers below refer to the numbered propositions in Chapter 5 of *Communities in Disaster*.)

> 1, 2, 10, 11, 12: The suddenness and severity of the deprivation and the number of victims make it more directly visible to community members and increase the likelihood of interpersonal discussion of the situation, as well as the willingness of the victims to communicate their distress.
>
> 3, 4. The more socially random the deprivation, and the more willing the victims are to communicate, the more likely an individual is to have personal contact with victims.
>
> 5, 6, 7. The closer the individual is to the location of the deprivation, the larger the individual's social network, and the more heterogeneous the individual's social network in terms of social categories, the more likely the individual is to have personal contact with victim.
>
> 8, 9, 13. Contact with victims and having a larger social network makes it more likely that an individual will serve as a communicator to others in interpersonal discussion of the deprivation, and conversely the greater the number of others engaged in such discussion the more likely each individual is to participate in it (a positive feedback from the group to the individual level, a "snowball effect.")
>
> 14. Mass media coverage of the deprivation promotes interpersonal discussion, generating a "two-step flow."

In the light of worldwide social developments since the original model was created, future research should look at the wider social networks created by contemporary patterns of intra-national and international migration and travel. We need to study how many people in the economically advanced countries are immigrants from poorer and more disaster-prone countries, how many have traveled in those countries on business, educational exchanges, or as tourists, and how many have resulting ongoing personal ties or sympathetic identification with victims of apparently remote situations of mass deprivation.

Easy telephone and internet connections now supplement the traditional letter-writing to remote relatives and friends. Organizations of fellow-countrymen or those identifying with an ancestral country, alumni groups from foreign study, missionary churches, and veterans of "peace corps" programs, and business organizations with foreign branches, can keep their members in touch with victims far away. In the 19th century, Christian missionary groups pioneered in international disaster aid, although sometimes with religious strings attached. Contemporary environmentalist, human-rights and labor-rights groups now supplement the religious groups in operating on a world scale to provide information on conditions of mass deprivation.

However when a situation of mass suffering is deliberately ignored or actually created by a government, or by competing elites engaged in civil war, these personal communications may be suppressed. This is particularly a problem in societies with authoritarian governments of left or right, or rule by predatory military groups. These elites use censorship of mail, surveillance of telephone calls, control of travel, and secret-police terror to isolate their populations from contact with the outside world, and from one another.

Mass Media Communication About Mass Deprivation

The mass media are also a major source of information for members of the society in which a mass deprivation occurs. Their coverage is a function of disaster characteristics and public concern, but also of interest groups which can control and limit news coverage, and the professional standards of media personnel.

> 15, 16. Mass media coverage is a function of the "disaster characteristics" of suddenness, intensity, and number of victims.
> 17. Mass media coverage is also a function of interpersonal discussion—a positive feedback from public concern to media concern, since the media adjust their content to their audiences' concerns.
> 18, 19. Deprivations which arise from conditions which benefit powerful social groups are less likely to receive news media coverage, to the extent that these groups exert control over the media.
> 20, 21. Sudden and socially random deprivations are less likely to arise from conditions in which there are socially "vested interests" than chronic deprivations and those limited to particular social categories, and are therefore the former are more likely to receive mass media attention than the latter.

Again looking at these processes in terms of response going beyond the local community, future research should emphasize the role of the media. Here again the "impact characteristics" of suddenness, intensity, and scale promote news coverage, while chronic deprivations are given only sporadic attention (Benthall, 1993). But even an enormous and sudden disaster like the earthquake at Tangshan, China, which killed 250,000 in 1976, went almost unnoticed in the world press (Young 1988). The first *New York Times* story appeared 9 years later, and included the information that the government had barred foreigners from the city for years after the disaster and that "the world was left to speculate about what had happened in Tangshan" (Burns 1985).

A content analysis of U.S. media coverage of natural disasters from 1964-1995 showed that disaster severity in numbers killed, numbers homeless, and estimated economic costs were the main predictors of *New York Times* coverage, with no significant bias concerning the race or region of the victims (Van Belle 1999). However the nature and consequences of media coverage of situations of mass suffering needs further research.

Media coverage of human suffering in countries with authoritarian regimes is subject to government censorship and control of both domestic and outside news media. The outstanding example is the largest famine in modern history in which somewhere around 30,000,000 Chinese died in 1958-61 as a result of Maoist mismanagement (Dreze and Sen, 1989, Becker, 1996). The famine was kept secret within the country and from the outside world, and indeed the highest levels of government refused to accept information on it and continued to demand extraction of food from the starving areas. Other examples of "secret famines" come from the Stalinist dictatorship in the Soviet Union. In the 1930s the government created the Ukraine famine to wipe out peasant resistance to collectivization, and a similar famine right after World War II, in both of which millions died under conditions of secrecy and state terror. The British colonial government imposed wartime censorship on the Bengal famine of 1943 in which over 2,000,000 died, to avoid pressure to divert resources from the war effort. Around 3 million are estimated to have died in the North Korean famines in the 1990s under conditions of secrecy and suppression of information (Devereaux 2000; Dreze and Sen 1989). Dreze and Sen argue that free news media are one of the most effective means of early warning and securing government action against famine, along with competitive multiparty politics which puts pressure on rulers to respond.

Even greater secrecy is attached to situations of mass suffering deliberately created by authoritarian regimes to control their people: concentration camps, labor camps, political killings, genocidal massacres, or death camps. However even in the presence of widespread knowledge, governments and peoples may be unwilling to pay the costs of "humanitarian interventionism" in other countries.

In capitalist societies where the news media's freedom is subject to market constraints, coverage of human suffering is limited by its lack of "newsworthiness" in the sense of ability to attract a paying or advertising-watching audience. This is more true of conditions of chronic suffering than of sudden dramatic "disasters." Chronic deprivations usually arise from institutionalized systems of either exploitation or neglect—in low-wage agricultural and industrial enterprises in poor regions or countries, in reservations into which aboriginal populations are driven, in urban slums, in "total institutions" for the mentally ill, the retarded, and the impoverished elderly, and in prisons. Those who profit by these institutions or who want to avoid paying taxes to improve them, are likely to have considerable influence over commercial media dependent on their advertising or tied to their corporate conglomerates. There is a tradition in democratic societies of media "crusades" exposing human suffering, but in the absence of powerful social and political movements representing the lower income groups, these crusades tend to be sporadic and have limited effects.

Dreze and Sen emphasis the role of a free press in preventing or mitigating famine, but they point out that premature deaths due to malnutrition, bad water supplies, lack of health care, lack of education and unemployment in a country like India cumulate year by year to equal those resulting from the sporadic governmentally-produced famines in authoritarian socialist systems like China, Russia, North Korea and Cambodia (Dreze and Sen, 1989: 204-225). These conditions clearly do not evoke the attention of the media or the media audience in the way that sudden natural disasters do, even where the media are legally free to report them.

Victims' Communication

The victims of deprivation do not necessarily play a passive role, but may actively communicate to others in the community.

Their willingness to reveal and discuss their plight is a function of a number of conditions.

> 22. There is a curvilinear relation of deprivation to communication by the victims themselves: the more severe the deprivation the more communication up to a point, beyond which the victims may be incapacitated or blocked from letting others know about their situation. This may be particularly true of victims of official persecution thrown into prisons or concentration camps, and killing people is especially effective in shutting them up, at least until the forensic experts examine the bodies.
> 23, 25 Socially connected victims can communicate more than the socially isolated, and social contact with other victims promotes communication by making people feel they are not alone and have social support.
> 24, 26, 27. There is a positive feedback between victims seeing that others share their deprivation, that others are freely discussing their plight, and the individual victim's willingness to communicate, which in turn increases the favorable environment for the others.

As an example of the "invisible poor" I quoted Woody Guthrie's "Pastures of Plenty," on the migrants who pick the community's crops and "come with the dust and go with the wind." More recently the social movements of AIDS victims had to work to get them to "come out" and overcome the silence of the stigmatized, using the slogan "Silence is death."

> 28, 29. Victims who accept blame for their own deprivation, and community members who blame the victims, are less likely to communicate about the situation.

This reflects the influence of ideology which makes certain kinds of deprivation shameful, and relieves other members of the community of concern with the victims. In a highly individualist culture, poverty is defined as individual failure, not social failure. Mental illness is defined as a personal weakness. Unemployment is concealed lest the person lose status (Newman 1988). AIDS is identified with shameful behavior. These considerations make it difficult for victims to organize, find allies, and press for collective action to improve their situation.

A set of derivative propositions linked the communications variables above to the individuals knowledge of a situation of mass deprivation. The level of individual knowledge of a given form of deprivation is related to the number of victims (33) and the suddenness of the deprivation (34), individual discussion of the situation (31), personal contacts with victims (32), the number of victims communicating (35), and the individual's sympathetic identification with the victims (36).

It is notable that in my 1960s analysis, done in the midst of all manner of activist social movements, I did not go further with the victims active role in dealing with their deprivation. I did mention the formation of self-help groups providing therapy and social support, but included no variables characterizing the extent of victim self-organization, or their ability to build coalitions to demand collective action on their behalf. To the extent that situations of racial oppression or class deprivation are part of the "collective stress" model, the whole *social movement* and *class organization* literature becomes relevant. This failure reflects the focus on community-level natural disasters in most of the research which I reviewed, in which the victims are seen as passive recipients of community altruism.

The role of a dominant ideology which blames the victims or stereotypes them as less than human is to reduce communication by and with them, to weaken their ability to organize themselves, and to make the rest of society unwilling to listen to them or talk about them. A society with institutions and values encouraging collective action by working people creates channels of influenced for the deprived (Korpi 1983; Esping-Andersen 1985; Franke and Chasin 1994).

DETERMINANTS OF MOTIVATION TO HELP

Sympathy With The Victims

Feelings of sympathetic identification with victims of deprivation, rather than indifference, are generated by several fairly obvious factors:

> Perceived severity of the victims deprivation (37), proximity to the victims (39), discussing the situation (41), direct contact (42), social randomness of the impact so that all types of people can identify with victims (44), and exposure to mass media coverage of the victims plight (40).
>
> Sympathetic identification is reduced by at least two factors. Blaming the victims for their own suffering (43), and the sheer number of victims (38). This is especially true if that number is so great that the onlookers are overwhelmed by the size of the problem and perhaps threatened by the prospect of having to sacrifice too much of their own living standard to do anything about it, perhaps of being forced into the same deprived fate as in a famine or epidemic.

The individual's own subjective deprivation may also reduce concern with other victims by giving priority to one's own problems (45). Subjective deprivation however is counteracted by the "relative deprivation" mechanism: if victims are surrounded by people even worse off than themselves, they feel their own deprivation less intensely and are more motivated to help those worse off in spite of their own sufferings. This is particularly likely to happen through helping the worse-off victims (propositions 46-52). This produces the anomaly that many severely victimized people may feel less deprivation than those on the fringes of a disaster who have little personal contact with the most severely deprived.

Blaming The Victims

A crucial element in the growth of an "altruistic community response" to deprivation is whether the victims are considered blameless or to blame for their own suffering. Situational factors which reduce blaming the victims include: the distribution and nature of the deprivation. Social randomness of the deprivation (53), and sudden rather than chronic deprivation (54) are important here. If "it could happen to anyone," then it is less likely to be considered a deserved result of moral failings or an inferior culture.

Political and ideological factors are also influential. Moralistic and individualistic ideologies emphasize individuals' responsibility for their own fate; even natural disasters may be considered divine punishment for sin. Altruistic and collectivist ideologies emphasize social or natural origins of deprivation (55). Religious groups like the Mormons may have a tradition and institutions emphasizing communal help (Fisher 1983; Golec 1983; Vogt 1953).

When there are vested social interests in the causes of the deprivation, powerful social groups and the communications media which they control (newspapers, churches, political organizations) try to spread the idea that the victims and not the social system are to blame (56, 57). This can happen also in nominally collectivist, socialist systems if there is a one-party regime which wants to shift responsibility for its failures to "capitalist elements" and "anti-party wreckers." And the more people in the community asserting the blameworthiness of the victims, the more each member is socially pressured to accept the idea (59). Personal contact with victims may counteract this, setting personal knowledge against community and media stereotypes (58). The normal segregation of personal contacts by class and race weakens this undermining of stereotypes, unless the disaster breaks down these social barriers.

Individual Obligations And The Formation Of Community Norms

Individuals in all societies are powerfully influenced by a sense of right and wrong, and going beyond feelings of sympathy are feelings of moral obligation to do something. The individual sense of obligation to help others is a product of a number of social factors.

Proximity to the victims is relevant. One's neighbors, people in one's community, people in one's own part of the country, are usually considered to be owed help as a matter of group loyalty, as distinct from the vaguer obligation to "help those in need" regardless of where they are (60). Competing with this group loyalty, however, may be the individual's own deprivation; the obligation to help others competes with the sense that one has to look after oneself and one's immediate family (64). As we have noted, however, subjective deprivation may be countered by the visibility of others worse off, reducing relative deprivation.

Ideological factors also influence the individual's sense of obligation; altruistic, egalitarian and collectivist values impose more such obligations than individualistic, aristocratic, or racist values (66). Related to this is victim blaming: those held responsible for their own miseries do not arouse an obligation to help except in the most charitable, while "innocent victims" move all but the most hard-hearted(65).

Perhaps most powerfully, there is an accumulation of individual reactions at the community level. As the number acting to help others grows, the perception that other people expect one to join the effort grows, so that however weak the individual motivation people feel obliged to "pitch in." (61, 62, 63). This is a positive feedback mechanism producing a "snowball" effect: the first helpers generate more helpers and yet more up to some saturation point. The formation of a high consensus on a powerfully expressed norm of mutual aid creates the psychological basis for the altruistic community, the therapeutic community, the "community of sufferers."

These propositions were perhaps the most oriented toward larger social systems in the original analysis, and point to cultural, structural and political factors of great relevance to national and global responses to mass suffering.

The remoteness, lack of direct contact, and "foreignness" of the victims makes the remote non-victim less likely to strongly identify with them. Impacts which are socially random within a community or region of a nation are by necessity not socially random in the larger society of the nation or the world: they happen in "the South," or "Africa," or to people very different from "us." These factors inherent in geographical and cultural remoteness have to be overcome. Hence the importance not simply of the amount of media coverage, but its ability to bridge these distances and bring remote victims vividly to life as fellow members of the national or world community. Pictures of the starving or the massacre victims in strange settings may not bring identification, but increase the sense of difference and of hopelessness. We need experimental research on the impact of "disaster stories" in the media.

As pointed out in the propositional model, communities or societies dominated by an economic upper class with individualistic, laissez-faire ideologies are less likely to encourage concern with the "undeserving poor" or the chronically miserable. Those who advocate the "spur of poverty" in getting their own poor to pull themselves up by their own bootstraps are likely to say "Let those foreigners solve their own problems because help would just turn them into parasites on more productive societies."

Societies with strong organization of their own working class and a welfare-state ideology are likely to transfer this orientation to the world society and devote more resources to foreign aid projects. The analysis of response to large-scale suffering needs to draw on the large body of research on the determinants of welfare-state policies. Aid to victims of disasters and economic crises is part of a larger welfare-state program. It is notable that the Scandinavian social-democratic countries now devote a larger portion of their national income to foreign aid than more conservative countries. On the other hand when there was competition between capitalist and communist societies in the Cold War, conservatives in the United States supported foreign aid, including disaster relief, to keep the Communists from winning over impoverished countries.

IMPLEMENTING THE HELPING COMMUNITY

Individual Role Competence And Access To Victims

The motivational basis for a helping community is established, resting on sympathetic identification with victims (67), individual feelings of moral obligation (68), and a perception of a community norm requiring help (69). Behavior however does not depend on motivations alone: it requires opportunity and resources. Individuals may be prevented from helping by their own injuries, loss of resources, or lack of skills (70). A severe enough disaster destroys the community's ability to help itself. Individuals who have resources need the ability to contact the victims, directly or indirectly, to offer help (71). Victims may be isolated by floods or destruction of roads; would-be helpers may find no organizations through which they can send contributions to far-away victims.

Chapter 3 of *Communities in Disaster* examined research on individual problems of implementing effective aid within a community under stress. Individuals within the community may suffer conflict between demands of their different social roles, particularly as family member versus organization member. Individuals vary in the occupational and personal skills which they can bring to bear on the disaster situation. A mass of highly motivated but poorly organized, trained and equipped individuals usually performs the bulk of the immediate rescue and relief work simply because they are *there* and professional helpers and formal organizations are not.

Organizational Relations And The Mass Assault

Chapter 4 looked at the major problem of how to relate skilled people and specialized organizations to this "mass assault." The most successful cases of rapid response coordinate the mass and the professional resources, rather than simply chasing away the "amateur" helpers when the "professionals" move in. The problem of ill-conceived media appeals for food and clothing was discussed, and the need to coordinate such public appeals with a realistic assessment of needs and delivery systems. Then there are problems of inter-organizational coordination which plague emergency responses. The need for well-practiced central coordination was clearly demonstrated.

There is now a large body of careful research studies and analysis of these implementation problems, not only at the community level but for world-wide disaster programs. In the problems of the most appropriate forms of aid in famines, Amartya Sen contributed a body of research that won him a Nobel Prize in economics.

Formal Organization, Mass Action, And The Restorative Process

Chapter 6 examined the problems of the period of restoration in a community that undergoes severe stress. It noted the weakness of many local governments when it comes to large-scale planning and implementing reconstruction projects. It also considered the strains which result from the carry-over of the "therapeutic social system and culture" into the longer term reconstruction process, and the re-emergence of social conflict. These problems are particularly important in dealing with large-scale famines, epidemics, and lowland floods, which may require changes in the social structure if they are not simply to reemerge a few years later. The analysis of how to effectively treat the chronic problems of poverty and ill health in the "Third World" inherently involves ideological and political problems.

We need to learn from cases of poor countries with successful programs of improving life expectancy, health, and education (Barton 2001). Such countries, like Kerala State in India, Sri Lanka, Jamaica and Costa Rica, have strong mass movements with socialist or social-democratic political parties competing successfully in multi-party democratic systems. Similar results on life expectancy, health, and education have been produced in some of the authoritarian communist countries—the Soviet Union, China, Cuba. These however have combined social welfare programs with political oppression and in the Soviet Union and China at any rate, episodes of some of the most massive famines in history, secret police terror, and massive imprisonment or liquidation of people defined as enemies of the system, including large number of intellectuals who initially supported their revolutions.

Still other countries starting out poor achieved vastly improved living standards and incomes through market-oriented capitalism: South Korea, Taiwan, and Singapore are the leading examples, with the first two of these moving to a democratic political system and development of strong labor organization and other reformist social movements for women's rights, the environment, and others.

The problems of response to natural disaster are part of a larger issue of how to prevent masses of people from being put in harms way from cyclonic storms, floods, famines, and epidemics, and how to deal with the chronic disasters of poverty in a world with unprecedented productive capability.

Those who want an extreme example of the convergence of these problems can apply the ideas raised in this paper to the enormous, deadly, and badly handled epidemic of AIDS in Africa. The homosexual communities of the United States and other advanced countries used their solidarity and resources to care for, and eventually save the lives of victims of this disease, and to educate their members in its avoidance. The disorganized aggregate of poor drug users in the United States became the primary victims, but they too are gradually being reached by public health agencies and minority communities. The expanding but still poor capitalist economy of Brazil developed a highly effective program of education and treatment of the epidemic, using the countries national public health system and domestic production of generic drugs in defiance of the wealthy countries' huge drug cartels (Rosenberg 2001). The conflict between the logic of capitalism and the desire to save human life was never more crudely displayed than in the issue of pricing life-saving AIDS drugs, and over providing socialized medical care versus profit-oriented medicine. The AIDS statistics from India show that the "welfare state" of Kerala stands out in its success in holding down the epidemic (US

Agency for International Development 2002); even the "sex workers" have a militant organization demanding state aid in preventive measures (Sex Workers' Forum Kerala 2002).

Finally, it would be useful to see if the model of altruistic community response and its wider version for national or international response can be applied to the reverse situation of genocidal behavior in a community or nation. The social and psychological processes which make for identification with victims and willingness to help appear in the negative when community members round up a religious or ethic segment of the community and murder them. A national society which rounds up Jews or suspected "enemies of the state" and sends them to death camps or deadly Siberian labor camps must have the negative of those features which leads societies to pour out aid for disaster victims.

Paradoxically some of the examples of state-created mass starvation occurred in societies which also provided collective welfare services for their members and achieve long life expectancies, high literacy, and economic security for those not sent off to camps or shot. The fall of the Communist regime in Russia opened the prison camps, but closed so many hospitals, schools, and factories that life expectancy fell ten years. Similar problems are arising as China "reforms" its economy and eliminates the collective institutions which supported the "barefoot doctors" and the urban health services.

At the same time some societies nominally dedicated to individual rights allowing masses of people to suffer poverty and unemployment, racial discrimination, and lack of health care. A crucial factor in avoiding both totalitarian and laissez-faire capitalist forms of mass deprivation seems to be the combination of political rights with effective economic and political organization of the mass of the people—the working class and the small farmers—to create a welfare state grafted onto a productive market economy. Some relatively poor societies like Kerala state in India, Sri Lanka, Costa Rica and Jamaica have achieved reasonably good conditions of health and life expectancy, along with the capitalist "newly industrialized countries" of East Asia, and the old social-democratic industrial nations of Europe.

CONCLUSION

Using the concept of "collective stress" to examine a wide range of situations of large-scale deprivation varying on several dimensions, with "local physical disaster" as one subtype, raises important theoretical questions and points to a wide range of empirical cases from which to learn answers. The wider concept relates the problems of preventing, mitigating, and coping with physical disasters to the general field of social problems and the means by which societies deal or fail to deal with them. It points to variables found important in research on the growth of welfare states (and the retreat from welfare states), on development or underdevelopment of poor societies, on human rights versus discrimination and genocide, on famine and epidemic disease and the social response thereto, on social movements creating institutions of self-help and of political pressure on governments to deal with social problems.

Quantitative studies of populations and organizations are needed to understand how to achieve policies to reduce vulnerability to both natural and technological hazards. A number of systematic studies of the process of adoption of social policies have been made in the last 30 years, summarized in review articles by Burstein (1981, 1991, 1998) and Amenta et al. (2001). Here again the problems of preparing for or avoiding physical disaster form a subset of the problems of collective stress and of social problems generally. Systematic comparative studies of how different societies deal with the "vulnerability" problem are needed, covering a wide range of potential collective stresses.

There are obviously specialized problems in specifically physical disasters in local areas, which need intensive study on which to base the "social engineering" of effective responses. This research needs the quantitative data which can only be provided by well-sampled surveys of the populations of people and organizations involved in response to disaster. Quarentelli pays tribute to the early National Opinion Research Center survey of tornado-struck communities as a "fountainhead study." (Quarantelli 1988a). Insightful field observations can guide the formulation of hypotheses for such quantitative research, but it takes numbers to create models for complex systems of community response. Given the social costs which natural and technological physical disasters are likely to continue to inflict even with much improved preventive and mitigative policies, there is a continuing need for cumulative, policy-relevant research on all aspects of physical disaster response. But the usefulness of specialized disaster research will be enhanced if it also draws on findings from the broader field of collective stress research and theory.

11

FROM CRISIS TO DISASTER: TOWARDS AN INTEGRATIVE PERSPECTIVE

Arjen Boin

INTRODUCTION: DISCUSSING DEFINITIONS

The collection of essays published in *What is a Disaster?* (Quarantelli 1998b) suggests a pervasive sense of unease with the state of the disaster studies field. In this landmark volume, key academics join in a remarkable self-study of their field, sparing few of the long-standing conceptual pillars that have supported the field throughout the 20th century. Unease here is both logical and understandable. The disaster community, dominated by disaster sociologists and U.S. practitioners, sits atop empirically grounded and theoretically interesting research findings that describe and explain individual, group and organizational behavior in natural disasters (i.e., hurricanes, earthquakes and floods). At the same time, little work has been done on other types of crises. Henry Quarantelli's (1998b) effort to engage the disaster field in discussion is therefore critical to the field.

The events of 11 September 2001 underscore both the relevance and irrelevance of contemporary disaster research. The 9/11 events spurred demand for both theoretical and practitioner-relevant research, not only in the U.S. but in Europe as well.

However, as the essays in Quarantelli's book make clear, the disaster field seems unlikely to deliver. In its enduring preoccupation with organizational and societal response patterns in times of natural mayhem, the disaster field has "missed" the signs of crises to come.

These signs are anything but new. The twin "manmade disasters," Three Mile Island and Chernobyl, were prototypes of the modern crisis; but they did not fundamentally reorient the field. Other time-defining crises were largely neglected. What were initially mysterious epidemics such as Legionnaire's Disease, AIDS, Veteran's Disease (Gulf War) and BSE (Mad Cow Disease); "new" terrorism such as Waco, the Empire State Building and the Alfred P. Murrah Federal Building in Oklahoma City; Black Monday on Wall Street; KAL 007, TWA 800 and the *Challenger*; the Heizel stadium tragedy and the LA Riots; Concorde and *Koersk*; the Millennium IT threat or the coming water crisis—this is but a list of crises that did not meet conventional disaster definitions.

The new and contemporary crises differ in fundamental ways from "classic" natural disasters (Rosenthal 1998; Rosenthal, Boin and Comfort 2001). The modern crisis is increasingly complex. It is not confined by boundaries of space or time. It entangles quickly with other deep problems and its impact is prolonged. Conventional disaster definitions do not capture the essence of modern adversity. Judging by the core definitions of the field and newspaper headlines of current crises, disaster sociology runs the risk of becoming a perspective whose time has come and gone.

Quarantelli's (1998b) book proves that disaster sociologists arrived at this very conclusion well before 9/11 permanently degraded the old disaster definitions to low relevance status (see especially the chapters by Gilbert and Quarantelli). The cautious suggestion at the end of the book now stands as a self-evident truth: a new perspective, or perhaps a paradigm shift, is required if students of disaster want to be heard, not only on the characteristics but also on the causes and consequences of today's and tomorrow's crises, such as smallpox threats and Anthrax scares, beltway snipers and economic meltdowns, eco-crises and all other "new species of trouble" (Erikson 1994).

This chapter discusses classic disaster definitions and insights in the light of new and very disturbing threats. It articulates the need to develop a new perspective that addresses both the classic disaster and the modern crisis in a consistent way, while bearing relevance for practitioners. In section 2, I briefly survey the 1998 discussion. In section 3, I focus on the relation between two key concepts: crisis and disaster. I argue that we cannot formulate a useful definition of disaster without a proper definition of crisis, as the two concepts are inextricably linked. In light of these insights, section 4 identifies key questions and the most promising corresponding perspectives that together lay the foundations for an integrative perspective on crises and disasters.

CLASSIC DISASTER DEFINITIONS AND THE SUBJECTIVE CHALLENGE

The question *What is a Disaster?* is a deceptively simple one. Most people associate a disaster with a destructive episode, involving death and damage. They are inclined to speak of *natural* disasters, as nature has traditionally played its devastating hand on mankind. The traditional pendulant of "disaster" is "war;" a concept that incorporates the same sense of loss and devastation (Gilbert, 1998). The founders of the disaster field primarily, but not exclusively, concentrated on public responses to natural disasters, but they also had a keen eye for war preparation relevance.

The classic definitions in the field, discussed thoroughly and perhaps exhaustively in Quarantelli (1998b), revolve around four key ingredients: agent description, physical damage, social disruption, and negative evaluation (Kreps 1998:110). Whereas more traditional definitions tend to emphasize agents and damage, younger definitions pay more attention to the social constructivist dimension of disaster definition and the social disruption that either follows or characterizes a disaster. But even the latter definitions still hint at damage and tacitly assume natural forces at work.

The question is whether this mixture of definitional elements is still adequate to capture the essence of disaster in today's risk society, which is characterized less by threat of devastation than by an obsessive fear for safety breaches (Beck 1992). In the modern Western society, people have become so used to physical safety that they get easily upset over the slightest challenge to their invulnerability. In the summer of 2001, for instance, a large crowd of 90,000 attended a popular dance festival in a large park area near the town of Velsen (north of Amsterdam). The beautiful day ended in cold rain. The absence of sufficient numbers of buses and taxis left thousands of scantily dressed people waiting in the rain. The next days, newspapers and radio reports spoke of a "near disaster." The municipal government of Velsen felt obliged to hire a consultancy firm in order to 'learn lessons' for the future. This silly episode illustrates how people in the risk society have become remarkably lenient in their labeling of adverse situations in terms of a disaster.

In the risk society, small glitches cause relatively large failures. These failures loom large because they are experienced in a context of near-invulnerability. The Millennium IT problem—soon to be entirely forgotten—marked a turning point in time: doom scenarios circulated, predicting depression, looting and other inconveniences, all because our computers would not work for, say, a week or two. In the risk society, a heat wave in Chicago then becomes a disaster, because the poor and the elderly do not have access to air conditioning (Klinenberg, 2002). A few hours of interrupted power in big city area create hazardous situations, because most people in the Western world apparently have no idea how to deal with such a situation.

When people die because of a malfunction in the risk society, we gasp for words to describe the traumatic dimensions of the occasion. The crash of an El Al Boeing in the Amsterdam Bijlmer suburbs (1992), the fireworks explosion in Enschede (2000) and the Volendam disco inferno (2001) had a combined death toll of less than a hundred; yet these commonly perceived as disasters that will define the modern history of the Netherlands. They may not meet the disaster definition of a U.S. sociologist and may appear little more than an accident to, say, a Chinese journalist; but in Holland these names—Bijlmer, Enschede, Volendam—spell disaster.

As the nature of modern disaster is changing and is becoming more a product of collective sense-making processes than of some exogenous agent, the definition of disaster must be adapted to preserve its correspondence with the phenomenon it describes. All authors in the Quarantelli (1998b) collection do indeed try to deal with the new disaster reality. "The main problematic for us," says Hewitt (1998:76), "does seem to be the social construction of disasters." The authors have done away with agent-driven definitions, but wrestle with definitions of modern disasters.

More specifically, they wonder how to study the mysterious processes through which people label a certain time frame or collective experience as a disaster. This is, of course, not what most disaster sociologists were trained to do. Many disaster sociologists were primarily interested to learn how people and organizations behaved in times of collective stress (Dynes 1998). Disaster as they knew it provided excellent, almost laboratory-like conditions, to test and develop their theories (see Merton's foreword to Barton's (1969) book). These academics very well knew that disasters were social constructions, but most were simply not interested in reconstructing the collective sense-making processes leading up to the disaster label (but see Stallings, 1995). This was seen as a political science activity. It is telling that the work of Murray Edelman (1971; 1977) is not cited in a volume heralding this subjective shift (see also 't Hart 1993; Bovens and 't Hart 1996).

Getting a grip on this subjective dimension emerges as the core challenge from this discussion. *I know a disaster when I see one* will not do, as the discussants readily admit. Theoretical purity induces a drive among them towards objectifying the subjective. Disaster theorists want to know when and under what conditions a certain percentage of people agrees on labeling some condition, event, or time period as a disaster. Such an exercise would require theorists to study how politicians, media, corporations, societal organizations, academics, and people in a well-defined social unit arrive at a common agreement—and maintain that consensus for some time—that "something" is a disaster (Bovens and 't Hart 1996). This is not an easy exercise, as participants in the

Quarantelli-led discussion have found. Disaster interpretations shift across time and space (Oliver-Smith 1998; Rosenthal et al. 2001), creating a sense of despair for those disaster students who had managed to stay outside the postmodernist realm.

One may well wonder whether a purely subjective perspective on disasters does not stray too far from the concept of disaster as we know it and as most non-academics understand it. It is, of course, clear by now that a "legalistic" or objective definition will no longer do (cf. Kroll-Smith and Gunter 1998). Defining a disaster in absolute terms leaves too much room for endless and unproductive discussion fueled by varying interpretations and cultural differences. An absolute definition also negates what happens in practice. In public administration, a disaster declaration is more an outcome of politics than of absolute measurements of death and destruction (Porfiriev, 1998). Moreover, a legalistic definition with "objective" indicators, rates, and scopes cannot capture the subjective feeling of loss, which rarely correlates consistently across time and space (Barton 1969; Ellemers 2001).

But an absolute turn towards a purely subjective notion of disaster would make us students of symbolics and semantics. It would require disaster students to follow and perhaps explain trends, polls, and hypes in order to understand the origins of a disaster. In other words, if the subjective is divorced from tangible and objectifiable features of collective distress, the relevance of the disaster definition and of disaster studies is completely diminished.

Yet all is not lost. The promissory notion of "social disruption" is the conceptual ingredient of existing disaster definitions that we have not discussed. All authors in the Quarantelli (1998b) volume agree that disasters must be defined in terms of social disruption, whether as cause, characteristic, or consequence. This is a promising concept, because it allows for objectification but also has unmistakable subjective connotations. This does not solve the problems outlined above, yet it provides an opening towards a fresh perspective on disasters. But it is necessary, then, to introduce a complimentary concept: crisis.

WIDENING THE PERSPECTIVE: DISASTER AS A "CRISIS GONE BAD"

The contributing authors in the Quarantelli book seem to agree that a disaster pertains to a period of social disruption, which is widely evaluated in negative terms (cf. Kreps, 1998). A disaster, then, indicates that the normal functioning of a human system—typically a community or geographically connected set of communities—is severely disrupted. Disruption in itself is not a sufficient condition for disaster sociologists to speak of a disaster. An economic boom, for instance, may disrupt normality in a rather pleasant way. Disruption becomes disastrous when the life sustaining functions of the system break down and people are deeply distressed as a result. This definition reflects the widest possible common denominator among disaster sociologists.

Any attempt to "objectify" or specify this definition ruins the consensus. It is easy to see and agree that a hurricane or earthquake disrupts a community by killing and wounding people, destroying houses, severing power lines, and undermining the response capacity of emergency services. The disruption affects the entire system. In many other cases, however, such clarity (for academics) is a formidable achievement. The Anthrax attack killed a few individuals and severely disrupted U.S. mail delivery, but it hardly affected the life sustaining functions of any social system. The *Challenger* explosion is still remembered as a national disaster, but its accident statistics do not fall within the definition by any stretch of the imagination. Very few events can be safely described in terms of social disruption of life sustaining functions. This does not mean that the dramatic events in question were non-disasters. It simply tells us that, even with the help of the "social disruption" concept, a disaster definition is rather devoid of meaning if it fails to capture what most laymen would consider a disaster.

If we leave it to the people to define disruptions in their life in terms of a disaster, however, the set of events becomes so large that the term disaster is devoid of its original meaning. A rained-out dance party may be experienced as a (near) disaster in the

Netherlands, whereas an explosion of a fireworks factory in China is accepted as a normal accident. The notion that disaster and destruction are God's punishment or Fortuna's pebble stones may be obsolete in today's disaster sociology, but many Africans reportedly view the AIDS scourge still in these terms. Such differences in perception provide food for thought to cultural anthropologists, but make it rather difficult for disaster sociologists to book theoretical progress.

Whereas the objective part of the disaster definition forces our attention to undeniable adversity (i.e., hurricanes, floods, and earthquakes), the subjective notion makes us chart all types of collective sensemaking (including hypes, trends and rumors). The challenge is to reconcile these perspectives on collectively defined epochs of undesirable system breakdown. This challenge does not require us to do away with "undesirable disruption" as a core element of a disaster definition. After all, it is clear that the prototype—typically natural—disaster fits this definition like a velvet glove. Our problem is the modern crisis, which is easily described in terms of disaster but rarely meets a mainstream definition of disaster. The very concept of crisis helps to solve this conundrum (see also Rosenthal 1998).

The Crisis Concept

The terms crisis and disaster are often mixed up and used synonymously by lay people, practitioners, politicians and journalists. In the world of theory, however, the concepts are rarely related to each other to build and sustain a comprehensive perspective on all forms of adversity experienced and to be experienced. The disaster field is the well-demarcated province of a recognized group of academics (mostly sociologists and geologists), selected policymakers (FEMA and state administrators), and field workers. It has its academic programs, journals, and meetings. The crisis field, on the other hand, resembles a hodge-podge quilt of specialist academics that are scattered over many disciplines (public administration, political science and international relations, political psychology, but also technical specialists such as epidemiologists and information technology experts). The two fields rarely meet.

The term "crisis" is typically used as a catch-all concept, which encompasses all types of "un-ness" events (cf. Hewitt, 1983). In this rather general perspective, the term "crisis" applies to situations that are unwanted, unexpected, unprecedented, and almost unmanageable, causing widespread disbelief and uncertainty (Rosenthal, Boin and Comfort 2001; Stern and Sundelius 2002). A crisis is, more precisely, defined as "a serious threat to the basic structures or the fundamental values and norms of a social system, which—under time pressure and highly uncertain circumstances—necessitates making critical decisions" (Rosenthal, Charles and 't Hart 1989:10).

The crisis concept thus helps to remedy at least one problem inherent to the classic disaster definition: it not only covers clear-cut disasters, but also a wide variety of events, processes and time periods that may not meet the disaster definition but certainly merit the attention of disaster students. As it relaxes the condition of collective assessment and thus makes way for situations of threat and successful coping efforts, it applies to all processes of disruption that seem to require remedial action. The label fits all the examples mentioned in the introduction of this chapter and covers all disasters one can remember or imagine. Eco-threats, IT crashes and economic adversity are joined by intrastate conflicts, prison riots, regional wars, exploding factories and, yes, natural disasters. The wide-ranging "case bank" of the Swedish research group, CRISMART, is filled with examples (Stern and Sundelius 2002)

To be sure, this crisis definition is not without problems. In the definition cited above, crisis is an elite construction. Authorities decide whether an event or process indicates progress or disruption of normality. This definition is, in effect, much closer to a preoccupation with a return to order than disaster sociologists are sometimes accused of being with their definition of undesirable social disruption (for criticism on disaster sociology, see Hewitt

(1998); see 't Hart (1993) for a discussion on the government-centric nature of crisis management studies).

This crisis definition does not solve the subjective problem of disaster students. We can only speak of a crisis if the actors in question perceive the situation as a crisis (the so-called Thomas Theorem). This subjective nature of crisis makes it impossible to neatly demarcate the beginning and end of a crisis, because different actors perceive a situation in terms of crisis at different points in time ('t Hart and Boin 2001). If we say that individuals or groups must perceive a situation in terms of crisis characteristics (threat, urgency, uncertainty), it automatically means that we "miss" certain events or processes that many of us would consider in terms of crisis just because the authorities do not recognize the situation in terms of crisis. As long as the authorities in question remain oblivious, analysts cannot treat this situation in terms of crisis. This problem is thus different from the subjective problem in the disaster field, where people on the ground see a disaster that does not meet the definition.

But the crisis field also harbors perspectives that offer objective definitions of crisis, which creates a new and promising perspective. The conceptualization of crisis as a period of discontinuity, marking the breaking point in a patterned process of linearity, builds upon classic lines of inquiry in sociology and political science (see Crozier 1964; Almond et al. 1973; Linz and Stepan 1978; Stinchcombe 1997). In this type of definition, crises are viewed as disruptions of normality. It is inherently suspect in the eyes of contemporary social scientists, as it smacks of structural-functionalist analysis. But if we sidestep this ancient battlefield, we can see that this type of definition helps to bridge the gap between disaster and crisis studies.

We can now define crisis in terms of a state of flux during which institutional structures of a social system become uprooted. In this definition, the main currency of crisis is legitimacy ('t Hart 1993; Turner and Pidgeon 1997). A crisis then occurs when the institutional structure of a social system experiences a relatively strong decline in legitimacy, as its central service functions are impaired or suffer from overload. Within a relatively short time, political and societal trust diminishes in the way a social system operates. At the heart of the crisis is an unremitting discrepancy between external expectations and perceived performance of the system. A combination of internal and external factors causes and sustains this gap. External stakeholders suddenly consider routines and outcomes that used to be satisfactory unacceptable or inappropriate. Internal deficiencies blind authorities to these new realities. This mismatch prevents timely adaptation, which erodes the legitimacy of sustaining structures.

A definition of crisis in terms of disruption fits the general disaster definition emerging from Quarantelli's (1998b) book. But whereas the disaster-related concept of disruption would require 'mental gymnastics of Olympian proportion' to translate it into measurable indicators (Dynes 1998:112), somewhat less effort seems necessary to make crisis-related disruption researchable. If we take shifts in legitimacy as a key indicator for disruption, it can be argued that the rapid decline in legitimacy for institutional structures that were previously widely valued helps us identify a systemic crisis. It is true that legitimacy itself cannot be precisely measured, but it is possible to gauge and document downward shifts by studying media reporting, political activity and other signs of societal mobilization.

By bringing crisis and disaster under one roof, we can have it both ways. We can differentiate between objectifiable processes of disruption and subjective processes of collective sensemaking without being relegated to the natural disaster niche or being turned into societal trend watchers. This only works if we share the concepts of crisis and disaster, which can now be sharply distinguished. Crisis, then, pertains to the process of perceived disruption; disaster applies to the collectively arrived-at appraisal of such a process in negative terms. In this perspective, a disaster is a crisis with a bad ending.

It could be said that disaster thus becomes a subcategory of the generic crisis concept (Quarantelli 1998b). This may seem a cannibalistic exercise with very little respect for the accomplishments of the disaster field. It is, in fact, nothing of the kind. It is merely a semantic reshuffling, freeing disaster sociologists from their subjective corset and inviting them to share their insights with the growing number of public and business administration scholars, political scientists, organization theorists, and social psychologists that study all forms of adversity and think of ways to deal with them. Disaster sociologists can return to studying causes, conditions and consequences of social disruption without having to worry about collective labelling exercises. The new paradigm would require disaster sociologists to reserve the term disaster for a specific subtype of crisis, but it would allow them to study all other types of crisis.

The joint perspective leads to a dynamic approach. A crisis has no clear beginning. The process of disruption is rooted in a combination of exogenous and endogenous factors. The consequences of crisis are felt in the future; a crisis may flare up long after it supposedly terminated. Sensemaking processes have very different dynamics. Sometimes they overlap with crisis dynamics, creating a widespread sense of disaster that Barton (1969) defined in terms of collective stress. More often, sensemaking processes follow different time paths; they are fragmented across time and space (Bovens and 't Hart 1996). A crisis is sometimes declared without clear signs of disruption, thus creating a crisis (and a disaster) in its consequences. Or a crisis is formally terminated, even though it is only beginning for some. The crisis dynamics and sensemaking processes affect each other in unforeseen ways.

This new perspective requires a multi-disciplinary approach. By relating the disaster and crisis concepts, we can encompass as well as categorize and classify a variety of events and processes that have long been the subject of distinct fields of expertise. The disaster category is widened to include all types of crisis with a bad ending: riots, stadium and crowd disasters; acts of terrorism; transport disasters; food poisonings; epidemics and massacres. The new perspective may do away with classic crisis categories on the basis of on-set (creeping crises versus sudden crises), agent, sector, process (slowly evolving versus fast-burning) and consequences (symbolic crisis versus disaster). More work remains to be done here. In the next section, we identify some common challenges awaiting us.

NEW QUESTIONS, PROMISING PERSPECTIVES

In the study of crisis and disaster, two types of questions dominate. First, we want to learn more about the causes of crises, the patterns of crisis coping, and the consequences of crisis. Second, we seek to find out how certain crises come to be labelled in terms of disaster. The joint insights of both fields go a long way in addressing these questions. Let us consider these questions in more detail and discuss some promising theoretical perspectives in addressing these questions.

Causes Of Crisis And Disaster

Most crisis and disaster researchers agree that today's crises cannot be explained by listing a few easily recognizable factors. Disaster sociologists have left the act-of-God explanation behind them (Quarantelli 1998b), but have not replaced it with other types of explanations. In the crisis field, the similar type of explanation—human error and lunatic motives—has given way to perspectives that better fit the context and process of contemporary crises. The research on causes of crises has become an interdisciplinary effort, paving the way for a multi-level approach that allows us to analyze the origins of any given crisis.

At the micro level, such an approach would focus on the role of individuals. In most, if not all crises, human errors are found at the roots of the crisis. Therefore we should study why and how humans err (Reason 1990). In addition, we should ask under which conditions the inevitable human error can cause a crisis.

At the meso level of inquiry, the focus is on organizational factors and processes that may play a role in causing crises. The crucial question is whether organizations can compensate for both human limitations and environmental factors that facilitate crises. On the one side, we can distinguish a group of researchers who argue that most organizations are unable to prevent human errors or alleviate the consequences of human failure. Quite on the contrary, they argue that organizations tend to bring other types of crisis-enhancing processes to the fore. Through a combination of sloppy management and an inherent blind spot for significant changes (for better or worse), organizations contribute to crises in the making (Turner and Pidgeon 1997). The extreme side in this debate is perhaps taken by those researchers who conceptualize the organization as a capitalist vehicle for egocentric leaders (see Perrow 1986; Wisner 2001).

At the macro level of analysis, theorists pitch in other powerful causes that seem to make crises more or less inevitable, and thus unavoidable, features of modern society (Beck 1992; Turner and Pidgeon 1997). One of the most persuasive authors in this vein, Charles Perrow (1999), argues that large technical systems will sooner or later produce a disaster as a combined result of sheer potential (for instance, nuclear energy), technical complexity (few people can understand what goes on inside a nuclear power plant) and tight coupling (one malfunction leads to another). Others argue that environmental pressures lead organizations to emphasize efficiency and output targets over safety goals (Sagan 1993). If we add such forces as globalization, ITC development and future terrorism, it is easy to understand this somewhat pessimistic outlook.

The so-called high reliability theorists present us with a more optimistic vision (Rochlin 1996). This group of researchers maintains that smartly designed and well-maintained organizations are capable of absorbing human errors and external pressures while preventing common organizational pathologies. Through a mixture of strategies, organizational leaders can turn their "high-risk systems" into high reliability organizations. This line of research finds support in the literature on institutions, which strongly suggests that the right kind of administrative architecture will lead to effective organizations (Selznick 1957). The debate between "optimists" and "pessimists" continues to generate powerful insights (*Journal of Contingencies and Crisis Management* 1994).

The challenge is to apply these static perspectives to the dynamic process of crisis, which leads a system from one temporary state to another. This process can take the form of linear escalation, moving from threshold to threshold and cumulating in severe adversity (Hills 1998). In the domains of information and communication technology and public utilities, for instance, blackouts or breakdowns rarely remain limited to their place of origin. Or they may take the form of 'reinforced feedback loops' that gradually or slowly—the creeping crisis—propel the system towards calamity (Ellis 1998: 146).

Most crises flow from unique configurations of individual errors, organizational failure and environmental flux. Because different crises follow different critical paths, crisis researchers need a methodology that allows them to reconstruct and compare each and every crisis process. What is needed is some form of critical path analysis, which identifies turning points within trends and thus key opportunities for policy intervention (Kouzmin and Jarman 1989). We may need "new" theoretical perspectives—the evolving field of complexity studies and the revived interest in evolutionary perspectives come to mind—to connect the various factors operating at different analytical levels.

Such an analysis may help us understand how human errors, organizational pathologies and environmental imperatives combine into system-disrupting processes, but it does not tell us why and when some tensions, problems or deteriorating circumstances come to be defined in terms of disaster whereas most are not. We need to understand how escalating crisis processes intertwine with political and societal sense-making processes.

An interesting body of research, mainly dealing with the understanding of so-called policy fiascoes, can help us understand these processes (Bovens and 't Hart 1996; Bovens et al. 2001). Therein, the key finding seems to be that negative labels such as "fiasco" and "disaster" are the product of social interaction between key players in political and societal arenas. The media play a crucial, controversial and hard-to-define role in this process. That is, as disaster sociologists know all too well, a political process: what is a disaster to some is a golden opportunity for others (Olson 2000). Some see the process as an unfolding play in which the various actors vie to dispose the blame, take the credit and emerge as a winner (cf. 't Hart 1993). The definition of disaster thus becomes separated from the impact "on the ground." It does, however, come closer to what people perceive to be the impact. This question clearly poses another challenge for disaster and crisis students.

Characteristics And Coping Patterns

The term crisis refers to a situation in which a threat to a system's basic structures or values is present, which must be dealt with urgently and under conditions of uncertainty or, as Yehezkel Dror says, inconceivability (Rosenthal et al. 2001:7). The threat of crisis can be the threat of death or damage, but it also pertains to the invisible and intangible perils that are feared to destroy a community (Erikson 1994). A crisis brings uncertainty with regard to the specific nature of the threat, people's responses, the dynamics of the situation, possible solutions and future consequences. Crises usually induce a sense of urgency, especially for crisis managers (Brecher and Wilkenfeld 1997). It is, of course, the perception of decision makers rather than some set of predefined conditions that counts.

Crisis management is the shorthand term for all activities—prevention, preparation, mitigation and recovery—that aim to deal with systemic disruptions (Comfort 1988). The combined insights of disaster and crisis research provide us with a good picture of both the challenges awaiting crisis managers and the routine patterns in their actual performance.

One of the pillars in a joint crisis and disaster perspective would undoubtedly be the realization that full prevention is simply impossible. It is true, of course, that technological progress and increased awareness go a long way in preventing certain types of crisis. But new technologies have a tendency to "bite back" (Tenner 1997). Moreover, public resources and political attention spans are inherently limited. Even if this were not the case, relatively minor disturbances can create immense effects in a society that banks on perfectionist prevention schemes. As we learn to prevent "routine crises," new crises emerge. The challenge, therefore, is to balance prevention and resilience, to organize for the unknown (Wildavsky 1988).

The practice of crisis and disaster planning bears out the enormity of this challenge. When organizations prepare for a crisis, their preparations are based on past experiences and routinized management repertoires. But crisis management techniques that worked in yesterday's crisis may not be effective today and may even have counter-effects in tomorrow's crisis. Planning and preparatory measures may fall prey to routinization or they may become part of the high politics game. Safety and security arrangements suffer from the reality of pro forma exercises, the lack of safety culture, and pressures to meet productivity standards. Moreover, the institutional tendency to routinize crisis management practices and procedures clashes with the necessity to operate in a flexible and adaptive way in the event of a crisis.

Responding to crisis is a challenge in itself. The research findings show how hard it is to make critical decisions under crisis conditions. Crisis managers must solve complex dilemmas without the information they require, in fluctuating organizational settings marked by bureau politics and under conditions of severe stress. Political leadership in times of crisis may well be qualified as an impossible job (Boin and 't Hart 2003).

The crisis aftermath is one of the most interesting and perhaps understudied phases of the crisis process. There is, of course, a number of technical issues that crisis managers must deal with in order to restore a new sense of normality, including relocation, insurance, grief counseling and reconstruction. Disaster and crisis research shows that these challenges are often underestimated in practice. The worst challenges often happen after the initial crisis has already occurred (Boin et al. 2001). This is also the phase in which the first evaluative notions begin to emerge with regard to crisis management performance. As the crisis process is still in a dynamic phase, the decisions and (perceived) actions of crisis managers feed back into the sense-making process that "decides" whether this crisis will be forgotten soon or will go down in history as a disaster.

Consequences

The consequences of crisis are often—understandably so—viewed as dysfunctional, undesirable, if not evil. This tendency is empirically grounded. People have to deal with material and immaterial damages. Houses must be repaired or rebuilt, the infrastructure restored, the dead must be buried and the wounded must be attended to. In that sense, there is an understandable need for restoration. The same is true for other types of crises, which often create a desire for stability, stocktaking, a new equilibrium or a temporary status quo. This inclination toward normalcy is supported by administrative reflexes.

But crises also present opportunities. A massive earthquake, killing thousands of people, may bring governmental failure to light and subsequently force incompetent politicians and administrators out of office—opening the gate toward much-needed development (Cuny 1983). In the long term, crises may thus set the stage for fundamental and drastic change of the system, tension release, open conflict and accelerated circulation of elites. We know that crises may accelerate social and political change, that they may bring latent forces of change into the open, that they may very well function as policy windows (Kingdon 1984), helping to reconstruct the policy or social agenda.

It is a mistake, however, to assume that a crisis is automatically followed by reform of some kind. Much depends on the actions of crisis managers and the evaluations of both these actions and the causes of crises among politicians, the media and the public. This process of evaluation and assessment is political in nature and driven by various factors ('t Hart and Boin 2001). It is in this phase that managerial challenges give way to political challenges, such as the "framing" of the crisis impacts processes of accountability and blame allocation.

An interesting question for further research asks how these political processes relate to "conventional" questions of learning and prevention. It appears that organizations often fail to learn (Sagan 1993), refuse to learn (Perrow 1999), learn only in symbolic ways (Clarke 1999) or in very slow ways. The challenge for crisis and disaster researchers is to identify conditions that facilitate effective learning that can improve future performance.

CONCLUSION

A discussion of crisis and disaster definitions can only be useful to either academics or practitioners, if it takes into account the changing nature of crisis. A definition that confines itself to a certain class of phenomena—be it natural mayhem, terrorism or riots—poses a long-term danger to the academic field working with the definition. As the 9/11 events have forcefully demonstrated, tomorrow's disaster is sure to differ in most if not all of its characteristics from today's. Common developments such as technology jumps, globalization, demographic shifts, media corporatization, and natural depletion are but a few driving forces that will create new and inconceivable crises in the near future.

Whether these future crises will become our future disasters, depends in part on our institutional crisis management capacity. It is clear that the rapidly changing nature of crisis poses fundamental challenges to this capacity and to crisis managers (Boin and Lagadec 2000). I would guess that the sense-making processes by which crisis events are classified as disasters are also subject to these change processes. All in all, disaster researchers must be prepared to deal with new questions in new ways if they want to be recognized as disaster researchers in the future.

The discussion initiated by Quarantelli (1998b) has led to a similar conclusion. The various contributions seem to underwrite the proposition that the disaster community would be better off by shedding its preoccupation with natural agents and by including non-sociological (and non U.S.) sources of insights in its search for organizational regularities. A merger of the hitherto strictly separated fields of disaster and crisis management—beginning with jointly operated journals, conferences and research programs—is a sensible option that should be explored. I believe that only by joining our efforts, will we be able to address the challenges awaiting both practitioners and academics.

12

DISASTER: MANDATED DEFINITIONS, LOCAL KNOWLEDGE AND COMPLEXITY

Philip Buckle

In re-reading the previous volume *What is a Disaster?* (Quarantelli 1998) it is clear that many of the papers put forward perspectives that while not incompatible with each other did illustrate the difficulty of achieving consensus on this question, and even showed the difficulties in working towards consensus on how we approach the issue of deciding what a disaster is. The variety of approaches is not unexpected. Efforts to come to an agreed understanding have been made, and continue to be made, without much significant progress towards a common and agreed understanding, witness the need for *What is a Disaster?* and this successor volume. This should inform us of the difficulty of trying to define or reach consensus on complex social phenomena, whether they are disasters or some other event or process.

Whether we need a precisely agreed perspective or a commonly accepted definition is open to debate. Of course it is useful when talking about an event, process or phenomena to have a common and shared understanding, but the level of precision we can achieve may be limited especially when dealing with complex social phenomena such as disasters. I acknowledge the circularity of writing about defining disasters and then using the term without defining it. It seems to me that this circularity is inevitable and reflects the nature of definitions. However, the fact that we can write about disasters and be understood before defining the term shows that there is a commonly accepted notion of what constitutes a disaster which exists intuitively and almost *a priori*. If by definition we mean identifying the uniqueness of a phenomenon by a description of its *critical and necessary elements* and the *ways in which they are related and interact* then it may not be possible to define anything precisely except for mathematical terms and some simple physical phenomena.

This is especially the case with social phenomena which, being influenced by the agency of human beings and their social structures and organizations and in turn and recursively influencing those same people, structures and organizations, may not be amenable to a precise definition which is constant over time and across different societies. This is emphasized by the capacity of humans to work in ways that are not necessarily or obviously in their own best interests, that are not necessarily rational and which may not be based upon a full understanding of the context in which decisions have to be made.

What we usually mean by definition is the analysis and description of something in such a way that we can use it, manipulate it or influence it so that we can achieve a particular purpose. This leads us into a paradox of relativism. That if we define things by how we want to influence them to achieve our goals then we may be exposed to the charge that definitions will vary according to the vagaries of our intentions and that validity derives only from utility (itself highly variable over time, space and society) and not from something inherent in the phenomenon itself. Perhaps then what we should seek is not a definition of disaster but "just" an agreed understanding. This may be still be fuzzy at its boundaries—as many concepts of social phenomena are—but its core, agreed meaning will provide us with a basic, commonly understood reference point.

This agreed core meaning will be important for at least two reasons. First, it will enable coherent policymaking (and management, programmatic action that follows) that in turn permits the development of a consistent approach to social phenomena that have common elements or other significant similarities. Second, it will allow us to develop a suite of theories of disaster causation, disaster development (how the social event/process unfolds and changes), and the relationship of vulnerability and resilience to each other, to broader social dynamics and to hazard agents. At the moment models and theories in disaster management are rarely robust, often not rigorous and use borrowed methods and perspectives from other disciplines without formally and coherently integrating them into an agreed perspective(s). This is not bad in itself and as a starting point—and may indicate the difficulty of deriving an agreed meaning and an agreed discipline for complex, varied events and processes—but it does not lend itself to intellectually or socially useful theory development. Much disaster management theory really consists of basic modeling of a limited number of the elements of the phenomena (so what is modeled is often a model itself) or, more commonly still, a simple description of key elements of the phenomena being studied whether these elements are of structure, process or agency. This paucity of theory does not allow us to develop models or theories that have much application to the real world or which allow us if not to predict then to indicate social responses across different times and different cultures. Without this capacity we are locked within a situational and pragmatic approach to conceptualizing disaster.[1]

We need to be clear about what it is we are trying to define. This appears circular. However, as we can see in the previous volume the authors of the various papers were coming from different positions, and had different purposes, in trying to define what is meant by "disaster". Do we mean the event itself (which may be defined variously as the impact or the consequences), do we mean the process of disaster causation or do we mean the organizational and social responses to the event?

Central issues for this debate and for practice are how we are to deal conceptually and practically with the boundaries of disasters.

At what scale and for what type of event, do disasters evolve from accidents, at what level of frequency to disasters become day-to-day disruptions to normal life—or is there a continuum that is defined by the context.

An equally important issue is how we deal with the complexity of disasters. This is not just the normal complexity, if it can be termed such, of social systems and social phenomena where the number of interactions between agents, the range of variables, the number and variety of processes and the multiplicity of structures combine to generate a complex, detailed panorama of social life.

Disasters are complex social events/processes, nested within a wider social context. The rapid rate of change, the level of unexpectedness of occurrence, the intensity of dislocation of social relations and networks and the uncertainty generated by damage to life, property, organizations and social networks combine to make disasters significantly more complex, over a given period of time, than most other social phenomena.

Key questions in sociology include how to relate the micro to the macro, the individual to the system, the household to the community; how to conceptualize the relationship between actors and structure and how to explain discontinuous and fundamental change. (Byrne 1998: 46). These are central issues for the sociology of disasters. How do individuals and broader levels of social organization relate and interact with each other, this is the case in particular during the period immediately after impact and for some thereafter until socially mandated agencies restore "order" when existing social structures are overcome or become temporarily irrelevant in meeting individual and community needs. Understanding the relationship between actors (whether individuals or groups or agencies) or more properly between action and structure is critical to understanding the dynamics of mitigation, response, relief and recovery and how individuals or small groups relate to each other and to broader social, political and economic strictures. Finally, a defining characteristic of disasters is the way in which they destroy existing linkages and processes and institute a period of change that is often not evolutionary but discontinuous.

Explaining the contingent conditions necessary for such change and the modes of change are important if management is to be more effective. I am not yet convinced by Byrne's claim that complexity theory offers a method for analyzing sociological issues, though I do believe strongly that it offers a framework within which to assess disasters in insightful, imaginative and powerful ways.

INTRODUCTION

What we, and by "we" I mean governments, public officials, not for profit organizations, commercial enterprises, professional and volunteer disaster managers and the community, mean by "disaster" is of critical importance. It is critical to policy development and implementation, program development and operations. It is critical to planning and to mitigation activities as well as to relief and recovery. It is critical to people affected by disaster to whom the turn of a legal phrase (as in the declaration of a state of disaster) may mean the difference between assistance and no assistance. It is critical because without a) consensus on the concept and phenomena we are addressing and b) an agreed conceptual understanding that more or less reflects what is going on "out there" (however socially constructed "out there" might be), we are not going to have basis for coherent and effective policy and programs. But we do not have a clear understanding, or at least we do not have a commonly agreed formal understanding, of what this word "disaster" means and nor do we, inclusively, have a good sense of what governments, organizations, communities and so on mean when they use the term.

Nonetheless, there is a semantic heart to "disaster" that disaster management professionals and lay people understand. We understand that it means unwanted loss, often but not necessarily death, injury, bereavement and trauma. Often the disaster has a rapid onset so opportunities for self-protection, evacuation and warning are constrained, (although slow onset disasters such as droughts and famines may approach imperceptibly and inexorably). We know that disaster is non-trivial but understand also that it may affect a single family, a community, region or a nation. So up to a point this common understanding has value and utility. But in some circumstances and at certain thresholds this common and shared understanding breaks down. At best this may lead to policy and programmatic confusion, in other cases it may lead to the loss of entitlements (at least as seen by potential recipients but not necessarily by donors) and it other situations it may lead to grief and suffering where action and expectation are predicated on an understanding that is not accepted by other agents.

I will approach this task from three different positions and in doing so and by a process of triangulation, make an attempt to clarify some of the meanings we attribute to "disaster" and to delineate the definitional boundary a bit more precisely. These three positions are first, mandated organizational operational definitions, second, community definitions and third, the emerging concept of complexity and its use by the social sciences to understand and explain process, change and multivariate phenomena. I shall draw on some examples to illuminate certain points. These examples will mainly be drawn from Southeast Australia, an area with which I am familiar. The points and issues so illustrated will have a wider relevance and will apply more or less directly to, any other countries in both industrialized and industrializing, North and South, developed and developing, countries.

When we ask for a definition we need to be clear what it is we are attempting to define, though as previously noted this may involve in a circularity. Disasters are not phenomena that occur as isolated, autonomous entities. They exist as the impacts on and consequences for individuals, families and groups of people within a specific social time and geography and a particular culture. We therefore have to ask what constitutes a disaster for the people of a particular society or group and how this may differ from the views of people from another society or group. I expect a very considerable degree of overlap, in most instances almost indistinguishable definitions of how disaster is understood.

A feature of all the definitions argued for in the previous volume was that they were put forward by researchers and academics. Many of them are eminent in their field and have worked conscientiously and with great skill for many years. Some, such as Ken Hewitt, have been among those who have transformed how we see disasters, in shifting our attention from the hazard agent to social impacts and in the process indicating to us that vulnerability and cause are linked, directly and indirectly, to broader and structural social processes and dynamics.

None of these definitions, or efforts to resolve the issue of whether a definition is possible and if so how it may be achieved, referred to the common sense definition employed by people who are not disaster management professionals. This definition may lack the rigor and clarity of other definitions but it does have at its core an agreed and understood meaning. We all know what "disaster" means when we use the word and when others use it. We all know what it is not. Its connotations include typically a sense of damage, a sense of loss, a sense of significance and a sense of irreversibility or at least of the need for long term recovery. However for the purposes of intellectual rigor, as well as policy development and program implementation, we cannot rely on this common sense meaning alone. But it serves as a touchstone or starting point.

It does highlight one issue that previous contributors ignored. That is the inclusion in the definitional process of local or community views of what disaster means. This exclusion has applied to other actors in the policy and program arena, including, governments, bureaucracies, disaster management agencies and the media to name some of the major actors. However, for my current purpose I shall confine my comments to the local, informally expressed views of the term "disaster" which, for convenience I shall refer to as community views.

MANDATED OPERATIONAL DEFINITIONS

Victoria is a State in Southeast Australia. It has a population of about 5 million people in an area the size of England and Wales. Australian States may be compared with the current status of

Scotland and Wales and USA states. Australian States have their own legislature, the capacity to raise certain taxes and are responsible for law and order and disaster management. The Federal Government holds powers for major taxation, defense and foreign affairs. Melbourne, the capital and largest city, has a population of about 2 million people in an area the size of Greater London.

When working, respectively as Manager and Assistant Manager of the then Disaster Support and Recovery Unit in the Victoria Department of Community Services, John Edwards and I developed the following working definition of disaster in 1985. A disaster is:

1. an unwanted, unintended event or process which damages property and/or threatens life and personal well being; and
2. an unwanted and unintended infrequent or novel event, process or set of circumstances to which communities are not adjusted; and
3. an unwanted event, process or set of circumstances that alters the functional conditions and relationships of a community to the extent that basic needs cannot be met satisfactorily; and
4. a set of novel conditions that result in the basic needs of individuals and communities being met less than satisfactorily and which can be altered only by the application of resources external to those affected and by the application of specific systems.

This effort to define disaster was developed as a pragmatic response to an operational need to delimit the boundaries of agency responsibility and operations. This effort occurred during a period of intense and creative revision of disaster management arrangements in Victoria following the catastrophic bushfires of Ash Wednesday, February 16, 1983, in which over 4000 house were destroyed, as many farms and business burnt out and over 60 lives lost. This definition was an attempt to move us beyond the limiting and unrealistic notation of rapid onset natural disasters as the only "authentic" disasters. This definition was never given widespread acceptance we succeeded in partly influencing the policy making process in Victoria and across Australia.

The key issues we tried to draw out are that:

1. disasters are unwanted and undesired,
2. that they may be processes as much as events which occur at a single moment in time (the clumsy phrase "set of circumstances" was intended to refer to disasters such as droughts which are not due to their duration disasters in a traditional sense nor are they obviously processes, being too diffuse),
3. they imply lack of social adjustment to a hazard of a given nature; they are novel in so far as they are not routine (When for example do drought conditions recur so frequently that "lack of rain" becomes a typical situation and so part of the expected, background environmental conditions that require social adaptation rather than emergency services),
4. they alter basic relationships, linkages and flows within society so that necessary requirements for health, safety, food, shelter and well-being are not met, and
5. in the short term at least these basic needs can only be met by the application of knowledge, skills and resources that are derived and/or coordinated from outside the affected area.

In retrospect I would alter this definition, in two ways particularly. I would give more emphasis, in contradistinction to the last point, to the contribution of local knowledge and skills. I would also try to find a way to logically include slow onset disasters (such as drought) and events such as riverine floods, and storms, that are more or less predictable within a defined probability at certain locations.

For a short time this was a serviceable, operational definition. As the review process continued in Victoria the *Emergency Management Act 1986* was drafted and passed by the State legislature. For the purposes of operations in Victoria and for this chapter "emergency" is synonymous with "disaster". This Act contains the following definition of disaster:

> ... the actual or imminent occurrence of an event which in any way endangers or threatens to endanger the safety or health of any person in Victoria or which destroys or damages, or threatens to destroy or damage, any property in Victoria or in any way endangers or threatens to endanger the environment or an element of the environment in Victoria, including, without limiting the generality of the foregoing: an earthquake, flood, wind storm or other natural event; and a fire; and an explosion, a road accident or any other accident, a plague or an epidemic, a warlike act, and a hi-jack, siege or riot, a disruption to an essential service ("essential service" means any of the following services: transport, fuel (including gas), light, power, water, sewerage, or a service (whether or not of a type similar to the foregoing) declared to be an essential service by the Governor in Council).

This legislative definition tried to deal with the dilemma of specificity (with the attendant risk that some events may be missed) and inclusiveness (with the risk of vagueness) by providing a generic definition and then indicating specifically certain types of hazard.

This definition has been in existence more or less unchanged for 16 years and has by and large proved a useful in describing boundaries to organizational responsibility, (always provided that you are not too close to the boundaries). There are particular difficulties with this definition. First it refers to potential disasters, which logically and practically are not actual disasters. But by referring to "imminence" and to "threats to endanger," it draws attention to disaster as process but otherwise refers implicitly to disasters as events and as events defined by the hazard agent rather than their cause or their consequences. This reference to process is to the procedures of agencies and not to the procedures and processes of communities or systems.

However, this definition has some more significant difficulties. Scale of event and process is not addressed. Hence, a fire that destroys a single house is the same type of disaster as a fire that destroys 1,000 homes. I think that most of us would agree that the latter event has a number of qualities that distinguish it by type from a single house fire. The scale of the event has significant resource and management implications for local emergency and medical services. The type of loss is different too. As well as losing a dwelling(s) in a major disaster local support systems, commonly owned infrastructure, community networks and relationships may be destroyed and local capacity to provide support is likely to be reduced in a large-scale event compared to a small or localized event.

Second and less importantly, the initial part of the definition is open ended in terms of the type of event. There are sound pragmatic grounds for this in terms of agency roles and responsibilities. It is impossible to nominate all potential events. An evolving society and environment will generate new types of hazards and risks. However, in operational terms this open-endedness is a mixed blessing. It allows scope for local interpretation and individual management judgment when an event occurs. But it gives little guidance on how professional, exert or lay judgment is to be exercised.

For this reason the following list of characteristics was developed by the Victorian Government (Government of Victoria 2001). Emergencies are characterized by some or all of the following:

> They are disruptive to individuals and communities;
> They are not part of day-to-day experience and are outside normal life expectations;
> They are unpredictable in occurrence and effects;
> They require a response for which normal local resources may be inadequate;
> They have a wide range of effects and impacts on the human and physical environment;
> There are complex needs in dealing with them;
> They can be of sudden onset;

> They are destructive of human, animal and/or plant life, health, property and/or the environment;
> They overwhelm normal prudent protective measures.

This is a useable list, but similarly to the list set out in the *Emergency Management Act 1986*, it gives no sense of scale.

Within the Department of Human Services and in response to municipal and regional requests for a clear statement of what sort of events managers had to deal with I developed (in my capacity as Manager, State Emergency Recovery Unit) the following criteria to guide operational activation. When any one of these existed, then at least a minimum level of activation was required to assess whether support and recovery services should be made available:

> Large numbers of people are involved;
> Numbers of fatalities occur and are public;
> Damage to homes or other essential property;
> Children or other vulnerable people are involved;
> Local resources are unable to meet needs;
> Police or response agencies request assistance;
> Public and media interest is high; or
> Horror element is high.

This list was prepared as an entirely pragmatic effort to set some working boundaries to a field which was growing at an increasing rate as success at providing recovery services generated an increasing demand from Government and the community for those services and assistance measures to be extended to small events and to be applied to an increasingly broad range of events. Apart from the logic and internal consistency of extending services to all similar types of events there were significant resource implications in this expansion of eligibility for services and assistance. There were increasing countervailing pressures to limit assistance to events of a certain size or type (typically large scale, destructive, rapid onset events that resulted in death, injury or loss of homes.). This countervailing pressure was driven almost entirely by resource constraints. Not logical, consistent or equitable, but reflective of a messy, corporeal world.

The purpose of these definitions was to set policy and operational boundaries for managers and practitioners could work to. As such these very practical definitions could perhaps to some degree relax academic rigor and logical consistency, though not much. However, they had to meet tests of public and political acceptability, equity and to be more or less workable in the local organizational context. These types of definitions are not unique or isolated. Alexander (1993 pp 4-5) writes:

> A natural disaster can be defined as some rapid, instantaneous or profound impact of the natural environment upon the socio-economic system . . . In general terms we are not only dealing with phenomena of high magnitude. In fact, we can define an extreme event as any manifestation in a geophysical system . . . which differs substantially or significantly from the mean.

Alexander cites a number of authors in support of this definition and reiterates it in a later work (Alexander 2000). Alexander is not an exception in his use of this sort of definition, but he refers only to events, and events that autonomously impact on human systems. His definitions (and those of others) give no sense of scale or type to the event or process that they are defining.

Without the capacity to deal with issues of scale and type it became impossible to differentiate on any defensible grounds between, for example, a transport accident in which 30 people were killed and a transport accident where one person was killed; though one was a rare event and the other a frequent, though no less personally tragic, event. Slow onset disasters, especially where the effects were compounded by inappropriate agricultural use (European stock and plants) in an environment adapted to a different regime of plants and animals, became hard to distinguish from background environmental conditions). How were criminal events that lead to death and injury, grief and bereavement to be separated (if they were to be separated in logic and practice) from other events that caused similar losses?

So the question was constantly asked: "which events are within the defined boundary, and which are outside?" To this there was no answer other than to say that sensitive, expert, managerial judgment was required to resolve this question. This really left the decision criteria to individual managers to evaluate on a situation-by-situation basis within the prevailing political sensitivities. This approach is pragmatic but hardly equitable or logical.

It must be emphasized that efforts to delineate "disaster" precisely occur across all sectors and all countries. For example the International Federation of Red Cross and Red Crescent Societies (IFRCRCS) accepts as a definition of disaster (IFRCRCS 2002 p181):

> A situation or event which overwhelms local capacity, necessitating a request to national or international level for external assistance, . . . 10 or more people reported killed, 100 people reported affected, a call for international assistance and/or declaration of a state of emergency.

At least one of these criteria must be satisfied for a disaster to be listed on EM-DAT, a database maintained by the Center for Research on Epidemiology of Disasters (CRED). CRED is supported by the IFRCRCS, World Health Organization (WHO), the United Nations Office for the Coordination of Humanitarian Affairs (OCHA) and the European Community Humanitarian Office (ECHO). These criteria are not situated in a context but are pronounced arbitrarily and there utility in any given situation is extremely limited.

To conclude this part of the discussion it seems clear that mandated definitions of disaster are of little value conceptually or practically, except as a road map indicating from where we have come. However, inclusive they try to be they fail in two key areas. They cannot anticipate all disasters types that may arise, partly because "disaster" is a social construct and as such its' meaning will vary depending on a specific culture and set of values and the broader social, economic and political context. Second for any given disaster type a mandated definition will not be able to set out robustly the limits to the event, that is the point at which a disaster is nothing more than an accident, or an event or process that is part of the expected background of day-to-day life. If what is meant by disaster is context specific then at best any boundary will be fixed only at a particular point in time within a particular society. This matters conceptually if what we require are clear cut definitions, and it matters in practical terms where disaster managers need guidance on which events they are allowed and required to deal with and to commit resources to.

COMMUNITY BASED AND INTERPRETIVIST DEFINITIONS

Interpretivism as a social science approach and methodology locates meaning and significance in the ways in which local actors themselves ascribe meaning and in how they construct (meaning both to build and to interpret) the world. If mandated lists, focusing on disasters as events, are inadequate in defining :disaster are there other perspectives that may be more rewarding in the sense that they can lead us to a broader and more robust agreement of the meaning of the term "disaster"? In this section I want to draw upon some recent research conducted by myself, Graham Marsh and Syd Smale within local rural, peri-urban, suburban and metropolitan communities (Buckle et al 2001a, 2001b). This research, sponsored by Emergency Management Australia, examined the perceptions, attitudes and values of local people (including emergency service personnel, volunteers and lay people) in a variety of settings across Victoria in Southeast Australia, but drawing also on relevant research in other parts of the country and internationally. This research is now being replicated in England.

These studies followed major bushfires in 1997 on the outskirts of Melbourne, extensive and difficult to manage floods in June 1998 in East Gippsland (a remote, mountainous area in the far

Southeast corner of Australia, reliant on agriculture, tourism and primary resource exploitation for its economy) and loss of the gas supply to 2 million households in September 1998. All of these events displayed characteristics that made them particularly difficult to manage. But the process of developing and working through a management strategy informed the process of vulnerability analysis, the process of linking disaster and development and caused us to reflect on the scope of disaster management in Victoria when it became clear with the gas shortage that we had moved into another realm of disaster management, the gas shortage being the first instance of a wide area utility failure whose impacts directly paralleled the impacts of "traditional" natural disasters. We employed a number of methods to triangulate our results. Interviews with local people, local municipal and emergency service personnel, local focus group sessions, interviews with State officials, Australian and international researchers were supplemented by a comprehensive literature review, expert focus groups and case studies.

In the first of a series of studies we examined vulnerability at local level. That is, the focus was sub-municipal, leaving it to local respondents to define the geographic extent of their community. We also examined perceptions of vulnerability and how these varied between areas and between municipalities, emergency management agencies and local people. The results surprised us in the strength and consistency of the views expressed across different communities. Emergency service personnel and municipal officers provided the answers we expected (based on our understanding of mandated organizational definitions) to questions about what constituted a hazard, local risks, local and regional disasters and vulnerable populations. In all cases the responses were predictable from the charter of their agency. So fire services saw hazards, risks and disasters in the context largely of fires, while flood control agencies saw floods as the most important threat. This is in one sense understandable since these agencies have a legislative mandate and statutory responsibilities to meet. Municipal officers had a wider view of hazards, risks and disasters that reflected the broader span of interests and responsibilities of local government. For all agencies a "disaster" was in effect what the legislation specified it to be and as we have seen legislative definitions are generally proscribed and reflect which events have been dealt with in the past and do not include those events which may have recently arisen or are emerging as significant threats to personal and community well being. For local people the situation was entirely different, both in terms of the events they considered "disasters" and in the priority they gave to the perceived risks they and their communities faced.

The background in all communities to their sense and understanding of "disaster" was their unequivocal and robust sense of their community. This sense of community embraced a geographical dimension; they knew where their community "was" and where its boundaries lay; that is they could differentiate between "them" and "us". They understood the environmental and ecological processes and status of their area. In addition to a geographical sense they had a sense of history and of the future. They knew where they had come from (this applied most strongly but not exclusively to rural) communities and they had a sense (usually filled with foreboding but not without some hope) of where they were going. Interwoven in this sense of continuity from past through the present to the future were a number of myths and fallacies about social processes, usually involving forced immigration of social welfare recipients from metropolitan areas and of Government bias against small and rural communities. This false perception of forced immigration was most a metaphor for the fear of unregulated and unwanted change in and of the community. Local people possessed a strong and determined sense of daily life. They knew who they were in the sense of having a coherent and confident set of values and norms, they understood local enterprises and the economic basis of their communities and they understood and participated in the many social and governance activities that make up the warp and weft of community life.

Allied with the sense of local community and of daily life local people had a strong body of hopes, aspirations and fears. Their feeling for a desired future was very much "more of the same", a continuation of contemporary daily life (or of daily life located in a recent past in which contemporary problems had not merged). Interwoven with this sense of history, culture, place and future was a very definite sense of what constitutes a "disaster". It was noticeable from our very first interviews and focus group meetings that when we introduced the notion of a "traditional" set of hazards and disasters, such as fires, floods, major transport accidents and similar rapid onset, physically damaging events. Local people acknowledged the importance of these events. But almost immediately all local respondents moved the discussion away from these events and towards their principal concerns which were typically long term social processes, which the respondents themselves clearly identified as disasters in the same way in which rapid onset, destructive events are disasters.

This point is critical to any definition of disaster. For local people a disaster was any event or process that significantly disrupted local daily life and which jeopardized the future. For these people the loss of young people to metropolitan centers for education or work, an aging population, environmental damage, changing agricultural practice, accelerating rural depopulation and the loss of government services were all of greater significance than "traditional" disasters. Local people made no distinction between traditional events and processes of (perceived destructive) social change. For local people unwanted change, however it was caused, was damaging and disastrous. But long term social change was feared more than events such as floods and wildfires because the social depth and the comprehensiveness of change was significantly greater for the continued well-being and the future of the community. Houses and roads can be rebuilt after a wildfire. Businesses and farms can be restored, but the loss of young people, the depopulation of an area or the loss of small businesses such as butchers and bakers and grocers is irreversible and impacts on everybody in the community. Of course there are substantial epistemological grounds for considering these events and process as more or less similar. Both generate uncertainty about the future, both put the present at risk, both attack contemporary values and aspirations to the extent that they invoke or are manifestations of uncontrolled and uncontrollable change and both may lead to systemic change.

Local people therefore specifically and obstinately set out a number of events and processes that they labeled "disaster" which emergency services and governments did not. This broadens what local people at least mean by "disaster". This also challenges Governments and emergency services to review and to redefine their understanding of "disaster". First, in a democratic, pluralist society account has to be taken, *de jure* or *de facto*, of sectoral opinions and values. Second, the processes of social change and development identified and nominated as disasters by local people are in significant ways indistinguishable from the impacts of events/processes that are already commonly acknowledged as (slow onset) disasters, such as droughts, soil erosion and land salinisation[2]. All have a long-term time-scale, all lead to social disruption, family stress and dislocation, and will often cause profound social, economic and environmental change. Third, the measures that need to be put in place to deal with structural change and dislocation are not day-to-day government or social support programs, or event supplemented programs. They are the same as the measures put in place to deal with major disasters and include additional or supplementary management arrangements (which may in time be melded with day to day arrangements), specific, targeted assistance measures and collaboration from local to national levels.

Local people also often saw clearly the linkages between vulnerability or populations, economies and environments at risk and the hazard agent which combined to generate a disaster, which, in other circumstances would not have occurred. For example, in East Gippsland, a remote, mountainous sparsely populated area, local people saw that their vulnerability was significantly increased not just by unreliable telecommunications, poor road access but also by processes of change, such as depopulation, that reduced local hazard knowledge and reduced community coping capacity.

To conclude this section, it is clear that local and community definitions of disaster are quite different to those of emergency management agencies and to government. Local people are as concerned with processes as they are with events; scale (that is "big" as against "small') is less of an issue for them, although they do have a sense of history and of the future and are able to place contemporary hazards and disasters in a temporal context. Local people are concerned with the totality of risks to every day life, and not just with a certain range of events. Local people understand the "significance" of losses, being the emotional and cultural weight of loss and incorporating intangible elements and items (such as mementos, photographs, wedding rings, trophies and certificates) that cannot be replaced even if the physical item itself is replicated. The original contains an irreducible and ineluctable emotional investment that can only be attached to, and only inheres in, the original and cannot be transferred to a facsimile.

For local people "disaster" overlapped significantly with change whose direction was not obvious and which was not controllable by local efforts. Globalization is a current example of this, where changes to agricultural practice induced by global markets remote from the source of production lead in turn to localized social changes that are not desired and which are having a demonstrable present effect on the local community through such mechanisms as changed land use, changed agricultural practice, changed communications (opening up the world and opening up the community to the world) and changed job opportunities drawing young people away from traditional occupations. This gives us not another perspective on "disaster" but an entirely different frame of reference for assessing whether an event or process is a "disaster". Where legislative and mandated definitions focus on events and to a lesser and less strong extent, some processes, local community definitions emphasize process over event and locate the meaning of "disaster" in losses (and not the hazard agent) and in particular to losses and damage and dislocation to everyday life.

COMPLEXITY AND DISASTER

Despite their differences both definitional epistemologies described above provide us with some criteria for deciding what a disaster is. These criteria are located within a social milieu and as such are contingent on the prevailing concerns and values of the society in which they are situated. In the one instance the definition is based on the mandate of an organization and in the other instance in the continuity of daily life. What is perhaps most important is not the differences between these "definitions" but how they and agencies and communities that use them are to be integrated into a shared and common purpose whose generic purpose is to improve public safety, reduce risk and sustain well-being.

One step to achieving this is perhaps to acknowledge in theory and practice that "disaster" is not a phenomenon that is susceptible to definition. This is partly because as disasters are socially constructed and as they are located at a particular but evolving social/historical point in time then any definition will have currency only for that particular time and place. This in itself may not be logically problematic, but it is difficult for agencies and communities if the terms by which they set standards and allocate resources are constantly, but not predictably, evolving.

Even the elements that contribute to "hazard", "risk" and "disaster" are not predictable. For example, which weather conditions may contribute to a "disaster" and how these conditions are nested within a broader climate which itself is changing are not easy to predict (Maslin 2002). In some situations acts of nature leading to "disaster" losses may be unpredictable and unforeseeable and even counter intuitive. (Berz 2002). One approach to resolving these difficulties of linking disparate views of what constitutes a disaster is to abandon the notion that disasters are susceptible to definition, at least in terms of carefully delineated lists and instead to locate meaning in the experience and values and norms of the community.

This acknowledgement that attempts to define and to delineate "disaster" in precise ways are bound to be incomplete and even misleading relates clearly to complexity theory and its' emerging use in the social sciences. David Byrne (1998, 2002) lists the following attributes that belong to complex social systems. The properties of complex systems and phenomena include:

The whole system is not reducible to its parts, and is not predictable from its' constituent elements;

Paths and modes of change, development and growth can be very sensitive to initial conditions;

Networks and interactions and processes are as important in understanding the whole as is understanding discrete elements;

Phase shifts (or thresholds) may arise where a significant change of state occurs often over an extremely short period of time and often unpredictably given initial conditions.

Emergence, the unpredicted development of new elements, characteristics and networks;

Systems are dynamic and change over time.

To which we can add,

Irreversibility. Development of complex systems cannot be "unwound" or reversed and in some cases it may not be possible to work backwards along a causal brachiation to identify causes and consequences (this relates in part to sensitivity to initial conditions, discontinuous change characterized by phase shifts and emergence all of which limit the capacity for retrospection.)

Those events and processes we characterize as disasters, starting with our commonplace, shared understanding of the term, clearly meet these criteria and even meet them in an exaggerated form. Events such as wildfires and processes such as droughts lead to and evolve into situations that are not predictable from initial conditions, not least because the dynamic of attempted control and mitigation, and the contingent political dynamic of mitigation and relief make the progress of each event/process non-identical. In addition, each event/process occurs within a specific social setting and with which it interacts in ways which make detailed prediction of outcomes difficult to achieve. Disasters are not reducible to individual elements. Death, injury, loss of homes and businesses and damage to the environment and infrastructure do not exist separately from each other. One loss will often compound another and in turn be amplified. Interactions and processes (how the hazard agent is transmitted, how information flows and is interpreted, how communities work together in new settings for example) are at least as important in understanding disasters and in their management as are a knowledge of static situations such as the number of dead or injured or the number of houses lost or the number of people evacuated at any given point in time.

Social systems during disasters often show emergence (where the system itself changes fundamentally) or emergent properties (new entities arise within a system) (Buckle et al 2001a). For example, local action groups that coalesce around particular issues may arise spontaneously after a disaster and unite disparate individuals and groups who would otherwise not work together or share a common interest. Equally, some groups may approach a threshold of membership (where numbers are insufficient to meet the functions of the group) or where new functions arise that the group is incapable of dealing with. In this case a threshold may be stepped over (a phase shift occurs) where the group is suddenly and unpredictably unable to function and collapses. This can occur on a broader scale with entire communities, where an existing community (and I am thinking here of particular communities affected by the 1983 Ash Wednesday bush fires just outside Melbourne) where a small proportion of homes may be destroyed but where this initiates a change process so that over the next few years the entire community population changes in what was once an apparently stable community. The same level of destruction in other communities may lead not to re-population but to greater social cohesion and a renewed sense of community togetherness and purpose.

What is the significance of this for understanding the nature of disaster? It is the case that those events and processes we characterize as disasters on the basis of "common-sense" meanings display most or all of these descriptors. It is the case also that there are a number of events and processes that we do not necessarily or at the present characterize as disasters but which do display these characteristics. Climate change and its attendant environmental and social changes, other environmental processes such as the decline relative to global population numbers, soil degradation are all processes in which can see the potentiality for most or all the points mentioned above. Animal population decline is a good example. Animal populations tend to decline in line with changes to habitat, normal population dynamics, pollution, externally imposed changes on environmental health as well as hunting and harvesting practices. At a certain point, however, stocks may fall so low that the population crashes spectacularly and often irrecoverably. The line at which population crash occurs is usually not discernible before the event.

CONCLUSION

Byrne (2002: 163) argues that social science needs to based on a new assessment of complexity as the central organizing principle of many social phenomena. He makes a number of points which include:

1. Complexity; understanding of the character of real complex systems in terms of wholes, parts, interaction of parts with parts, parts with wholes, and of systems with other systems in their environment, within which they are embedded and which they contain:
2. Non-linearity; recognition that interesting and significant shifts in the trajectories and hence characters of complex systems are those that involve radical shifts of kind
3. Localism; the recognition that knowledge is inherently contextual and that a crucial component of the specifications of any of any item or system of things and relations known is the delimitation of the spatial and temporal boundaries within which that knowledge might hold good . . .

4. Connectionism; the recognition that any useful description of real complex systems must itself be complex. This does not preclude the representation being less complex but it must incorporate some element of complexity, for example in the form of explicit interaction, within itself.
5. Action research—the recognition that knowledge is always used in the reconstitution of the social world and that we must take specific account of this in our research processes and practices.

We have seen that mandated, linear descriptions, usually composed of lists, of the apparent elements of disaster fail to adequately deal with complexity, change (predictability), thresholds (phase shifts) and emergence. These definitions are arbitrary and reflective of past events (process is often ignored and covertly transmuted to event) and do not even acknowledge, let alone take account of, changing contexts, values and the social construction of disasters and what we mean by disasters. Mandated definitions have a clear but limited, purpose in informing agencies what actions they must and will be engaged in. But the list is rarely complete or consonant with existing and foreseeable social, cultural, economic, environmental and political trends.

> De Greene (1996:9) has indicated that:
> ... complex systems are dynamic rather than static, evolve or are driven into domains of instability, and emerge into new structures. There is now a growing gap or loss of fit between our systems-management capabilities and the real world. Policymakers and decision makers must deal especially with severely reduced time frames, consequences-of-action uncertainty, and actions that produce diminishing returns.

He goes on later to emphasize this (De Greene 1996:11):

> The concept of evolution is finding increasing application in physics, chemistry, astronomy and

astrophysics, as well as, of course, in biology, geology and paleontology. But it appears that all too few behavioral and social scientists use the evolutionary framework, and that all too many theories, hypotheses, and empirical research efforts are directed toward the static, the cross-sectional, the linear, the equilibrium seeking, the stable, the reversible, and the structurally constant. These efforts . . . operate within a prevailing but exhausted paradigm.

Local community definitions of disaster locate disaster much more firmly in the context of daily life and in systemic and long-term changes. These definitions however are rarely explicitly stated and may often resort to the descriptive "I may not know what a disaster is, but I know what is disastrous to me and my family and my community". It is this local context in which agencies and governments have to act and we can see how over recent decades even the mandated definitions of disasters have moved from focusing on large area, physically destructive and rapid onset natural disasters to include other types of events and processes such as environmental change, complex humanitarian emergencies and terrorism. This change has occurred as a result of community expectations that local assessment will influence central perceptions of disaster and that local values and needs will influence central priorities.

All definitions of social events, processes, structures and action have no eternal and objective validity, they are fixed in a particular culture at a particular time. Given the in ability to formally (mathematically or logically) define disasters—given the nature of complex systems—by identifying autonomous, constituent elements we are left with definitions that are specific to a particular perspective and given that social, cultural and political perspectives are value-laden then these definitions must explicitly or implicitly represent a particular point of view, a particular view of the world. And this being the case, then all definitions contribute to Byrne's "action research" whereby any definition and any action based on that definition is intended to effect some change in the world even if he intent is conservative aiming to avoid further change.

There is nothing invalid about definitions that reflect and are derived from a particular stance; all definitions in social science are such. But it is important that we acknowledge this and acknowledge that if definitions and the events and processes they are intended to define do derive from a specific stance then we must assess whose definitions we should be using. We can reduce this discussion to a few statements.

1. Mandated lists do not completely account for all types of disasters, do not address emerging disasters and treat disaster as an event rather than a process.
2. Local people locate disaster in the context of daily life and of broader society and see disaster in terms of process at least as much as they see them in terms of events. Disasters are defined by their consequences and not by the hazard agent
3. In a democratic, pluralist society account needs to be taken of local norms, values and definitions and organizations and governments have to acknowledge the rights of local people as well as the practicalities that unacknowledged, extraneous definitions cannot be successfully imposed.
4. Disasters are complex events and are typified by characteristics of complexity, such as emergence, the total is greater than the sum of its parts and cannot be estimated by aggregating the parts, phase shifts and irreversibility.

Accepting these statements offers a new view on what a disaster is. For operational purposes it may be located within the mandate of an organization, but this is insufficient when the organization has to deal with the community (and which do not?) who will often have a profoundly different perspective on what constitutes a disaster. Communities locate disaster in daily life and in the interaction of daily life with change, both short term and long term. However, given the nature of disaster as a complex social phenomena

NOTES

1. I have bypassed the issue of whether social science is able to develop theories for the real world. My view is that theories are generally relatively weak in their predictive power, but often much stronger in explanation.
2. This sort of systemic change can also be generated by rapid onset disasters where the disaster is on a sufficiently large scale and is destructive or where it destroys key elements such as entire settlements of essential infrastructure or where the event occurs at a time of pivotal social change and the disaster "tips the scales" in one direction.

13

IN THE EYES OF THE BEHOLDER? MAKING SENSE OF THE SYSTEM(S) OF DISASTER(S)[1]

Denis Smith

Disasters, as a broad category of phenomena, have been important in shaping the nature of many communities and societies. As a consequence, there is a considerable body of literature that has focused attention on the impact that physical (sometimes expressed as environmental) disasters have had on human activities (Alexander 2000; Chester 1993; Davis 2001; de Boer and Sanders 2002; Fagan 2000; Hewitt 1997; Pelling 2001; Smith 2001; Steinberg 2000). The selection of these "physical" disasters for investigation has largely been a function of the extent of their destructive capability, the speed of their onset and the impact that they have had upon human communities.

In definitional terms, the focus on the human element has been an important defining factor in the classification of an event as a disaster and investigations of other cataclysmic events have often remained outside of this categorization (see, for example, work on mass extinction) (Benton 2003; Boulter 2002; McEntire Fuller et al. 2002; Moran 2003; Walker 2003). Other areas of research that have often been excluded from classification as a disaster have involved the impact of intentional human destruction, notably war (Hewitt 1998), and, until events of 9-11, much of the work on terrorism, despite the extent of the damage caused by these events. The scale of the devastation imposed upon the population of German cities during World War II, for example, is captured by Sebald (2003), who observes that the UK's Royal Air Force alone:

> ... dropped 1 million bombs on enemy territory ... of the 131 towns and cities attacked, some only once and some repeatedly, many were almost entirely flattened, that about 600,000 German civilians fell victim to the air raids and 3.5 million homes were destroyed, while at the end of the war 7.5 million people were left homeless, and there were 31.1 cubic metres of rubble for everyone in Cologne and 42.8 cubic metres for every inhabitant of Dresden—but we do not grasp what it all actually meant. The destruction, on a scale without historical precedent, entered the annals of the nation as it set about rebuilding itself only in the form of vague generalizations. It seems to have left scarcely a trace of pain behind in the collective consciousness (Sebald 2003: 3-4.)

By any physical measure, the devastation caused by such bombing would justify the inclusion of the event as a disaster. In addition, the last part of Sebald's description of the bombing also raises an important issue relating to the trauma of such catastrophic events and the manner in which it is dealt with by those who experienced it directly. He argues that the devastation caused by such bombing seemed to have generated a degree of "self amnesia" with the result that the "images of this horrifying chapter of our history have never really crossed the threshold of the national consciousness" (2003: 11). Such a psychological-social impact of an event would also be a characteristic for its classification as a disaster. Similarly, there is little doubt that the terrorist attacks on New York and Washington in 2001 have led to considerable physical damage and trauma and a re-conceptualization of "disaster", at least in terms of public consciousness (Cohen et al. 2002; Greenberg 2002; Walker 2002). One might question why the academic integration of such deliberate, human-induced disasters into the mainstream literature has been seen as limited (Hewitt 1997, 1998), when many other disasters have been shaped and influenced by human in/action. It is clear, therefore, that the definition of disaster needs to be systematically undertaken if we are to include or omit certain groups of catastrophic event from any taxonomy. These phenomena include plagues, viruses and disease (Barnett and Whiteside 2002; Berridge 1996; Cantor 2001; Epstein 1996; Hooper 2000; Karlen 1996; Rhodes 1997), environmental impacts (Davis 2002), medical and health catastrophes (Davis 2001. 2002; Rhodes 1997; Smith 2002; Stephens and Brynner 2001; Vass 2001), and a range of technological accidents (Bird 1962; Chiles 2001; Perrow 1984; Reason 1997; Sipika and Smith 1993; Smith and Sipika 1993; Turner 1978; Turner and Pidgeon 1997). The question of what, if anything, unites these diverse events in such a way as to provide insight into the manner in which disasters are generated and "managed", has been the subject of considerable discussion and debate (Etkin 1999; Gilbert 1998; Hewitt 1997, 1998; Kreps 1998; Pelling 2001, 2003; Porfiriev 1998; Quarantelli 1998b; Turner 1976). It is the unification of key constructs around the term "disaster" that this, and previous volumes (Quarantelli 1978a, 1998b) have sought to address.

The aim of this present chapter is to explore the elements of the term disaster, by working through the analytical lens provided by literatures relating to crisis management (including systems thinking and, to an extent, management). Whilst this focus on a specific set of literature for such a multi-dimensional problem is inevitably artificial, the rationale for the primary focus on crisis management is two-fold. In the first instance, a considerable amount of the disaster literature has focused on the social dimensions of such "events", with any discussion of "management" as a contributory factor being largely framed in terms of the nature of the response to the event by the various regulatory and controlling authorities. Secondly, the work on crisis management has not had a significant impact upon the traditional literature on disasters, with some notable exceptions (Rosenthal 1998; Shrivastava 1987; Turner 1978), and there are several key theoretical concepts relating to incubation and latent error that can be seen to be relevant to the wider debate (Calman and Smith 2001; Reason 1990, 1997, 2001; Turner 1976, 1978; Turner et al. 1997).

IDENTIFYING BOUNDARIES

Given the nature of the problem addressed here, there are several assumptions and caveats that need also to be made clear, in order both to clarify the approach taken and to explain the boundaries imposed upon the discussion. This is not done in an apologetic way, but rather to ensure that there is a reduction in any ambiguity around the arguments. The first caveat concerns the perspective offered by the crisis management approach that is adopted here. In many respects, this body of literature offers some potential to extend the existing work on the sociology of disasters, by including additional material relating to organizational vulnerability and resilience. It also serves to raise the profile of a range of management processes that act as core contributors to the development of that vulnerability, both for organizations as well as for communities. The second caveat is that the crisis approach generally sees the physical "triggers" (i.e. the events themselves) as secondary factors in the overall process, with the issues of primary concern often being expressed in terms of the incubation of systems vulnerability and the constraints imposed upon coping strategies as a consequence. In the context of disasters with a "natural" (or more accurately, an environmental) trigger, the generation of coping strategies for damage reduction (engineering responses, population zoning and contingency planning) are all processes in which "management" has a significant role to play. In addition, a whole series of managerial and organizational assumptions are inherent within the development of such contingent responses and these have been largely ignored, or relegated in importance, within certain segments of the disaster literature. This is not to say that the managerial aspects of disaster research should have primacy, but rather that they should be given more prominence than at present. The third caveat is that the systems perspective heavily influences the crisis literature that is drawn upon here, as well as being important in influencing much of the work within the earth sciences, human factors and crisis management. The approach can also be seen to allow for a greater integration of the "human" elements with the physical-technological aspects of a disaster and, as a result, offers the potential for a more holistic approach to complex events. A systems approach also allows for the integration and consideration of such concepts of "space-place-time", "vulnerable-resilient" and "emergence" as explanatory/analytical constructs within a disaster context.

Inevitably, the approach taken here will prove too constraining for some and, possibly, too diffuse for others! By surfacing these underlying assumptions, however, an attempt is being made to define the limits of this inquiry in the hope that subsequent debates around the boundaries may generate additional insights. As such, this essay tries to bring a range of literatures together in an attempt to "make sense" of the issues raised by disasters.

DISASTERS IN TEMPORAL AND SPACIAL CONTEXT: A SEARCH FOR BOUNDARIES

". . . in social theory simplicity should not displace the complexities of tension" (Law 1999: 1).

One of the obvious difficulties that exist within any attempt at defining a disaster is the risk of over-simplifying what is an extremely complex and highly emotive term. One might argue that, given their diversity and complexity, disasters are not easily reduced to a simple definition. However, in order to frame the debates in this essay, it is proposed to establish an early definition of the term disaster and to test the suppositions within that definition against subsequent insights developed from the literature. As a starting point, it is proposed that we establish an early "straw" definition of disasters that can be used as a basis for discussions around the term. Disasters can, therefore, be seen as:

> multi-level issues that unfold through the impacts that they have on elements of society via processes of agency (and in some cases because of the actions of agents), the networks of inter-dependence that they expose or damage, and through the consequences that they generate for actors (as victims of the physical processes of generating harm). (Definition 1)

This definition identifies several important elements that are worthy of further discussion and elaboration. Firstly, disasters are complex, "multi-level issues" (Yammarino and Dansereau 2002) and, as such, should be seen as having impact beyond the immediate physical damage that is normally associated with a "disaster event". In any disaster, it is likely that the physical impacts of the event will trigger the emergence of several issues that also require intervention and action. In exploring the implications of such multiple levels for disaster research, Haggett (2000) has identified three strands that are seen to be important. The first of these strands involves a focus on location and the importance of space as a conceptual and practical framework. The second focus is concerned with the human-environment relationships and the impact of the various "processes" of production, consumption and destruction on ecological systems. Hagget (2000) argues that it is important to remember that this interaction is a two-way process and it is also possible for human activities to impact upon physical processes. The final element in Haggett's definition of the discipline is the notion of place, on the unique character of particular places... [which]... fuses the social and ecological strands on to a specific area or region (Hagget 2000:2).

Secondly, the notions of space-place-time relationships have also permeated other research relating to issues of risk and hazard, notably the work on post-modernity and globalization (Giddens 1990). Urry, for example, argues that there are five key elements within the processes of globalization, which can be seen to have a relevance to our current discussion. These elements are seen as structure, flow, ideology, performance and complexity (Urry 2003) and they can be used as a framework through which to illustrate the "multi-level" nature of "disasters" (see table 1). This mosaic of elements serves to generate a dynamic, emergent set of issues that will face any community or network exposed to the disruption and damage associated with a disaster. The impacts of globalization should not be underestimated in terms of both disaster causation (incubation) and mitigation. [Of course, "Globalization" has also proved to be a concept that has been subject to debate and disagreement.] This is especially important for technological disasters, due to the actions of trans-national corporations in exporting hazard, but it also has implications for "natural" disasters (Blaikie et al. 1994; Pelling 2001, 2003) and terrorist acts (Baxter and Downing 2001; Vidal 2002). What emerges from the interaction of these elements is a sense of the complicated nature of disasters (see Table 1 and Figure 1) and the manner in which networks of connections can shape the dynamics of catastrophe.

Table 1: Globalization, modernity and their implications for disaster

	Characteristics of the elements (source: Urry 2003)	Relevance to disasters
Structure	–increased interconnections between agents –compression of space-time	–increased interconnections may generate emergence associated with both the creation of and response to hazards –structural factors may inhibit the various organizations' abilities to learn lessons from events –the creation of immediacy, in terms of the manner in which disasters are communicated and responded to, generates demands on decision making –greater internationalisation of disaster agencies removes the power of localised control

Flow	–flows occur within scapes –increased communications processes with the compression of time and space –importance of nodes within scapes –information, images and messages transferred quickly –revised flows create inequalities of access across social groups –relative location may be seen as more important than absolute	–importance of disaster/aid agencies as key conduits of resource and information –relative location may increase access to information and expertise and serve to exclude other elements of society –imbalances within confined zones of disaster may exhibit inequalities, especially in more economically challenged areas –the interactions between key agencies is seen as being important in shaping the complexion of a particular disaster –nodes may become key barriers to the effective response to hazardous events –a focus on the frequency, (natural) occurrence and type of hazard, rather than on their social and economic impact upon communities, may serve to distort the nature of the problem and shift policy negatively
Ideology	–transnational corporations assume greater power within globalized economies –generates problems of regulation –organizations' lack long term commitment to place –erosion of the power of the state –emergence of technocratic elites	–technological risks may be increased as a function of the power of capital to evade regulation and control (e.g. Bhopal) –hazardous activities may be exported from the point of production as a means of maximising profitability and reducing interference –expertise becomes a surrogate for democracy and groups are disenfranchised from debates concerning the nature and acceptability of hazards and policies towards their mitigation –the legitimacy of technical elites negates and minimises the role and importance of local (expert) knowledge –the power of global capital may escalate the physical impact of a disaster by spreading its economic impacts –assumptions are made about the power of technology as a means of mitigating the consequences of a disaster
Performance	–nature has become a global, interconnected and political process –"This global nature has resulted from fusing various social practices that are remaking space"	–disasters have become a global rather than a local issue and the political infrastructure may be seen to by-pass local controls and systems –resource availability may be enhanced by reference to global networks –issues exist with regard to absorption capacity both locally and globally, especially in terms of recovery and rehabilitation –the level of interconnectivity with regard to disasters (and their impacts) increases with globalization –communication factors increase the severity of an event and widen the scope of its impact

Complexity	–systemic and dynamic character of globalized processes –dynamic and shifting processes generate new and emergent issues for management and control –patterns of networks generate emergence and complexity –cause does not equal effect as a consequence of emergence	–disasters can no longer be seen in isolation and there is a considerable degree of interconnectivity between events and the damage that they cause –there is a growing and ever more complex global network that seeks to deal with disasters –knowledge around disasters becomes more the domain of the expert and may be beyond the access of local publics –power relationships change and evolve to meet the demands of the globalizing society

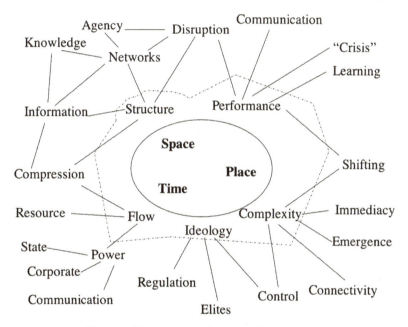

Figure 1. Disaster: towards an initial construction

Another aspect to emerge from our opening definition is that disasters can also generate impacts across a considerable distance and over a long time period and this raises further issues within the structure-performance-complexity aspects of Urry's framework. The causal factors that serve to shape the event may also incubate over time and space and will be shaped by social, political and economic factors in addition to the geo-physical or technological issues that are in operation (Alexander 2000; Bird 1962; Chiles 2001; Davis 2001; Fagan 2000; Fisher et al 1997; Turner 1978).

The connected nature of disasters has become all the more apparent within a globalized world. The images of a disaster and the sense of human suffering take on a new dynamic when they are transmitted in real time into our homes. The sense of being one step removed from a disaster has been eroded.

The connected nature of the system in which disasters occur also allows the consequences of one event to influence the conditions that will shape the complexion of other disasters in different spatial and temporal settings (Davis 2001; de Boer et al. 2002; Fagan 2000). In addition, one disaster may influence the resilience or vulnerability of a community to the consequences of other events (Davis 2001; de Boer et al. 2002; Elliott and Smith 1993). This interconnected dynamic of a disaster is an important element in the inclusion of an event within any taxonomy of disasters.

An additional element that emerges from this perspective sees disasters as also having a sense of place—they cause damage within a community that is located in a "place", although in a globalized and e-enabled society, this notion of place has taken on a new dimension (Auge 1995; Hudson 2001; Jackson 1994; Urry 2003). The interaction of networks, both within and between communities and organizations, and the impact of "culture" upon the reactions of those "communities" generates a set of socio-political-cultural dynamics that provides a unique element to the environmental aspects of the event. In this setting, the notions of "communities of practice" are also important, as a disaster will shape the subsequent behavior of those professional groups who have a role to play in disaster management and prevention. Finally, our initial definition also recognizes the importance of actors and victims within the process. It does, however, see them not as passive entities but rather as dynamic, interconnected elements in a socio-physical setting.

By taking these discussions into account, it is now possible to refine our opening definition in the light of the material reviewed thus far. As a result, our second definition of a disaster sees the events as:

multi-level, complex and damaging systems-related events that unfold over time and space, through an emergent complex interaction of elements involving structures, connections and networks and which are shaped by ideological, economic and social factors to generate impacts on elements of society that changes the performance of the "normal" order of that societal setting. The damage that occurs is shaped via processes of agency (and in some cases because of the actions of agents), the networks of interdependence that they expose or damage, and through the consequences that they generate for actors (as victims of the physical processes of generating harm). (Definition 2)

In order to test and refine the assumptions within this revised definition, it is necessary to explore this "system" of disasters further. For the purposes of this paper, a system will be defined as "a set of interconnected elements that interact together to generate emergent properties". The notion of a system serves to help conceptualize, frame and explain the phenomena under investigation.

SYSTEMS OF DISASTER

The use of a broad systems approach is adopted within this paper because it allows both for the abstraction of complex ideas and concepts as well as the subsequent "testing" of those abstractions. As such, it is argued that the approach has considerable benefit within debates around "disaster". One of the techniques that has been developed to deal with complex, ill-defined issues is the "soft systems methodology" (SSM), that has emerged out of the work of Checkland (Checkland 1981; Checkland and Holwell 1998; Checkland and Scholes 1990). Using a framework developed by Checkland, it is possible to shape the discussion of disasters around the CATWOE framework in order to move towards a root definition. At the core of the CATWOE framework are six elements that are deemed to be of importance in shaping the characteristics of the system and these elements need to be outlined in turn.

In the first instance, we need to consider the *"customers"* of the disaster. Whilst at first glance this might seem to be a somewhat bizarre expression of a group within a disaster setting (due primarily to the transactional and economically based nature of the term "customer" in common usage), the customers here are seen as those individuals who are the victims or recipients of the activities and costs generated by the disaster. The second group are the *"actors"*, and these play a direct and active (as opposed to a passive) role in shaping the nature of the events. The actors are important within the context of a disaster as they have a major part to play, both in terms of the incubation of the event, as well as influencing the aftermath of the disaster. Clearly then, it is likely that the nature, composition and actions of these actors will change in terms of the time-space-place relationship and may be closely identified with the various phases of a disaster as a consequence.

The third component of our root definition centers upon the *"transformations"* that take place during the timeline of any disaster. Clearly this is a complex and potentially ill-defined process, especially due to the importance of emergence within a system that is operating under conditions of traumatic change. Inevitably, the sheer complexity of a disaster generates conditions that are both difficult to predict and yet which can be shaped both by the physical manifestation of the event as well as the intervention of human agency in the processes of incubation, mitigation and recovery. An obvious transformation within a disaster is the destruction that is invariably associated with an event and it is clear that for certain types of phenomena this destruction can span generations as well as geographical borders. In some cases it is possible to see the disaster as a trigger for further manifestations of the event's consequences. For example, AIDS, whilst a major catastrophe in terms of loss of life and more general humanitarian issues, may also generate a crisis for any health care system that does not have the resources to cope with the demands generated by the scale of the illness. Another example would be the UK's BSE crisis, which indirectly had an impact upon the nature of the 2001 Foot and Mouth outbreak, largely as a consequence of the reduction in the numbers of abattoirs, but also in terms of regulatory change. Whilst BSE, and its human variant VCJD, has resulted in a considerable number of deaths, these have occurred over a long timeframe and across a diffuse geographical area. This led to greater distances traveled for the slaughter of the animals and seems to have contributed to the spread of the disease. Thus, one might argue that the notions of space and time are also important elements in this transformation process.

The fourth element of the CATWOE definition centers on the "*Weltanshuung*" or World-views of people involved in the events. This is very much an exercise in "sense-making" (Weick 1988, 1993) and is an important element of the disaster process, particularly so given the perceptual and stress related aspects of the phenomenon. The earlier observations about the denial or reconstruction of events within the disaster timeline are important elements of the human aspects of the process. These may, in turn, add a different interpretation to the phase that follows on from the initial destructive period of the disaster (Sebald 2003).

The fifth element concerns the "*operators*", those who are seen to have control of the event, or can help shape the responses that are made to it. The notion of control implicitly raises issues relating to power relationships within organizations, between organizations, and between organizations and those who become victims of a disaster. Once again, the dynamics of control are important here and they will change throughout the timeline. There is a sense in which any disaster may represent a loss of control on the part of one group over elements of their environment, and an attempt by another group at reasserting that control. The processes by which disasters can be incubated will also have significance in terms of our concepts of control. In this case, it could be argued that the assumptions and beliefs that people have about control will be critical in allowing system defenses to be bypassed. Alternatively, they may create a false set of assumptions concerning the nature of the risk (in terms of its probability of occurrence and the associated consequences) and the manner in which it can be managed. Clearly, the worldviews of these actors are important in shaping the "configuration" of a particular disaster.

Finally, a root definition has to consider the *Environment in which the disaster is contextualized.* The environment is important in providing a set of (local) conditions within which the rest of the CATWOE framework is set and it will inevitably shape the manner in which the event unfolds. An attempt at developing a CATWOE root definition framework for the notion of a disaster is shown in 7. It should be noted at this point that this is a general attempt at dealing with the issues and each specific disaster will generate its own character that makes it unique. The broad framework provided by such a root definition could also be extended across the timeline associated with the event and the dynamics between the CATWOE elements would invariably change over time as a result. In order to illustrate this argument, it is necessary to explore the notion of a "timescape" (Adam, 1998) of disasters in more detail.

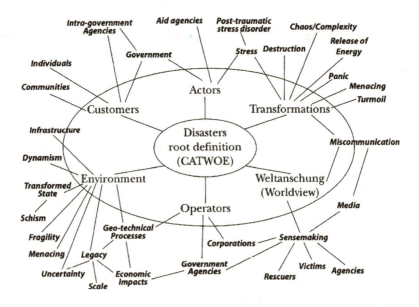

Figure 2. Elements of disaster research

TIMESCAPES OF DISASTER

> *"a timescape perspective conceives of the conflictual interpenetration of industrial and natural temporalities as an interactive and mutually constituting whole and stresses the fact that each in/action counts and is non-retractable"* (Adam, 1998: 56).

In discussing the role of time in shaping environmental hazards, Adam (1998) uses the term "timescape" as a means of conceptualizing the role of time as an influencing factor on the nature of hazard. For an organizationally based crisis, the timescape could be seen in terms of three distinct but related stages: the crisis of management, the operational crisis and the crisis of legitimacy (Sipika et al. 1993; Smith 1990a, 1995; Smith et al. 1993). The notion of control implicitly raises issues relating to power relationships within organizations, between organizations, and between organizations and those who become victims of a disaster. In order to explore the implications of time on our discussion of disaster, this framework can be analyzed in more detail. There are a number of analytical frameworks used within crisis management and most of these make use of a staged framework in order to examine the differing mix of processes in operation in each phase (Pauchant and Mitroff 1992; Reason 1997; Smith 1990a, 1995; Turner 1976, 1978). With that in mind, it is important to recognize that each of these phases will offer a different perspective on the nature of the event. They will also be shaped by the manner in which the various networks of association operate within the space-place-time frameworks and these will help to generate multiple interpretations and understandings of the disaster.

The existing literature on disaster makes the distinction between various forms of "time" (social, industrial, geological) (Adam 1998; Jackson 1994; Le Poidevin 2003; Repcheck 2003) and disasters provide us with a useful context in which to illustrate the impact of the different timeframes on the configuration of the event itself. In discussing the nature of volcanoes, for example, Fisher has observed that,

Our lives are single frames in the moving picture of the constantly changing earth... Volcanoes, however, are geological systems operating in real time" (Fisher, 1999:4).

Thus, the notion of time is seen as important in understanding the particular construct that is a volcanic disaster, but there are clearly two timelines in operation; the geological and the human. The build up to the disaster can take place invisibly over many thousands of years but the event once it occurs is marked by its rapid onset and catastrophic impact and the resultant disaster is shaped by its immediate and long-term impacts upon human activities (Davis 2001; de Boer et al. 2002; Fagan 2000; Keys 1999; Kreps 1998).

There are also subtle dimensions to the disaster timescape in terms of the generation and emergence of the event. The first concerns the processes of incubation for the event (Turner 1976, 1978), which can take place over a considerable period of time for socio-technical disasters and considerably longer for natural hazards. This timeline would also include the process of recovery after such an event, which can, in certain circumstances, also take place over a long time frame. The second dimension concerns the immediate responses to the event itself, which is typified by the high-energy release and the immediate demands for containment, control and remediation. One analogy that tries to encompass all of these elements is the notion of a "vibrating string" (de Boer et al. 2002). A disaster can generate a series of effects over time, in a process by which the initial event triggers a series of subsequent impacts. These can clearly have consequences beyond the immediate timeframe of the specific disaster and may span generations of "victims". These impacts will invariably contain less energy than the initial catastrophic event but they may last for considerably longer periods and, thereby, cause greater damage (de Boer et al., 2002).

Despite the multiple time frames at work in a disaster, there are often early warnings of the impending catastrophe which can provide prior indications of the event (Ravilious 2001; Reason 1997; Scarth 2002; Turner 1978) although it is obvious that these warnings are not always clear and unequivocal in their message. For example, Scarth (2002: 31) observes that:

... volcanic eruptions rarely behave like clockwork and follow exactly the same pattern. Sometimes, indeed, the preliminary symptoms do not even lead to an eruption, but at least they warn that something sinister might be brewing in the entrails of the volcano.

Issues of connectivity and interaction are also important within the generation of the disaster event. It is important to consider the holistic process of damage, rather than the narrowly confined timescape that is associated with trigger of the eruption, earthquake or explosion. For the purposes of our current discussions, it is proposed to outline a particular framework for considering a timescape that sees such events occurring in three overlapping stages.

The "crisis of management" (Smith 1990a) phase is that period prior to the generation of damage. It is typified by a gradual erosion of capability and resilience, and will involve the creation of "pathways of vulnerability" within both organizational and community defenses and capabilities (Smith 2000b). It is this phase of a "disaster" that has attracted the attention of those who seek to create resilient organizations and communities, although the problems of developing an effective audit framework remain elusive (Smith 1995, 2002; Smith and McCloskey 2000). Similarly, the search for predictive indices of disaster has also attracted attention (Ravilious 2001) but may ultimately prove to be something of a "Holy Grail"(Smith 1995). The second phase of the timescape—the operational crisis—is that phase in the disaster timeline where the destructive event itself occurs. This phase is typified by damage, disruption, confusion, the need to implement contingency plans and the failure of control systems (Smith 2000a). This phase is also typified by the intervention of "rescuers", who can be individuals (including victims of the disaster), or organizations with responsibilities to act as first responders in a disaster. This phase becomes somewhat complicated, however, if we include the more chronic types of disaster in our discussion. Here, those events in which the phase of damage generation takes place over a long time period, will not have the clearly defined timescape typically associated with a disaster. These events are more diffuse and tend to be marked by disputes and debates concerning the nature and extent of the hazards. Problems associated with "public health" disasters illustrate the diffuse and complex nature of such events (Angell 1996; Baker 2001; Brown and Duncan 2002; Redfern, Keeling, and Powell 2000; Smith 2002; Stephens et al. 2001). The final stage, "the crisis of legitimation", is concerned with the aftermath of the event itself and is typified by the processes of recovery, reconstruction and rehabilitation, organizational learning and regulatory change (Sipika et al. 1993; Smith 1990a; Smith et al. 2000; Smith et al. 1993). This period is also often marked by a search for culpability and the processes of learning and to a degree scapegoating (Smith 1990a, 1995). This search for culpability is often undertaken by government(s) through the formal public inquiry/presidential commission process as a means of ensuring that learning takes place or, more cynically, that blame is apportioned and state legitimacy is maintained (Smith 1990a, 2000b). Whilst the framework has been applied to technological disasters and organizational crises, rather than "natural" or environmental disasters, it is felt that the issues have a validity within that broader setting.

Table 2 seeks to outline the main characteristics of each of the three phases. This table is adapted from the collective work of several scholars (Reason 1990, 1997, 2001; Smith 1990a, 1995, 2000a, 2000b; Smith and McCloskey 1998; Smith et al. 2000; Smith et al. 1993; Turner 1976, 1978). Each stage of an event brings with it its own subtleties and nuances, and the energy levels associated with each stage will also be significantly different across the timeline. What a crisis framework brings to the discussion is a greater emphasis on the role of human agency and, in particular, the role and importance of management as a contributory factor in the generation of the event. Obvious examples of such a role include, amongst others, decisions taken around hazard zoning, additional engineering for structures, and the development of contingency plans. It can be argued that such a framework has a relevance to natural as well as technological disasters although the role of human agency prior to a natural disaster may not always have the clarity that can be provided by a socio-technical event.

Phase of the event	Characteristics and Processes
The Crisis of Management	-role of assumptions and beliefs in shaping decision making for disaster prevention (group think) -assumptions and beliefs shape the defences that are put into place -reluctance to consider and plan for worst case scenarios due to perceived low probability of occurrence (and high cost of intervention) -distraction of decision making bodies by other issues which are given higher priority -trade-offs made between "risk" and benefit–risk minimisation -failures in "management" to identify and prevent erosion of defences -excessive power given to technocratic elites in decision making -difficulties around communication inhibit early warnings of potential disaster -emergent properties in complex systems generate conditions beyond the tolerance of control systems -creation of pathways of vulnerability and fractures within control -erosion of resilience
The Operational Crisis	-trigger events expose weaknesses in the "system" developed in the crisis of management phase -release of "energy" or problems relating to emergent properties cause severe damage and disruption -emergent properties exceed capabilities of contingency plans -need to utilise additional resources to deal with demands of the event -need for containment and control -recovery and rescue teams mobilised -disruption of "normal" procedures and services -additional demands placed on other organizations to deal with damage and disruption; potential for knock-on effects is high (may serve as an incubation mechanism or trigger for another event) -high task demands from vulnerable populations generates "political" problems of resource allocation -"crisis management teams" mobilised to deal with the task demands of the event -constrained communications and control may compound initial problems -prior failures to train rescue and crisis teams may lead to an escalation of the event -involvement of media increases the profile of the event and heightens stress levels for those charged with "management" of the problems -mobilisation of aid and resources from outside of the "region of damage"

The Crisis of Legitimation	-need for rehabilitation, stabilisation and recovery -investigation of causal factors and lessons to be learnt–high level of government involvement -re-evaluation of control mechanisms and contingency plans -heightened possibility of scapegoating through a search for culpability -organizational learning constrained due to assumptions of those "managing" the process -media investigations into the cause of the event and the attempts at dealing with its demands -impact on financial performance of organization or state though rehabilitation and recovery demands -failure to address the core problems of assumptions and beliefs leading to single-loop learning

If we consider the relationship between the CATWOE framework and the three stages of crisis model then it is possible to capture something of the complexity of the interactions that take place within any disaster, by tracking the timeline of the event relative to the changing root definition of the disaster. Again, this adds a layer of complexity associated with the concept of a disaster and is an important reflection of the ways in which such events unfold in reality. One of the distinguishing events of a disaster is the manner in which emergence plays a major role in shaping the event. By framing a disaster using these concepts, the potential for that emergence—expressed in terms of the interactions between elements of the event and the generation of new and unforeseen characteristics as a consequence of that interaction—is considerable.

If we take the key elements from the CATWOE analysis, expressed in figure 2, and test them against our opening definition, then it is possible to identify a number of further omissions within the definition. The first set of issues that challenge our definition emerge out of the transformations that take place within a disaster. These events clearly bring with them emergent properties that often contain a tremendous amount of energy, much of it negative, and they also generate considerable fear, confusion and misunderstanding (Bird 1962; Raphael 1986; Weick 1993). The second issue concerns the multiple phases and layers that are inherent within a disaster. This, in turn, also generates a sense of the complexity associated with the event and this is compounded by the manner in which the event is reported through the media and social networks. Thirdly, there is a sense in which collaboration is required in order to allow the various groups to cope with the demands of the disaster.

By incorporating these elements of the analysis into our discussion, it is possible to move towards a third iteration of our evolving definition. Disasters can now be seen as:

> "multi-phased and multi-level, complex and damaging systems-related high-energy events that unfold over time and space, through an emergent complex interaction of elements involving structures, connections and networks and which are shaped by ideological, economic and social factors to generate impacts on elements of society that change the performance of the "normal" order of that societal setting. The damage that occurs is shaped via processes of agency (and in some cases because of the actions of agents), the networks of inter-dependence that they expose or damage, and through the consequences that they generate for the psychosocial well-being of actors (as victims of the physical processes of generating harm). These events create considerable problems associated with complexity, communication, stress and sense-making. (Definition 3)

As a working definition, this has clearly evolved from our opening attempt and it now has a strong sense of the psychosocial dynamism of a disaster associated with it. Of particular interest here are the difficulties that the notion of disaster generates in terms of "sense-making", an issue that will be returned to later. At this point, it is necessary to calibrate our working definition of disaster by reference to attempts made elsewhere to define the term.

EXPLORING THE BOUNDARIES: SETTING THE FRAMEWORK FOR ANALYSIS

In order to test our third working definition of disaster against the literature, it is proposed to set out a series of spray diagrams (commonly used in systems research) as a means of identifying the key elements of the construct. Figure 3 represents a first attempt at framing this "networked nature of disasters", by making a simple expression of the issues dealt with in this paper thus far. What is clear from this diagram is that no single definition could provide the richness that is encapsulated in the issues identified within Figures 1-3. Above all, what is of interest is the manner in which these elements interact together to generate a construct that is richer and infinitely more complex than the simple sum of the parts. In employing a human centered approach to the term, the importance of the physical phenomenon becomes relegated in importance and is seen largely as a trigger event for the disaster. In this way, human agency can be seen to provide input into the incubation process for the disaster in a way that could be lost within a more event-centric approach. The key elements of our expression of disaster, emerging from figure 3, would suggest that emergence, resilience and vulnerability are important in shaping the nature of an event.

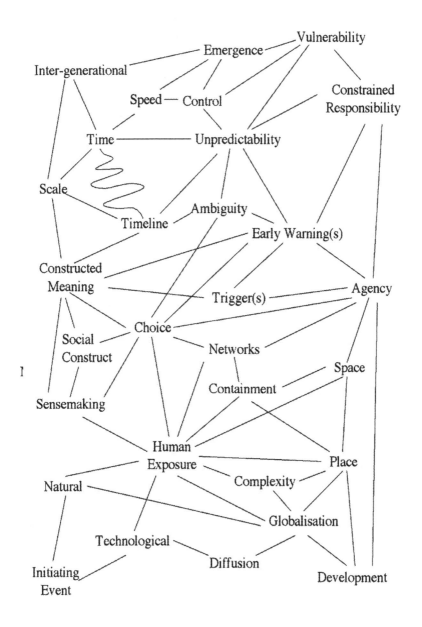

Figure 3. Towards a root definition of disaster

In earlier explorations of the term "disaster", a number of core elements were identified by several authors and an attempt has been made to capture many of these elements in figure 4. Again, there is a clear human-centered dynamic to the process and there is also a considerable degree of overlap between the various constructions of the term. One of the key elements to emerge from this work concerns the networked nature of disasters and this needs to be examined in more detail.

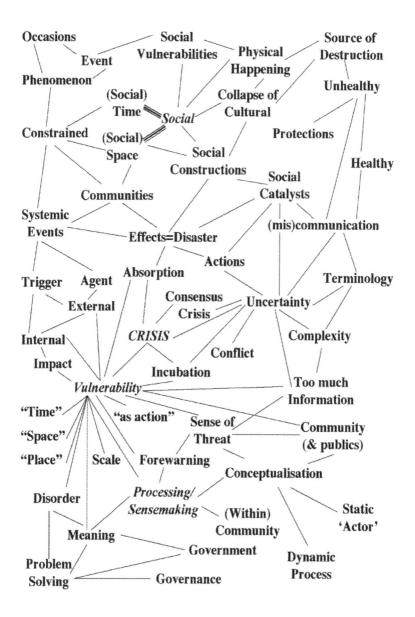

Figure 4. Shifting definitions of the disaster process in three stages

SPACE AND PLACE: NETWORKS AND AGENCY

Research in crisis management has also indicated how important social frameworks, or "networks of association", can be in both generating the conditions for the crisis, as well as impacting upon the ability of the organization to deal with the task demands associated with the event. The interactions between the elements within these networks, as well as with elements of the broader system itself, are seen as important mechanisms by which emergence is generated. In the crisis of management phase (Smith 1990a, 1995), this emergence helps to generate the conditions that "allow" the event to unfold, or to make the consequences of an event even more significant by eroding gaps in the controls that are put in place to deal with the disaster (Reason 1997; Smith 2000b). During the "active" or operational phase of the crisis, emergence can also generate conditions that will escalate the consequences and severity of the event by, for example, increasing the population at risk or affecting its vulnerability. However, it is also clear that emergence is also important in generating organizational capability (resilience) to deal with the task demands of a crisis event. There have also been several crises where the interaction that took place between individuals or groups served to create additional capability beyond that normally associated with the activity. This has proved to be particularly important in terms of sense-making and problem solving capabilities of the organizations or groups involved in the event. The crash at Sioux City in the USA, for example, illustrated how the combination of expertise held by the crew, the technical and piloting capabilities of individual crew members, and the chance presence of a senior DC-10 training instructor as a passenger who was co-opted into the "team", all combined to generate a unique capability to deal with the task demands of the event (Krause 1996). Emergence within the context of a disaster is, inevitably, a double-edged sword.

A second aspect of the network dynamic of disasters concerns the abilities of the various individuals and agencies to communicate around the dynamic elements of the event. This can be seen both in terms of the early warnings associated with the disaster and also around the response strategies developed for dealing with issues of containment and control as the precise nature of the disaster unfolds. Again, there are important issues here that relate to the language used to communicate, the nature, role and importance of technical expertise in decision making and the power structures associated with the organizations involved in the event(s).

A further issue concerns the relationship between the customer-actor-owner elements of the system (as expressed within CATWOE). Clearly, these terms have been developed for use within an organizational setting and might be seen as somewhat limiting within our present discussions. As a consequence, a distinction is made here between the various "actors" within the system and one that encompasses the roles of "operators" and "customer".

There are seen to be three principal, overlapping groups of actors; victims, rescuers and agents. The victims in a disaster are those who are directly faced with the consequences of a disaster event. These victims should not, however, be seen as passive, but rather as operating within an enacted environment in which their choices and actions are seen as important influencing factors in the shaping of the disaster (Weick 1988, 1990, 1993, 1995). The second group is those rescuers who respond to the immediate task demands generated by the event. These will include the emergency services and various disaster agencies, but it will also include elements of the victim group who act as first responders and provide assistance to others. The final group are termed agents and these are individuals and/or groups who play an active role in shaping the emergence of the disaster as a function of their decision-making and actions. These groupings are dynamic and inclusion in one group does not preclude inclusion in another. Each group will also interpret, or make sense of, the disaster in different ways and they will also be important in shaping the transformations that take place around the event (see figure 5).

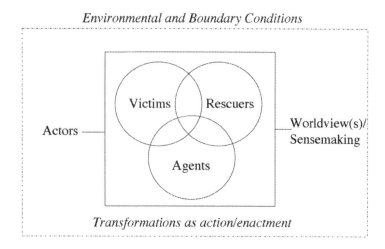

Figure 5. Space-place-time and the development of disaster potential

What does emerge from the discussion so far is that, irrespective of the trigger event for the disaster, there is a strong and convincing argument, which suggests that disasters have a strong human component in terms of their causality and that this needs to be embedded within the definition of the term. This human-centered focus extends to an argument that sees decision-making and "management" (including the generation of both latent and active errors) playing significant roles in the generation of, and response to, disasters. The reconstruction of the event as a narrative and the difficulties that often face groups and individuals in terms of their sense-making for a disaster, also adds a layer of psychological complexity to the use of the term. Once we see disasters as human centric, then the interplay of space-place-time and the subtleties around human networks and agencies takes on a new dimension.

At this point, we can see the role of the human element in the causation of disasters; these are no longer events caused by a third party or some higher being, but result from a complex interplay of human activities around the attempts at controlling both nature and science/technology (Epstein 1996; Esser and Lindoerfer 1989; Shilts 2000; Shrivastava 1987; Smith 1990b). Put another way, the complex set of interactions will themselves generate complex relationships around the interactions between elements. A related process here is that of tight coupling and interactive complexity, issues that were seen by Perrow as causing catastrophes to escalate quickly once they begin, and to follow pathways that had not been considered prior to the event (Perrow 1984). The interaction between these elements will generate "pathways of vulnerability" (Smith 2000b) which can lead to an erosion of the main systems of control that organizations believe are in place to deal with the demands of the event. The interaction of these factors, operating within the space-time-place framework, will generate pre-conditions for a disaster that will help to shape the manner in which the event unfolds. This, in turn, relates to the manner in which the contingent processes that are developed to deal with such events are used and, in many cases, fail to deal with the demands of a disaster. There will be changes in the role of human agency throughout the timeline of a disaster and this will impact upon the sense-making process that the various "groups" undertake (figure 6). The various actors will have a role to play across the timeline of the event but their relative importance will shift according to the phase that the disaster is in. Similarly, the sense-making processes will also have different implications in each of the stages of the event.

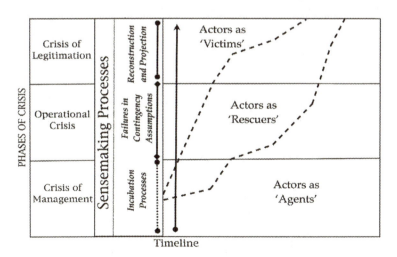

Figure 6. Learning and the incubation process within disasters

If the processes of the crisis of management phase can help to shape the configuration of a disaster, then the elements of the operational crisis may serve to compound those initial processes of incubation. One of the key elements in responding to the demands of a disaster concerns the processes of communication that are in place. Clearly, communications are important in the dissemination of information once a disaster has begun, but they are also a key factor in shaping the success of any early warnings that are raised prior to the event. The language used to describe these processes is an important issue here, especially so around the discussion of technical issues and the communication of risk in the incubation of disaster potential. These processes of communication are also obviously of importance in dealing with the interaction between the elements of the root definition (CATWOE). Another important element that can exacerbate the problems associated with a disaster is the lack of a suitably trained and experienced crisis management team that will assume responsibility for dealing with the task demands of the event once it occurs. Again, a poorly trained team will make decisions, or fail to make sense of events, that will allow a bad situation to escalate further (Smith 2000a). The third related issue is that of containment and control. One of the key tasks of any crisis team is to prevent the existing situation from escalating to a point where it gets significantly worse. These processes have to be considered prior to an event and the teams trained accordingly. All too often, crisis teams fail because of the assumptions and beliefs held by senior planners within the organization, who become cognitively blind to the hazardous scenarios that they might have to face (Smith 2000a, 2003). Finally, the process of interconnectivity will inevitably prove to be problematic for those responsible for managing the demands of a disaster. The increasingly interconnected nature of modern society means that even disasters in remote locations can have serious implications on a global scale.

The interactions between these elements, operating across the S-P-T relationship will generate a complex mosaic or kaleidoscope (Pidgeon 1998; Weick 1998) of factors that will ensure that each disaster has its own fingerprint. Such a view risks the implication that there is little that can be undertaken by way of intervention. However, this is not the case and many organizations have sought to address the manner in which they learn from adverse events as a means of dealing with the processes of incubation.

BOUNDARIES AND BOUNDS: MAKING SENSE OF THE CONTEXT OF DISASTERS

The processes of defining a disaster obviously represent an activity that is fraught with potential problems. There have been several attempts at the process and they inevitably come up against the bulkheads of disciplinary perspectives. The boundaries of the term in both theory and practice are constantly called into question by events that challenge our worldview(s) about the nature (and limits) of the construct. There should be no surprise in this statement because, by their very nature, disasters are highly emotive events that are often viewed in terms of outcome rather than process. The sheer complexity and emotional impact of a "disaster in practice" often seems to serve to confound our use of the term in theory.

It is clear from our discussions thus far that the notion of a disaster is a complex, multi-dimensional concept that is often used to describe a sub-set of events that involve multiple fatalities and which arise from natural, technological or socio-political causal factors. Even within those broad categories, there is considerable debate and disagreement concerning the nature of the term and its relevance across the portfolio of events that are considered to be "disasters". Perhaps more important from our perspective here, there is considerable debate around the particular significance of the various elements of the term, their relative significance and the manner in which they interact with each other to produce the complex mosaic that becomes a disaster event.

Inevitably, disasters are emotive and yet an inherently ill-defined phenomena. As discrete events, disasters span a range of natural-technological boundaries and yet remain at their core, human, socio-political and economic phenomenon. Disasters, by their very nature, serve to challenge the assumptions and core beliefs (Mitroff et al. 1989; Pauchant et al. 1992) of individuals, groups and even whole societies, around such issues as the nature of the risk itself, its assessed probability of occurrence, or the ability of the "system" to contain the demands generated by the event once it occurs. Given the range of disciplines involved in any such discussion, it is not surprising that there is debate and disagreement around the focus of research attention, the locus of control within and following on from such events, and the nature of the impact that disasters have upon the "spaces of destruction" that they occupy.

From an academic perspective, such discussions are important in shaping the manner in which research is undertaken into the processes through which disasters are generated, evolve and can be "managed". They are also important in shaping knowledge around such phenomena and the construction of that knowledge is an important process in itself. From a practice perspective, the definition of an event as a disaster can be important in shaping the level of resource that is made available to those who are trying to deal with the aftermath of the event. Consequently, the literature is broadly divided into those studies that focus on the practical characteristics of disasters, either as individual events or as categories, and those that focus on the theoretical underpinnings of disasters as process and the implications that theoretical development has for our understanding of the phenomenon. This duality around disaster research is not unique. Some academic disciplines, geography being an obvious example, have long had to consider the problems created by examining large-scale phenomena across the "physical-human" interface. In commenting on the link between physical and human geography, Clifford (2001) outlines five issues that have a relevance to our current discussions.

The first is that there is a complexity around the interface between the physical and human perspectives on "environmental" issues. This complexity creates difficulties in terms of interpretation, sense-making and apprehension (Clifford 2001). The world does not behave as expected, and this seems to be more apparent when dealing with the role of human agency in physical phenomena. In addition, the particular issues of scale, time and space generate further problems for interpretation. The second issue raised by Clifford concerns the manner in which knowledge related to physical and human problems is constructed and disseminated. For those problems approached from a multi-disciplinary perspective, the dissemination of such knowledge is important. The purpose of earlier attempts to define disasters was to ensure that the knowledge generated by research in this area was disseminated as widely as possible (Quarantelli 1978a, 1978b, 1998a, 1998b). Clifford's third point is somewhat related to the issue of dissemination but is focused on the lack of theoretical convergence between the various perspectives taken on "environmental" phenomena. From a disaster perspective, this is clearly of importance. If we take the work related to "physical" disasters and compare that with research on organizational or technological "crises" then it is clear that there has been little *effective* transfer of theory. Where convergence does take place is in practice. The emergency services have begun to recognize that the contingency planning process has relevance beyond the confines of geo-physical phenomena to include socio-technical disasters. The duality of the debates around theory and practice seem, at one level, to be somewhat redundant. For the victims of a disastrous event, the debates concerning definition and the theories used to analyze disasters are essentially meaningless as they are concerned, as victims of the situation, with issues of containment and recovery. For these victims a disaster represents a severe disruption of their daily lives as well as considerable damage to people, property and services. However, for policy makers and regulators the definition and designation of an event as a disaster can have major implications both in terms of planning for a range of events and the release and mobilization of resources to deal with the task demands that disasters generate.

Returning then to the process of definition, our final attempt at capturing the essence of the term disaster sees such phenomena as: multi-phased, multi-level, complex and damaging systems-related events that unfold over time and space, through an emergent complex interaction of elements involving structures, connections and networks and which are shaped by ideological, economic and social factors to generate impacts on elements of society, represented within a particular "place". These changes are brought about by the destructive, high-energy nature of the phenomenon in such a way that it changes the performance of the "normal" order of that societal setting and the networks and associations that operate therein. The damage that occurs is shaped via processes of agency (and in some cases because of the actions of agents), the networks of inter-dependence that they expose or damage, and through the consequences that they generate for the psychosocial well being of actors (as victims of the physical processes of generating harm). These events create considerable problems associated with complexity, communication, stress and sense-making. (Definition 4)

At a simple level, disasters are events with too much negative energy, in the wrong place, at the wrong time and which exceed the host "society's" abilities to cope. Of course, disasters are not simple and the sheer complexity of the definition expressed above is not one that will change the public consciousness about the nature of a disaster but rather might provide a framework in which academic research can be undertaken. For any working definition of the term "disaster" to have validity, there is a need to test it against a range of environmental and socio-technical events and across different timelines in order to explore the limitations and nuances that such empirical verification brings to the term. The pitfalls facing disaster research that were identified by Clifford (shown in Figure 7) provide some fundamental questions to be asked of the process of research itself. If disaster research is to have the impact that many within the community hope that it will, then it needs to be inclusive rather than too narrowly defined in terms of "scientific" methods of inquiry. The theories that are developed in one situational context need to be applied to other forms of disaster, including those where intentional human agency is involved. Finally, research needs to be more embracing of different paradigms and disciplines if it is to become more holistic in its approach to dealing with the complexity of disasters.

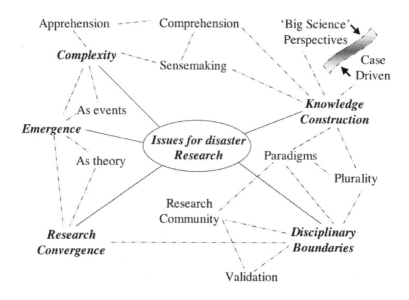

Figure 7. Issues for disaster research

CONCLUSIONS

"We now know without question that global natural catastrophes are a normal part of our planet's history and evolution, and that our modern world has yet to experience their devastating effects. The big question then is: are we living on borrowed time?" (McGuire, 1999: 51).

This paper has sought to examine the nature of the term disaster by reference to a diverse, and some might argue, unrelated set of literatures. However, the reason for bringing such literatures together was to explore the implications that different perspectives could bring on a complex problem. The use of a systems approach represented an attempt to frame the complexity inherent in the term disaster and to try to illustrate the dynamics of the underlying processes.

What is clear from this discussion is that there are several core elements of the term and that these transcend the physical-political-technical boundaries of disasters that some disciplinary-focused studies tend to impose. The attempts here have been to capture the richness associated with the term rather than try to narrow the discussion down on a number of key elements. For this, some will inevitably be critical. However, the contention here is those complex phenomenon simply do not lend themselves to reductionist modes of scientific inquiry and analysis without losing the richness that they hold within them. The argument here has been that disasters can be seen as "spaces of destruction" in which issues of space-place-time have an important role to play in shaping the fabric of a disaster. Many disasters result in harm being generated as a consequence of the processes of production that takes place; whether this is as a function of the occupation of hazard zones for the production of goods, services or commodities or through the generation of hazardous process for the same ends. The distinction between the natural and technological hazard has been relegated in importance and the argument developed here is that it is the impact upon human networks and agencies that should be the dominant element of the construct. What is clear is that disasters are not going to reduce in importance for those "actors" who have to deal with their consequences. By turning the kaleidoscope of analysis, it is hoped that a different set of perspectives have been brought to bear on the complex "scapes" of disaster research.

NOTES

[1] This paper is dedicated to the memories of Carol Smith (1966-2003) and Edward Lloyd (1936-2003). This loss of two wonderful people, occurred much too close in terms of emotional space, place and time.

14

DISASTER, CRISIS, COLLECTIVE STRESS, AND MASS DEPRIVATION

Robert Stallings

> *"Quite clearly what has happened is a disaster."* Right Honourable Tessa Jowell, MP, Secretary of State for Culture, Media, and Sport, United Kingdom, commenting on the plundering of museums in Iraq (quoted in Gottlieb 2003)

Why worry about the term disaster? The authors contributing the four chapters to this section provide two different answers to this question. One answer is *practical*: A definition of disaster triggers the provision of special goods and services. The chapter by Buckle ("Disaster: Mandated Definitions, Local Knowledge and Complexity") deals with practical definitions in the context of public policy-making and disaster management. The other answer to the question is *analytical*: A definition of disaster is important in conducting research. Such a definition affects all aspects of the research process from the selection of cases for study, to what data are to be collected, to what to make of the findings. The chapters by Barton ("Disaster and Collective Stress"), Boin ("From Crisis to Disaster: Towards an Integrative Perspective"), and Smith ("In the Eyes of the Beholder? Making Sense of the System(s) of Disaster(s)") are concerned with analytical definitions of disaster. Each type of definition, practical and analytical, requires the resolution of interesting issues and the answering of important questions. All four authors make contributions along these lines. I will endeavor to identify what I think are the most significant contributions of each author, taking issue where I disagree with them, and at the end of the chapter offer my own assessment of where we stand on the question. I will devote more attention to the chapter by Boin because it raises important issues not found in most of the other chapters in this or the previous volume (Quarantelli 1998).

PRACTICAL DEFINITIONS

Buckle on Mandated and Local Definitions of Disaster

Buckle begins with what he calls "mandated" definitions of disaster. These are the legal definitions written into public policy. They are *event-based*, meaning that they assume disasters to be events bounded in space and time, that is, located geographically by physical destruction and temporally by a distinct beginning (onset), middle (emergency period), and ending (recovery). They determine the types of situations to which governments respond and the forms of aid they can provide. Because their function is inherently practical, they are of interest primarily to disaster professionals and disaster victims, actual or potential. They are of interest to analysts in the same way that other lay conceptualizations of disaster are of interest, as subject matter.

Halfway through the chapter, Buckle shifts his attention to what he calls "community-based" or "interpretivist" definitions of disaster. These are equivalent to what I call laypeople's definitions. Such definitions are more open-ended than mandated ones, meaning that they are less bounded by the physical destruction of place and less easily delimited in time. Buckle appropriately calls them *process* definitions. An interest in broadening legal or mandated event-based definitions to include some of the circumstances identified by process definitions is clearly one of the author's goals.

This is a worthwhile objective, but it needs to be placed in some sort of context. From my perspective as analyst (i.e., disaster sociologist), there is a bit of naïveté in efforts such as this that I am sure Buckle would admit. This is especially true in the extreme when public officials and policy-makers (read: politicians) are assumed to pay attention to anything that academics write or say. Buckle clearly knows this, but some readers of his chapter may not. While disaster professionals in nongovernmental organizations (NGOs) and public agencies may welcome the assistance of academics' definitions in clarifying or expanding the mission of their organizations, it is the politicians who determine both the core and the boundaries of mandated definitions. The calculus for politicians simultaneously involves fiscal responsibility on the one hand and aiding constituents in times of need on the other. Too much emphasis on fiscal responsibility, especially in the midst of a disaster, makes politicians appear heartless. Too much emphasis on expanding the scope of emergency operations and public aid makes politicians look fiscally irresponsible. A clear mandated definition of disaster gives politicians "cover" in denying aid, but victims may suffer unjustly and unnecessarily as a result. A vague definition gives politicians "wiggle room" but may make life miserable for emergency managers, as Buckle notes. Fear of setting a precedent by extending disaster aid to novel situations—and thereby expanding the boundary of a mandated definition of disaster—is a major impediment to the goal of making such definitions more inclusive.

The case of the Mariel boatlift (see Aguirre 1994) is an illuminating one involving mandated definitions and suggests the kind of analytical work that remains to be done on them. Emigration from the Port of Mariel between April and September 1980 resulted in the arrival in the U.S. of nearly 125,000 Cubans, most of whom made their way to Miami. This massive influx of Marielitos put a severe strain on both nonprofit organizations and public agencies, including law enforcement. The governor of Florida requested federal aid, and the Federal Emergency Management Agency (FEMA) was named to coordinate a federal response. The

Carter Administration, seeking ways to provide federal funds, initially considered declaring south Florida a major disaster area under the Disaster Relief Act of 1974. However, due to opposition in Congress as well as inside the administration itself, the president instead chose to declare an emergency rather than a major disaster. FEMA's top administrators were opposed to expanding the scope of the act to cover a refugee crisis by means of either form of declaration (Rivera 1991: 42). "[T]he definitional term 'other catastrophe' [in the definition of "emergency" in the act] gave the [Carter] administration enough of a loophole to justify using the act to handle the Mariel boatlift" (Engstrom 1997: 171-172, footnote 23). Members of the Congressional committee with oversight responsibility for FEMA protested that the act was "... not designed to provide assistance to incidents of strictly a social or economic nature..." (Rivera 1991: 73, footnote 2) and came close to calling for a formal amendment to prevent such use in the future before finally deciding "... against altering the language until [it] could study the matter further" (Engstrom 1997: 172, footnote 27). (The Mariel boatlift took place just months before a presidential election, one that Jimmy Carter lost to Ronald Reagan.)

Mandated definitions of "emergency" and "major disaster" are worthwhile subjects for research. Here, for example, are the U.S. versions from 42 U.S.C. 5122 (1) and (2):

(1) Emergency—"Emergency" means any occasion or instance for which, in the determination of the President, Federal assistance is needed to supplement State and local efforts and capabilities to save lives and to protect property and public health and safety, or to lessen or avert the threat of a catastrophe in any part of the United States.

(2) Major disaster—"Major disaster" means any natural catastrophe (including any hurricane, tornado, storm, high water, wind-driven water, tidal wave, tsunami, earthquake, volcanic eruption, landslide, mudslide, snowstorm, or drought), or, regardless of cause, any fire, flood, or explosion,

in any part of the United States, which in the determination of the President causes damage of sufficient severity and magnitude to warrant major disaster assistance under this chapter to supplement the efforts and available resources of States, local governments, and disaster relief organizations in alleviating the damage, loss, hardship, or suffering caused thereby.

Understanding the process of their enactment, their application, and even their wording is an important aspect of a politics of disaster (e.g., Olson 2000; also May 1985). However, the roles of analyst (i.e., researcher) and practitioner are very different, as are the purposes for which each develops definitions of disaster. Analysts *as advocates* may have an interest in seeing the mandated definition expanded (or contracted). It is far less clear why practitioners would have much interest in academic definitions—with one exception. Practitioners—including policy makers/politicians—would have use for an academic definition if it were consistent with and supported their previously determined position on the issue of altering or amending an official definition of disaster. Any academic definition contrary to that position, however, would be of no political value. One can easily imagine the effect of an attempt to inject an analytical definition into the Mariel controversy. Since mandated definitions are products of power politics, it is difficult to see how else academic definitions figure into them. This is not to say that Buckle's presentation is not worthwhile. On the contrary, his discussion of mandated definitions in the first half of the chapter is the best treatment of these issues that I am aware of.

In the second half of the chapter, Buckle turns his attention to laypeople's definitions of disaster. The basis for this discussion is research conducted in Australia by the author and a colleague. Here the striking thing is the similarity between locals' sense of process-type disasters and Barton's discussion of mass deprivation. The key feature of both is a perceived threat to the quality of life, a threat that seems open-ended. It is the open-endedness of unwanted change that distinguishes this type of disaster from the classic type and gives rise to the event/process dichotomy. Buckle writes: "Houses and roads can be rebuilt after a wildfire. Businesses and farms can be restored, but the loss of young people, the depopulation of an area or the loss of small businesses ... is irreversible and impacts on everybody in the community." The fear of unwanted, long-term change articulated by Buckle's respondents is laypeople's expression of the system failure component in Barton's definition of collective stress. Both are centered on expectations about quality of life in accordance with historical circumstances and social location. Placing the source of these fears in the "dislocation to everyday life" and "in the [dis]continuity of daily life" is consistent with other writers who identify the phenomena we all are grappling with, however we label them, as disruptions of the routine.

The problem is that the label *does* matter. Buckle gives two reasons why this is so, one explicitly and the other perhaps unintentionally. First, he points to the fact " ... that we can write about disaster and be understood before defining the term shows that there is a commonly accepted notion of what constitutes a disaster which exists intuitively and almost *a priori*." Here he has put his finger precisely on the reason why "disaster" should not be stretched to try to cover all instances of unwanted disruption. Its widely understood and accepted meaning makes it resistant to redefinition. Like other constructs in the social sciences such as class, status, or institution, "disaster" can be given a new and more precise or more expansive definition than it enjoys in popular linguistic convention, but effective communication—even among disaster scholars—requires the repeated insertion of adjectives such as "man-made," "conflict-related," or "chronic" to clarify how the revised term is being used.

Buckle perhaps unintentionally illustrates the second reason why labels matter. To fit the chronic forms of unwanted and irreversible change under the disaster tent, he borrows a model of complex social systems. The assertion is that disasters as events and as processes have the same characteristics as social systems. They are complex entities that exhibit emergence and thus unfold in unpredictable ways. In the process of attempting to reconceptualize "disaster" so that both event (mandated) and process (local) definitions are included, Buckle does the same thing that Barton, Boin, and Smith do (see the next section): he turns to a different, more abstract, and therefore more general concept, that of the complex social system. While disasters, whether as events or as processes, "display most or all of these descriptors [of complex systems]," so, too, do "a number of events and processes that we do not necessarily or at present characterize as disaster." The concluding section of his chapter discloses more interest on his part in change processes in complex social systems than in disasters per se (however defined).

The use of a complex systems model to subsume the two types of disaster circumvents the problem with using "events" versus "processes" as a way to distinguish mandated from local definitions. This distinction is in the "eye of the beholder," that is, it is subjective. Phenomena are not objectively events *or* processes. Rather, analysts can choose to *view* phenomena either as events or as processes. A tornado may be a physical or a social event, delimited in time and space, but it is also a series of events that form a process from warning to onset to rescue to rehabilitation to recovery. Process models of disaster have been around for a long time (see, for example, Neal 1997). Long-term processes such as depopulation also may be viewed as a series of discrete events (the closing of a factory, the departure of a family, etc.).

In sum, to identify the phenomena and the empirical questions that Buckle believes both analysts and practitioners should be interested in, he turns to a higher-order concept of which disaster is a subtype. This characterization also succeeds in integrating the challenges facing both analysts and laypeople. For analysts, as we have said, the challenge is to link research on both old and "new species of trouble" with research on classic natural disasters. For practitioners, including politicians, the challenge is not so much to tinker with existing mandated definitions of disaster as to think of disaster in a larger context. The kinds of organizational actions and resources triggered by a disaster declaration may be inappropriate for dealing with other forms of disruption, but thinking of disasters as one element of a larger picture may be politically advantageous if it leads to a new mix of fiscal restraint and appropriate resources to address the needs of victims of unwanted disruptions.

ANALYTICAL DEFINITIONS

Barton on Collective Stress and Mass Deprivation

Barton's chapter is a significant updating of the framework he first developed in a monograph written for the U.S. National Academy of Sciences-National Research Council (Barton 1963) and later in his more widely known book (Barton 1969). In all three he treats disaster as one of several types of collective stress situations, defined as "... those in which 'many members of a social system fail to receive *expected conditions of life* from the system'" (from the second section of the chapter in this volume; emphasis added). It is of more than merely historical interest to note, as he does, that most disaster research prior to the mid-1960s was intentionally comparative. Natural disasters, especially those with sudden onset, little forewarning, and proportionately high levels of physical destruction, were of special interest to funding agencies because they were viewed as peacetime analogs of a possible surprise nuclear attack on the United States (Quarantelli 1987b; see also Quarantelli 1988). Lessons learned from studies of such events could be applied in the nation's civil defense effort. Social science research on Allied bombing of German and Japanese cities during World War II, especially its effect on civilian morale (USSBS 1947a, 1947b), was important for the same reason and was accorded a category in Barton's typology (see Table 1.1 in Barton 1963: 6; see also Table 1 in Barton 1969: 44). The typology arrayed stress situations along four analytical dimensions: speed of onset, scope of impact, duration, and degree of preparedness. It was an early attempt to facilitate the comparative analysis of seemingly different events for the purpose of generalization. As Barton puts it, "The intent is to locate a particular type of social unit or phenomenon in a wider theoretical context, allowing more general social theories to be brought to bear."

Barton's chapter in this volume, including its reprise of selected portions of his earlier work, has much to offer the current discussion of the term disaster. "Collective stress" is a useful construct for generalizing across a broad range of troubling events having different labels. Indeed, his propositions from forty years ago are remarkably nimble, as demonstrated by his easy extension of them to late twentieth-century concerns such as state-generated mass starvation, AIDS, and the effects of globalization. Also impressive is the fact that Barton recognized early on the importance of the mass media in shaping perceptions of stress situations for both victims and nonvictims and built the effects of media coverage into his propositions.

One noticeable difference from his earlier work is Barton's more sophisticated treatment here of the role of the state in collective stress situations. In addition to being one of the mechanisms for preventing or responding to such situations, the state is now depicted as equally capable of being a passive bystander that willfully fails to prevent or mitigate catastrophe as well as itself a direct cause of mass deprivation. He offers a sobering proposition about the ambivalent effects of "formally democratic" polities as "means of preventing mass emergencies or chronic situations of oppression." There are also now several references to the influence of an ideology of "blaming the victim" that "relieves other members of the community of concern with the victims" of collective stress. There is more emphasis on the role of victims in general, whether playing an active part in addressing their deprivation or acquiescing to their situation, and on the relationships, both social and psychological, between victims and nonvictims.

Beneath the surface, Barton makes even bigger contributions in his chapter. He does not attempt to redefine "disaster" to encompass a wider, more "modern" range of troubling situations. (When I enclose terms such as "crisis" and "disaster" in quotation marks, I am doing so to make it clear that I am referring to conceptualizations or definitions; when the same words are used without quotation marks, they refer to events, situations, or phenomena.) Let "disasters" be what we've always taken them to be, he says implicitly. Tweaking the term disaster is not going to improve our ability to study future calamities. Instead, he shifts the debate to a term that is already more abstract and less closely associated with images of specific tragedies. This allows him to give precise meaning to this other term without first having to clear away a thicket of preconceived ideas. He is then able to spend his time conceptually developing "collective stress."

The section on "Reconceptualizing Disaster as a Form of Collective Stress" is actually a careful working out of issues associated with identifying *mass deprivation* as the core of what all collective stress situations have in common. Some of these issues are: the fact that deprivation can be the result of either sudden concentrated stresses, "larger and less sudden stresses," or chronic conditions; that deprivation includes the "psychological" as well as the physical and the physiological; that deprivation can only be judged in relative terms, that is, relative to "a socially defined normal way of life"; that "normal" has to be judged "relative to the standards of a given society and historical period"; that this means "there may be disagreement on whether conditions are normal or create undue stress and require a remedy"; that victims may recognize their deprivation but be resigned to "what experience tells them is their lot"; that nonvictims (i.e., "the rest of society and its leadership") may or may not identify with victims or "feel psychological or social pressure to do anything about the situation"; and that there may be conflict over the existence of deprivation or the necessity to do something about it along lines of class and status cleavages.

We may not resolve these issues the same way Barton would, but he is thinking through what it means to define collective stress in terms of mass deprivation. By implication, he invites the reader to think about these and other issues as they emerge in the reader's own conceptualization of the essence of collective tragedy. Barton actually may be moving away from "collective stress" to "mass deprivation" and seemingly wants to place both under the rubric of "social problems." Whatever the ultimate direction of his thinking, his chapter deserves careful study, and *Communities in Disaster* deserves rereading.

Boin on Crisis

Before getting to the specifics of Boin's chapter, I must offer the following disclaimer. I enthusiastically endorse his choice of "crisis" as a general concept under which "disaster" and other calamitous phenomena should be fitted. In fact, I have made this argument myself (Stallings 1997, 1998a, 1998b, 2001). As promising as Boin's chapter is, however, it contains two shortcomings that hinder its contribution to the present discussion. One problem is the inconsistent use of the distinction between the *objective* and the *subjective*. This makes it difficult to understand exactly how "disaster" differs conceptually from "crisis." The other problem is harder to articulate. Let me call it one of failing to keep distinct or at least to be clear about what *level of analysis* or *focus of attention* is being discussed. This makes it difficult to be sure in many instances whether Boin is referring to the nature of disasters as phenomena, to laypeople's perceptions of disasters as phenomena, to analysts' conceptualizations of disasters, or to analysts' conceptualizations of laypeople's perceptions of disasters. The terms "layperson" (singular) and "laypeople" (plural) will be used throughout in place of more commonly used terms such as "actor" or "the public." These terms refer to people who do not formally study disasters (as do, for example, disaster sociologists) but who themselves are the subjects of study by disaster sociologists and others, herein referred to collectively as "analysts." This distinction between laypeople and analysts is used to separate clearly, for example, people's perceptions of disaster and analysts' conceptualizations of people's perceptions of disaster. It does not presuppose that analysts are not in all other respects also laypeople, that is, members of the same society and participants in the same culture as the people they study.

The central arguments that Boin makes are that "disaster" and "crisis" are complementary concepts that can and should be linked and that the former is a subtype of the latter. Unfortunately, these straightforward arguments are obscured by Boin's attempt to advance them using the objective/subjective dichotomy. I will go into this in some detail, not to "beat up" on the author, but because I agree completely with his goal and its potential benefits. Rather, I do so because a more solid foundation for the disaster/crisis nexus needs to be laid. Ultimately what Boin argues for is "a merger of the hitherto strictly separated fields of disaster and crisis management." This is a sound proposal, but the arguments for it need to be clarified.

Boin's first argument is that the nature of disasters as phenomena has changed. The "classic" disaster was about (objective) nature. Modern disasters are about (subjective) "sense-making." The classic disaster was concentrated in space and time, whereas the modern disaster is "not confined by boundaries of space and time." The classic disaster was an isolated event, whereas modern disasters quickly become entangled "with other deep problems" and their impact "prolonged." In short, the objective character of disaster is changing, and a new definition is needed to keep pace. "Conventional disaster definitions do not capture the essence of modern adversity." Most of the authors in the first volume (Quarantelli 1998) would agree with this assessment.

I have no quarrel with the contention that there are many more forms of adversity in the modern world than those conventionally labeled "natural disasters." I also agree with Boin's contention, made both implicitly early in his chapter and explicitly later on, that many of them do not fit "disaster" as conventionally defined and, more importantly, that they are better referred to as "crises" rather than "disasters." However, I disagree with the contention that the *nature* of disasters *as phenomena* is changing from the external and the objective to the internal and the subjective. In the second section of his chapter, Boin notes: "... the *nature* of modern disaster is changing and is becoming more a product of collective sense-making processes" (emphasis added).

My disagreement with Boin on this has two parts. First, classic disasters are neither more or less "objective" than modern ones nor more or less "subjective." A tornado may rip the roof from a house, but the experiencing of it by the occupants of the house is as subjective as is the experiencing of any other event. "Nature" or the "objective environment" is never experienced directly by human beings. It is never purely "exogenous." All human encounters with the objective world take place through the intervening filter of culture, the historic residue of collective sensemaking as received by the individual, and in this sense are always subjective. Furthermore, sensemaking is as characteristic of disasters in historic times as in modern times. Biblical accounts of disasters of various kinds were written by prophets who were engaged in sensemaking for themselves and for members of their sects. Job in particular suffered all manner of adversities and struggled faithfully to make sense out of each one of them. St. Augustine of Hippo tried to make sense out of the calamities befalling the Romans (e.g., *The City of God* [413-426]). Second, modern "disasters" such as terrorist bombings and the SARS (severe acute respiratory syndrome) outbreak are just as "objective" as classic disasters. The explosives and metal fragments of the terrorist's bomb and the germs broadcast during an epidemic are as objectively real and "exogenous" as are tornadic winds and rising flood waters.

Boin seemingly wants to link his subjective, sense-making characterization with Ulrich Beck's (1992) conceptualization of the risk society. In the second section he states that " . . . the essence of disasters in today's risk society, . . . is characterized less by the threat of devastation than by an obsessive fear for safety breaches." However, the fact that some types of events (e.g., accidental releases of radiation, diseases) take their toll in human lives without damaging structures or the fact that comparable earthquakes kill fewer people in some parts of the world than in other parts or kill fewer people today than in previous decades does not mean that they are more about (subjective) sense-making than external (objective) physical forces.

This is reminiscent of the erroneous distinction that persisted for decades between "real" (objective) risk and "perceived" (subjective) risk (see Freudenburg 1988). Objective risk supposedly is what analysts can count and convert to a probability. Subjective risk is what laypeople perceive as threatening to them. The former is supposedly a "true" measure of risk, while the latter is presumably "false." Glassner's (1999) well-known book purportedly identifies many of the discrepancies between objective and subjective risk, in other words, between "real" and "exaggerated" fears. Unfortunately, things are not this clear cut. *Both* analysts' risk probabilities and laypeople's perceptions of risk are subjective (see Best's [2001] review of Glassner's book). More generally, the quantification of risk or of loss does not make either more objective—or less subjective.

Nor can the argument be made that classic disasters differ from modern ones because the fear of victimization is now out of proportion to the "objective" chances of victimization. An oft-cited example is the falloff in commercial air travel in the U.S. after the attacks of September 11, 2001. People supposedly were reluctant to fly for fear of becoming victims of the next terrorist hijacking. "Experts" rated these fears as exaggerated. Presumably, this is the nature of all modern disasters—fear out of proportion to objective risk probability. However, this high fear/low probability disparity also applies to classic natural disasters and therefore cannot be a distinguishing feature of modern ones. Hotel bookings and theme park attendance in southern California fall after damaging earthquakes as tourists change their vacation destinations out of fear of becoming victims in a future major earthquake. Many Californians for their part refuse to travel to the Midwest during the summer months because they fear becoming victims of lightening strikes or tornadoes. Subjective fear of victimization that is estimated by experts to be in excess of "objective" indicators of risk is as characteristic of classic natural disasters as of modern "sense-making" ones.

There is a sense in which one can say that change is affecting the objective character of disasters. Take earthquakes as an example. Earthquake disasters involve damage to human settlements. Absent the human settlement, the energy released by movement of tectonic plates only rearranges elements of the natural environment. An earthquake can only threaten high-rise buildings when there are high-rise buildings to be damaged, for example. It can only cause the release of radioactive material by damaging a nuclear reactor when there are nuclear reactors in proximity to epicenters. Likewise with underground hazardous materials storage sites. This is the essence of so-called compound disasters or complex emergencies. To describe these as changes in the nature of disasters is misleading. They are better described as changes in the nature of society, or in the built environment, if you like. They are, in other words, *social changes* affecting the characteristics of disasters, not changes in nature.

Having argued that the nature of disasters is changing from "some exogenous agent" to "more a product of collective sense-making process," Boin argues that "disaster sociologists," who "very well knew that disasters were social constructions," are either not trained or not interested in studying them as such. What disaster sociologists are trained for and interested in, apparently, is "objectifying the subjective," having primarily studied disasters from the "outside" (i.e., their objective features, with "objective" now referring to a behavioral perspective)—"how people and organizations behave in times of collective stress." In other words, disaster sociology if it does not undergo a reorientation will only be capable of studying the objective indicators of collective sensemaking. This is because students of disaster have managed to avoid postmodernism. So disaster sociologists are becoming irrelevant because, while disasters are changing from objective (previous meaning) to subjective in nature, they are unable or unwilling to change from studying the objective (behavioral meaning) to studying the subjective. Call this disaster sociologists' "objective corset."

By the third section, the tables have turned. Here we find disaster sociologists being described as hindered by their confinement in a "subjective corset." Now disaster sociology is in danger of being left behind because it is trapped into studying the main *subjective* questions about modern disasters: What do people (including "politicians, media, corporations, societal organizations, academics, and people in a well-defined social unit") label disaster and under what conditions? Now it is crises rather than disasters that have objective features that can be studied by analysts, and a merger of the disaster and crisis perspectives would successfully blend the subjectivism of the former with the objectivism of the latter.

Boin initially gives "crisis" as precise a definition as possible. He moves from Hewitt's (1997) "catchall" sense of "un-ness" (unwanted, unexpected, unprecedented, and unmanageable) to "'a serious threat to the basic structures or the fundamental values and norms of a social system'." Crises are situations that require making crucial decisions under conditions of uncertainty and time pressure. The crisis perspective offers the possibility of "objective definitions of crisis." Basically, crises are periods of "discontinuity" or "disruptions of normality that result in the uprooting of the institutional structures of a social system." (For a similar discussion, see Stallings, 1998a.) The core of a crisis is legitimacy, or rather de-legitimation. Discrepancies arise between expectations and system performance, leading to an erosion of "the legitimacy of sustaining structures." Thus, crisis is legitimation crisis (cf. Habermas 1975 [1973]).

It is because crises are characterized by rapid withdrawal of legitimation that they can be "objectified," that is, translated into measurable indicators. Because disasters are subjective, they cannot be similarly objectified. An "absolute," "legalistic," or "objective" definition of disaster fails because it "cannot capture the subjective feeling of loss." Crises, on the other hand, are "researchable" because disruption is indicated by rapid (downward) shifts in legitimacy which can be documented "by studying media reporting, political activity and other signs of societal mobilization."

The very next paragraph in the third section after this passage displays another flip-flop. Crisis now becomes subjective: it is "the process of perceived disruption." Earlier in the same section, this subjective conceptualization is affirmed. "Authorities decide whether an event or process indicates progress or disruption of normality," that is, whether or not a crisis exists. "It is, of course, *the perception* of decision-makers rather than some set of *predefined conditions* that counts" (emphasis added). Thus crisis is a "top-down concept." But it could also be a "bottom-up" concept (see "societal mobilization," above). "We can only speak of a crisis if the actors in question perceive the situation as a crisis." Boin states that "[t]his crisis definition does not solve the subjective problem of disaster studies." "The *subjective nature of crisis* makes it impossible to neatly demarcate the beginning and end of a crisis, . . ." (emphasis added). Furthermore, unless "authorities" label a situation as a crisis, " . . . analysts cannot treat this situation in terms of crisis."

The reader thus concludes that "disaster" will not do because it is too closely linked with "exogenous agents" and disaster sociology is becoming irrelevant because it has been bypassed by recent theoretical trends such as constructionist theory and postmodernism. On the other hand, "disaster" will also not do because it is confined in its "corset" of subjective perceptions of disruption and thereby compelled to devote its energies exclusively to the study of cultural conventions in the linguistic use of "disaster." At the same time, "crisis" has the same subjective meanings and therefore the same problems as "disaster." What is different is that "crisis" can be liberated from its subjective meaning by quantifying the visible signs of declining state legitimacy in the form of protests, newspaper editorials, speeches, and the like. This, however, seems exactly like Quarantelli's suggestion thirty-five years ago that one way to "gauge and document" the disruption accompanying disasters is by such "researchable" indicators as the timing and geographic dispersal of lost and restored utilities, rerouting of local buses and commuter trains, interruption and restoration of mail and newspaper deliveries, duration of event cancellations, and the like.

In other words, the objective/subjective distinction that Boin uses neither helps us differentiate between "disaster" and "crisis" nor succeeds in fitting these two concepts together. What we are left with is that both "disaster" and "crisis" are objective *and* subjective concepts. In the final analysis, however, Boin chooses to treat both as subjective concepts in order to again try to distinguish between them. Both pertain to processes of "perceived disruption."

"[D]isaster applies to the collectively arrived-at appraisal of such a process in negative terms.... [A] disaster is a crisis with a bad ending.... [D]isaster thus becomes a subtype of the generic crisis concept." The term "disaster" is reserved "... for a specific subtype of crisis,..."

Thus, crisis is a generic concept characterized by the subjective perception that normal routines have been disrupted. Disaster is one of the subtypes of crisis, specifically the one associated with *negatively* perceived disruption. If disaster is a negative subtype of crisis, then there must be at least one other subtype of crisis that is appraised in *positive* terms. Otherwise "crisis" and "disaster" would be indistinguishable, that is, one and the same. Put differently, if disasters are the negative type of crises and if there are no other types, than all crises are disasters. That there are other types of crises besides disasters is made clear toward the end of the third section when Boin states that to reserve the term disaster for a "specific subtype of disaster" would make it possible for disaster sociologists "to study all other types of crisis." Since crises are characterized by a decline in legitimacy, does this mean that a legitimation crisis is a good thing (positive appraisal) or a bad thing (negative appraisal)? If the latter, then declining legitimacy is a disaster (bad ending). But declining legitimacy is the defining property of crisis, not disaster. Clearly, in the messy real world legitimation crises can be good for some (oppressed masses, for example) while at the same time being bad for others (e.g., ruling elites). But disasters also have "winners" as well as "losers" (for one description, see Scanlon, 1988). What else fits under the "crisis" rubric besides "disaster"? One could readily respond by listing the events that Boin mentions in his introduction: terrorism, AIDS, Black Monday on Wall Street, the loss of the submarine *Koersk* and the *Challenger* space shuttle, etc. By any reasonable standard, these, too, would be appraised in negative terms. Does this mean that they, too, are disasters? If not, then how do they differ from disasters since they, too, have bad endings?

Having treated both crises and disasters as subjective phenomena in order to try to differentiate them, Boin then returns to treating both as simultaneously objective and subjective phenomena. With the semantic reordering of the two concepts, "[D]isasters sociologists can return to studying [the objective] causes, conditions and consequences of social disruption without having to worry about collective labeling exercises." Those who study crises now have a new conceptual tool, "the joint perspective," which makes it possible to separate "crisis dynamics" (the objective side) from "sense-making processes" (the subjective side). However, only if "crisis" has both objective and subjective referents can one create propositions such as " . . . a crisis may flare up long after it supposedly terminated" and "[a] crisis is sometimes declared without clear [objective] signs of disruption, . . ." As these propositions show, there is a second set of issues that need to be sorted out.

The second set of issues in Boin's argument for shifting from "disaster" to "crisis" has to do with levels of analysis. This may not be the technically correct way to describe it. Focus of attention may be a better way. What I find confusing is a lack of clarity among the following: the *nature* of phenomena (objective), specifically of disasters and crises; *laypeople's perceptions* of these phenomena (subjective); *analysts' conceptualizations* of the phenomena (subjective); and analysts' conceptualizations of *laypeople's perceptions* of the phenomena (subjective).

The lack of a clear distinction among these runs throughout the chapter. Most importantly, it is not always clear when Boin is referring to the nature of disasters as phenomena (such as when he states that disasters have changed from exogenous agents to collective sense-making) and when he means perceptions (and conceptualizations) of disasters. His frequent references to disasters as no longer about exogenous agents sounds like a characterization of the phenomenon of disaster, while references to disaster as collective sense-making sound more like the nature of people's perceptions of that phenomenon. That the distinction between phenomena and perceptions or conceptualizations of phenomena is important to him is revealed in those passages where he worries that the two will be out of "synch" unless the conceptualization of disasters is brought up to date.

The apparent confusion of these different levels or foci results in what can only be described as an erroneous assertion. In discussing the causes of crisis and disaster near the end of the chapter, Boin concludes: "Disaster sociologists left the act-of-God explanation behind them (Quarantelli 1998), but have not replaced it with other types of explanations." In the preceding section he makes the same point in reference to the spread of AIDS in Africa: "The notion that disaster and destruction are God's punishment or Fortuna's pebble stones may be obsolete in today's disaster sociology, but many Africans reportedly view the AIDS scourge still in these terms." Since the subjects of these two sentences are different—disaster sociologists in the first, disaster sociology in the second—I will deal with each separately.

First, in what role are we to consider disaster sociologists: as the sociologist-as-layperson or as the sociologist-as-analyst? *As laypeople*, I have never known or known of a disaster sociologist who personally believes that disasters are acts of God. Those who do may exist, but, if so, none has ever shared such a religious belief with me or made me aware that they held such a belief. (Undoubtedly there were many sociologists in the late nineteenth and early twentieth centuries who held such beliefs, and they may exist today, but none of them, past or present, are known as disaster sociologists.) Therefore, the assertion that disaster sociologist's as laypeople have "left the act-of-God explanation behind them" makes no sense to me. I suspect that, if you asked them today, most would either cite the laws of nature or human agency or a combination of the two as explanations for disaster, so I also disagree with the other assertion about the lack of a "replacement."

Second, the assertion that the idea of disasters as God's punishment or as acts of God is "obsolete" in *disaster sociology* is also erroneous as is the further assertion that "such differences in perceptions" between disaster sociologists and laypeople in Africa "provide food for thought for cultural anthropologists, but make it rather difficult for disaster sociologists to book theoretical progress." While sociologists-as-laypeople may not personally subscribe to the view that disasters are acts of God, sociologists-as-analysts have always and still today continue to deal with acts-of-God explanations *held by the people they study*. The disaster sociology literature is full of examples. The pioneering survey done after a tornado in Arkansas by the National Opinion Research Center contained a series of questions that probed respondents' naturalistic versus supernaturalistic (i.e., acts-of-God) interpretations of the disaster (Marks and Fritz 1954: 423-424, 484-485). Dynes and Yutzy's (1965) early article remains a useful source both for conceptualizing the problem and for propositions about it. Turner et al. (1986) used survey data to unravel the complex mixture of religious and secular interpretations of earthquakes and earthquake predictions in southern California. Schmuck (2000) used ethnographic materials to show that the presence of deeply held beliefs that disasters are "acts of Allah" did not foreclose engaging in practical forms of disaster mitigation in rural Bangladesh. Dynes (2000a, 2000b) studied the clash between the Roman Catholic Church and secular officials following the 1755 earthquake and tsunami in Lisbon to underscore the Enlightenment's impact on laypeople's sense-making about disaster. Disasters as acts of God are alive and well in disaster sociology, and disaster sociologists, whatever their personal beliefs may be, are as able to study and theorize about this interpretation of them as are representatives of any other discipline.

At some points in his chapter, it is not clear whether Boin is referring to laypeople's "definitions" of disaster or analysts' definitions. He insists that, unless the two are aligned, an analytical definition of disaster is worthless: ". . . a disaster definition is rather devoid of meaning if it fails to capture what most laymen would consider a disaster." In the very next sentence, however, he recognizes one of the dangers in aligning lay and analytical definitions: "If we leave it to the people to define disruptions in their life in terms of disaster, however, the set of events becomes so large that the term disaster is devoid of its original meaning." He cites as an example the "near disaster" of the rained-out dance party in Velsen. Here the failure to distinguish the two different levels or, better put, the failure to recognize the different definitions of disaster held by laypeople and analysts, results in unnecessary confusion. Laypeople's uses of "disaster" seem twofold: to make sense of the world around them, as Boin correctly identifies; and to communicate their experience with the world around them to others. Many of the metaphorical uses of "disaster" fall into the latter category, such as: "The wedding reception was an absolute disaster!" Analysts' uses of "disaster" are less about sensemaking (except perhaps in their personal lives) and more about research. Only when research deals specifically with the question, "How do people use the term 'disaster' in sense-making and in everyday conversation?" do lay and analytical definitions need to coincide. Otherwise analysts are not obligated to restrict their definition to only that of laypeople. This principle obtains for any theoretical construct (class, social movement, civil society, etc.). Analysts' "sensemaking" takes the form of theory construction, and their communication is with peers in their field of research. (I would not argue that laypeople's sensemaking is not a form of theory construction, only that it is less explicit, less formal, and less systematic. Some have called laypeople's sense-making "quasi-theories"; see Hewitt and Hall 1973.) Analysts are thus bound by norms of replication (Kaplan [1964: 127-128] prefers the term "repeatability"), not by the definitions of the people they study (see, for example, Hoover and Donovan 2001: 1-11).

The distinction between lay and analytical definitions becomes confounded with the objective/subjective dichotomy. Boin's point seems to be this: Analysts (disaster sociologists, for example) cannot stray too far in their formal definition of disaster from laypeople's understanding of disaster without producing a meaningless concept. Yet, because laypeople's definitions—including those in the media—are likely to include all manner of "hypes, trends and rumors," aligning analytical with lay definitions will produce a meaningless concept anyway. This is because "disaster" contains two parts, an objective part that we supposedly can all agree on (that is, "classic" disasters representing the "undeniable adversity" accompanying hurricanes, floods, and earthquakes) and a subjective part that contains "hypes, trends and rumors" as well as rained-out dances that analysts may not want to label disasters. But the distinction is also problematic because there are events beyond the objective part that laypeople may *not* call disasters but that analysts do (or could). These are modern crises, and they are " . . . easily described in terms of disaster."

Despite the uncertain distinction between objective and subjective parts of "disaster" (and disaster) and the dubious requirement that lay and analytical definitions be isomorphic, Boin makes the right call here. His recommendation is the same as Barton's: namely, let's not fool around any longer with the definition of disaster. Let's instead use a different term to cover these "new species of trouble" (from Erikson 1994). I concur in the selection of "crisis" for this purpose (as does Quarantelli 1998: 251-254), but in my judgment the same two problems that mar Boin's re-conceptualization of "disaster"—the unclear objective/subjective distinction and the unrealistic connection between lay and analytical definitions—undermine his argument in favor of "crisis" as well. In a concluding section, I will outline my own views on how these two terms differ and how "crisis" might be conceptualized to do what needs to be done with it. Here I will simply say that the distinction between objective and subjective perspectives is not appropriate for this nor will referring to "bad endings" work.

Smith on Complexity and Sensemaking

My reaction to the latest version of Smith's chapter is the same as to the earlier version that he has withdrawn. Smith believes that, because disasters are complex phenomena, a definition of disaster necessarily must be complex as well. I believe that Smith is mistaken about the necessity for an isomorphic relationship between phenomena and analytical definitions of them. In addition, Smith believes that in his chapter he is constructing a definition, whereas I believe instead that he is constructing an analytical model or perhaps a theory.

One difficulty in critiquing this latest version of Smith's chapter is in knowing whether to take literally certain key phrases that he uses or whether they should be treated as merely figures of speech.

For instance, he refers repeatedly to "testing" his evolving definitions (sections three, four, five, six, and eight), sometimes with a body of literature (as in sections three and six) or with a model such as CATWOE (section five) and sometimes "against a range of environmental and socio-technical *events*" (eighth section; emphasis added). Whether or not this and other terms used in reference to his evolving conceptualizations such as "investigating," "calibrating," "validity," and "empirical verification" are figures of speech, there are other clues that his is an effort at theory construction (or model building) rather than definition. One glaring example is Smith's choice of a quotation to serve as a preface to the third section of his chapter. The section begins: "One of the obvious difficulties that exists within any attempt at *defining* a disaster, . . ." (emphasis added); the quote that introduces this section—and this sentence—is: " . . . in social *theory* simplicity should not displace the complexities of tension (Law 1999)" (emphasis added). Conflation of definition and theory also explains this passage from the concluding section:

> What is clear from this discussion is that there are several core elements of the *term* [disaster] and that these transcend the physical-political-technical boundaries of disasters that some many [sic] disciplinary-focused studies tend to impose. The attempts here have been to capture richness associated with the term rather than try to narrow the discussion down on a number of key elements. For this, some will inevitably be critical. However, the contention here is that, complex phenomenon [sic] simply do not lend themselves to reductionist *modes of scientific inquiry and analysis* without losing the richness that they hold within them.

Smith's stated goal is to create a definition that makes sense of disasters. One of the ways in which Smith pursues this goal is to inject "the human element" (introduction) into the characterization of disasters. This is necessary "to avoid omitting certain groups of catastrophic event [sic] from any taxonomy" (introduction). He also wants to add the ideas of vulnerability and resilience. Each seems like a reasonable proposal. However, the principal technique for achieving sensemaking that Smith employs is to ensure that his definition is sufficiently complex to capture the complexity of disasters, a definition that will avoid narrowness and oversimplification. Because disasters are complex, emergent, processual, and unique—in a word, unpredictable—a definition of disaster must also be complex in order to make sense out of these phenomena. But the question is: Is sense-making the function of a definition or of something else? Is it the function of a definition of unemployment, for example, to make sense out of the complexity associated with the so-called jobless economic recovery in the U.S.?

I will not trace the issues of theory-versus-definition and of the relationship between a phenomenon and its definition across the four iterations of Smith's evolving definitions. Instead, I will focus on the fourth and final definition (near the end of section eight) and on the paths that led to it. Note the verbs in this definition: the term disaster "*sees* such phenomena *as*"; "unfold"; "are shaped by"; "generate"; "are brought about by"; "changes"; "is shaped via"; "expose"; "damage"; "generate"; and "create." Apart from the first two, the other nine are transitive verbs that are all synonyms for "cause." In other words, this one hundred-fifty word definition is more a series of causal hypotheses than a definition.

In fact, a close reading of the text discloses that most of the discussion of the complexity of disasters and what this implies for a definition is actually a discussion of *etiology*. A few exhibits: management is a "contributing factor" in disasters, not merely a "response to the event" (introduction); "a range of management processes ... act as core *contributors* to the development of ... vulnerability" (second section: emphasis added); disasters give rise to "a dynamic, emergent set of issues" (third section; see especially Table 1); globalization is one of the causes of disasters (third section); disasters are part of a sequence of cause and effect in which the "causal factors" that shape them "incubate over time and space" and which in turn "also generate impacts across a considerable distance and over a long time period" (third section); "each specific disaster will generate its own character that makes it unique" (section four); "disasters have a strong human component in terms of their causality and . . . this needs to be embedded within the definition of the term" and "we can see the role of the human element in the causation of disasters" (both from section seven); and finally, "Perhaps more importantly from our perspective here, there is considerable debate around the particular significance of the various elements of the term, their relative significance and *the manner in which they interact with each other to produce the complex mosaic that becomes a disaster event*" (section eight; emphasis added). What started out as an attempt to create a definition has morphed into the construction of a causal theory.

If we remove the causal hypotheses from Definition 4, what elements of a definition remain? The definition becomes this: Disasters are events. They are events that are complex, and they unfold. (There are three additional adjectives that modify "events.")

Definition 4 also raises a third issue. This one is about the relationship between definitions and etiology, about the definition of disasters and their etiology in this case. My own view is that a definition should not preclude any specific form of etiology but that it should not advance any specific form of etiology. Making etiology part of the definition itself runs the risk of making any theory based upon that definition tautological. In other words, it would be impossible to falsify any hypotheses derived from it.

I continue to disagree with Smith that complex phenomena require complex definitions in order to effectively identify and isolate their subjects from other phenomena. (Are there any simple phenomena?) The causes of unemployment may be multiple and complex, defying easy sense-making, but a definition of unemployment need not be: "A person is said to be 'unemployed' if he or she is looking for work, is willing to work at the prevailing wage, but is unable to find a job" (McCain 2004). Such a definition does not tell us *why* people who want a job are without one. That is the function of a *theory* of unemployment.

Adding complexity is necessary for elaborating and strengthening theory, but the opposite strategy is needed for formulating a definition. Simplification is required. The complexity and nuances of individual historical cases need to be pared down to the element or elements that are the signature qualities—the defining properties—of the phenomenon in which one is interested.

CONCLUSION

The model for doing this is Max Weber's construction of *ideal types*. Weber begins with existential definitions (Schutz 1967; McKinney 1969)—that is, laypeople's definitions—and produces a constructed (analytical) definition in the form of an ideal type " . . . by abstracting and accentuating certain conceptually essential elements" (Weber 1949: 100). The ideal type need not identify a single element as its defining property. Weber's ideal type of bureaucracy, for example, contains seven elements characteristic of the modern legal-rational form of organization (Weber 1978: 956-958). An ideal type is not meant to capture all the details of any concrete situation. It is a pre-theoretical tool for isolating the phenomenon of interest from other phenomena outwardly similar but fundamentally different from it. Weber, for example, distinguishes rational capitalism from all other previous forms of economic arrangements (Weber 1958: 47-78, esp. the example of the "putter-out," 66-68).

Let me offer my own attempt at a definition of disaster following the logic of the ideal type. A disaster is *a social situation characterized by nonroutine, life-threatening physical destruction attributed to the forces of nature, regardless of what other causal factors may seem to be involved.* Others may take issue with all or part of this definition. Regardless, it will serve my purposes here. "Social" separates disasters from tragedies that befall individuals or individual small groups such as a family. Disasters are collective in nature. Barton's typology of *collective* stress emphasizes this point and also demonstrates how one can identify analogous situations affecting progressively more inclusive collectivities. "Situation" may or may not be equivalent in meaning to the term "event" as used by some of the contributors to this volume. It locates disaster within a subjective framework rather than implying that it refers to either physical destruction per se or to the natural forces that contributed to it. Disruption of normal routines and social structures is the defining element of these situations, as several authors in both this volume and the previous one have noted.

The verb "attributed" is used deliberately to denote that the important link between cause and effect—between natural forces and physical destruction—resides in people's minds. Whatever the "true" causes, people see nature as playing a hand. They may also come to see other people as responsible, such as incompetent bureaucrats or corrupt politicians. Even if they do, lack of intent is assumed (intentionally causing a building to collapse is a crime, not a disaster), but this does not mean that no one will be blamed after the fact. "Nature" is also identified subjectively. Natural processes are as involved in an act of terrorism (chemical reaction, physical motion of projectiles) or an epidemic (transmission of germs) as in a tornado or an earthquake. What separates disasters from terrorism and epidemics is not only the absence of intent or human control but also the social conventions rendering wind, chemical reactions, and microorganisms, for example, into conceptually distinct linguistic categories.

"Life-threatening" remains an ideal-typical element of the definition of disaster. This applies whether deaths actually occur or not. "It's a miracle that no one was killed" spoken after a tornado has destroyed a mobile home park suggests the expectation that death is part of the accepted meaning of "tornado disaster." A runaway train that derails, crashing into several houses and causing injuries but not fatalities, described by an excited television field reporter, "It could have been a disaster," means that without fatalities the reporter finds it inappropriate to apply that label. One of the main issues involved in the what-is-a-disaster? debate can be addressed in light of the life-threatening element of the definition and the relationship of the definition itself to other troubling situations. Many of the participants in the debate would extend "disaster" to include situations that are neither immediately nor directly life-threatening. I believe that it is analytically inappropriate as well as counterproductive to do so. In fact, it is this extension of the life-threatening element of the term that makes its use metaphorical when applied to situations such as wedding receptions and the looting of museums.

By abstracting each of the elements in the ideal-typical definition of disaster presented here, other types of situations can be identified that are not conventionally labeled disasters. For example, "life-threatening" is an extreme form of threats to life-quality, that is, quality of life. Situations involving mass deprivation can be studied in comparison to life-threatening situations such as disasters, as Barton has shown. Calling them disasters, however, does not help us to identify them or to study them. We are able to identify and study them in comparison to disasters because we are able to imagine an entire spectrum of situations involving threats to life at one extreme (such as genocide or the Holocaust, for example) to other, non-lethal but still unwelcome threats at the other. A definition of disaster helps us do this, not when we change the definition itself but when we (a) simplify the definition to capture the essence (the ideal, in Weber's sense) of the term and (b) are able to abstract or make more general each of its ideal-typical elements. This process of abstracting is a logical one carried out by the analyst. It is not an empirical process requiring us to sift through an ever-widening variety of types of situations in search of some elusive quality that they all have in common.

Each of the ideal-typical elements in the definition of disaster offered here can be used for abstracting in this way. I will illustrate with two additional examples. Disasters are nonroutine situations. Readers may object that what is routine and what is exceptional is too "subjective" a distinction to make the definition a useful one. In fact, this is what makes the definition useful for research and for theory construction. What is routine and what is nonroutine is not an issue for analysts to decide *a priori*. Routine and nonroutine are "in the eyes of the beholder" (see the discussion in Stallings 1998c). One's house or apartment does not catch on fire every day, but responding to house and apartment fires is routine for firefighters. Nonroutine fires from the standpoint of firefighters can occur. When they do, they are likely to have some unusual or unprecedented feature (not universally or historically, but from the standpoint of that particular local fire department) such as the kind of combustible material, the scale of the conflagration, or the number of lives threatened or lost. Similarly with tornadoes: the same community is not devastated regularly by killer tornadoes, but disaster relief specialists from a variety of regional and federal agencies are routinely deployed to tornado-stricken communities each year. From a different direction, Barton in his chapter provides an excellent illustration of how "consciousness-raising" is related to the distinction between the routine and the nonroutine in types of mass deprivation situations that would not be labeled disasters.

The second example of abstracting using the ideal-typical elements in the definition involves the attribution of causation. People's beliefs about the etiology of disasters and how those beliefs have changed over time is a fascinating subject. (For some examples involving earthquakes, see Stallings 1995: 111-116.) However much such beliefs may have changed, one component that has remained is that of natural forces. Nature still is perceived to be the agent directly responsible (in the sense of the most proximate cause in a sequence of causation) for death and destruction and the social disruption they produce. Human agency has always been part of the causal chain, even in ancient times. An angry god such as Poseidon may have made the earth tremble, but it was some disrespectful act by human beings that caused his anger in the first place. There are numerous examples of the Judeo-Christian God's wrath in both the Old Testament (e.g., Noah and the flood [Genesis 6-9]) and the New Testament (such as the plagues in Revelation [e.g., Revelation 9]). Subtracting nature completely from the definition of disaster adds nothing to the usefulness of the redefined term. On the other hand, labeling as disasters those situations wherein human intent is obviously involved may be undesirable for both theoretical and moral reasons. Does labeling the bombing of Dresden (see Sebald 2003; for an interesting personal perspective, see Vonnegut 1968), the torpedoing of the *Wilhelm Gustloff* (see Grass 2002), or the Holocaust (Hewitt 1997:

321-348) disasters make us more rather than less likely to think of these events in terms of their perpetrators and to hold them accountable?

There are two alternatives. One is to broaden the definition of disaster to include every unwanted change or situation with a bad ending that we may want to study. The other is to choose a broader term already capable of encompassing the circumstances involving "bad-ness" that attract our attention. As I have argued throughout, the latter alternative is the only one that makes sense to me. Let me offer a further, seemingly farfetched example. Rather than continuing to explore the possibility of expanding the term disaster for this purpose, let us choose the term "flood" to refer to the new and troubling threats we have been discussing. A radiological accident could then be a "radiation flood," a terrorist incident could be a "flood of shrapnel," an epidemic a "flood of germs." The problem with this is obvious: "flood" by linguistic convention involves water, too much water for the place where it is now located, whether it got there by nature alone or was aided and abetted by human agency (poor landscaping, mountaintop removal, unwise land-use decisions, etc.). "Flood" and "excess water" are so closely linked as to make other uses of the term metaphorical (e.g., a "flood of emotion"). It is the same with "disaster." Both terms are so tightly connected to specific referents by linguistic custom as to be considered *definitive concepts* (Blumer 1954: 7). This makes them unsuitable for use as *sensitizing concepts*, which is the use for which a new definition is being sought for disaster research. Selecting a different term that can be used for this purpose is the preferable alternative.

Quarantelli (1998: 251-254), Boin (here and elsewhere), and I (e.g., Stallings 2001) among others have recommended that this alternative sensitizing concept be "crisis." Just as earthquakes, floods, and tornadoes are subtypes of "disaster," so too are disasters, terrorist attacks, and epidemics subtypes of "crisis." "Crisis" is already a broader term signifying the arrival of a turning point between possible good and bad endings, between triumph and tragedy, and the necessity of suspending "business as usual" in pursuit of a resolution. "Crisis," "disaster," and "flood" are concepts differing in level of abstraction, not phenomena differing in order of magnitude. Actually, the use of the term crisis in this way predates the modern field of disaster studies by half a century. William I. Thomas developed a theory of crisis and social change early in the twentieth century (see Thomas 1909: 13-22). This "standpoint," as he called it, was the theoretical underpinning of the forerunners of the disaster sociology of mid-century. The earliest work in disaster sociology by Prince (1920), Carr (1932), and Kutak (1938) was grounded in Thomas's crisis model as was, in a roundabout way, the chapter on disasters in the early textbook by Queen and Mann (1925: 422-441).

There is a useful property of "crisis" that is not generally associated with "disaster." When one speaks of "crisis," there is an implied reference to a specific *social unit* characterized by this condition. Disasters are more likely to imply a geographical location (e.g., the Northridge earthquake, the Mississippi River floods) than a social unit. There can be a crisis in a marriage, a family crisis wherein a parent's behavior is becoming intolerable to other family members, a crisis within an intercollegiate athletic conference when some schools threaten to leave in order to join another conference, a school system facing a severe budgetary shortfall, and so forth. All of these situations, as varied as they may appear in substance, have one essential characteristic in common: some of the key members of that social unit (a wife, a son or daughter, an athletic conference commissioner, members of a school board, etc.) have publicly proclaimed the existing situation to be intolerable and in need of immediate change. (Whether or not participants or key bystanders such as news reporters actually use the term crisis is unimportant. This also does not presuppose that all participants agree that the label is appropriate for the situation or that they behave accordingly.)

This conceptualization of crisis is broader than Boin's and more inclusive than Barton's "collective stress." Boin's examples of crises have in common threats to life, even though they are not all limited in time and space or linked to natural forces. Some are "man-made"

threats such as mechanical systems breakdowns (TMI, Chernobyl) and terrorism (Oklahoma City, World Trade Center) while others are more chronic threats to life (Agent Orange, Gulf War Syndrome, AIDS). Marital problems and the breakup of an athletic conference can be considered crises under the broader notion, even though they are not inherently life-threatening. This does not mean that some of those who deem the situation intolerable might not engage in violent or self-destructive behavior (suicide, substance abuse, etc.). Only a subset of crises involve life-threatening circumstances, whether immediately or in the long-run.

Barton's contribution is helpful here. His working through the implications of "mass deprivation" provides some useful conceptual distinctions and identifies some of the empirical questions that need to be answered in order to understand the dynamics of crises. Conceptually, Barton identifies the essence of what is intolerable and threatening in crisis situations. At risk is not life or health but *quality of life* or, more simply, *lifestyle*. When a wife tells her husband that she "can't go on this way any longer," she is proclaiming a marital crisis, not because she feels that her life is at risk but because the *quality* of her life is threatened. (Spousal abuse is a different matter, but not all marriages "in crisis" are so because of physical violence or the threat of it.) Similarly, an athletic conference commissioner who responds to the threatened withdrawal of some member universities is in "crisis mode" not because lives are at stake but because both the prestige and the financial future of the remaining member institutions are at risk. An excellent example of a non-life-threatening form of crisis is graffiti (see Austin 2001). By placing threats to the quality of life as the essence of the urgency and intolerability of "crisis," we are now able to encompass the events that otherwise seem out of place such as the sudden drop in the stock market and fears about the consequences of Y2K. Parenthetically, these examples show that crises do not have to end badly, as Boin notes in calling attention to the potential effectiveness of crisis management (and as Thomas posited more broadly a century ago). Not all marital crises end in divorce. Sons and daughters can get help for a misbehaving parent.

Commissioners can succeed in keeping their athletic leagues intact. Stock markets eventually go up after a fall, and some threats such as those associated with Y2K fail to materialize.

Barton's discussion of collective stress and mass deprivation makes another important contribution to this discussion. Many of the issues associated with the development and use of such terms are empirical questions. How many people need to define a situation as intolerable and requiring fundamental change before special actions are taken? If not how many, then what kinds of people need to hold this belief? In what public arenas (from Hilgartner and Bosk 1988) do they need to speak out? What strategies, rhetorical and otherwise, are needed to mobilize for change and which are effective for defending the status quo? (For examples of the latter in environmental controversies, see McCright and Dunlap 2000). Many permutations are likely: specialists (e.g., scientists) identify or predict the existence of mass deprivation, but elites reject their analysis; laypeople believe they are experiencing it, but analysts view conditions as vastly improved over earlier periods; outsiders (sometimes called "outside agitators") believe circumstances to be intolerable, but those who should be most affected by them see nothing out of the ordinary; etc. Boin makes similar points about the dynamics of crises.

I would go farther than Barton does in his chapter, although he seems to be thinking along the same lines. I would locate "crisis" squarely within a *conflict perspective.* Crises are not just about contested definitions of the situation, such as between scientists and elites, analysts and laypeople, or outsiders and victims. Proclaiming a situation to be a crisis of unacceptable proportions is part of a contentious process of demanding fundamental change in the status quo. The wife demands that the husband behave differently, the conference commissioner demands that the would-be renegade universities abandon their selfish pursuits and honor their existing obligations, etc. Even "consensus" situations such as natural disasters can become crises if change is sought because the belief arises that death and destruction could have been prevented or that conditions that led to the tragedy must be changed to prevent future reoccurrences. Politicians are keenly aware of the crisis potential in disasters. Tours of disaster sites, public expressions of compassion and sympathy, and promises of aid are standard practices for ensuring that demands for change appear to be unnecessary. More extreme measures also exist, such as the appointment of a committee of experts to study the situation and make recommendations for consideration at some future date. Conflict suppression is a part of crisis management.

The most important question in these discussions has yet to be addressed squarely. Why do we need a definition of disaster or any other similar term? The practical answer, that is, the reason we need a legal or mandated definition, is to provide goods and services in designated situations. The analytical answer is in order to *generalize*. The aim of analysis is always generalization, even with case studies. (The case under examination is interpreted in light of similarities—patterns—holding for other comparable cases.) The method making generalization possible is *comparison*. One can choose to study the individual case because it is interesting or historically important (e.g., the assassination of Abraham Lincoln), but one cannot generalize about political assassination without defining the term. As Kaplan (1964: 83) put it, "Generality is a trait of all meaning. The individual case is but a resting place for the movement of thought . . ."

The logic of comparison upon which generalization rests was described as well as it has ever been nearly two centuries ago by Mill (1872 [1843]). In his First Canon (the Method of Agreement), Mill (1872: 451-452) describes the logic of comparing " . . . two or more instances of the phenomenon under investigation [that] have only one circumstance in common . . ." In the Second Canon (the Method of Difference, known more contemporaneously as the comparative case study), two instances, one in which the phenomenon is present and the other in which it is absent, are contrasted (Mill 1872: 452-458). The Third Canon, the Joint Method of Agreement and Difference (Mill 1872: 458-460), is the logic underlying the controlled experiment and, by extension, all scientific and social scientific research:

If two or more instances in which the phenomenon occurs have only one circumstance in common, while two or more instances in which it does not occur have nothing in common save the absence of that circumstance; the circumstance in which alone the two sets of instances differ, is the effect, or the cause, or an indispensable part of the cause, of the phenomenon. (Mill 1872: 458)

Identifying "instances" is the purpose of a definition as is distinguishing them from "noninstances." I include this quotation here to make two points. First, calling everything a disaster makes it harder rather than easier to find the patterns that hold across "instances" because they may have little or nothing in common. Second, calling everything a disaster makes it impossible to contrast cases because (by definition) they are all disasters, that is, instances in which the "phenomenon" is present. These barriers to generalization can only be overcome through the use of *subtypes* identified by adjectives that modify "disaster." "Rapid-onset" disasters can be studied separately or in contrast with "chronic" disasters, "natural" disasters by themselves or compared with "man-made" disasters, and so forth. But this brings us back to our starting point. In other words, expanding the boundaries of "disaster" negates rather than facilitates the comparative strategy that is the foundation of generalization. It takes the reintroduction of the same analytical distinctions (natural versus man-made, rapid-onset versus chronic, etc.) that we tried to obliterate by expanding the definition in the first place.

By moving to a move abstract term such as crisis, collective stress, or mass deprivation, we can identify logical subtypes for comparing and contrasting. These subtypes all share the ideal-typical quality or qualities of the more general phenomenon but differ in fundamental ways among themselves (e.g., in attributed causes, characteristics, or consequences). The working model may well be Weber's (1958) study of the relationship between religion and economic behavior. After differentiating religions into major historical types to isolate ascetic Protestantism and then distinguishing premodern from rational capitalism, Weber formulated a fundamental generalization about the religious antecedents of modern civilization. It is not necessary to have universal agreement on either the terms to be used in our analyses or their precise definitions. Certainly this has not been the case with Weber's hypothesis about the unintended consequences of the Protestant ethic. Scientific norms of replication ensure that others can examine for themselves the terms we use and either agree or disagree with them as well as the generalizations based upon them.

It is the goal of generalization and the logic of comparison that are central. Generalization is what the social sciences are all about. A coeditor of this volume (Quarantelli) used to put it succinctly to us when we were beginning graduate students: in a word, it's about "patterns." Social science is about the identification and confirmation of patterns or regularities, whether in the behavior of individuals, the interaction between individuals, or the relationships among groups. Having described a pattern, one hopes to be able to explain it by being able to answer such questions as: Why does this pattern exist?; How did it originate?; What has caused it to change over time?

Even if one is unable to offer satisfactory answers to such questions, the mere existence of an identifiable pattern is useful. It helps us make sense out of what is going on around us. We are not surprised by the unfolding of events because we recognize that "this is the way such things typically happen." (We also may be less shocked or outraged than others by each new event because we have seen the same pattern repeat itself many times before.) We may be able to predict what will happen next, before it occurs, if events follow their typical course. The fact that we know—or think we know—what is typical also alerts us to unusual developments. When a new twist arises, a challenge has presented itself. What does this atypical element mean? What are we to make of it? By definition it means that our understanding of the pattern is inadequate to some extent. But to what degree, precisely? Have we identified an exception that confirms the rule? If so, we have added to our understanding of the pattern by being able to specify some of the contingencies that affect its course. Or has the unusual development so badly shaken our confidence that we now question whether we actually have a useful generalization at all?

The importance of the question "What is a disaster?" from my perspective is that it is about our ability to identify and explain patterns of human behavior, interaction, and intergroup relationships that are associated with ruptures of the routine. Many things can disrupt the routines of everyday life. Not all of them should be called disasters. Those that meet our definition of disaster should be separated from those that do not. *If* something has the characteristics that we designate a disaster, *then* we expect to see a certain pattern unfold. We *understand* what is happening *because* this is what typically happens "in a disaster." We expect different patterns to hold in situations that are not disasters. Successful generalization requires that we identify both similarities and differences, that is, both instances and noninstances of disaster. There are all manner of *contretemps* for us to study. It is not necessary that they all be called disasters.

15

A RESPONSE TO ROBERT STALLINGS: IDEAL TYPE CONCEPTS AND GENERALIZED ANALYTIC THEORY

Allen H. Barton

Why do social scientists worry so much about defining concepts of social conditions and processes, when the society already has a set of labels that it applies? Because clarifying general concepts allows us to construct theories applicable to a wide range of social phenomena that have historically been hard to understand and deal with. Robert Stallings' discussion of how the contributors to this volume respond to the question of "what is a disaster?" points to important questions in the methodology of theorizing.

As he says, my concept of "collective stress" is designed to help us "generalize across a broad range of troubling events having different labels." The core of my definition is indeed "mass deprivation," and it asks us to consider a wide range of social situations that involve this core. Looking across these situations suggests a set of generalized variables or attributes, whose combinations define types of collective stress. Within this "attribute space" we can locate traditional "natural disasters" (sudden, localized, unintended physical destruction of the environment in which people live, with consequent loss of life, injury, loss of housing and possessions, perhaps of employment), along with other types including "social disasters" (such as chronic conditions of bad housing, bad health, and unemployment of large numbers of people resulting from failures of the economic and political system) and situations of mass deprivation imposed on populations by deliberate human action: ethnic discrimination, genocide, military invasion, or bombing from the air. Further there may be "cultural disasters" in which a population is simply demoralized by the invasion of powerful and culturally different people: an example is Anthony F. C. Wallace's account of *The Death and Rebirth of the Seneca*, in which a Native American society was first overwhelmed by demoralization and alcoholism, and then recovered through the leadership of a native "prophet."

It is by sorting these situations into types in terms of theoretically relevant dimensions, and reviewing the different kinds of social responses historically observed, that we can develop a theory of social response to collective stress. This theory will then help understand response to traditional "natural disaster" along with many other types of "troubling events." The important question to ask about a "troubling event" is not "is it a disaster?" but where it falls on a set of variables that have been shown to influence the ability of society to respond. Among these are:

1. size of the deprivation relative to the resources of various social units involved,
2. extent to which non-victims care about what happens to the victims,
3. ability of the victims to demand action from those who control resources,
4. preparedness of social organization to respond to the speed and scale of the problem,
5. extent to which there are powerful interests in maintaining the state of deprivation, and
6. extent of blaming the victims for their deprivation.

Similar variables apply to analyzing social response to *potential* situations of mass deprivation, either in terms of developing preventive policies or preparedness to respond.

Stallings points out that collective stress as I use it falls under the even broader rubric of "social problems." I would emphasize however that that term is not limited to "mass deprivations" but includes a range of social issues with little in common except that *some group* in the society is "troubled" by them. Often one group's "cure" for a "social problem" is another group's social problem. The heterogeneity of these "problems" makes it unlikely that there can be a theory of social problems.

Stallings concludes by proposing to use Weber's method of ideal types to construct a definition of disaster. He follows Weber in abstracting a set of conceptual elements from observed phenomena which differentiate disasters from "other phenomena outwardly similar but fundamentally different".

> "A disaster is a social situation characterized by nonroutine, life-threatening physical destruction attributed to the forces of nature, regardless of what other causal factors may seem to be involved."

The abstracted elements are:

1. Social: collective, on a larger scale than a small group;
2. Nonroutine: disruptive of "normal" behavior and relationships;
3. Life-threatening: having at least the potential of death, rather than simply involving inconvenience or economic loss;
4. Attributable to nature rather than essentially due to human intent, even though human incompetence may contribute;
5. Physical rather than involving infectious disease.

For a broader term covering a greater range of troubles, Stallings suggests "crisis" as a term which brings out the element of social decision-making in dealing with troubles generally. On the other hand "crisis" may generate as heterogeneous set of observations as "social problem," since it seems to refer to any threat to the functioning of any social organization which is recognized by the leadership or the underlying population.

For disasters as he defines them, Stallings advocates systematic comparison of observed cases in order to develop generalizations. By limiting the cases to be studied by his ideal-type definition, he argues that it will be possible to identify the variables that help us understand how society reacts to these situations. However comparing within this limited range of cases may make it harder to identify important variables influencing response.

At the same time he agrees on the importance of using a more abstract term like collective stress, crisis, or mass deprivation in order to identify logical subtypes and the behavior patterns that go with the subtypes. I would suggest that this is a more important step toward theory construction than creating an ideal type definition of "disaster." Talcott Parsons in *The Structure of Social Action* has a long discussion of Weber's "ideal type" approach to theorizing. He warns:

The formulation of class concepts, including ideal types in Weber's sense, is an indispensable procedure. But it is not usually possible for scientific analysis to stop there. To do so would result in a type atomism—each type concept would be a unit of analysis by itself. But in reality these units are systematically related to one another. This is true because they are formulated in terms of combinations of relations between the value of a more limited number of properties, each property being predicable of a number of different type concepts. Above all the values of the general elements concerned are not always combined in the particular way that any one type concept involves; they are independently variable over a wider range . . . . For on the type basis it is necessary to have a separate general concept for every possible combination of relations between the values of the relevant elements, while in terms of an element analysis it is possible to derive all these types from a much more limited number of element concepts. Indeed it is impossible to work out a systematic classification of ideal types without developing at the same time, at least implicitly, a more general theoretical system (Parsons 1937: 618-619).

This points to the basic problem of trying to create a theory of "disaster" considered as an ideal type of situation characterized by a particular set of values of elements like speed of onset, type of causation, extent of physical damage to the environment in which people live, and extent of deprivation of the people in the social unit affected. Both laypeople and social scientists can then argue as to whether "natural" and "man-made" damage should fall into this ideal type or be treated as two categories, whether sudden, slow-moving, and chronic deprivations are or are not "disaster," whether massive physical damage where no people are affected is a disaster, whether massive "social" damage in the absence of physical destruction is a disaster, and so on.

My approach was to consider the variety of situations of collective stress (or mass deprivation) which are observable, ranging from "natural disasters" to famines to depressions to chronic poverty to genocide, and look for general analytic dimension on which they could be characterized. Then, having located the observable cases in a multidimensional typology or "attribute space," one can examine *social responses* to the various types of situations: whether there is widespread individual effort to help victims, whether large-scale organizations or government take action, whether actions are rational or irrational, coordinated or poorly organized, based on knowledge tested by experience or guesswork or ideology. One can also look at *preventive actions* taken to avoid future occurrences of such situations, or to be better prepared to respond.

16

BACK TO NATURE?
A REPLY TO STALLINGS

Arjen Boin

BLACKOUT

On August 14, 2003, the Northeastern regions of the U.S. experienced a massive power failure that sent cities such as New York and Detroit into chaos. The breakdown caused an immediate crisis for city officials, electricity companies, emergency services, airport authorities, hospitals and, of course, media workers. But the crisis faded soon, as the next day brought power and a sense of relief because nothing bad had happened. President Bush spoke of a "wake-up call" and bickering with the Canadians was temporarily hushed by installing an investigative committee. After the weekend, the U.S. slid back to normal and memories of the crisis faded rapidly.

The 2003 Blackout presents crisis researchers with a very interesting case. The ancient power grid failed just when many Americans were returning home after work. It was hot. Metro cars and elevators got stuck. Airports grounded to a halt. Yet, panic remained absent. In orderly waves, New Yorkers crossed the bridges on their way home. The authorities appeared calm and in control. Did effective crisis management help to avoid a disaster?

Disaster research offers arresting insights with regard to the mass behavior observed during this power outage. This case, however, is unlikely to trigger much interest from the disaster field, as I argued in my chapter and Bob Stallings confirmed in his detailed reply. In my chapter, I observed that traditional disaster definitions do not apply to this type of "modern" crisis, which—for reasons that should interest us all—did not result in casualties, chaos or major damages. I subsequently proposed to reserve the term disaster for "crises with bad endings" and suggested that traditional disaster research be broadened to include precisely these episodes of modern threat to our well-being. For disaster researchers can teach us—laypersons and analysts alike—a thing or two about self-organizing behavior in times of collective stress, which may be the key to understanding the peaceful outcome of this crisis.

Bob Stallings critiqued my chapter in the fine tradition of the author and editor Samuel Johnson (1709-1784), informing the readers that my ideas are both good and original. Unfortunately, Stallings (echoing Johnson) then proceeds to tell us the good ideas are not very original and the original ideas are not very good. Stallings enthusiastically endorses my "choice of 'crisis' as a general concept under which 'disaster' and other calamitous phenomena should be fitted;" he has made the argument himself. My more original idea to exploit this convergence of disaster and crisis minds contains "shortcomings that hinder its contribution to the present discussion."

The outcome of Stallings' inspired review of my argument is enlightening if rather disappointing. It is enlightening, because Stallings actually solves the *What is a disaster?* puzzle. The rejection of my argument forces Stallings to offer an alternative line of reasoning, which, I argue, underscores the very concern that started this whole discussion. This alternative is subsequently disappointing, because it relegates the field to obscurity.

DISASTER AND CRISIS RESEARCH: BRANCHES OF THE SAME TREE

Crises happen all the time: the SARS threat, the Blaster worm, and the 2003 Black Out are the most recent reminders of Western society's vulnerability to disruption. These modern threats find traditional counterparts in natural agents of destruction (the 2003 killer heat in France) and war-caused tragedy (Iraq). Some of these episodes enter the book of disasters, many do not. Hence the question: What is a disaster?

If we momentarily sidestep this question, I think we can all agree that disaster sociologists have much to offer in understanding these episodes of disruption. The disaster field harbors a well-developed body of insights and findings with regard to the behavior of people in the face of these unforeseen and threatening situations. Disaster sociologists have many meaningful things to say about— I cite arbitrarily from their catalogue here—evacuation behavior, early warning systems, the interaction between media and the general public, the organizational capacity of emergency services, and, as Stallings helpfully reminds us, about the religious beliefs underpinning the perceptions and behavior of disaster-stricken populations.

The problem, of course, is that disaster sociologists routinely deprive themselves of this opportunity to enlighten us, as their definition of disaster does not cover all sorts of crisis events. Many contemporary crises do not involve huge casualties nor do they find their origin in the forces of nature. The authors of the preceding volume all agree that a new (or adapted) definition is necessary (Quarantelli 1998). Their efforts, however, are marred by the reality that laypeople, journalists and many analysts reserve the term "disaster" for a situation that is collectively defined as really bad.

Both crises and disaster are subjectively defined by those who experience them, hear about them, deal with them or report on them. The challenge for analysts is to define them in a way that analysts can agree on the nature of the phenomenon in order to facilitate meaningful research. In other words: analysts try to define subjective processes (collective sense-making) and their outcome ("It's a disaster!") in an objective way, which allows for valid research findings. It may be easier to define crisis than disaster, I suggested, because the latter definition somehow must pinpoint the collective arrival at a shared disaster notion (how many people must feel "something" to be a disaster before analysts can speak of one?). I also ventured—perhaps a bit too carelessly—that disaster sociologists should not get too embroiled in tracing this mysterious process of sense making, as their expertise and interest seems more congruent with the analysis of collective behavior. Stallings assures us that disaster sociologists can study both perceptions and behavior, which must be considered good news.

It appears that everyone agrees that crisis and disaster are related concepts, but precisely how they are related remains a matter of dispute, as Stallings makes clear. I defined crisis in terms of a discontinuity, which usually (but not always) causes authorities to engage in critical decision-making under conditions of uncertainty and time pressure. The term thus applies to earthquake threats, heat waves, bush fires, computer worms and terrorist attacks. Thus defined, the outcome of the threat is left open: a smooth evacuation may minimize casualties of an approaching tornado and timely intervention may prevent computer viruses from infecting our critical information highways. In other words: crisis management matters. Obviously, crisis management sometimes matters not quite enough, which leaves us with a big mess that many laypersons call a disaster.

If we could all agree that this proposed distinction works, research capacities can be bundled, re-divided and applied to the pressing problems at hand; the questions ranging from causes to responses, from early warnings to collective appraisals. The labels separating crisis and disaster researchers would become irrelevant and the question *What is a disaster?* would be more or less resolved. It is here that Stallings draws a line in the sand.

COMING FULL CIRCLE?

Stallings is happy to connect disaster and crisis, but in an entirely different way. His definition of disaster clarifies the distinction he proposes: "A disaster is a social situation characterized by nonroutine, life-threatening physical destruction attributed to the forces of nature." Disaster is thus not a *negatively defined* subtype of crisis (a "crisis gone bad"), as I assert, but a specifically defined *subspecies* of crisis. A disaster occurs when we think that wind, water, earth tremors or meteors will destruct something physical that subsequently can destruct us. Stallings presents us with an admirably concise and clearly formulated definition of disaster, thus making future editions of this book unnecessary. We have natural disasters and other problems, which we can refer to in terms of crises or collective stress; as long as we refrain from the term disaster. By analogue reasoning, it appears that we have disaster sociologists and other "analysts."

Why does Stallings bring us full circle to a definition that the participants of the previous discussion seemed to have left so far behind them. To understand his position, we must return to what he refers to as the two shortcomings that hinder my contribution.

The discussion of the first problem—"the inconsistent use of the distinction between the *objective* and the *subjective*"—reveals what appears to be a pillar of opposition to the idea of mixing crisis and disaster. students of crisis have little to offer disaster sociologists in the eyes of Stallings. This may very well be the case. After all, disaster sociologists have consistently and persistently studied natural disasters for well over half a century. The resulting insights—and this is my point—would greatly enhance our understanding of crises, modern or not. Stallings refuses this courtship, however, as my argument reminds him of some "erroneous distinction that persisted for decades" that has been long since corrected. The disaster church has no room for untrained zealots.

The second problem Stallings identifies in my argument has to do with the distinction between lay and analytical definitions of disaster. I argue that an analyst's definition cannot stray too far from the definition used by most laypersons, at least if analysts want lay people to take them seriously. Stallings refers to "a dubious requirement that lay and analytical definitions be isomorphic." From a discourse community perspective, Stallings is absolutely correct. It would be ludicrous if astrophysics would strive for a definition of, say, dark matter that would be "aligned" with the thinking of lay persons. Correspondingly, it is entirely defendable to maintain a time-honored definition of disaster even if the term has taken on a different, more encompassing meaning among the general public than the one prevalent in the academic ivory tower.

The price for this principled stance is paid in the currency of societal relevance. If we adopt Stallings's definition of disaster, the field of disaster sociology will sponsor conferences and fill journals in which one will look in vain for analyses of 9/11, the Anthrax scare and the 2003 Black Out. Stallings engages in a little conceptual gymnastics to broaden his disaster definition to include these types of events: "natural processes are as involved in act of terrorism (chemical reaction, physical motion of projectiles) as in a tornado or an earthquake." To no avail, I am afraid. Declining societal relevance tends to translate in academic obscurity. For it is precisely these types of events that motivate young, talented students to pursue a career (as an academic or practitioner) in disaster management. Stallings may wish to study disaster management without studying the 9/11 disaster, but he may find himself in a very small and well-hidden niche.

This is the last place where I would wish my respected opponent and his many, extremely capable colleagues in the disaster field. Judging from his constructive suggestions as to where the crisis field should go, Stallings is not principally opposed to a tighter cooperation between all those studying social disruptions with serious potential to do harm. Indeed, he welcomes a merger between the two fields as a "sound proposal." Hopefully, our exchange of views has helped to clear the path toward such a merger. There is, after all, very little reason to draw iron curtains around any field of research. For it is these protective walls that tend to become the gates that separate the declining niche from the evolving world.

17

RESPONSE TO ROBERT STALLINGS

Philip Buckle

First let me reflect on Stallings observation that mandated (or legal as Stallings refers to them, though mandated is a broader concept that includes legislative authority, enunciated policy and dominant authority consensus; typically the Government and disaster management policy makers) definitions are event based. Often they are, though in some circumstances they may not refer to events, at least not to events that are rapid onset, discrete and easily identifiable phenomena. Droughts, the collapse of financial institutions, environmental degradation and other disasters are more processes than they are events. They have no easily discernible start or end and they may, indeed often do, modify their own context so that at their "cessation" the social, economic and physical environment in which they have occurred may itself have changed and changed as a result of these processes. Mandated thus refers not just to events or to legal authority but also to a limited number of procedural disasters and includes less formal but no less significant and influential modes of the expression of authority besides the legislated.

Stallings suggests that there is some naiveté in trying to broaden mandated definitions to more clearly include process and processes. I don't agree. Idealism perhaps, but not naiveté. Research by me and my colleagues, Graham Marsh and Syd Smale, indicates that practitioners welcome advice, critical analysis and criteria for effective policy and practice. Increasingly policy makers are commissioning such research or are drawing upon expertise and research findings conducted independently. If they do not make use of it immediately and fully this is for a number of reasons. The most significant of which are that differences between research finds may suggest ambiguity or uncertainty or error and therefore need further comparative assessment of the findings themselves before they can be used as a basis for policy and second the constraints of day to day practice (practitioners doing the job) which leave little time for critical reflection and the testing and implementation of new ideas. There is still a long way to go in bringing research and practice together (if this is an admirable aim, and this is open to question if it results in the compromise of research independence) but my view is that by small steps, practitioners and researchers are moving closer.

I disagree that process models can be broken into "discrete events". Perhaps this is necessary for disaster management operations. But even in this context the inappropriate classification of "elements" and the inappropriate arbitrary disaggregation of process has often led to equally inappropriate and harmful responses. This has often arisen where the disaggregation of process has been attempted on the basis of agreed but arbitrary temporal and spatial criteria and have not taken account of how these elements have arisen in the first place nor how they are related to other elements. Where the disaggregation is arbitrary but argued for the grounds of operational expediency it is no less constrained by artificial and inappropriate conceptual boundaries where convenience overrides the dynamism and complexity of the world beyond policy and operational practice. This seems to me to be the sociological equivalent of atomism, Newtonian physics when what we need is the quantum theory of Planck, Einstein and Bohr.

I want to address some specific points that Stallings raises. He writes that " . . . it is politicians who determine both the core and the boundaries of mandated definitions." This is an incomplete picture. Politicians (but agencies, and other constituents must also be included in the political process) do not exist in isolation from their society. Through a variety of ways, the media, local constituent groups of the political parties, the dialogue between government and opposition and political responsiveness to the communities' needs and concerns, politicians do take (some) account of community definitions of disaster. In some instances politicians may be in advance of their community. Because the interaction between politics and community is more of a dialogue and exchange than Stallings suggests it is important to understand the different approaches and the ways in which the parties may interact. Hence my description of mandated and community definitions and my efforts to suggest a mechanism for understanding the linkages. Each definitional domain has a significant part to play in the exchange and dialogue between "politics" and "community". Complexity theory is one means of understanding this exchange.

Related to this point about the role of the politician and the practitioner Stallings asks why—unlike academics—they would have an interest in academic definitions unless that definition supported their existing position. My experience is that typically politicians—whatever other shortcomings they may have—are responsive to their constituents and to their communities and have a commitment to social change and progress (though they typically disagree among themselves on what progress means and should be). They are often interested in what academics say because they want to move forward and in the context of disaster management make them safer places. But politicians too exist in a world constrained by competing interests and limited resources which limit their capacity to achieve the change they often desire. Hence they are not always able to or willing to accept the advice and recommendations of researchers.

Also, communities are often not passive and will vigorously pursue a political agenda. My experience is that communities have driven much of the debate about improving disaster management over the past two decades. Often the most original thinkers and the groups most committed to change arise from local communities and not from the political arena or academia. Perhaps the dialogue is more of a conversation between academics, politicians and agencies and communities. None of these have entire freedom of action and none are entirely persuasive (there is even disagreement within each of these groups) and it is little wonder therefore that advice is considered, weighed and assessed before being taken up; if it is taken up after being evaluated.

I use the conceptual framework of complexity as a means of understanding the commonalties of different types of disasters (natural, technological, rapid onset, slow onset etc.) but I do not see disasters as replicates of complex social systems. I see complexity and the concepts that exist beneath its' heading as a means of dealing with four issues. The first is the definition of disaster. Efforts so far in the research community have not been overly successful in generating agreement about what is meant by or what constitutes a disaster. Efforts have been more successful in the practitioner community but only because of a pragmatic approach that *de facto* includes some events and processes and excludes others without empirical or theoretical justification. Success here denotes the mandatory imposition of a working definition, with the emphasis on and the rationale arising from "working". Second, complexity as a method of analysis allows us to better understand how social processes are created, unfold and develop and are transformed. In particular, complexity allows us to deal with process and processes where much previous analysis has dealt only with events. Third, complexity as a tool for analysis and also as a meta-tool, if I can be excused for a clumsy phrase, allows us to understand the interactions between a disaster and its social, political, economic and environmental contexts. Much analysis has not investigated how disasters, events and processes, are related to their broader environment. Blaikie and colleagues put forward a model that situates the disaster in the flow of local unsafe conditions and more strategic and structural processes and structures of a society. This model is widely accepted and used and has contributed very significantly to our understanding of the nature of risk, vulnerability and disaster. It does not give us tools for better understanding how root causes, dynamic pressures and unsafe conditions interact with each other and how one is converted into another.

I tried to show in my paper that there are two conflicting approaches to defining disaster. The mandated (government) approach and the interpretivist (community or lay) approach. These are in many ways at odds with each other in terms of the priorities they give to risk, the emphasis of one on events and the other on processes and the ways in which they evaluate and respond to disasters, however defined.

As Stallings notes my discussion of complexity does " . . . disclose(s) more interest on his part in change processes in complex social systems than in disasters per se (however defined). This is right. But it is not lack of interest in disasters. It is because disasters are agents of change and do arise from the structure and dynamics of the complex social systems in which they are a part.

An example of this is the heat wave in Europe in the northern summer of 2003. In France about 10,000 people died prematurely because of the unusual hot summer. In the United Kingdom, which recorded its' hottest day ever, the number of dead is not known because there was no central recording of the figures. There is now broad acceptance at political and community levels that heat waves are disasters. But heat waves have been with us since time immemorial. So why the change now to move heat wave from a weather condition to a disaster. The excessive heat perhaps, breaking records and the number of people that died; but there have always been heat records broken and people have always died from excessive heat. The role of media possibly—but this begs the question—why were the media interested? Why is heat wave now a disaster when a year ago it was not? Perhaps because we have an increasing understanding and greater concern with climate change which leads us to be more interested in existing processes (global warming). Whatever the reason heat wave has become a candidate for disaster through social processes of perception and evaluation and risk assessment. But it is indisputable that heat wave is now a condition for disaster. What are the social processes (driving cars for example) that gave rise to global warming/climate change and the increased incidence of heat waves? What are the physical processes (the chemistry and physics of CO2 emissions), and what are the processes of risk perception and risk evaluation that labeled heat wave as a disaster now, and not previously? Disaster studies so far have not been able to link these diverse issues.

Definitions of disaster are of no use unless they recognize that disasters are social events, that they are the products of both local and structural conditions. Disasters cannot be understood outside their contemporary social context. We need a mechanism and tools to help us understand how disasters are situated in society, how they unfold and develop and are resolved and what linkages exist between the event/process, the community and politics.

18

THROUGH A GLASS DARKLY:
A RESPONSE TO STALLINGS

Denis Smith

There is something inherently difficult about writing a reply to a commentary that is made on one of your own papers. When that initial paper is grouped together with three others (that you haven't seen), then the interpretation of the overall thrust of the commentary paper takes on a somewhat surreal perspective! This is the position in which each of the four authors found themselves in attempting to structure their reply to Stallings. Unfortunately, one's interpretation of the work of the other three authors is then carried out through the lens provided by the commentator. This reply attempts to draw upon both the broad canvas and the specific points made by Stallings in his paper, although constraints of space limit that discussion. These caveats are not made as an attempt to "opt out" of a full discussion and neither should it be seen as a reflection upon the quality of the commentary provided by Stallings, quite the contrary. Instead it is an expression of the constraints that exist around this reply, as well as a statement of concern regarding the potential risks of misinterpreting the arguments of others, especially when they are viewed though someone else's eyes. With these constraints in mind, it is important to set out some opening comments about Stallings' commentary.

Stallings makes several important points in the course of his paper. Whilst some of these are directly related to the arguments made by others in this volume, they are sufficiently generic to justify further discussion here. In addition, there are also several specific comments that have been made on my paper that also need to be addressed. However, before dealing with the specifics of these issues, it is important to say that there is much in Stallings' commentary that I find myself in agreement with, although inevitably there are some elements of the piece that I take issue with also. In the main, the comments made here are concerned with the points of disagreement rather than with those of acceptance. Again, this tends to generate a set of comments that seem, on the surface, to take a counter position to that set out by Stallings and it should be recognized that the margins of disagreement are less than might appear at first glance. In order to attempt to provide some clarity over the main issues of debate, it is important to set out the agenda for discussion attempted by this paper. For our current purposes, I would like to address the following issues.

In the first instance, there is the question of the *relationship between "crisis" and "disaster"*, which Stallings discusses at some length. The semantics of each of these terms are obviously important, as they both influence research (as a means of including/excluding events for analysis) and are also a means of shaping broader policy frameworks for dealing with such "events"[1]. However, the relationship between "crisis" and "disaster" is potentially confused and a number of points need to be made around that relationship.

Secondly, Stallings takes issue with the notion of disasters as complex, multi-level phenomena. Perhaps more to the point, Stallings seems to take issue with the use of the terms *"complex"* and *"complexity"* within the frameworks for analysis used in the earlier paper. This reply, therefore, seeks to clarify further the nature of complexity and its relationship to the definition of disasters. Invariably, this will be a limited discussion around what could prove to be an area of considerable debate.

Thirdly, some comment is needed concerning the issues of *triggers and consequences* within the processes of disaster generation and escalation. This discussion touches upon the key issue of vulnerability, both within communities and organizations. Vulnerability has been generally seen in terms of those "victims" of a disaster and the communities in which they live. There are, however, other perspectives that would see vulnerability as playing a role in the generation of disasters. In other words, the decision making that takes place around disaster policy and contingency planning may well increase the level of vulnerability within communities and other organizations.

Finally, it is worth remarking on the criticism made by Stallings around the issue of theory *construction* relative to the processes of *defining* the term "disaster". The relationship between the definition of disaster and those underlying causal processes that help to shape the morphology of the specific catastrophic event, are worthy of consideration.

These four issues are examined here, although the constraints of space will inevitably prevent a detailed discussion around each of them. As such, this rejoinder cannot do justice to the breadth of Stallings' paper and there are other issues worthy of discussion which, unfortunately, remain outside of the remit of this response.

A RUSSIAN DOLL OF DEFINITIONS: EXPLORING "CRISIS" AND "DISASTER"

There is little doubt that the semantics of the terms "crisis" and "disaster" have been important points for debate within their respective literatures for some considerable period of time. Whilst there is some overlap within the literature between the two terms, they have generally evolved from within different paradigms of research. Crisis management can be seen to have its origins in political science/international relations as well as within the broad area of "management". Disaster research, in contrast, has primarily emerged from the geological/geographical sciences and sociology. There are, therefore, many different perspectives that are brought to any construction of a definition. The manner in which a definition of the term is constructed clearly impacts upon both research and policy making, hence the debates within this and previous volumes (Quarantelli, 1978a, 1998b). However, the relationship between "crisis" and "disaster" remains potentially confused and a number of points need to be made concerning their relationship.

In his commentary, Stallings sets out his own definition of "disaster" in which he sees the phenomena as ". . . a social situation, characterized by non routine, life-threatening physical destruction attributed to the forces of nature, regardless of what other causal factors may seem to be involved." There are some important aspects of this definition that need to be discussed further.

In the first instance, this definition does not exclude those catastrophic "events" that do not involve human fatalities; as long as such "social situations" are seen as being "life threatening". This notion of the "threat" associated with an event, raises a question concerning whether fatalities (expressed in terms of the scale of the "event") should have primacy within any definition of disaster. I would argue that the presence of fatalities is an important element in a definition of "disaster" and one might question whether "life threatening" is sufficiently powerful to serve as a barrier to "inclusion". Life threatening implies that the "events" have the potential for escalation to a point where fatalities occur but, I would argue, does not suggest that fatalities are a pre-requisite for the definition of "disaster". In part, my position has shifted slightly, as my original framework for a disaster would have allowed for a consideration of "mass extinctions" episodes within a conceptualization of disaster. The logic being that these events involved fatalities (albeit not human) and, as such, they were on a scale of damage that should be considered as extremely significant. Within their historical context, these mass extinction events resulted in fatalities amongst the dominant species at the time. Philosophically, one might question whether any approach to categorizing 'disaster" should limit it to events that affect humans. Thus, my argument with Stallings is that potential harm should not be considered but that fatalities involving humans should be the primary criteria for inclusion.

Secondly, the focus in Stallings' definition is on natural causes and therefore excludes all technological "events", despite the number of fatalities that they might generate. There are problems associated with this approach. For example, a volcanic eruption that kills no one, but which had the potential to cause many fatalities, would be classified under the Stallings' definition as a disaster. In contrast, a toxic gas release that kills in excess of 3,500 people would, according to the logic inherent within the definition, be classified as a "crisis". Such a crisis would then be inevitably categorized along with other events that involved no human fatalities or may even simply involve economic cost rather than physical damage. Such an approach is, to my mind, problematic. In the first instance, the response of the communities affected by the destruction might prove to be the issue that should interest disaster researchers. If disasters should be seen to involve human fatalities (as a function of the definition), then one might question why the *mode of death* should be the determining factor for inclusion. Of course, this would open up a debate around the threshold number of deaths that would be required for classification, as well as the manner in which the deaths occurred.

There is a need, however, to consider carefully the nature of "technological" or "social" catastrophes that one might include in any disaster taxonomy. For example, a case could be argued for the exclusion of intentional acts (such as war and genocide) from any definition of disaster. However, this too brings with it some fundamental problems. It would, for instance, exclude the deaths of some 250+ patients, within a well defined catchment area in the UK, at the hands of a local physician, Dr Harold Shipman. Shipman was actually convicted of only 15 of the murders. The committee of inquiry found that he had killed 215, with a further 45 being highly probable. There were also a number of deaths for which no judgment could be made (Smith 2002). In many respects, these deaths (within a defined geographical space) would satisfy many of the criteria for disaster within Stallings' definition, apart from the "natural" dimension. There is clearly a sense of community involvement in the tragedy, along with considerable loss of life and a sense of social disruption. If we exclude catastrophes of this type, then we should also exclude terrorism and war (including all forms of armed conflict). Whilst the case for such a wholesale exclusion of such catastrophes is not completely convincing (Hewitt 1997, 1998), we can for the sake of argument, remove such intentional acts from our definition. This still leaves us with a group of technological accidents and certain types of pandemic that could be classified as a disaster. For example, the Spanish Flu pandemic of 1918 has been estimated as having killed some 40 million people and AIDS is continuing to kill at an alarming rate, with estimates of current fatalities and rates of infection being in excess of 35 million people, although Estimates of the number of infected individuals vary considerably. The scale of these "outbreaks" alone should justify their inclusion in any categorization of "disaster", irrespective of the root cause of the catastrophe. This is especially so as both of these cases could be seen as physical events that arise from natural causes.

There is not a convincing case, either, for the exclusion of technological accidents from a definition of disaster. The "natural-technological" boundary has become somewhat blurred, as both have the potential for widespread destruction and both are embedded within modern society. The central importance of technology to modern societies and their impact upon the notion of "self" has led Munro to observe that " . . . . technology is not simply a means to an end but is fundamentally bound up with how we understand ourselves" (1999: 514). As a consequence, perhaps it would be logical to include technological triggers within any attempted taxonomy of disasters. The limits imposed by Stallings upon a definition of "disaster" by the use of the phrase "forces of nature", may well prove too constraining in a technologically advanced society.

Perhaps a more convincing argument for inclusion within a categorization of disaster might well be the notion of the *scale* of the event rather than the triggers that generate the fatalities. *Scale*, along with *time* and *place,* provide a set of constructs against which to frame a discussion of a disaster. Time and place will interact with the scale of a disaster to generate an intensity that should serve as one of the "defining signatures" of a disaster required by Stallings. The notion of place (serving as a context for communities, or networks of association, that are at risk from the disruption caused) and the emotional impact of the disaster (arising from the scale of the event) will combine to generate an intensity that should provide such a defining signature.

The third major issue raised by Stallings concerns the relationship between "disaster" and "crisis". The existing literature does suggest that there is some measure of agreement with the view expressed by Stallings (following on from Boin's paper) that the term "crisis" should be seen as the broader, more encompassing, term and that "disaster" should be seen as a sub-set of this group of "events". Whilst agreeing with Stallings (and, therefore, Boin) that the term "crisis" is an appropriate overarching term, I find myself at odds with Stallings' arguments about consigning technological catastrophes to the category of "crisis", irrespective of the number of fatalities. The distinctions and overlaps between the terms "crisis" and "disaster" have been discussed extensively at various times within the literature (Hewitt 1997, 1998; McEntire et al.2002; Shrivastava 1987; Smith 1990a; Turner 1976, 1978) and both terms retain something of an elusive nature around their strict definition.

Perhaps the reason for this is that there is naturally a considerable amount of overlap between the two terms, due in the main to the interconnected nature of relationships between them. Disasters invariably bring with them a sense of place. We tend to think of "zones" or "regions" of disaster and the physical damage caused is often confined spatially. Crises, on the other hand, are often seen as being organizationally based (Mitroff et al. 1989; Pauchant and Mitroff 1992; Shrivastava 1987), although it is obvious that they can also be set within communities and regions (Smith 2002; Turner 1976, 1978). At one level, a crisis can be seen as an event that threatens an organization's abilities to operate, or which has the potential to cause damage (in social, political, physical and economic terms) unless "resources" are used to contain the potential damage (Sipika and Smith 1993; Smith and Sipika 1993). In many respects, the notion of a crisis is seen as being a broader concept than that of "disaster". However, the sheer breadth of the term can also generate problems of interpretation, especially when our "boundaries of consideration" around space and time are allowed to stretch. The ambiguity, especially around cause and effect within environmental and intergenerational hazards, is not untypical of crisis events. In many respects, the timeframe over which these "crises" occur generates much of the ambiguity concerning exposure to the hazard and the generation of harm. In disasters, such ambiguity is not normally present. It is invariably clear what caused the harm, although some of the underlying geophysical processes may be more ambiguous. Again, a focus on acute, rather than chronic impact, would not prevent the inclusion of certain types of technological catastrophes within a definition of "disaster".

Crises and disasters are also interlinked. A disaster, by virtue of the scale of its destruction, will generate crises for those organizations that are directly "affected" by the consequences of the "event". It may also serve as a trigger for a "crisis" elsewhere. For example, if an organization is within a disaster region but is not directly affected by the physical damage of the event, the disruption within the geographical region (or the region occupied by its supply chains) may well severely impair the organization's abilities to operate normally and may exceed its abilities to cope with the task demands facing it. A disaster could therefore be seen to indirectly generate a crisis for the organization.

The fourth observation concerns the *non-routine nature* of disasters (although the same could also be applied to crises as well) and in this case, I find myself again in agreement with Stallings. The notion of disasters as non-routine phenomena is important for several reasons. If disasters were routine events then it is unlikely that they would have the same psychosocial impact upon social groups that rare (i.e. "shock") events have. If a threat is frequent or continuous, then one might naturally expect that people exposed to the hazards would adapt to the threat; presumably by not occupying the hazard zone! However, there is considerable evidence that hazard zone occupancy does not always display such a "rational" approach to decision making, as evidenced by the number of people who occupy flood plains, volcanic "slopes" and earthquake zones. The trade-offs that individuals and groups make around the various sources of hazard and the benefits that they perceive to exist, are important therefore in shaping our understanding of their sensemaking processes and these may shape their subsequent responses to disasters. Again, the point about technologically-induced "disasters" is important here, as a comparison of public responses across the main groups of triggers for disaster would allow for a greater understanding of sensemaking and coping strategies within communities at risk.

The notion of the "non-routine" also breaks down in certain types of "crisis;" especially those involving biological agents, where there is a high risk of re-infection or migration of the virus over time. One might also question whether the notion of routine is sufficiently well defined in human time frames within Stallings' definition. For example, the nature of "routine" in geological time takes on a completely different dynamic relative to that used within a societal context.

The fifth aspect of Stallings' definition that raises important issues for our present discussion concerns the *situational context and the associated damage* associated with disasters. What Stallings' fails to do in the definition that he offers (although he does touch on it in the paper) is to explicitly deal with the issues of space-place-time and scale in providing boundary limits on the conceptualization of a "disaster". However, if we take a broader perspective on the nature of disaster, and include within our taxonomy such events as the AIDS epidemic or even BSE, then clearly this changes the relative importance of space-place-time as causal elements in the make-up and escalation of the disaster, by moving from a focus on spatially and temporally well-defined disasters and acute disasters to include more diffuse forms of damage.

Finally, Stallings also objects to the argument that suggests that the nature of disasters have changed over time. Clearly, if we restrict our definition of a disaster to include only those caused by the "forces of nature" then such events have not changed considerably in a physical way over time. What has changed, however, is the increased number of people who occupy the hazard zone and the resources available to them to mitigate the hazard. In addition, our awareness of the technical aspects of the disaster "triggers" has also changed as the depth of our understanding increases. The point that has been made by several authors is that there are new and emergent forms of "disaster" and that many of these arise out of the activities of modern societies (Barnett and Whiteside 2002; Chiles 2001; Giddens 1990). If these emergent forms result in significant numbers of deaths within a short period of time, then perhaps they should also be classified as disasters. To an extent, the core issues around definition, and the exclusion of more "modern" types of disaster ties into the second principal issue for discussion, namely the question of disasters as complex phenomenon.

DISASTERS AS COMPLEX PHENOMENA

Stallings seems to have an objection to what he sees as the "complexification" of disaster. He observes that in defining disasters, " . . . simplification is required. The complexity and nuances of individual historical cases need to be pared down to the element or elements that are the signature qualities—the defining properties." The earlier chapter was an attempt to identify these signature qualities, and a systems approach was used to generate the key elements of a disaster as a starting point for the discussion. What is of interest, however, is the manner in which these elements interact together to generate emergent properties. There is, however, a potential problem the simplification approach that Stallings suggests. Whilst identifying the defining properties is a core goal of the systems perspective, a failure to explore the interactions between these elements can lead to a reductionist approach that will prove to be flawed. At their simplest form, disasters can be seen as: "catastrophic events that will kill and injure people and cause considerable social, political and economic disruption within defined community settings."

Such a definition could be seen, however, as being too simple, especially as it leaves open the notion of the disaster "triggers" as a means of categorization. Whilst such a definition may capture the essential elements of a disaster (around the scale of deaths, destruction and disruption), it is the interaction between these elements that generate the complexity associated with any study of the phenomenon. For the purposes of our current discussion a complex system can be defined as

> a group of interacting elements, which are not identical even if from the same class. The elements can learn and change; the forces and connections between the elements may not be simple and may themselves change with time; the boundaries of the system may be ambiguous and may change with time (Allen 2003).

A natural disaster would clearly satisfy the criteria within this definition and the notion of a "system" has been prevalent within work on natural hazards for decades. As such, the notion of "complexity" is not simply a metaphor for the description of disasters but is an attempt to illustrate the features of disaster. However, on this point, Stallings makes the following observation: "The fundamental problem, it seems to me, is the assumption that somehow by examining the features of disasters as phenomena we will eventually produce a new and better definition of them." Whilst such an assertion may have some validity, it is difficult to see how failing to explore the complex nature of disasters will advance our understanding of the phenomena either!

There is little doubt that the complex, multi-dimensional nature of disasters generates problems in terms of both the generation of effective definitions and for theory building. However, I have to take issue with Stallings' assertion that simplification is the answer to the generation of a definition of "disaster". If that were the case then a definition of disaster, which stated that they were "events that generated excessive energy, located in the wrong place and at the wrong time, thus causing harm", might well suffice. Clearly such a definition would fail to capture the subtleties of such events and would inevitably lead to problems of interpretation. Indeed, some of Stallings' arguments on simplification and complexification are, in part, negated by some of his own arguments within the paper.

In addition, I would also argue the there is little point in trying to develop a definition of disaster without trying to explore, at least in part, the theoretical implications and contradictions that are associated with such a definition. Thus, the complexification of disaster definition, as Stallings puts it, is simply an attempt to show the emphasis on the elements of the term that already exist in the literature and to assess some of the implications of that research. The elements of complex, non-linear adaptive systems that are relevant to our discussion of disaster are as follows:

1. Cause and effect relationships are not linear in their orientation, and both space and time can shape our understanding of these interactions by shrinking our "boundaries of consideration".
2. Such systems are typified by emergent processes and properties. Elements of the "system" (in this case geophysical, human and, I would argue, technological) interact to generate problems that had not been previously considered as credible outcomes or had simply not been considered at all.
3. Agents are important in helping to shape the manner of that emergence and may mitigate or escalate the consequences of the "event".
4. There is an interconnected nature associated with different types of crisis and "disaster". It is possible for a disaster to create the conditions in which a crisis is generated further down the timeline. Vulnerability is either created or exposed in the wider socio-economic context in which the initial event takes place.

There are some important issues around the interconnected nature of both crises and disasters. Whilst there is some acceptance that lessons can be learnt from disasters, it is also possible that failures to learn from previous events may make an event worse (Alexander 1993; Elliott et al. 2000; Smith and McCloskey 2000) What is less clear, however, is the manner in which one event, and the response to it, can incubate another crisis or disaster further along the timeline (Sipika et al. 1993). An interesting research question might concern the role of "disasters" in stimulating volatility in the marketplace, or changes in social structures, that might, in turn, provide some of the preconditions for future "disasters" through the erosion of vulnerability. There is some acceptance of the interconnected nature of natural disasters with socio-economic events (Bolt 1999; Cantor 2001; Davis 2001; de Boer and Sanders 2002; Fagan 2000) but the manner in which socio-technical events and economic crises interact has not had the same level of research attention.

TRIGGERS, CONSEQUENCES AND ESCALATION; ELEMENTS IN THE CONSTRUCTION OF DISASTER

Stallings correctly identifies and comments upon the duality of disaster; with disasters being seen as both the trigger and the outcome. Disasters are interconnected events and any attempt to remove them from their spatial and temporal settings severely constrains our understanding of them. Stallings acknowledges this and argues that: "If something has the characteristics that we designate a disaster, then we expect to see a certain pattern unfold. We understand what is happening because this is what typically happens in a disaster." The notion of emerging patterns of disaster characteristics have not always generated the understanding that Stallings feels is a central component of the use of the term "disaster". The inhabitants of Pompeii, for example, had no obvious understanding of the nature of the disaster that unfolded before them. Even in more modern times, disasters have been typified by a sense of confusion by many of the victims. The sensemaking process (Weick 1988; Weick and Sutcliffe 2001) is an important element of any disaster.

In order to address the points made generally by Stallings, I will set out a brief framework that might serve to stimulate further discussion. In the first instance, the potential for destruction within any disaster occurs as a result of decisions and actions taken prior to an event. This arises from decisions to occupy hazard zones, the foresight to develop contingency plans and the strategies adopted with regard to early warnings. This "incubation" of disaster potential (Turner 1976, 1978) takes place within the communities at risk and runs parallel to the physical process that take place prior to a disaster. In this framework, the physical event can be seen as the trigger for the social disaster. The next stage occurs when the physical event exposes the vulnerability within the community at risk. The physical characteristics of the catastrophe determines the nature of the damage and disruption; much of which it may not be possible to develop effective mitigation strategies for prior to the disaster (this will be, in part, a function of the speed at which the physical destruction occurs). The final stage of the disaster involves the processes of clean-up and recovery and the return of the community to a degree of stability (including recovery from psychological trauma). Throughout this process, there will be a considerable amount of emergence within the interactions that take place and this emergence will give the disaster its own unique characteristics.

IN GLASS HOUSES: DEFINING A CONSTRUCT OR CONSTRUCTING THEORY

". . . developing a definition is not the same thing as constructing a theory. Attending to one does not accomplish the other."

Clearly, this not a statement that one can find much to argue with. However, it is also clear that one must pay close attention to the processes that underpin the definition of the term under investigation in order to have any chance of developing a theoretical framework that is robust. Such a definition must also have relevance to practice as well as theory. Although the brief for authors was to address the question "what is a disaster?", the answer to that question inevitably requires a consideration of the theoretical elements of that definition. I, for one, am not certain that any of the authors in this volume claimed that by defining disaster they were constructing theory. Both processes are independent but linked and a consideration of one inevitably requires that we look over the picket fence to consider the other!

CONCLUSIONS

Disasters are important phenomena, both in terms of the manner in which they emerge and can be "managed" in practice, and the manner in which they are researched. The debates within this volume have sought to examine some of the different interpretations that can be made of the term "disaster" and, whilst it is likely that the outcome of these debates will be inconclusive, the "emergence" of ideas and concepts that result from these interactions may well prove to be of importance in the longer term.

In his comments on the four papers in this section, Stallings categorizes the main thrust of the various contributions in terms of their "practical" and "analytical" dimensions. In some respects, any such classification is arbitrary as both approaches are necessary in order to deal with the real-world issues that are generated by disasters. There is considerable merit in arguing that research in this area must have practical validity and should not be undertaken simply for the sake of it. Of course, coming from a management school, I am likely to argue for the role of research into practice! One might argue that the practical-analytical dimensions should be overlapping and if the papers fail to do that then there is an obvious criticism that can be made of us all.

NOTES

[1] Stallings objects to the use of the term "event". However, it should be noted that the term was used in the initial paper as shorthand to encompass a variety of phenomena. It is in that context that the term is also used here. The term is not being used as a defining label as Stallings seems to imply! One might also point to Stallings' use of the term "situation" in his own attempt at definition, which is also open to misinterpretation.

PART III

19

DISASTERS, DEFINITIONS AND THEORY CONSTRUCTION

Ronald W. Perry

As several of the contributors have noted, this volume represents the most recent in a series of efforts organized by E.L. Quarantelli to gather scholars and ask them how they define disasters. Of course, none of these efforts had the goal or aspiration to achieve an immediate consensus on a definition. Instead, the purpose of this effort and those before focuses upon sharing. The notion is to create a forum to exchange, among many of us in the field, what we meant when we used the label disaster. Thus, all of these efforts are part of a process: A process of critical examination of the phenomenon that we all study. Indeed, one might say phenomena that we study, because we have highlighted the dimensions along which the disaster events we scrutinize are different and similar. The progressive exercise has also caused the community of disaster researchers and practitioners to examine where we are going and what structures—intellectually and otherwise—we must build on our journey.

For me, the ongoing exercise has demanded that I confront my own views of what social science is and how disaster research fits into that framework. It has brought home to me the notion that many of my colleagues view the world and profession differently than I was taught to view either. Like most intellectual exercises of this magnitude, the process of examination has produced controversy, disagreement, agreement and questioning of what the field is, where it is headed, and what paths will take us forward. Without doubt, the discussion has caused many of us to reflect and attempt to order our thoughts and outlooks.

I am concerned in this paper with the definitions offered especially in this book and the previous book (Quarantelli, 1998b). I will survey my vision of the extent to which they overlap and are changing. I also believe that the purpose of definitions needs to be briefly explored as an element of theory and in relationship to taxonomy and classification. Because so many authors seem conflicted about social science (and various "isms," including positivism, post-positivism and post-modernism), the third section of this paper will address notions of epistemology and metatheory. Finally, I will close my paper with a discussion of prospect: where are we likely to go from here?

THE DEFINITIONS

I was a discussant for five papers in Quarantelli's original book published by Routledge in London in 1998. At that time, I noted that for me it was appropriate to separate the fundamental definition of disaster offered by authors from the elaboration each scholar offered to support the conception they offered. Part of the reason for this tactic was the fecundity of definitions. The fundamental theoretical statements themselves are exercises in nominal definition; not operational definition. They are attempts to capture and share *meaning*. This is important at a theoretical level and guides many other decisions related to concept development; visions that are appropriately abstract. Elaboration of definitions is an attempt—in most cases—to demonstrate the definition in the world of experience; an operational endeavor. I saw the issue then, and still see it now, as about theory and therefore about abstraction.

My original assessment of the definitions I reviewed that were offered by Russell Dynes, Robert Stallings, Uriel Rosenthal,

Anthony Oliver-Smith, Steve Kroll-Smith and Valerie Gunter as possessing common themes (Perry, 1998). Those common features included the definition of disasters as social events in social time, acknowledgement that disasters are disruptive to social intercourse, and that disasters should be understood in a context of social change (human and institutional adaptability). I also see these common points in the work of the other authors in that volume; Claude Gilbert, Wolf Dombrowsky, Gary Kreps, Boris Porfiriev and Kenneth Hewitt. Although I did not dwell on it at the time, there were also significant differences among the definitions advanced. But I saw the differences as resting in issues other than basic nominal definition. Thus, in my opinion, some differences rested in (1) the view of the context of the phenomena as disasters or hazards; (2) questions of *whose perspective* is used as a definitional referent; the public, the victims, researchers, policy-makers; (3) the definer's vision of social science; and (4) issues that should be addressed in terms of taxonomy and classification. There was greater similarity among authors that were similar on these four features and less similarity among those who differed. Perhaps the consistency that I read in the articles of the first volume stemmed from the consistency among those particular authors along issues of the role and philosophy of science.

In the present group of definitions, generated just half a decade later, I see less congruence among authors. I believe that this may stem from a greater variation among authors along the dimensions described above. Across the work of several authors in this volume, I still see the basic agreement that I observed in 1998: disasters are disruptive, understood in social time as social events (not agent based), and that they are intertwined with change. Yet I think the disagreements among these authors are more extensive and substantive that those among the 1998 authors. As Quarantelli has noted (1998c), some of the apparent increasing disagreement may be a function of sampling. Authors have not been chosen randomly. Instead, there was an effort to represent a wide range of thinkers from many different social science and national contexts. In some ways, given the sampling goal of diversity, the level of consensus about what is defined as a disaster in each volume is positive. A critic would indicate, however, that the systematic patterning of differences indicates the need for more discussion among disaster researchers and greater attention to what research and social science are about.

Both Wolf Dombrowsky and Robert Stallings, in their roles as discussants, captured a key dimension of difference among the definitions they reviewed. That is, that variance exists in terms of the author's view of the perspective of the definer. Some focused upon "practical" or policy enabling dimensions, exploring definitions that could serve as a basis for government or institutional definition. Neil Britton, with his long experience as both scholar and practitioner, concentrated upon blending the academic with the practical, citing Australian and New Zealand governmental conceptions. Likewise, Buckle and Smith deal with practical definitions (Buckle calls them "mandated"). Susan Cutter is less concerned with practical and theoretical issues than with implications for social action and disaster management; her approach places the meaning of disaster in understanding the resilience and vulnerability of communities. Alexander, Barton, and Boin offer essentially analytic or social scientific definitions of disasters, with Barton and Boin exploring the critical issue of classification. Rohit Jigyasu's definitional excursion is more difficult to characterize along this dimension. He deals with the notion of disaster in a perceptive, almost religious, context in which he seeks to suggest that both the concept itself and the experience of victims needs to be expanded.

There are other differences as well. The authors vary on the importance of using a definition of disasters for disaster researchers that also makes sense to the public at large. An extreme of this position can be found in Kroll-Smith and Gunter (1998) who essentially tell us that a disaster is what people say is a disaster. Alexander, Cutter and Smith embrace a hazards perspective somewhat more than other authors. Boin, Barton, Britton, Buckle, Dombrowsky, Jigyasu and Stallings approach the problem from an "occasion instant" or disaster point of view. Furthermore, Barton,

Boin, Stallings and Dombrowsky emphasize the need to specify meaning through taxonomy and classification. These scholars argue that the term disaster—particularly the vernacular—is ambiguous and researchers need to redefine the "conceptual" space into theoretically meaningful units. In his closing chapter for this volume, Quarantelli also embraces and demonstrates the need to elaborate types of disaster occasion or collective stress situations as a means of making intelligible apparently conflicting empirical findings. Finally, there are at least implicit differences in perceptions of the value of definitions, theories and what (if any) social science model may be appropriate as a model for moving forward.

Where do these observations leave (or lead) the collectivity of disaster researchers? The consensus that exists is encouraging, but highly limited. One must move to a very abstract level to find it. There remains agreement that disasters are defined as social occasions, that they are disruptive, and that they are related to social change. At this level, most of the authors writing for each of Quarantelli's volumes agree. On the other hand, the differences are also profound. And most of the patterned differences rest in fundamental notions—hazards versus disasters, appropriate perspective for definitions, the need for taxonomy and classification and the way knowledge accumulates and is stored. These latter differences are especially important, because as Professor Cutter says it is possible to talk past one another on definitional issues, but one's view of social science controls our ability to talk to one another. My perception at this juncture is that disaster researchers are spending more time talking past one another than talking to one another. In an effort not to resolve the challenge but to simply clarify it and encourage dialogue, the following section looks at the problem of definition.

DEFINITIONS, TAXONOMY AND CLASSIFICATION

If disaster research is to continue to develop, must there be consensus about a definition of disasters? Cultural Anthropology has long thrived in the face of considerable controversy regarding the definition of culture (Oliver-Smith, 1998: 177). One may make the same observation about the term "leadership." Yukl (2002: 2) points out that "the term leadership is a word taken from the common vocabulary and incorporated into the technical vocabulary of a scientific discipline without being precisely redefined." He subsequently indicates that there has been disagreement among researchers about the meaning of the term since the 1950s and that the ambiguity has interrupted efforts to develop a real theory of leadership. To disaster researchers, the situation, as well as the consequence should be familiar.

Definitional consensus (or the lack thereof) is not a major deterrent to the conduct of research. Indeed, most research is not about the term "disaster." Research can be descriptive or model testing, but its object is usually a particular social response to some set of circumstances (or some change in circumstances). The author may or may not label the response a product of disaster or the circumstances a disaster. For the particular research project at hand, the label "disaster" has been applied directly or indirectly, and the focus is upon the findings regarding social behavior. Research on such social phenomena form the empirical basis of knowledge in many fields. The era of "dust bowl empiricism" in sociology was one reflecting many studies of many communities with little integration of the outcomes. The body of knowledge in disaster research in particular resides in the individual contributions of many such studies.

The challenge comes when one seeks to assemble the body of knowledge. Whether the assemblage takes the form of theories or models or even an elaboration of findings, one must "know" what a disaster is to accomplish the goal. Over the years, Barton, Quarantelli, Drabek and others have created such assemblages. Each scholar has observed that, when one attempts to gather findings together, there must be some level of organization if meaning is to be conveyed. In the early 1960s, Barton devised (and has since revised) a classification of collective stress situation. In 1986, Drabek developed an inventory of propositions, but still had to define dimensions of disaster behavior to do it. Specifically, faced with the findings of many studies, one must have a system for classifying them even to describe them at the simplest level. To begin to interconnect the findings and create meaning requires an even more sophisticated arrangement.

To some, the need to connect findings is a call for models and theories. These are the structures from which one derives explanations and predictions in social science. Yet the object of explanation is normally the behavior of some unit of analysis in connection with social structural or conditional circumstances. Hence, explanations tend to focus on decision-making under crisis conditions, or on information seeking behavior of warning recipients, or on disaster planning behaviors. Rarely does one see a "theory of disasters." While taxonomists see taxonomy and typology (classification) as a fundamentally theoretical endeavor, one can distinguish it among theory construction activities. Classically, taxonomy is the theoretical reasoning behind the creation of typologies. It is a process involving abstract thinking and conceptualization. Typology or classification is the act of creating types or ordering schemes, and of identifying empirical findings (objects) that lie within the types.

For me then, the need to arrange empirical findings meaningfully is a call to taxonomic thinking; of deciding what is a disaster and what are its theoretical dimensions. Based on this thinking, one creates categories of disasters that reflect the definition of the term and that identify important concepts and relationships. Subsequently, these concepts and relationships form the bases of models and theories. This tactic has been used effectively by Barton (1963), Drabek (1989) and Kreps (1989). Others, including Boin in this volume, have also developed classification schemes. Of course, social science is not linear and one can develop theories without typologies and typologies with a minimum empirical record. But the point is that disaster is a term with many dimensions and if we are to make sense of the empirical record (not to mention defining future direction), classification schemes represent an important step.

Indeed, classification is itself a way of defining disasters more precisely. Even primitive phenotypic typologies—now seen as very naïve—like classifying disasters as "manmade" versus "natural," begin the process of specifying what a disaster is. At the most basic level, this distinction was useful in its time as a means of grouping human response differences. Further research and reflection has caused us to realize that issues in addition to what precipitates the event in simple terms are important. Many disaster researchers are ready to begin thinking about genotypes: expressing classification in terms of social impacts, social time and the like. As this process continues, one can expect more sophisticated typologies that will allow researchers to group and compare their findings with those of others in theoretically meaningful ways.

The development of classifications is not a path to homogeneity, either for theories or for research. Many different typologies of the same phenomenon can exist simultaneously and still be constructive. Indeed, they can be dealt with much like different theories of the same phenomenon: evolve criteria for evaluating their utility and make a selection. Over time, those classification schemes that are most useful will enjoy a greater consensus. At any given time, new theoretical thinking or new findings may become the basis for a new typology. In all cases, the community of researchers gains specificity. Instead of fitting findings under a potentially ambiguous term like "disaster", findings can be fitted into the relatively greater specification of (whatever variables compose a) classification system. In fact, even if a researcher doesn't explicitly place findings within a classification, it can be done after the fact by a reader.

The promotion of classifications does not address the notion of the perspective of the definer directly. What I've written above is largely concerned with the idea that a researcher or social scientist is developing the meaning of disaster to be used in a social science context. Certainly, one would not expect laypersons to use the same definition, except perhaps in a general way. And that to me poses no particular problem; the fact that I may see an occasion as a crisis and a layperson call it a disaster is only an indicator of differences in our perspective and use of the term. For reasonable communication to take place, laypersons need not fully embrace my definition nor me theirs. A social scientific definition can also reasonably differ from a mandated or policy definition. The use of different definitions achieves different objectives. In fact, many terms as used by policy-makers are distinct in meaning to some degree from the definitions used by a technical audience. Those who work with technology transfer argue that over time the definitions of policy makers converge on those of the technical specialists. The next steps toward defining disaster are taken—for me—whenever one distinguishes among types of collective stress or even distinguishes a disaster from a crisis.

EPISTEMOLOGY AND METATHEORY

There is considerable controversy among social researchers about how knowledge is accumulated and ordered in social science. We read about "alternative epistemologies" and the death of positivism and wonder with what it has been replaced (Denzin, 1986). There appears to be considerable confusion about the concepts and terms in this controversy that promotes claims unrelated to practice (Agnew and Pike, 1994). For disaster researchers, it is important to remember that an epistemology is simply a way of viewing and understanding the world, and that many different epistemologies exist simultaneously. This point in particular was made by Jigyasu in his commentary. These concepts are generally treated as within the purview of philosophers.

In the broadest sense, science and social science constitute epistemologies (Bunge, 1998). Long ago, Sjobert and Nett (1968) concisely summarized the postulates that underlie social science as a world view in the form of several assumptions. These assumptions are:

1. There is a nonrandom order to the recurrence of events in the social and natural world;
2. Knowledge is superior to ignorance;

3. An empirical assumption that the external world can be known through human senses;
4. That cause and effect relationships can be identified;
5. Science should be used to improve the condition of humans;
6. Societies will sustain the efforts of scientists to understand the world.

Taken in the context of the scientific method—that research should be replicable and that knowledge must be tested in the world of experience—these assumptions form a social scientific epistemology. Anyone, whether a disaster researcher or otherwise, who claims to be operating with an "alternate epistemology" to science or positivism or whatever, needs to specify and contrast the elements of the alternative epistemology.

For any epistemology—but particularly for social science—two issues are important in accumulating knowledge: the logic of discovery and the logic of proof. The logic of discovery focuses upon how knowledge is found or how conclusions are drawn when observing the social world. The logic of proof addresses the process by which conclusions are tested and subsequently accepted. These processes are interdependent and can be captured under the umbrella of metatheory, a model of how knowledge accumulates in social science (Alexander, 1991). Von Bretzel and Nagasawa (1977) provide a comprehensive discussion of metatheory as a process that connects basic inductive reasoning with deductive reasoning. They point out that social scientists observe in the world of experience toward two ends: first to collect information and second to test predictions. The logic of discovery begins in the world of experience with observation of social behavior and proceeds to the cognitive world of abstraction (in the researcher's minds) where observations are grouped and ordered to produce concepts. Still in the abstract world, concepts are linked to form propositions, sometimes propositions are linked to form models or theories. The discovery process ends—so to speak—when the researcher has collected observations in the world of experience and moved to the world of abstraction to group and order them into concepts and/

or propositions. The logic of proof is deductive. It begins in the world of abstraction, when we examine the concepts, propositions or theories and evolve a prediction. This process ends in the world of experience when research to test the prediction or claim is designed and executed. In terms of the scientific method, our confidence in a given proposition, model or theory increases to the extent that it is repeatedly tested and not found to be false.

The life of social science is captured by individuals following the logic of discovery and/or the logic of proof over time. On a more macro level, theories (models) are constructed as we accumulate propositions that have been frequently tested. One can juxtapose metatheory with the goals of social science: description, explanation, prediction and control. Description tends to be inductive (part of the logic of discovery) and by far makes up the bulk of research done on disasters and disaster behavior. There is no particular problem with an abundance of descriptive studies. Indeed they sharpen our view of the phenomenon under study, serve to identify new issues for investigation and document changes in previous patterns of behavior. Note that this kind of work is often described as "qualitative" and some claim it reflects—somehow—an alternate epistemology. While it is explained here as a component of social science, it also might be used in some alternative approach to understanding the world, but the burden is upon the user to explain that alternative.

Drabek (1986) has emphasized that disaster researchers have taken few forays into explanation. In social science, explanation is based in deductions from knowledge and usually assembled in the form of models and theories. Describing a phenomenon is a step toward, but by no means the same as, explaining why the phenomenon operates or what factors cause it to operate. In itself, explanation forms the basis for making predictions and forms the knowledge upon which control of phenomena can be undertaken. The protective action decision model (Lindell and Perry, 2004), for example, offers an explanation of individual decision-making that can be used to make predictions about citizen response to disaster warnings or the adoption of protective measures for future disasters. Such theories can also form the basis for designing prevention programs that address mitigation issues as an extension of the concept of control.

Clearly, the growth of disaster research as a legitimate discipline will be contingent upon increasing efforts at assembling our findings into models and theories (explanations) and testing those theories to identify those that accurately explain and predict. In turn this will shape the applied or practitioner side of the field, since accurate explanation and prediction, lead to better control of the negative consequences of disasters. I believe that much of what Cutter and Britton have discussed can only be accomplished with the growth of such theory. And still there is a classification or typology dimension to this discussion. As Quarantelli points out in his concluding chapter, in some "disasters" we have documented and offered rationales for the presence of looting. In others we have documented and offered rationales for the absence of looting. His point is that in the face of such apparent empirical contradiction, we need a system of classifying occasions that enables understanding and meaningful interpretation of such disparities. In this case, he suggests a fundamental distinction between conflict situations and those not involving conflict. There is much nuance in understanding the extent to which classification (reflecting taxonomy) differ from and compliment modeling as paths to explanation that can't be addressed here. Certainly one does not supercede the other necessarily, but given the extensive accumulation of empirical observations that characterize disaster research and the "ordering" power of classification, there is a special appeal to the development of typologies.

MOVING ON WITH DISASTER RESEARCH

Prognostications about the future often look silly in retrospect within a relatively short time. I shall leave predictions for the most part to observers who are senior to me. There are some assumptions and conclusions I would like to share at this point. For me, a primary assumption is that disaster researchers are not homogeneous and not likely to become so. We are geographers, urban planners, sociologists, psychologists, geologists and anyone else who chooses to study the phenomenon. We reside in different types of institutions, on different continents, and have different emphases when we think of mitigation, preparedness, response and recovery. To believe that disaster researchers will speak with one voice on any except the most generic issues is probably more hallucination than imagination. Diversity and difference in opinion and interpretation are important and constructive, especially if there is consensus about scientific method.

By simple deduction from the above, there will continue to be differences in the way we define disasters. I do expect that over time, and as a function of exchanges like those engaged in this volume, the level of consensus will increase, but at the most generic level initially. What are the consequences of the lack of consensus? Certainly the result will not be the destruction of the field. It would be a major setback if the goal was to generate a theory of "disasters" and we were unable to define them. But we are focused upon the specific social behaviors and phenomena that attend disasters, crises, or collective stress situations (or whatever categories interest us). As a metaphor, there is a "germ theory of disease" but, except in a most general way, it does not directly inform the understanding and treatment of particular ailments. Disaster research, particularly descriptive studies, can easily continue in the face of only a little consensus regarding what is meant by a disaster.

As disaster researchers, we can probably continue to very slowly build models and theories of disaster behavior. For this activity however, the absence of consensus on what is a disaster poses significant difficulty. For theory construction that produces viable explanations, there is a need for interpretation that requires a clear vision of disasters. Consequently, without basic consensus on the phenomenon, the field of disaster research will not be able to develop the power to predict and to ameliorate disaster outcomes. What one will see under these conditions is a stagnant field of disaster research that continues to generate interesting but unconnected case studies.

In my opinion, at this point, much will depend upon the appearance and use of typologies. These will allow us to meaningfully arrange (if not integrate) the vast backlog of descriptive studies generated over the years. Typologies will also serve to formulate modeling and theory building efforts more precisely. This will place the field in better stead with public policy makers who define the resources and strategies for disaster management. But how will we know we are moving in this "right" direction? In a sense, there are signs that we are now moving in this direction. It can be found in the work of Barton, Drabek, Kreps and Quarantelli and in Boin's and Dombrowsky's work in this volume, to name just a few. Will we move in a linear fashion toward the development of typologies and other products of theory construction? Of course not. There is no precedent for this path in the physical, social or natural sciences. The first sign that the field is moving in this direction in a serious way will come when researchers themselves routinely classify their research in terms of some typology. Another sign will be the more frequent appearance of theoretical reviews that classify findings in terms of one or another typology. Barton's work or Drabek's 1986 inventory are examples of the latter. Progress will be measured when many typologies exist—some complimentary some competing—and when researchers use them. Ultimately, without regard to the level of consensus on disasters, to move from description to explanation and beyond, disaster researchers will have to increase their collective understanding of social science and metatheory. It is certain that without this road map, it will be difficult to arrive at any consciously chosen destination.

20

A SOCIAL SCIENCE RESEARCH AGENDA FOR THE DISASTERS OF THE 21ST CENTURY: THEORETICAL, METHODOLOGICAL AND EMPIRICAL ISSUES AND THEIR PROFESSIONAL IMPLEMENTATION

E. L. (Henry) Quarantelli

INTRODUCTION

This chapter differs from the previous ones in one major respect. The authors, following the mandate they were given by the editors of this volume, mostly tried to indicate where they agreed and where they disagreed with earlier conceptions of disasters that existed in the literature and then indicated how they thought disasters ought to be conceptualized. As such, the focus was on a relatively delimited although very important matter—how the concept of disaster had been and could be theoretically addressed. The chapter authors did what they were asked to do, discussing the concept of disaster or related terms.

Our goal in this chapter is much broader. We do deal with theoretical issues in disaster studies. We do agree that the theoretical issue of what is a disaster is a significant matter. However, in this chapter we are arguing that improvements in disaster studies requires going considerably beyond only theoretical issues. Whatever theoretical advances are made, they will have to be simultaneously accompanied by major changes in the methodological and research arenas as well as improvements in the professional infrastructure of the field of social science disaster studies. Put another way, our position is that there has to be an across the board improvement in disaster studies. Theoretical advances are necessary, perhaps more than anything else, but are not sufficient to bring about the overall changes we think should occur in the social science studies of disasters.

The authors of the chapters in this volume, as well as those that wrote the two reaction papers were not asked to deal with the broader issues in the larger framework we are using. They were given a more focused goal and can not be criticized for focusing on what they were asked to do. Therefore, we will not evaluate what they wrote. That was a major part of the two reaction chapters (by Dombrowsky and by Stallings), and in a different way in the concluding chapter by Perry. No purpose would be served by our covering again the same grounds.

However, we will use some of what the different authors have written as jumping off points for our own comments. In fact, it was only after reading the previous chapters that it occurred to us that we could build on what was written and suggest a broader framework for students of disasters.

OUR STARTING POINT

Systematic and extensive social science work on disasters started in the very early 1950s. Thus we now have half a century of studies in the area. Much has been learned. How much we now understand can be documented by looking at some recent publications, particularly the series of books emanating from the Second

Assessment of Natural Hazards Research undertaken at the University of Colorado (e.g. Burby 1998; Mileti 1999; Tierney, Lindell and Perry 2001) as well as other writings independent of that effort (e.g., Dynes and Tierney 1994; Hewitt 1997; Turner and Pidgeon 1997; Quarantelli 1998; Godschalk et al. 1999; Alexander 2000; Waugh 2000; Cutter 2001; Hoffman and Oliver-Smith 2002; Rosenthal, Boin and Comfort 2001; Alexander 2002; Nigg and Mileti 2002; Stallings 2002; Boin 2003; Perry and Lindell 2003; Lindell and Perry 2004)). Topics and questions are discussed in these publications that were not in the 1950s and 1960s even on anyone's agenda for the future. By any criteria, the field of disaster studies has accomplished much (an interesting assessment of self progression can be seen in a comparison by Allen Barton of his 1963 publication with a 2003 publication partly set forth in his chapter in this volume).

But in our view, as we move into the 21st Century, we need some major rethinking in the area, if scholars are going to continue to develop new knowledge and understanding of disaster related phenomena. Pioneering work has the advantage that anything that is a research observation contributes to the field, slowly filling in the huge vacuum that always exists when anything has not been previously studied. Not unexpectedly, many such early findings tend to be critiques of previously held but popular notions (e.g. that panic flight or looting behavior is a major characteristic of disasters). However, such an accretion of knowledge by establishing empirical generalizations, eventually hits a point of diminishing returns. Work has to go beyond mere critique. More important, past the pioneering stage, an area advances by generating new theories, models, explanatory schemes, and/or master hypotheses over and beyond empirical generalizations of a descriptive nature. The start of the maturing of a field is characterized by the development of explicit analytical frameworks or what we just called them, namely theories, models, schemes and hypotheses. Some of this currently exists and a few workers in the area have already advanced relevant ideas on these matters, including what has been said in earlier chapters in this volume by authors such as Barton,

Dombrowsky and Perry. But in the field as a whole this work has barely started.

To move in such a direction requires addressing old questions that have not yet been adequately answered or posing new questions not yet explored. As has been said by others as well as us, major scientific advances require some fundamental rethinking of how to proceed, not just simply doing more traditional studies. If what the field knows on the basis of studies is to markedly increase, we must think through what we could do that is different in fundamental ways from what disaster scholars have done and are currently doing. New knowledge requires new or at least different questions or issues addressed up to now.

This paper poses 20 questions or issues that if adequately dealt with, could get the field moving intellectually in the ways we have just mentioned. In no way are we advancing a completely new work agenda for the next 50 years. However, we do ask questions and indicate issues that if dealt with, would force disaster studies to be different in major ways than it is for the most part from how they are currently conducted.

For purposes of presentation we ask separate questions about the theoretical, methodological, and research-empirical issues, as well as what might be needed professionally to implement what could be done (or in terms of the last idea, putting in place a better professional structure or organization than currently exists). As already noted, there already have been some slight movements on some of these matters. Not all disaster students are stuck in the last century. However, our position is that advances along all four dimensions are necessary if the first half of the 21st Century is to match the outcomes and products of the first 50 years of pioneering work.

OUR INTENDED AUDIENCE

We are not writing for everyone. This paper is not directed at everyone interested in the disaster area. Our intended audience is primarily scholars in the area. As we have written extensively elsewhere the goals and procedures of researchers and research users (i.e., practitioners) are distinctively different (Quarantelli 1993b). Actually, a failure to understand this is currently subverting some of the basic work in the area. It is not that applied questions are meaningless. They are not. However, asking and even answering them can do very little to advance basic knowledge and understanding per se of disaster phenomena. As far as we can see, practical concerns have never been the primary engines for scientific advances in any area. But there are mixed opinion on this (see Rossi 1980). Also very good observations can be made by operational officials (as an example see the appendices in Roberts 1994). However, in our view, despite exceptions that might be noted, practitioners or users of research seldom ask basic questions or produce work of scientific value. So why should disaster studies be different? There is a need for good social engineering, but let us not confuse it with social science.

In our widely ignored Presidential address (Quarantelli 1987) to the International Research Committee on Disasters during the World Congress of Sociology in 1986, we paraphrased Benjamin Franklin, who said we needed more astronomers—or to change the metaphor—social science students to study the skies, the stars, the galaxies and the universes of disasters, rather than more carpenters helping to build better lifeboats for floods, better buildings for earthquakes, or better shelters for radiation fallouts. We need more disaster scholars to look up and dream, and not look down and do. We need more theory and abstract thinking and less mucking around in practical matters and concrete details. The heart of any scientific activity is basic knowledge and curiosity driven, and is not concerned with immediate outcomes or products. (However, Britton in his chapter earlier in this book makes a case that the latter may not be completely unimportant).

Our call for new ideas is applicable to all the social sciences. However, we have been trained as a sociologist and we wear sociological glasses in looking at the world. This will be reflected in our remarks. Along many lines, this is a sociological paper for sociologists doing sociological research. In our view, the

Durkheimian position is the raison d'etre for sociology. That is, we are to identify and explain social facts by other social facts. Our view is that at least sociologists working in the disaster area should take this disciplinary principle quite seriously. After all, we have been shown the light, and do not have the excuse of those living in intellectual darkness. We will do better disaster studies by being better sociologists.

Taking this position is neither an instance of nor an argument for sociological imperialism in scientific work on disasters. We hope to see and would welcome other scholars from anthropology, geography, economics, political science and psychology bringing their own disciplinary perspectives to bear on the questions and issues we discuss. In fact, it might be a very interesting exercise to see the similarities and differences in what representatives of other social science disciplines would set forth for a disaster work agenda for the 21st Century. Cutter in her chapter earlier in this volume does seem to imply that such a path might be worthwhile following.

From our perspective, in a way we are arguing that sociologists in the disaster area should be doing more and better sociological work than they as a whole have done so far. Unfortunately, a great deal of what sociologists (including us) do in the disaster area is not sociology at all—in fact, it is sometimes very difficult to identify the work in any disciplinary terms since it lacks, at least explicitly, any of the assumptions, models, theories, hypotheses, concepts, linkages to the non-disaster literature, etc. that is the corpus of present day sociology or any other social science. Some of it is good journalism, some is excellent social history, some is fine descriptive inventorying—all worthy endeavors, more of which are desirable. But such work is not sociology in intent, execution or end result even though we use the term "sociological" in a broad way as some of our later examples will exemplify. As such, if you take sociology seriously as a scientific enterprise, this should bother you if you are a sociologist (as it seems to bother Dombrowsky in his reaction paper earlier in the volume).

Almost all of the 20 questions and issues that we discuss challenge many current assumptions and traditional ways of doing work on disasters. In some instances we explicitly indicate our own specific views or position about the matter discussed; in short, we sometime advocate taking a particular direction. That some of what we advocate is very controversial should go without saying. If this is seen as deliberate provocation, that may not be incorrect. In other instances, our presentation is primarily an exposition about a particular question or issue, with no indication of how we think the matter ought to be dealt with in the future. However, whether or not an "answer" is proposed, in all cases the hope is that something worthwhile is being presented for thoughtful consideration by disaster scholars.

THEORETICAL ISSUES

As said at the start of this chapter, theoretical issues were addressed by all the earlier chapter writers in this book. Some of the questions below were addressed here and there by these authors. But most were not, and we have problems with some of the answers or ideas presented. As such under theoretical issues we discuss five things which for purposes of exposition we initially set forth in question terms.

They are: 1.How much conceptual clarity about the concept of disaster is needed? 2. If disasters are viewed as inherently social phenomena, what are the implications of taking that position? 3. What are the advantages of decoupling the concept of disaster from its long time linkage to the concept of hazard? 4. To what extent should the larger social context be taken into account in thinking about disasters? 5. What unused theoretical models and frameworks might be particularly appropriate for disaster research?

How Much Conceptual Clarity is Needed?

There is a lack of conceptual clarity in the disaster area (see Quarantelli 1998; Kelly 2000). As some of you probably know, we have long argued that unless we get a better conceptual grasp of "disasters", there are going to continue to be serious problems in our data gathering and analysis. Thus, for example, much of the disagreement on the mental health effects of disasters (see Goode 2003 and Lee 2003) stems from different conceptions of "disasters" that various parties to the argument take. It has far less to do with empirical findings per se. Thus, the more there is the inclusion of conflictive types of crisis occasions in an analysis—such as war and terrorism—the more heterogeneous the social occasions looked at, the more likely negative consequences will be found. The larger and the more differentiated the social net used—and a concept in many ways is a word net—the greater the certainty that more non-positive features will be found. We say this to highlight the point that definitional and conceptual issues are not side matters, but go to the very heart of what we will find in our studies.

> Let us state what Robert Merton, a long time ago, wrote concepts constitute the definitions (or prescriptions) of what is to be observed; they are the variables between which empirical relationships are to be sought . . . it is . . . one function of conceptual clarification to make explicit the character of the data subsumed under a given concept . . . our conceptual language tends to fix our perceptions and, derivatively, our thought and behavior.

He then notes that:

> The concept defines the situation, and the research worker responds accordingly . . . conceptual clarification . . . makes clear just what the research worker is doing when he deals with conceptualized data. He draws different consequences for empirical research as his conceptual apparatus changes (1945: 465-467).

As Pittman, still another sociologist has written: "concepts are categories that help to establish the origins and perimeters of activity. At best they can mirror only part of reality. They abstract and encase representative selections from phenomena, help to organize the frame of reference, and represent description". (1960:34). The concepts used are especially crucial for new scientific understandings.

As Huff wrote three decades ago: "the history of natural science . . . repeatedly shows the central role played by concept formation. He then goes on to say that: "From this perspective, theoretical innovations is heavily indebted to the postulating or "conjecturing" of novel relationships between "old fact" and "new entities". Or:" stated differently, innovation is the result of discovering new ways to conceptually organize previously known but puzzling and inexplicable phenomena" (1973: 261).

Much could be said here. For example, definitions and concepts are not matters of empirical determination. Both terms have to be independently identified apart from whatever conditions are seen as generating whatever the phenomena are. Similarly, effects or consequences of whatever the definition or concept encompasses, have to be separated out or otherwise the outcome are true by definition or concept. Thus, in a volume on children and disaster, many of the formulations are such that disasters can only exist if there are widespread negative effects. This is so by definition (see Saylor 1993). Conceptually we need to keep independent in our thinking the conditions for something from the characteristics of that something, from the consequences of such characteristics. These three aspects are often badly intermingled in much current disaster research, and usually unrecognized by the researchers involved. However, of all the possible conceptual issues let us single out three.

First, in our professional view we often are trying to use only one concept, that is, the label of disaster to attempt to capture too much. For instance, elsewhere we have suggested conceptualizing "disasters" and "catastrophes" as two different although related phenomena since there are both qualitative and quantitative behavioral differences in the references of the two terms. At least four different dimensions are involved. Let us illustrate this. In a catastrophe, most/all of the total residential community is impacted, thus making it impossible for the homeless to go to friends and relatives who in a similar situation. Likewise, most of the facilities and operational bases of emergency organizations are themselves impacted. Also, local officials are unable to undertake their usual work roles not only in the crisis period, but also into the recovery period. Finally, most of the everyday community functions are sharply and simultaneously interrupted across-the-board. In disasters, these four features do not clearly appear. In the United States, it was the presence of these characteristics that distinguished what appeared in Hurricane Andrew from other hurricane impacts, and in Japan what separated out the Great Hanshin earthquake (popularly called the Kobe quake) from most other earthquakes in that country. The two just named would best be viewed as catastrophes, the others as disasters.

If our view is correct, we should stop trying to squeeze relatively heterogeneous phenomena under one label. That would improve not only our theoretical understanding of disaster phenomena, but create knowledge useful for planning and managing purposes. As a practical example, if victims cannot go to friends and relatives in a catastrophe as they typically do in a disaster, there are different operational implications for emergency or crisis managers. At a more theoretical level, Barton in his earlier chapter clearly differentiates numerous subtypes of his more generic concept, collective stress situations.

Second, we should question why we in the area mostly conceptualize disasters as primarily focused occasions, both in terms of time and space (in chronological and geographic terms). Barton in his chapter in this volume clearly is an exception. Even Jigyasu who eventually proposes a philosophical view of time and space, starts his chapter with the notions of chronological time and geographic space. Many of the other chapter authors as do most disaster scholars implicitly take or assume the traditional viewpoint.

But a different perspective can be taken. We grant that some of us are uneasy in thinking of famines and droughts as disasters. Yet since these happenings do not occur in traditional form in developed societies, many of us can blithely ignore them in our theoretical musings, justified to an extent because these phenomena are not in the sights of our research sites. However, it is no accident that at meetings of the World Congress of Sociology there is always a formal group, called the Famine and Society Working Group which has an existence independent of the International Research Committee on Disasters (and there is almost no overlap of any kind between the two groups of researchers involved; for instance, it is our impression that we are the only person that is a member of both groups!). Maybe the separation of the two groups may have to do that those interested in "famines" come from developing countries that have to deal with that phenomena. But clearly the two groups of disaster scholars are using a different time/space framework.

However, the developing country base does not explain why we are not studying the AIDS epidemic. Not one as far as we know has ventured into that area, although an occasional scholar is willing to allude to the Black Death as a well-known historical "disaster" (a happening very spread out over a continent and lasting over decades). This begs the question of what is the theoretical justification for the exclusion of AIDS. To be certain, there is always a danger in our area of labeling all negative social and collective negative happenings as "disasters", an equation which enlarges the concept to almost a meaningless and useless one. Personally, we are inclined to exclude from the concept of "disaster" all very diffused events, including traditional droughts and famines and certain kinds of epidemics. We would do this because in our view it is best to think of the concept of disaster as an occasion involving an immediate crisis or emergency. Using that kind of thinking in some of our other writings, we have also tried to distinguish ecological problems from disasters (Quarantelli 1995b).

However, leaving this last distinction aside, we think there is considerable murkiness in how we deal with diffuse situations like those that have just been mentioned. It leads to our odd intellectual ignoring of such phenomena as famines. And we do ignore them. Very seldom is the existing literature on famine or drought used or cited by self-defined disaster researchers. Actually it would be difficult to use, because some research findings from famines/

droughts are inconsistent with a number of empirical generalizations from the "disaster" area that presumably applicable to all such occasions. In part this is because, as we see it, famines can be meaningfully conceptualized as "social problems" (illustrated in the 1987 discussion of McCann about the vulnerability to famine of northeastern Ethiopia, which has one of Africa's most efficient and traditional agricultural systems) in ways that distinguish them from what we would prefer to call "disasters". At any rate, far more systematic work needs to be one on this whole matter of inclusion or exclusion of diffuse happenings from the category of disaster.

Third, and last, there is the perennial issue or problem of whether or not to include conflict situations such as "disasters" (see Stallings 1988). This matter has been even more pushed to the forefront by 9/11. Was what happened at the World Trade Center as a result of the terrorist attack, conceptually a "disaster"? (Fischer 2003). Anyone who does not seriously asked that question clearly has not thought through very well what the core of a disaster is. The same is true of the Oklahoma City bombing. There is a very complicated issue here. Certainly many scholars including Cutter in her remarks in her chapter earlier in the volume seem to think that 9/11 was a benchmark historical happening with major consequences for how researchers will have to think about crises, disasters, etc. Alexander in his chapter also alludes to the importance of the attack on the World Trade Center as possibly affecting how we will subsequently think of disasters.

About a decade ago we published a review article that compared behavior in natural/technological disasters and behavior in riots and civil disturbances in the United States (Quarantelli 1993a). We compared behavior at the individual, organizational and community levels in the preimpact, impact, and postimpact stages of both kinds of occasions. Overall, our conclusion was that while there were some behavioral similarities (especially at the organizational level) there were far more differences, some of a rather marked nature. For example, we noted that when disasters occur, individuals actively react and in a mostly prosocial mode; there is far more variability in riots with antisocial behavior frequently surfacing. Also, while the experience of a disaster is a memorable one, and there are differential sort run effects, there does not appear to be too many long lasting behavioral consequences among survivors; riots seem to leave more residues. Similarly, there is somewhat more likelihood for organizational changes after riots than after disasters. At the community level, disasters involve massive convergence behavior by people and groups; this is far less true of riots. While there are some selective longer run outcomes and changes in communities impacted by crises, the impact is less in typical disasters than riots.

Thus, our comparative summary of a range of empirical data supports conceptualizing at least major conflict situations in a different way than disasters. However, we do not think this issue in the long run is primarily a matter of empirical determination. The very analysis we undertook in part found differences from the very way we defined and differentiated disasters and riots. In our view, a position of some kind on the matter of theoretical exclusion and inclusion of conflict situations is better based on the basic imagery one has of what processes hold social systems together. Of course in sociology and vastly oversimplifying, there has been the functional point of view that mostly holds that systems are held together by commonly shared values and norms, and then there is the Marxist point of view that conflict is what binds a social system. Professionally, we would be willing to take a third position by borrowing from the "garbage can" model of organizations. This argues that organizations (and in our view, societies) instead of having clear and consistent goals and values operate instead from a variety of inconsistent and ill-defined preferences. Different social entities at different social levels have different and incompatible views at different times; preferences may not be known until after choices are made. In addition, different parts of the system do not know what others are doing; what happened in the past and why it happened is not clear, and the connections between the actions taken and the consequences of such actions are obscure (see March and Olson 1986).

Our overall point here is that it is possible to arrive at drastically different conclusions about whether consensus occasions and conflict situations should be treated within the same definitional or conceptual category. Much depends on the scholar's more basic assumptions about what processes serve to integrate social systems at the community/organizational levels. Since this an unresolved question in sociology and in political science generally, it is also probably irresolvable in the particular area of disaster studies. Yet we should be aware of our starting points and be consistent in our approach. For example, we are puzzled why students of disaster who include conflict situations as part of the disaster arena, for the most part, do not study civil disturbances, or why they do not take advantage of the rather substantial body of theoretical and empirical literature in the sociological specialization of collective behavior that deals with crowds and riots (e.g., Goode 1992; Curtis and Aguirre 1993; Marx and McAdam 1994; Melucci 1996; Reshaur 1998; Turner 2000). Of course, from our perspective, as someone familiar with the collective behavior literature, we think that they would find that much which is empirically known about crowds and riots would be difficult to square with what is known about behavior in natural and technological disaster occasions. For example, there are at least four major behavioral differences between looting in disasters and in riots. (Elsewhere, we have noted also the marked behavioral contrast in the delivery of emergency medical services in disaster and riots, see Quarantelli 1993a)

It would be difficult to deny that there is a substantial lack of consensus among scholars about the concept of disaster. There clearly are major differences about how to think about disasters among all the authors of chapters earlier in this volume. For example, in this volume, Stallings using a traditional positivistic orientation, and Jigyasu with an almost mystically approach—at least from a Western cultural perspective—appear to be almost in different intellectual worlds. Nevertheless, there are a few central ideas about the referent of the term which seem to be at least broadly shared at an implicit level. We thus turn to a discussion why the implications of viewing the concept of disaster as having a basic social nature is not always followed through in thinking and behaving.

Implications Of The View That Disasters Are Social Phenomena.

At one level, we would say the implicit basic paradigm in the disaster area is acceptable (although not unchallengeable). The current paradigm involves a number of interrelated notions, but two of the more fundamental ones are that: (1) disasters are inherently social phenomena, and (2) that the source of disasters is rooted in the social structure or social system.

Nevertheless, while most scholars would generally accept these notions, we do not seem to always take them as seriously as we should. For example, if we did with respect to the first, we would see all processes associated with disaster occasions as also inherently social. Thus, instead of talking about chronological time and geographic space (as mentioned in our earlier discussion), we should use the concepts of social time and social space in looking at the temporal and spatial aspects of disasters. We suggest our understanding, for example, of response to warnings and emergency time protective behavior as well as informal search and rescue activities would be considerably enhanced if we saw them in the framework of social time and social space. Anyone interested in these notions can look at the ideas advanced more than a half century ago by Sorokin and Merton, and more recently the work, both theoretical and empirical, done by sociologists and social psychologists on the topic (see Zerubavel 1981; McGrath and Kelley 1986; McGrath 1988; Young and Schuller 1988; Pronovost-Giles 1989; Baker 1993; Flaherty 1993; Adam 1995; Levine 1997; Bluedorn 2002; Crow and Heath 2002; Zerubavel 2003). There is also a major journal dealing with social space, namely, *Space and Culture; International Journal of Social Spaces*. It is also perhaps not amiss to note that dealing with social space and time is increasingly spreading in other areas of social science research (e.g., there was a June 2003 special issue of *Mobilization*—the specialty journal for social movement and collective behavior papers—with the title of "Special Issue: Space, Place and Contentious Politics).

As an instance of what we might learn from this new perspective, there is a sociological analysis that suggests nighttime life and work has characteristics also found in frontier life, that is, social space and time at night is similar to what exists in a frontier type community with the according manifestations of certain kinds of behavior. Actually the frontier notion that implies a degree of unstructuredness and much informal emergence is not a bad metaphor to apply to the crisis period of disasters. The general point of our example is that by using the concepts of social time and of social space we will be forced to think of disaster phenomena in somewhat different ways than we see them when using chronological time and geographical space.

As a somewhat related kind of example, Forrest (1993) used sociology of time framework to explore how six coastal and inland communities acknowledged the first and second anniversary of Hurricane Hugo. He reports on how past events surrounding the disaster were reconstructed to have meaning and utility for the present. Our analyses of disaster recovery would be better informed if we took this general notion that it is not the passing of chronological time or the placement in geographic space that is crucial in the process, but that of social time and social space.

With respect to the second point, that disasters are rooted in the social structure, it is necessary to note that what we "really" mean is that disasters are consequences of social change since structure is simply change analytically frozen by a scholar at a particular point in time. The notion of disasters as being inherently related to social change goes as far back as one of the very earliest theoretical articles on disasters ever written, the paper by Carr (1932). This is a work known by name to a fair number of disaster researchers but as far as we can tell has been unread by almost everyone (except for a few European disaster scholars with theoretical interests such as Dombrowsky 1995 and Gilbert 1995).

More important, it is of interest that most students of disasters in developing countries, these days almost automatically link disasters to the development process. The link to social change in that context is "obvious," but the great majority of students of disasters come from developed countries so it is not that apparent to them (instead some try to make a link to "social problems that is more "obvious" in their social systems). If disasters are rooted in the social change processes of developing countries, is it not reasonable to assume they are also similarly embedded in the social dynamics of developed societies? We would urge all our colleagues interested in theoretical aspects of disasters to answer that question.

Our overall point is that if we start out with a theoretical assumption that disasters are inherently rooted in social change, we will be far better able to explain, for instance, the sources and loci of resistances to disaster mitigation measures, for instance, instead of looking at the psychological makeup or attitudes of realtors, community planners or policy makers. The social dynamics and processes of communities and societies are where we should seek answers. Unfortunately, the few who have ventured down this path, have sometime tended to reify social structure, a frequent but badly misleading approach.

At a more general and futuristic level, our feeling is that if we press the current paradigm to its fullest, we will be forced to a worthwhile paradigmatic shift. What this will involve is not totally clear to us at present. However, in earlier writings we suggested the value of incorporating into our view of disasters, the notions of genotype and phenotype as developed in the biological sciences (Quarantelli 1987). Essentially making this distinction argues that less obvious or visible characteristics are far more important than surface features. Our prediction is that our eventual new paradigm will involve far more genotypical rather than the phenotypical features we now almost exclusively use.

One way of proceeding in that direction is to decouple the concept of disaster from the concept of hazard. A focus on the former, in our view, forces a focus on more intangible aspects than the former. Thus will require an in depth discussion to which we now move.

Decoupling Disasters From Hazards

In our view, there should be a very explicit focus on disasters rather than hazards, along with the implications of such an orientation being taken seriously. Our suggestion might seem to involve a quibble about which of two words to use. But our view is that "what's in a name? to paraphrase Shakespeare, actually makes important assumptions about the phenomena being labeled. Our position is that the word which is used indicates the strategic approach which should be used, and as such is a very crucial assumption and starting point. From our perspective, the prime focus should be on disasters not hazards. It is no accident that the UN Decade, after initially being labeled "for hazard reduction" was eventually changed to "for disaster reduction." Also, the very recently formed Congress Directorate holding its first meeting in 2001 entitled it the 1st World Congress on Disaster Reduction. A focus on disaster calls attention to the social nature of such happenings; a focus on hazards tends to emphasize physical and natural phenomena. With rare exceptions little can be done about the latter; much can be done about the former. What has to be lessened or at least reduced are the negative social happenings which are called disasters.

A focus on hazards also often leads to treating disasters as *epiphenomena*. This is a philosophical notion. In terms of what we are discussing, this is the idea that disasters are secondary to or a by-product of other more important phenomena, in our context, this being hazards. Or put another way, in dictionary terms, a disaster is "a phenomenon which is a mere accompaniment of some effect, but can not itself be considered as either cause or effect" (Funk and Wagnall's College Standard Dictionary) because it is secondary to a hazard. In our view, this is a poor way of visualizing disasters.

In fact, the imagery of hazards as leading to disasters is a very misleading one. To be sure, a hazard may at times be involved. However, the hazard, to the extent there is one (they are very difficult to see in famines, blizzards, many technological disasters, space shuttle explosions, acts of terrorism such as in 9/11) is one factor at best, and not necessarily the most important one. Studies which show, for example, that earthquakes of roughly the same magnitude are accompanied by drastically different negative social effects (as illustrated by comparison of the Armenian and Loma Prieta earthquakes where the fatalities and the destruction in the latter were but a small fraction of those in the former happening), are implicitly making the same point. A hazard might have been involved but it was not the most important elements in the disasters that occurred.

This general point is consistent with the view of social science scholars that all disasters are primarily the result of human actions. Actually this view precedes those disciplines. Thus, A. C. Bradley nearly a hundred years ago wrote: "No amount of calamity which merely befell a man, descending from the clouds like lightning, or stealing from the darkness like pestilence could alone provide the substance of [this] story . . . the calamities . . . do not simply happen, nor are they sent: they proceed mainly from actions, and those the actions of men" (1906: 11 cited in Hewitt 1997: ii)

A disaster is not a physical happening. As said earlier, it is a social occasion. Thus, it is a misnomer to talk about "natural" disasters as if they could exist outside of the actions and decisions of human beings and their societies (interestingly this is always recognized in the case of technological disasters). For instance, floods, earthquakes, and other so-called "natural" disaster agents have social consequences *only* because of the activities of involved communities, before, during and after the impact of a disaster. Allowing high-density population concentrations in flood plains, having poor or unenforced earthquake building codes for structures, permitting housing on volcanic slopes, providing inadequate information or warnings about tsunamis, for example, are far more important than the disaster agent itself in creating the casualties, property and economic losses, psychological stresses, and disruptions of everyday routines that are the essence of disasters. The character of past, present and future disastrous occasions stem from social factors (Quarantelli 1999c). That is the image that we should keep in the forefront of our thinking about disaster planning and managing.

In one sense, the recent shift in much of the literature from a primary focus on hazards to one on vulnerability is a step in the right direction (and is explicitly advocated by Cutter in her chapter earlier in this book). Mary Anderson in discussing the historical shift in how the understanding of vulnerability to disaster has shifted and enlarged notes the following. She indicates that "early disaster studies identified natural hazards as the cause of vulnerability" (1995: 43). From another perspective we can say that this was the early time period when disasters and hazards were more or less treated as the same phenomena. As a current example, Degg, a geographer, says "a natural disaster is the actual experiencing of loss due to the occurrence of natural, but hazardous process" (1992: 199).

The next stage according to Anderson is when there was a focus on "costs as cause. Economists assess how much vulnerability reduction is rational" (1995: 44). This again from a different perspective is when researchers recognized that losses could not be seen as simply being of an economic nature. For understanding there was a need to take other variables into account. According to Anderson, the third stage is when there was recognition that disasters had differential impact on populations who live in hazard-prone areas. There was an attempt to account for how "loss of life, health and property varies widely among people who experience the same disaster and among people who experience disasters of the same size and scope at different times and in different parts of the world" (1995: 45). The conclusion was that more than just hazard and exposure needed to be considered in any accurate assessment of vulnerability. From another perspective, this is saying that the different lifestyles of impacted populations, especially at the lower socioeconomic levels, made a difference in the negative effects that appear in disasters. In short, human beings are responsible for vulnerability.

In our view, this kind of thinking is definitely on the right track. However, it does not take the final step which we think is necessary. Others also sometime hesitate to take this additional step. This is true in the following quotation which while it indicates the direction which we think should be taken in the second step, does not take the final step but regresses back to a limited vulnerability argument. "Most flood-related literature analyzes floods as natural disasters. In contrast the social sciences consider floods as a social category. Neither concept is broad enough to encompass the vast complexity of the issue. Floods are actually a link between society and nature, in the same way that natural resources and environmental problems are" (Sejenovich and Mendoza 2000: 24).

From our perspective, the next necessary step is to argue, as expressed for some time now by different disaster researchers and theorists that disasters stem from the very nature of social systems themselves. Disasters in this framework are overt manifestations of latent societal vulnerabilities, basically of weaknesses in social structures or social systems. The source or origins of disasters are in the very system in which they appear. They should not be seen as the result of an external force from outside impacting the social system. Likewise, the appearance of a disaster goes beyond the effects of a hazard on different lifestyles among victims. Rather a disaster is rooted in the weaknesses of a social system that manifest themselves depending on the dynamics of that system.

In considering disasters, one should start with the social systems involved instead of looking at the victims, the current traditional approach. One of the advantages of such a stance is that forecasts about possible disasters can be made ahead of time. There is no need to wait for a disaster to happen, to see what might be the casualties and losses. One of the few who indirectly seems to recognize this is Albala-Bertrand (1993:204) who observes that the effects of disasters are to be sought not in casualties and losses, but in how much the disaster reflects a damaging of ongoing social processes, that is, the pre-disaster structure and dynamics of the social system involved.

In a parallel fashion, but looking at lower social levels and focusing more on risks rather than disasters, Perrow argues that accidents in nuclear plants which have the potential to become disaster are not the result of human errors by the builders or the operators of the plant, or because of mechanical errors or the plant design. Thus, with respect to the Three Mile Island disaster, he says: "The cause of the accident is to be found in the complexity of the system. That is, each of the failures—design, equipment, operators, procedures, environment—was trivial by itself... it is the *interaction* of the multiple failures that explain the accident" (1984: 7)

Equally as important, Perrow sees accidents as normal in the organizations that run nuclear power plants, space missions, nuclear weapons systems, recombinant DNA production, ships carrying highly toxic or explosive cargoes, genetic engineering, chemical plants, or any other high-risk technology because: "If interactive complexity and tight coupling-system characteristics—inevitably will produce an accident, I believe we are justified in calling it a *normal accident* or a *system accident.* The odd term *normal accident* is meant to signal that given the system characteristics multiple and unexpected interactions of failures are inevitable... System accidents are uncommon, even rare; yet this is not all that reassuring, if they can produce catastrophes"(1984:100).

Our own view is that disasters are similar in that they latently exist in the larger social systems, and are the result of a convergence of a variety of social factors none of whom might be very important in themselves.

To emphasize disasters is to put the focus on the social nature of the phenomena. Disasters are when all is said and done, social happenings. Their origins, their manifestations, and their consequences are all basically social. In fact, disasters can occur independent of the impact of any physical hazard. They can happen just from rumors of a possible threat or a possible but never a realized threat. For example, in late 1999 there was a news story that:

> For months scientists have been predicting devastating volcanic eruptions in Ecuador prompting a series of evacuations and school closings that have disrupted life for hundreds of thousands of families here in the capital and in other parts of the country... while there have been some relatively minor eruptions, no cataclysmic event has yet taken

place . . . predictions of an imminent eruption have prompted officials to close 600 public land private schools in and around the city three times over the last two months, each time for several days, putting 320,000 students behind in classes . . . [in] the latest episode, officials said schools and the capital's airport would close for at least six days . . . The forced evacuation was an economic disaster for Banos, which makes much of its income from tourism (Ecuadoreans 1999:5)

Also, some disasters, such as famines and many computer system breakdowns have no identifiable, originating agent. More generally, disasters cannot be identified in terms of any geophysical, hydrological or atmospheric aspect. An earthquake is simply a physical happening, a movement of land. According to one report, there are more than 3,000 such perceptible happenings every year; but only 7-11 of them involve significant loss of life (*Guidelines* 1994: 32). If there are no negative social consequences, there is no disaster. We see disasters only in the unwanted behaviors of persons and groups. As Albala-Bertrand (1993: 10) observes, it may be a truism, but without people there can be no disaster.

Focusing on disasters does not mean that it is not worthwhile studying hazards (but even geographers with their traditional focus have increasingly recognized that more and more in the discipline have shifted to a "disaster" view rather than a "hazards" (White, Kates and Burton 2001). It should go without saying that there are many good theoretical and practical reasons for such research. But much of what goes under "disaster" research, planning, policy or even thinking, is really hazards research, planning, policy or thinking. As an example, studies of earthquakes are worthwhile. But the large bulk of it should not be confused with research on disasters that are associated with earthquakes. Sometimes even a conference or workshop that is labeled as one on disasters when looked at in detail will show that it is really about hazards. In essence, such a focus misses the essentially social nature of disasters.

Also, there are very important questions and issues which are purely social in nature and have no relationship to any kind of hazard. For example, the cooperation and cooperative interaction of multiple groups or organizations is not only important but crucial for decision making, the setting of policies, the carrying out of programs, and the implementation of specific measures in all phases of the planning and managing cycle, that is, in mitigation, preparedness, response and recovery. The study and understanding of such key interorganizational relationships require a social science approach and a basic assumption that disasters are fundamentally social phenomena.

It should be noted that the idea of stressing "disasters" rather than "hazards" is also starting to spread among emergency and disaster managers themselves. An Australian official, Buckle—author of an earlier chapter in this volume—but writing from the perspective of the State Emergency Recovery Unit in Victoria very recently said:

> Governments, disaster management agencies and the community are increasingly accepting that the proper focus of disaster management is not the hazard agent in itself . . . but rather the community and the consequences for individuals, groups and communities. Successful application of this approach requires a better understanding of the resilience and vulnerabilities of various levels of human systems and social activity (Buckle 2003: 110)

See also Buckle, Marsh and Smale 2002; Gabriel 2002, who reemphasize that the focus is shifting more and more to a focus on the community and away from a hazard management paradigm to one on management per se. The result is necessarily a concern with social factors rather than the physical characteristics of a hazard. Said in different words but saying somewhat the same thing is a statement from a British writer:

> There appears to be a very significant resistance to the analysis of socio-economic factors in disasters, and their socio-economic causes. Instead the scientific and policy emphasis,

> measured by spending, is on the "natural" causes of disasters . . . Why is there such reluctance to examine socio-economic causes of disasters, and to understand them in relation to "normal" everyday life? (Cannon 2001:

Increasingly, as another researcher originally from New Zealand noted, more and more the emphasis has come to be on "management" rather than "emergency" (Britton 2001:1). This comment of course is from Britton, who also elaborates on his earlier statement in his chapter in this volume. From our perspective this means there has to be more attention paid to disasters than hazards.

There are also other positive effects from emphasizing disasters rather than hazards. There are certain implications in moving to primarily focusing on disasters. In particular, such a focus calls for taking into account even broader social aspects of disasters. We now turn to this issue.

Failure To Take The Larger Social Context Into Account

The world is currently undergoing a massive transformation in its social life. This has been well described in summary statements by such sociologists as Smelser (1991a) and Tiryakian (1994) and in a somewhat different way on a global scale, by Omen (1995), in his Presidential Address to the World Congress of Sociology. Massive social changes are happening in the political, economic, familial, cultural, educational and scientific areas everywhere in the world, developing as well as developed countries. As examples, we can note the new family and household patterns that are emerging, the basic alterations occurring in the role and status of women, the move almost everywhere to a market type economy to produce goods and distribute services, the spread of at least nominal democratic patterns of government, the growing dominance of nontraditional artistic and musical forms as well as a globalization of popular culture, the escalating employment of computers and related means for training and educating people, and the growing diffusion and expanding use of applied social science to many areas of life.

We mention these massive transformations, because as far as we can see few in the disaster area are incorporating them into their research designs. Interestingly, a majority of the authors in this volume *do* note the major changes going on in the contemporary world with Boin in his chapter in this volume being perhaps the most explicit about this matter. Despite the fact that earlier chapter writers do pay attention to social change, they are atypical. The general lack of attention by most disaster scholars is rather odd. Among other things, clearly these changes will transform the numbers and kinds of disasters that will occur and the nature of the disaster planning and managing necessary in the future (Quarantelli 1994a). Among other authors in this volume, Denis Smith exemplifies in his chapter the idea that the very nature of disasters are changing as a result of the larger social changes the world is undergoing.

In part, this neglect of the larger social setting reflects the generally ahistorical approach dominant in disaster research since its beginnings. To be sure, this again this partly reflects more general sociology. While there has always been a minority point of view around, it is only relatively recently that there has been increasing acceptance as Fischer recently wrote:

> Sociology, like biology and geology, is a historical science. Specific historical conditions and events, as well as lawful processes, determine current life ways. Sociologists of American society ought, therefore, to know American social history; too often, we do not. But there is help. Within the last three decades or so, historians have amassed a bounty of studies on American society, culture, and behavior. Focusing upon the everyday life of the "masses' instead of the dramas of the elite, this "new history" is informed by sociologists' questions and methods. So much and such diverse research has appeared that leading practitioners now call for a synthesis (1994: 226).

The same general notion is set forth in a statement in 1994 by then current President of the International Sociological Association, Immanuel Wallerstein. He quotes from Durham who in the very first issue of the *Annals of Sociology* looked forward to an inevitable merger of sociology and history into a single discipline. This was because:

> as soon as history compares, it becomes indistinguishable from sociology [and] as long as the sociologist is a stranger who intrudes in the domain of the historian in order to help himself, so to speak, to the data that interest him, he will never do much more than skim the surface rather superficially . . . It is virtually inevitable that the sociologist will not pay attention to, or will consider as disturbing, the data most worth noticing.

Wallerstein concludes: "I personally agree with Durham. I cannot imagine that any sociological analysis is valid without placing the data fully within their historical context" (1995). Dombrowsky in his reaction paper in this volume seems to take the same position.

If we take all of this seriously, does it not suggest some different theoretical studies than are now being undertaken? For example, if market driven economics has or is moving to the fore everywhere, what is the implication for the disaster area of such a trend? Even confining ourselves to the United States, we would suggest that, for instance, the recent emphasis on disaster mitigation by FEMA probably reflects the macro level economic orientation that the last three national administrations have taken. Yet who in the disaster area is doing such macro level studies? (For a speculative essay on market forces and disasters see an article by a non-disaster specialist, Horwich 1990). Whether there will be empirical support or not for our specific example, our general point is that we need to take the larger social context into account especially since it is a very dynamic one.

Let us note in what way the neglect of the larger framework of social change actually underlines the assumption that disasters are socially dysfunctional. Belief in the "badness" of disasters is very widespread. A common sense notion, it is widely shared among very many disaster researchers. In fact, as said earlier, some definitions of disasters characterize a disaster primarily in negative terms and much of the mental health literature on disasters including that used by many sociologists implicitly. The American Psychiatric Association definition of a traumatic event, which includes disasters, is that is one that is outside the range of usual human experience and that would be markedly distressing to almost any one. We think that inhabitants of many areas of Bangladesh would find the first phrase interesting; we probably badly underestimate how many of our concepts and ideas in the disaster area are not fully reflective of the full range of human experiences around the world. The second phrase seems to include a prejudgment instead of making the statement a matter of empirical determination.

In our view this implicit assumption about "badness" is also one factor that leads some scholars to view disasters as some kind of social problem; even in the social constructionist approach to social problems, the perceived "badness" of the phenomena by claim makers is a crucial element (see Schneider 1985; Hilgartner and Bosk 1988). However, our argument is that this issue is a complicated one, which needs far more attention and some rethinking. Definitions aside, the matter can partly be approached at an empirical level. And the evidence on that clearly is that there are many positive aspects of disasters at all social levels (see the work by Scanlon 1988 and others). Disasters can and do have positive characteristics and we should have more systematic studies on such features and not leave it to newspaper accounts to document the matter (e.g., a New York Times article once had a headline of "Winners as well as losers in the Great Flood of '93" and did a very good job of illustrating that point; see Feder 1993). In many cases, we do not find other than negative consequences because that is all we seek. For example, in the mental health area most studies cannot find the positive outcomes of disasters because, simply put, they do not search for them. For those who might be concerned about focusing on functional aspects of disasters, it might be noted that sociologists have already written on such topics as "the positive functions of poverty" (see Gans 1972).

However, at another level, in our view, the question about the dysfunctionality assumption is more of a theoretical issue. It rests on the basic imagery we have of what constitutes, what is the sociological heart of a disaster. For example, many disaster scholars assume that a disaster is a traumatic event occurring to an existing social system. This conjures up an image of damage, and efforts to react to an external agent. This is an understandable view and was implicit even in our earliest writings on the subject matter. On the other hand, there are other scholars who see disasters as evolutionary manifestations of ever changing social systems. This evokes, we would suggest, a rather different image, of efforts to adapt to internal system dynamics. The first image emphasizes the negative and reactivity, the second the positive and proactivity.

Our more up to date view now is that we would do better by using the semi-Darwinian model of evolutionary change. It would force us to consider the more positive aspects of disasters (all but impossible to consider in a social problem context that focuses on the negative). We would necessarily need to think about and look at both the functional and dysfunctional aspects if we see disasters as part of the evolution of social systems. A French sociologist, Touraine, in a paper that examines the future of social movements makes roughly the same point in writing that: "Many social problems or political issues are not related with social movements; many of them, in all kinds of societies, are related with processes of societal change, especially of modernization" (1994).

If social problems are socially constructed as many sociologists have long argued (see, Spector and Kitsuse 1977; Mauss 1992) it follows that a social change approach should be more fruitful for theoretical research purposes (We should note that Stallings 1995, has done a masterful analysis of why at least earthquakes have *not* come to be perceived as social problems in American society).

Apart from using a general framework such as the social change one just discussed, there are also other particular theoretical ideas that could be usefully employed in disaster research. We discuss five such unused ideas in what follows.

Ignoring Relevant Basic Theoretical Orientations

There are many theoretical models and frameworks in the social sciences. However, disaster researchers have explicitly used very few of them, although several of the chapter authors do use more than is typical. Even implicitly, the range of what has been employed has been rather narrow. For example, symbolic interactionism is the social psychological approach most used (Nigg 1994); it is even the one that has been implicitly our approach and as such probably the correct way of doing things. But there are other social psychologies around that could be used.

Our point is there are other kinds of formulations or orientations that at least might be brought to bear on certain questions, because they would seem on the surface level to be particularly relevant. As examples, let us first mention two that could be applied in studies of decision making in disasters, then three others that could deal with certain kinds of social relationships often involved in disaster behavior.

"Attribution" Theory In Social Psychology.

Without getting technical about it, this approach is fairly simple. Essentially it says that practically every person commits the "fundamental attribution error," that is, explaining the behavior of others on the grounds of personal disposition to behavior in particular ways across a variety of situations, rather than—as we interpret our own behavior—as a response to circumstantial and contextual pressures.

If we seriously accepted this theoretical formulation, it should influence how we might study decision making at any level in disasters. (However, we should note that attribution theory has very recently been used to examine how judgments of responsibilities for disaster consequences are made, see Hans and Nigg 1994). It suggests that the research focus should be on what actors see as the circumstantial and contextual pressures rather than looking for some predisposing attitude or motive that moves them to action.

Of course the general point was made a long time ago by the Russian novelist, Leo Tolstoy who wrote:

> One of the most widespread superstitions is that every man has his own special, definite qualities; that a man is kind, cruel, wise, stupid, energetic, apathetic, etc. Men are not like that . . . Men are like rivers; the water is the same in each, and alike in all; but every river is narrow here, is more rapid there, here slower, there broader, now clear, now cold, now dull, now warm. It is the same with men. Every man carries in himself the germs of every human quality and sometimes one manifests itself, sometimes another, and the man often becomes unlike himself—while still remaining the same man.

Although some social scientists would disagree, it is our view that there are times when we can learn even from fiction writers.

"Satisficing" Theory In Social Organizational Theory

Although the basic notion won the Noble Prize for Herbert Simon, it too states a fairly simply notion. It is that organizations instead of trying to optimize or maximize goals, settle for "good" enough or satisfying decisions. They stop at that point instead of attempting to do better.

If we would take this theoretical formulation seriously, it too could affect how we might study decision making with respect to organizational learning from disaster experiences. The limits of learning are clearly indicated by the satisfying theory, as well as why organizations are unlikely to initiate massive disaster mitigation measures.

Diffusion Studies

For another example apart from decision making, let us mention diffusion studies. The diffusion of innovations and the decisions involved in their adoption has generated a substantial literature in sociology and related disciplines (Valente 1993 a, 1993b). However, we are not aware of a single use of this theoretical framework or idea in any disaster study. Yet it would seem a particular relevant approach for studies of mitigation, especially since recent work in the area has produced a PAR score, that is, a potential for adoption score representing the likelihood that any one innovation will be adopted (see Dearing and Meyer 1994). The spread of GIS or geographic information systems would seem an obvious candidate for diffusion studies (for an initial work on this topic, see Gatreil and Vincent 1990; more indirectly see Dash 2002). In fact, any disaster related phenomena that involve social networks could be well approached with a diffusion framework.

Networking Theory

It has been around for a long time, with systematic thinking on the topic going back to the 17th Century, long before the existence of any social science discipline. However it has especially come to the fore in recent years in discussions of the supposed networks of terrorists or the networks around the world that mobilized to oppose the war by Iraq. In fact, the very idea of networks has spilled over into journalistic discussions (e.g., Eakin 2003) as well as social science tomes on the matter (e.g., Albert-Laszlo Barabasi 2002; Buskens 2002; Buchanan 2003; Watts 2003). The basic notion again is a simple one. It is that such collectivities consist less of organized groups, but more of informal linkages in strings and chains of social interaction (Miller 1998). As such, the implication is that less attention should be paid in research to formal groups and more to the links between informal groupings. A study of relationships is a rather different than one focused on entities. Social networks particularly involve questions about interpersonal trust, reciprocity and shared subcultural meanings. There are research manuals available on how to study networks (Schensul et al. 1999).

The Concept of "Social Capital"

It refers again very simply put, to the resources that an individual or group has a result of their existing relationships and personal networks. In a somewhat broader context, social capital are the features of "social organization (networks, norms, and social trust) that enable cooperative efforts for mutual benefit" (Karner 2000: 2637). The concept has increasingly been applied to a range of social behaviors from the macro issues of modernization and organizations, to its implications for families, community life, work, and governance (Dasgupta and Serageldin 2000). From our perspective, social capital might be a very useful concept to capture one major kind of resources that those involved in disaster-related activity might or might not have. Clearly those social entities with the most social capital available would be better off than those with less. Or in the context of our earlier discussion, the more an entity is involved in networks, the more relevant social capital is likely to be available for planning and managing purposes.

The overall point we are making is that we should explicitly use far more than we currently do of the more relevant theoretical orientations around. The examples we gave are just that, examples. Actually there are many more notions around rooted in larger theoretical frameworks that could provide us guidance for the testing of important hypotheses (e.g., the notion that ignorance is not absence of knowledge but is socially structured, see Stocking and Holstein 1993; that changes have occurred in collective self identities of different ethnic and racial groups in Western societies; and, that we are moving into a time of post bureaucratic types of social organization with more participatory decision making). One idea which would be particularly applicable to formal groups in the disaster area is the notion of organizational decay which attempts to explain how some organizations function (see Schwartz

1990 who applies it to the US space agency). More generally, some might argue that we could learn much by applying "chaos theory" not because the term is somewhat homologous to the word disaster, but because that theory is particularly applicable to irregular cyclical phenomena.

Our view is that disaster scholars should start applying theoretical notions that have shown their value and usefulness in other areas of life. Let us use the theoretical guidance provided by those who have preceded us in all the social sciences.

No matter how good the theoretical apparatus a researcher might bring to a study, the end result can be no better than the methodology used to collect relevant data. There seems to be no particular research method or technique that disaster researchers have not used (see Stallings 2002). However, we have questions about whether there has been an appreciation that some ways of gathering data might be used more than they have been and/or in different ways. We discuss some of these matters in what follows.

METHODOLOGICAL ISSUES

Under methodological issues, we want to discuss the urgency of taking more advantage of the computer/high tech information revolution, the value of experimenting with less traditional sampling and unorthodox interviewing techniques, the need to obtain better and more systematic field observations, examining how we might learn from historians how to gather more diverse and better documentary data, and in what ways we could obtain more valid and better statistics. Some of these points are not new. Taylor, about 25 years ago wrote that: "work in the field of disaster studies needs some exercise of the sociological imagination in the use and development of research techniques and procedures" (1978: 276). Unfortunately, there has not been much following through on what she advocated.

It signifies something, although we are not sure exactly what, that for about three decades there were only a handful of publications on general methodological issues in doing disaster research (there is, for instance, very few between Killian 1956 and Mileti 1987; only in 2002 did a full volume appear on methods of disaster research, Stallings 2002; see also King 2002). Perhaps this is because there are no special or unique problems in undertaking disaster studies. However, we think most veteran field researchers in the area, including us, would argue that there are both advantages and disadvantages in doing disaster studies compared to what is present in normal times. For example, it is often much easier to get into organizational headquarters and to get to higher level officials at the very height of the crisis time in a disaster than would be possible during routine times (although our French colleagues such as Patrick Lagadec might disagree with this, but perhaps that signifies some cross-societal differences that we need to explore). On the other hand, there is also no need to document that there are significant sampling problems if one is interested in search and rescue activities during the crisis period. If our general perspective is anywhere near correct, we need considerable more attention to methodological issues in the area.

We leave aside, in considering methodological issues, the view increasingly being expressed that positivism in sociology is in massive retreat (Baldus 1990; Brown 1990), and that an emerging postmodernism approach is changing the very nature of the knowledge being obtained (see Sassower 1991; Christopher 2002). If this is a true reading, someone ought to consider the implication of this shift for future disaster studies. There would seem to be important consequences if we do shift from a scientific positivism that sees scientists as noninvolved "spectators," to a postmodernistic stance that views researchers as "participants" (see Toulmin 1981)

The Computer/High Tech Information Revolution

We should take advantage of the computer/high tech information revolution. It needs little documentation to note that we are at the start of a massive information/knowledge/communication revolution that is transforming the world. What differences is this making in what is, or perhaps better stated, what should be used in our research? It seems obvious that the recent flood of technology as manifested in products and processes such as computers, digital cameras, satellite dishes, modems, cell phones, Email, virtual reality, the Internet, broadband downloading, CD-ROM disks, two way pagers, instant messages, digital imagery, video games, electronic journals, search engines, DVDs, etc., are creating a built environment that is fundamentally different from any the human race has lived in up to now (see e.g., Heap et al. 1995; Jones 1995; Chowdbury 2001; Amor 2002; Rosaman and Singh 2002; Smith et al. 2002; Ratner 2003). In fact, there is an argument that an even more drastic revolution is ready to occur with the development of a wireless technology which is unwiring the Internet and linking many devices that are not directly linked (Anderson 2003). In any case, at the disaster research level, as we have discussed elsewhere, it is clearly creating massive changes in disaster phenomena themselves, as well as in the planning for and managing of such occasions (Quarantelli 1994a).

However, in this paper we want primarily to point out that the computer/high tech revolution is also opening windows of previously unavailable opportunities in the gathering of, the analyses done, and writing of reports from data on disasters. This is not to say that everything that is occurring is all to the positive for study purposes, but there are some potentially very positive aspects for research purposes. Only a very few have even addressed these possibilities (e.g., Butler 1994; 2002 and n.d., but who in writing several comprehensive summary articles on the current communication and information revolution focuses mostly on the implications for disaster management rather than for disaster research which is typical, e.g., Disaster Information Task Force 1998; Hearth 1989).

There are at least three ways through which studies could be improved by more and better use of the outcomes of the computer/high tech information revolution. For one, we can obtain data now that previously was impossible or very difficult to collect. For instance, it is currently possible to tap into in much real time organizational and interorganizational information and communication flow. As an example, we ourselves became aware of this when surfacing the Internet a few years ago, we ran across the information that the US Center for Disease Control was sending out to all state and local public health agencies during a flood in Iowa. Also available were the reports about health problems such agencies were reporting back from every county in the state of Iowa. Talk about availability of primary data! The already collected data were there, all a researcher had to do was to analyze them! (Suggestions on how to do research on the Internet can be found in Mann and Stewart 2000).

It is also now possible to obtain via computers much of the disaster related information that FEMA in the US currently issues to citizens as well as press organizations. In terms of the examples given, we would say we can get a much better picture of the content of such communications than we could by interviewing the communicators themselves. To be sure, there are problems even of just making a content analysis of such data, but any data has problems. There are many disaster related electronic bulletin boards currently in existence. For example, it is now possible to tap into information put out by US federal government agencies besides FEMA, such as EPA, USGS and NOAA (see Butler, 2002 for various sources that can currently be monitored). While these examples are from American society the same kind of possibilities ought to be available in other social systems that have any kind of computer operations.

At the international level it is possible to keep very current with situation reports on disasters issued by international agencies such as the UN Department of Humanitarian Affairs or as it is now called, The U.N. Office for the Coordination of Humanitarian Affairs. When we first started monitoring these reports we were struck on how blind disaster scholars from Western societies probably are to constantly occurring major disasters elsewhere, especially in developing countries. For instance, although there was not one referent to them in the American mass media we were exposed to, there were five massive disasters in about 10 days of July 1995. These included one in Togo where torrential rains made

75,000 people homeless; floods in Ghana that made over 200,000 homeless; monsoon rains in Pakistan that affected more than half a million of the population in 1,018 villages; torrential rains in Bangladesh that affected 12 million persons and destroyed or damaged nearly one million homes; and very heavy rains that destroyed and incapacitated the sewer systems and heavily polluted the main sources of drinking water in a city of two million residents in the Ukraine.

To put it as politely as possible, students of disasters, who are mostly from developed countries, seem to work with a very limited range of disaster occasions. The universe of such happenings is being very badly sampled. To indicate that the above examples from 1995 were not an atypical instance, in 2002, there were massive floods in Bangladesh, China and India involving millions of people (see the *Disaster Database* in volume 12 Number 2 issue of *Disaster Prevention and Management* for some data on these happenings) that were basically ignored in press reports in Europe and North America. In contrast, floods of large but nonetheless less consequential floods in the Czech Republic and Germany were paid at least some attention.

A second possibility is that we can much more easily now locate and obtain comparative data from the same or similar occasions by other researchers. Many note that the high tech revolution is not only generating more information, but has an interactive quality to it that renders it qualitatively different from previous information/knowledge distribution systems. In short, scholars can find and communicate more quickly and much better with other researchers now than ever before.

For example, it is now possible to learn very quickly who else besides oneself might be undertaking studies on the same disaster. Thus, when we became interested in the Northridge earthquake we used at that time an Earthquake Information Gopher easily reached by our own PC. In doing so we were able to find the Northridge Earthquake Research Directory that led to a file called the Northridge Earthquake Research Coordination Project Participants. Entering this file, it was possible to generate a listing of the names and titles of 119 researchers on the earthquake. Clearly the existence of such information allows quickly making links and tying in to networks of researchers that previously either could not have been done or would have been much more laborious to establish.

As another example, is anyone interested in learning who has worked on disaster aspects of cultural properties? Using the keyword "disaster" on the Veronica system, we was able to find again using our own PC an annotated bibliography of 102 publications of work done on protecting and restoring cultural artifacts in disasters. In a similar kind of search we found listings of children's literature on floods and natural disasters, publications providing examples of disaster-related emotional problems, abstracts of TV coverage of natural disasters, and statistics on financial assistance for disaster-related schools and tourism problems, and also similar information on chemical disasters and droughts. Many similar kinds of information can be obtained through the EPIX system, that is, the Emergency Preparedness Information Exchange Gopher accessible via the Center for Policy Research on Science and Technology at Simon Fraser University in Canada (see Anderson 1994, for a good summary of EPIX).

Sometimes it is possible to directly get written papers and reports. Some research centers such as NCEER allow direct computer access to entire texts that are available on line. Other information sources provide the information in different ways, such as the PAHO/WI-IO Disasters Documentation Centre in San Jose, Costa Rica, which has set up a CD-ROM library especially for professionals in the Americas. (However, as an aside it has been surprising to us, how many such data sources come and go and what is in place can suddenly disappear. In fact, we are not sure that all the specific references to particular sources we cite in this paper do still exist! Gophers appear to have disappeared from cyberspace).

Even if we had the technical knowledge, which we do not have, we do not have the time here for anything resembling a full discussion of all these matters we have alluded to above. Interested parties, therefore, are especially urged to look at, besides the references already provided, the 1994 November/December issue of the *Stop Disasters Newsletter* put out at the Osservatoiro Vesusviano in Naples, Italy for the IDNDR Secretariat, which has a number of articles on the communications/information technological revolution and its implication for the disaster area.

Our point is that what would in the pre-computer era have taken months of searching and probably ending up with less information, can now be found in minutes. We have been particularly impressed by the real time nature of much of the information that currently can be found through a computer. For instance, there were 16 WWW sites, three Gopher sites, four newsgroups and one relay chat room available on various computer nets that focused on the Great Hanshin earthquake in Japan, as of January 18, 1995, and many came into being within days of the disaster.

This kind of computer generated data and study sources would seem to considerably enhance, facilitate and quicken the linkages between researchers interested in the same disaster or disaster topic. In fact, a very worthwhile project would be to examine the quantitative and qualitative implications of the computer revolution for the development of critical masses of disaster scholars, their informal colleges and the professional networks involved. Earlier sociology of science studies on these topics, totally apart from the disaster area, strongly suggest that the computer revolution will significantly accelerate intellectual exchanges among students of disasters.

Of course we want to stress that no technological innovation can be any better than what human beings contribute by way of substantive content. For instance, more than once after a major disaster has occurred we have been able to monitor on our own PC discussion groups that have emerged regarding that particular occasion. It was disturbing to us how many simply incorrect notions about disasters are circulated among the participants. In another instance, there were a number of disaster scholars exchanging ideas on how to define disasters and hazards. The active participants came from Mexico, England, Canada and the United States. To put it mildly, the degree of sophistication, substantive knowledge and awareness of the existing literature, shown by the interacting parties was extremely uneven. Nevertheless, even such a mixed intellectual exchange suggests the exciting new potential that exists for learning from others that is for the first time now possible via certain modern technologies.

Finally, a third possibility that now exists is that we can improve the writing up of data, not so much in the word content as such of reports, but in how some data could be displayed. By this we mean we can use better graphics, visual displays, photographs, and similar means to describe and depict our data about disasters; with imagination even more could be presented on video tapes.

More than a decade ago we were very impressed in seeing in Japan a computer generated depiction of the dynamics of where victims had moved and died in a nightclub fire. However, that is one of the very few times that we have seen disaster researchers go beyond words, simple graphs and tables, and occasional photographs. Actually the last was once more prominent even in sociology generally; thus in the early days of the *American Journal of Sociology*, from 1896 to 1916, a total of 244 photographs accompanied 31 articles (Stasz 1979). That kind of depiction became rarer after that time period.

In our view we could make substantial improvements in our description and depiction of data if we were to utilize some more recent technologies that have been developed and can be used for graphic and visual displays. Actually sociologists have written extensively on some of the older mechanical means available, such as those who have employed film records to judge the presence and extent of collective behavior (see Wohlstein and McPhail 1979). In addition there have been those who more recently have discussed the use mostly in anthropological field studies of visual images from photography and film (e.g., Image-based Research 1998; Mirzoeff 1999; Emmison 2000; Malcolm 2001; Sturken 2001). However, it must be admitted that the social sciences as a whole has made very little use of even these older audiovisual ways of presenting our data. If August Comte, the founder of sociology were to return today, however surprised he might be along certain lines, his attention would not be distracted by any exciting visual displays (about the only exceptions are some interesting photo and graphic displays that appear in introductory sociology texts).

Given that, it is not surprising that disaster researchers in writing reports primarily display data using only means that preexist not only disaster studies, but also sociology as a field. For anyone interested there are two social science oriented journals which could provide many good ideas (see *Visual Studies* and *Visual Sociology*). There are also some recent books on the presentation of visual images such as one by Pink (2001) with the title of *Visual Ethnography: Images, Media and Representation In Research* which discusses photography and video and hypermedia in ethnographic and social research (see also Rose 2001; van Leeuwen and Jewitt 2001).

Our point is not so much that there is a need "to jazz up" our presentations, but that if we used some imagination readers and viewers could both better see what we are analyzing as well as conveying a much better picture to our audiences. As an example, we should make far more use of the graphic depictions that some Japanese researchers have recently employed. We do not have the capability here to reproduce the different colors that they used in the illustrations employed to give an overall picture of the dynamics of different disasters. Anyone interested should look at a Japanese publication, *Long Road Toward Mitigating Earthquake Hazard (Learning From the Past)* Tokyo, Japan: SEEHM, Kajima Corporation, No. 2 September 1992.

Apart from incorporating new ideas, scholars need also to experiment more with old ways of doing things. The argument here is not instituting change just for the sake of change, but because doing some things in a different way might have more research payoff.

Different Sampling Frames and Interviewing Techniques

Extensive experiments using less traditional sampling frames and also more unorthodox interviewing techniques should be undertaken. Few scholars would question the fact that particularly in studying impact time disaster behaviors, we are usually faced with major problems of sampling and interviewing, for reasons quite familiar to any experienced field researcher. Yet, there would appear to be better ways of sampling and interviewing disaster relevant populations than what is usually done in the standard survey study. It should be noted that Bourque and her colleagues note that many present day researchers do not take advantage of all that can be done with even standard surveys (2002). That aside, we ought to make some attempts to experiment with less traditional sampling procedures and frames as well as interviewing.

For instance, there already exists a literature that discusses in detail a variety of existing methods, in the felicitous phrase of one article, for "sampling rare populations" (Kalton and Anderson 1986). Among established techniques available are screening methods, the use of disproportionate sampling, multiplicity sampling, multiple frames and snowballing. Except for very rare and isolated uses of disproportionate sampling (this oddly enough was used in the very first systematic population survey of disaster population, namely the 1954 NORC study of the Arkansas, now recognized as a classic, see Marks and Fritz 1954), and of snowballing (used in some NORC studies and early DRC research on search and rescue and emergent groups), the other techniques are not used on any scale by students of disasters.

Many of these techniques are not that new; for instance, household surveys with multiplicity sampling where respondents report not only on their own behavior but of other persons as well such as friends and neighbors, are at least three decades old (see Sirken 1970). Researchers from the Disaster Research Center (DRC) did use results from one multiplicity technique in their study of the 1985 earthquake, but honesty requires noting that this was only because the Mexican polling organization carrying out the population survey, solely on their own initiative, employed the technique. Nevertheless, from 567 randomly selected, treated as informants who provided information on earthquake-related behavior of every member of their household. Therefore, DRC obtained data on the nature and extent of volunteer activity for a total of 2,965 individuals (Dynes, Quarantelli and Wenger 1990).

In addition, we would argue that we should try using some unorthodox or little used interviewing techniques that are different from the standard procedures typically employed in both open-ended and structured survey interviewing. For instance, we have always thought although admittedly never have tried, that it might be worthwhile to do personal interviews of several persons together, in a semi-focused group setting. Also, while we would not for sociological purposes utilize Rorschach type techniques, it could be worthwhile experimenting with the use of maps, photos, diagrams, etc. in conjunction especially with open-ended personal interviews (geographers for instance have obtained some fascinating data from having respondents draw maps of their "neighborhoods" or communities). What about showing actual disaster scenes that have been caught on tape or film to victims that were involved in such recorded happenings? In fact, given that today it is possible to use cell phones to take photographs of scenes, it seems to us that with a little imagination such a procedure could be incorporated into some on the scene interviewing formats. We leave aside here the very important crucial and significant moral, ethical as well as legal questions that would have to be addressed, but in principles we are suggesting that combining different media recordings with interviewing is something worthwhile thinking about.

Also it is a deeply embedded notion—at least in American disaster research circles—with respect to interviewing that the interviewer not openly challenge what respondents and informants say. But one only has to look at the legal system in many societies, including the United States, where consciously challenging witnesses is seen as the best way to obtain the "truth". Should disaster scholars automatically reject what might be called conflict type interviewing? At least some thought might be given to using that kind of interviewing and maybe even some field experiments to see the similarities and differences in data that the two interviewing styles typically evoke.

Better and More Systematic Field Observations

We should obtain better and more systematic field observations. For a whole variety of reasons, including the increasing legal problems of protecting the confidentiality of data (see Tierney 2002), it has become more and more difficult to conduct personal interviews on almost any subject matter in North America. Until recently, sociological disaster researchers have depended heavily on face-to-face or personal interviewing (although in recent years, there has been a marked shifted to greater use of survey interviewing, either by phone or mail). Our view is that whether we want to or not we will have to look for other data gathering methods to complement if not to supplement our primary reliance on the interview per se.

For a long time we have thought that, far more might be done to develop field observation teams, especially for obtaining systematic information regarding the crisis time periods of disasters. In fact, if we were to be reincarnated and started working in the disaster area afresh, it would be an interesting challenge to try to develop such teams of observers. This would require extensive training on how to conduct systematic observations on site, and in particular how one could take advantage of and collate the multiple perspectives of different team members (although we have strong doubts about the theoretical value of the notion of "the assembling process" for collective behavior analysis as developed by Clark McPhail (1991), there is much we can learn from the systematic coding systems he has produced for studying the process, see McPhail and Wohlstein 1983, 1995).

Such systematic observing would probably be limited to looking at certain phases of the preparedness and response phases of the crisis periods of disasters. Yet, we think we might learn more from such data gathering than relying as we do now mostly on retrospective and after the action interviewing. As Mileti has written of disaster behavior: "what people say about behavior and how they actually behave are not the same thing" (1987:69). Moreover, such teams would have an advantage today compared to the past.

In part, this is because such groups could now use video cameras and laptop computers in their data gathering, and there have been texts for more than a decade on using computers in qualitative research (e.g., Pfaffenburger 1988; Fielding and Lee 1991; Gibbs 2002). We should also note that with some sociological imagination it is possible to visualize a gathering of observational data concurrent with a simultaneous analysis at a central computer base that would allow a shifting of observational points to capture the dynamics of the processes being observed, such as in search and rescue efforts. Is this too grandiose a formulation? Perhaps, but even now it is technically feasible although the social infrastructure necessary may be beyond our current willingness to attempt. However, it is the kind of research design and equipment that we think will be commonplace in the mid or late 21st Century.

One frequently raised objection to observational data is the supposed limitation of what can be done with the end product. Personally, we have never assumed, as is true in a very strict positivistic viewpoint, that observations are useful only in the preliminary stages of scientific exploration and can only generate but not test hypotheses. Our view, hardly unique today in sociology (see Lofland and Lofland 1984 for this position nearly two decades ago), is that as a form of data collection, observations can be useful: "for measuring concepts, testing hypotheses and/or constructing causal explanations" (Jorgensen 1989:7). If that is your position, collecting and analyzing observational data poses no problem for scientific advances.

Also, the probability that much observational data might have to be qualitative also does not bother us. In part, this is because we as sociologists, as we see it, have never taken full advantage of the kinds of qualitative measurements that have long been available (and this applies to other than the disaster area). As examples, we might cite several writings on methodology by Paul Lazarsfeld and Allen Barton, which despite being decades old, are still highly relevant for qualitative observational data gathering and analysis. (see Barton and Lazarsfeld (1955) reprinted in McCall and Simmons 1969, and Lazarsfeld and Barton 1962). For more recent discussions on the analysis of qualitative data, see Miles and Huberman (1994), Denzin and Lincoln (2000), Ellis and Ellingson (2000) and Lincoln and Denzin (2003). While unstructured interviews and more recently focus groups have been used in disaster research, more off beat techniques such as textual and narrative analyses, personal essays, discourse analysis (Phillips and Hardy 2002) or autoethnography (see Reed-Danahay 1997) have very rarely been used. There are even qualitative models for data gathered in a non-quantitative way (Heise and Durig 2000; see also Wengraf 2001), as well as computer CD-ROMs for analyzing qualitative data (e.g. MAXqda, Software for Qualitative Data Analysis which exists both in English and German versions).

Systematic observational data might be especially useful for cross-societal and cross-cultural research. Anthropologists and others have long done comparative observational studies of behavior such as are involved in "body language" and spatial distances between interacting human beings (e.g., Bull 1983). Much has been learned. Who knows what disaster scholars might learn if they made comparative examinations of some disaster behaviors in such ways?

Learning From Historians

We can learn from historians on how to gather more diverse and better documentary data. There is a need for not only better but more diverse documents. We use the term document in a very broad sense going considerably beyond official reports, written records, census statistics and mass media contents. Many of those are often gathered in disaster studies.

Less frequently obtained are such items as organizational minutes of meetings, informal group logs, business transaction data, etc. Seldom, moreover, does one find disaster researchers systematically collecting and using letters, diaries, graffiti and informal signs, bulletin board items, family albums, religious sermons, and much of what have been called nonreactive items (see the classic work on the last, Webb et al. 1981; for the use of personal documents, see Plummer 1983; Burgess 1984: 123-142; Prior 2003; also, Hodder 1994).

The best that can be found is that occasionally there are fleeting references in studies to "gallow humor" or jokes, or the songs that follow disastrous occasions, but no one has attempted much of a collection of them. However, studies of the popular culture of disasters have recently emerged (see Webb, Wachtendorf and Eyre 2000). In fact, an edited volume (by Webb and Quarantelli, forthcoming in early 2004) has chapters discussing such phenomena as disaster related songs, on-site graffiti, movies, quilts, religious explanations, etc, and suggests that more attention ought to be paid to folk legends and beliefs about disasters, disaster novels and poems, memorial services of certain kinds, cartoons and comic strips with disaster themes along with video games of a similar nature, survivor buttons and hats, and World Wide Web chat rooms that develop around disaster occasions. For those who argue that disasters ought to be looked at more from the perspective of victim individuals and groups, this would seem a logical path to explore. At any rate, our general point here is that we should not equate documentary data only with formal and written reports, and statistics. Our data scooping efforts ought to be broader.

We do not need to start at ground zero on this matter. One discipline has had to depend mostly on documentary data in the broad sense of the term. That of course is the field of history. Historians have been at their craft decades longer than have social scientists. It is not inconceivable that perhaps they have learned how to gather, assess and use documentary data (the classic and still relevant work in historiography is Lang Lois and Seignobos 1898; for more current references, see Pitt 1972; Hodder 1994; and especially Dymond 1981, an English publication which deals with the use of local sources and would be particularly good for community studies). We ought to look at what historians can teach us about how to deal with documents of all kinds.

Even at present, a few disaster scholars, using mostly historical sources, have done rather good studies of past disasters. Scanlon (2002), for example has reconstructed in very fine detail, much of the behavior during and in the aftermath of the Halifax explosion, which occurred over 80 years ago. If nothing else, his work shows how persistence and imagination can uncover data that superficially one might think never existed in the first place much less survived the years.

Another good historical study with a larger goal is one by Perez (2003) who has written a book with the title, *Winds of Change: Hurricanes and the Transformation of Nineteenth Century Cuba*. Written by an historian, historical documents such as contemporary eyewitness accounts and agricultural and economic records are used to depict the land tenure forms, labor organizations and production systems in the Cuban political economy. There is then an analysis of the social characteristics of three major hurricanes in 1842, 1844 and 1846 and lesser natural disasters, and how these led to a transformation of the social system in Cuba as well as the development of Cuban identity and community. In short, this study using a historical framework and data moves from looking at an existing social system, to the related social characteristics of the disasters in that system, to the later related social transformation of that society.

Perhaps others ought to try their hand at historical reconstruction of disasters. After all, many major works in sociology recognized as classics and by such sociologists as Weber, Marx, Durkheim, Thomas and Znaniecki, Tonnies, etc., are primarily historical studies based mostly on documentary data. What we have just cited also implies that a historical analysis of documents need not be confined to a single case study.

In these days of tight research budgets, it is perhaps not amiss to note that much, although not all, documentary data collecting is often very inexpensive. Much can be found in university libraries or organizational archives. There is a very good discussion about how to go about mining such sources, in an old publication by Glaser and Strauss (1967: 161-184).

Further, we would suggest that it might be worthwhile for some disaster scholar to put together a detailed statement on the methodology of gathering documentary data. All of us would benefit from such an effort. We cannot afford to continue to ignore the need for and the value of more diverse and better documentary data in our studies.

There is currently a rather large database that in one sense is historical but is currently unused. Let us mention something very briefly. In some ways, it can be seen as an effort to salvage something from a considerable expenditure of societal resources.

Up to a few years ago and for about three decades, hundreds of millions of dollars were spent and thousands of studies were done on nuclear war effects, including those on the civilian population in the United States (and apparently from what we have been told by Russian colleagues, this also happened in the former Soviet Union). From a cursory perusal we have made of the American studies we would say that substantively such studies are probably not very useful for any purpose that we can think of, since almost all of them projected an unknown postnuclear war world (for a typical such study see, Chenault, Engler and Nordlie 1967; for general summaries of these studies that attempt to use a social science approach to the post-attack problem, see Nordlie 1963; Lybrand and Popper 1960).

However, in most of the research undertaken, for a fairly obvious reason, a consistent overall (nation state) social system approach was used. This is a framework only rarely employed in past or current disaster studies. So perhaps to the extent we move to undertake more macro level studies, there might be some clues on how to proceed from this war-oriented research (cf. Perry 1982). More important, from our perspective, is that very many of these war oriented studies used elaborate and sophisticated research techniques and methodologies for social system analyses that clearly in our view would warrant and be worthwhile looking at for insight and ideas especially for macro level studies of regional disasters or catastrophes.

The Need For Better Statistics

There is a very great need for better disaster statistics, with emphasis on the word better. There is no absence of quantitative especially statistical data in the discussion of disasters. As we gave written elsewhere (Quarantelli 2001) there are numerous statistics and figures around with respect to disasters generally and/or for specific disasters. It is very, very rare in the reporting of a major disaster not be to be presented with specific numbers on deaths, casualties, and property and economic losses. There are numerous estimates of negative results from disasters in the research, policy, professional and operational literature, as well as in press news reports. We are not lacking quantitative estimates and data with respect to disasters.

But as we have also written in the same publication (Quarantelli 2001), how reliable are such statistics and are they as precise as they seem to imply? Our blunt answer to those two questions is: The statistics are not at all reliable; their precision is even more dubious. We do not have the time here to document these points. But we should note that we are hardly alone in our very negative view. Thus, as one analysis of the political economy of large natural disasters has noted: "Most disaster analysis is based on shaky foundations. Institutional bias, political interests, and technical insufficiencies make disaster statistics unsatisfactory and unreliable . . . This contributes to preserve myths about the effects of disasters on the economy and society (Albala-Bertrand 1993: 39).

Some of the better gatherers of disaster statistics actually are among those most skeptical of the data they gathered. For example, with respect to the data reported in *World Report 2002* which primarily uses figures from the Center for Research on Epidemiology of Disasters at the Catholic University of Louvain in Belgium (probably the best of its kind anywhere) it is noted that: "Disaster data . . . [have to be] handled with care . . . data . . . remain at best, patchy . . . Relative changes and trends are more useful to look at then absolute, isolated figures . . . the lack of systematic and standardized data collections disasters in the past is now revealing itself as a major weakness for any long-term planning" (2002: 179).

What can be done about dubious statistics? For one, researchers should not set forth figures that in no way can be as precise as stated. Is it really valid to say as does a summary (Dilly 2000) about floods between 1970 and 1998 that 1,721 such occasions killed 186,736 people and affected 2,002,201,949? A partial rechecking of the 2 billion plus figure on those affected appears to be a correct reporting in terms of the data source used, which of course does not make the figure a precise one in fact. Second, there should be a conscious recognition that differentiation should be made with respect to the validity of data that are about different phenomena. Everything else being equal, the number of deaths reported are more likely to be "correct" than about injuries (although both can be off not by percentages but magnitudes of three or four; see Quarantelli 2001). And both are more likely to be "correct" than property damage figures and economic costs, although the former is more likely to be valid than the latter.

Organizational specialists have long taken the position that all statistics are all socially constructed. Without understanding how, when and why the statistics are gathered in the first place, little face-value credence can be given even to figures derived in fairly controlled situations. This has led experts in these areas to make the following statements about the US census. One involved demographer openly said: "I say the census is an estimate of the truth" and "The census is probably precise to the millions" (Scott 2001: 22, 23). It is not surprising that there was much controversy over the last US census since there was widespread agreement that millions of inhabitants of the country were missed even though the issue was almost exclusively if someone was or was not physically counted. If this is true of such a relatively controlled situation, what can one expect about trying to make counts of people in disasters, especially in developing countries?

However, and third, as an occasional study here and there have done, if considerable effort is put into collecting and assessing the statistics around, much more reliable figures can be obtained. See, for instance the analysis done by Olson his colleagues (1999) for the figures that existed from Hurricane Mitch; see also Mushtaque and his colleagues (1993) and Haque and Blair (1992), about the figures circulating for a 1991 cyclone that hit Bangladesh. In the latter the official figures of deaths were off by at least a magnitude of two. In an instance of a flood disaster in Venezuela, which we our self looked at, the dead may have numbered 3,500 rather than the published figures of 50,000. This means that the deaths were probably overestimated by a magnitude of 14! But since better statistics can be obtained as just indicated in the two studies mentioned just above, many more efforts of this kind should be undertaken.

We are especially disturbed by efforts to assess the quantitative value of mitigation or preventive measures in lessening losses form disasters. Of course the goal is very laudable and ought to be kept in mind as the ideal for which scholars ought to strive. But we also recognize that there is considerable "political" pressure from legislative bodies and international organizations such as the World Bank to come up with costs-benefits analyses to justify putting money into mitigation measures. But given all the problems and difficulties in putting together any reasonable disaster relevant statistics, it is all but impossible in the first instance to estimate what might be lost and what might be saved by appropriate measures, and what has been lost and has to be restored. Can researchers continue to pretend that is not the case? Something really has to be done on this matter, but more imaginative persons than us with perhaps some very innovative ideas will have to take the lead.

RESEARCH OR EMPIRICAL ISSUES

It is not our intent to present a laundry list of research or empirical studies that might be undertaken. Instead, we present a more strategic rather than tactical approach to this matter. While some specific topics are suggested, it is our intent here to stress general themes on how we ought to approach empirical research. These include a need to do more studies on disasters that cut across governmental and political boundaries, do far more in depth research on topics about which our data base is really weak, look at many important disaster phenomena of a social nature on which we have done almost no studies, examine for their significance the "deviant" cases we encounter, and look at institutional areas that have been neglected so far.

Studies of Disasters Across Governmental and Political Boundaries

There is a need to do more intensive studies of disasters that cut across governmental and political boundaries. Many disasters these days cut across international, national, regional or other formal governmental boundaries. Many good examples of this happening surface in the operation of lifeline systems, a few of which have been studied (see Tierney 1992; Nigg 1995). Other recent but different examples are the radiation fallout from Chernobyl that fell on many countries in Europe, the pollution of the Rhine River that started near Basel, Switzerland and affected six nations along an 800-mile course, and the spread of the SARS epidemic in 2003 which originated in China and leaped to Canada and then other places in the world. On a less extensive scale, even relatively small disasters such as the sinking of the ferries at Zeebrugee in Belgium, or the Estonia in the, Baltic Sea, necessarily affect in a direct fashion organizations and citizens from many different societies. We think we can take for granted that such noncommunity disasters will be more frequent in the future. In fact, Rosenthal and his colleagues (2001) argue that will be a major characteristic of future disasters, and it is of course a point that Boin addresses well in his chapter.

In what ways and what do we study in such disasters? Just as risk analysis and preparedness for disasters that start in one locale and have consequences far away pose difficult operational problems for emergency managers, we in the disaster area also clearly will have difficulties in designing research to span such diffuse disaster occasions. Yet it is something that we increasingly will need to do. We need far more studies of those disasters whose effects are not community focused or locused, but cut across all kinds of political/ governmental boundaries.

For empirical studies too, we must consider theoretical developments in sociology on this matter of the blurring of social boundaries. There are also research problems we need to attend at the other side of the spectrum, not where the disaster impacts but those groups that have some responsibilities for responding. For example, what is the empirical research implication of those who like Skocpal (1992) argue that we should move from a "state centered" explanation of social policy to a "polity centered" model. She essentially believes that while the state itself remains important, nongovernmental organizations, institutions and movements that are politically active—for example, unions, veterans' groups and women's voluntary organizations—may also crucially affect policies about benefits for veterans and family welfare programs. What should we be studying if her position is a valid one and generalizable to the disaster area? In more general terms, what studies are suggested by the blurring of traditional domain lines and the evolution of important groups with other than formal governmental boundaries. From our viewpoint, this approach would appear particularly important for disaster mitigation research.

Although we will not specifically address here the consequences for empirical work, there is something happening to all scientific activity generally, which someone ought to examine for its implication for studies in the disaster area. This is what has been called the internationalization of social science research and knowledge (Smelser 1991b). Just as organizational and political boundaries are becoming vaguer and less consistent with formal legal boundaries, so too is science becoming less rooted in particular nations or social systems. We find it difficult to believe that our empirical work in the disaster area is not being affected by this internationalization process. Our surface reaction is that overall the effects will be positive for research studies (and elsewhere we have suggested it will lead to improvement in disaster theory, see Quarantelli 1995a).

Yet we feel that unless we do a better job of addressing problems in doing cross-national, cross-societal and cross-cultural studies (and the three are different), and ask how we can develop transnational teams of researchers, we will not progress very far along this line (although sometime ago we once wrote one of the few articles yet available on this topic, it is now clear to us that our approach was very superficial (see Quarantelli 1979; but see the recent proposal to coordinate domestic and foreign post-earthquake field studies, Holzer et al. 2003). Also, the more we moved toward cross-studies of any kind, the more we will discover that researchers elsewhere have frequently done more work than many of us realize (To North American and European disaster researchers, we would call attention to the Annotated Inventory of the social science research literature on disasters in the former Soviet Union and contemporary Russia, which list over 100 publications; see Quarantelli and Mozgovaya 1994).

In Depth Studies Where the Data Base Is Very Weak

Far more in depth studied are needed of many topics and questions about which the data base is very weak. There are many empirical generalizations about disasters that are widely accepted by social scientists. But if one looks closely at the research data base on which such generalizations rest, one can become a little disturbed because in many case the data base is very small or weak.

Some sociologists have said that we do not do a good job in sociology generally in the accumulation of knowledge. As Gans has written: "even the normal science that is conducted while paradigms remain dominant is not cumulative, at least in sociology, for empirical researchers regularly carry out research that repeats findings already reported by earlier researchers (1992: 701). There is certainly a degree of that in sociological disaster studies, although we will forego giving anecdotal examples of failures to recognize that something more recently "found" had been consistently reported by much earlier researchers (elsewhere, Quarantelli 1988, we indicate how the famous NORC study of the Arkansas tornado in 1952 sets forth very many propositions about behavioral responses in disasters, some of which are sometime advanced as "new findings" in current studies).

However, we think our problem on this matter is slightly different. There are many topics in the disaster area that we think we know a lot about but for which the data base if really very weak. For instance, probably all disaster researchers believe that there is considerable convergence of people, goods and information to a disaster site after impact. We personally have no doubt about it. Nevertheless, the empirical data base on this is remarkably weak. The pioneering disaster researchers such as Fritz and Moore made major attempts to empirically document the phenomena (see Fritz and Mathewson 1957; Moore 1958). However, after that initial work, the notion that convergence existed was taken for granted and never reexamined in any systematic way.

Only about a decade ago did Scanlon (1992) revisit the topic. While his findings did not basically challenge most of the widely held ideas about convergence, he did considerably refine, better detail, and made further important distinctions about the phenomena. However, our point here is that several decades went by between the initial work on convergence and the much later restudy by Scanlon; that should not have happened. If US Today can obtain numbers on certain kinds of convergence in the Loma Prieta earthquake (see, Stone and Castaneda 1990) or a British newspaper can report that after the Zeebrugge ferry disaster, the Kent County police in England received 1.4 million phone calls, why cannot social scientists do better and more systematic studies? To be fair, some very recent studies in connection with particularly the organizational context of convergence during the 9/11 occasion in New York City have done some sophisticated analyses that go beyond the earlier literature on the topic of convergence (Kendra and Wachtendorf 2003). Nevertheless the question that we are primarily asking here is "why do we accept 'conclusions' in our area when even a superficial search would uncover the weak database?"

As another example, what do we know about crime in connection with disasters? We do think we are certain that looting does not generally occur or that violent antisocial behavior is very rare at least in developed societies at the crisis time period of disasters (Quarantelli 1994b). But there are many anecdotal observations that white collar crime (for a recent general discussion of this topic from a sociological perspective see Croall 2002) is widespread in disasters. Here again journalists have been ahead of us. For instance, while the official death toll for the Northridge, California earthquake was 58, the state received 374 requests for grants to pay funeral expenses for quake victims (Simon 1994)! Also, not too long ago there was an investigative report in the *New York Times* about massive fraud in agricultural disaster aid programs in the United States (Frantz 1994:1), and there have been consistent rumors about malpractices in international disaster relief and recovery programs. As far as we know, researchers have not looked at all at such criminal behavior (although we have a major monograph underway on the topic).

Here and there, a few researchers have built upon and extended previous work. Our own studies of panic flight go back as far as our Master's Thesis on the subject matter (Quarantelli 1954, 1957), nearly a half century ago. These early writings in the area came to be generally accepted as canon on the topic (Nigg and Perry 1988). However, Norman Johnson and his colleagues a few years revisited the topic and employing a far more sophisticated approach than we had used, substantially advanced our knowledge of panic behavior in disasters (see Johnson 1987, 1988; Johnston and Johnson 1989; Johnson, Fineberg and Johnston 1994). Equally as important, they grounded their conclusions in a solid body of data. Our pioneer work on panic behavior now is mostly of historical value only rather than substantive, since the implication of their research is that "panic" ought to be discarded as a worthwhile scientific concept (Quarantelli 2002).

We need many more similar in-depth studies of widely believed findings about disaster phenomena that have a weak empirical base. A list of such topics could probably be developed through a perusal of the *Inventory of Sociological Findings* on disasters compiled by Drabek 1986 (an updated version is in the process of being put together), or some of the chapters in the *Sociology of Disaster* volume (Dynes, De Marchi and Pelanda 1987) or those in the recent tome by Dynes and Tierney 1994.

Research On Disaster Phenomena Only Very Little Or Not Studied.

There are many aspects about disaster behavior where we have extremely little or no knowledge at all. Research should be initiated on such disaster phenomena. In fact, unlike the empirically weak but nonetheless widely held beliefs that we discussed above, we are talking here of where such beliefs do not even exist. Can any disaster researcher cite any widely held beliefs, for example, about disaster-associated aspects of death, sex, or humour? (To be sure there are problems of identifying something as humour such as the current saying circulating in the Los Angeles area, namely, "downtown's a great place to work but it has its faults"). Their absence can be documented by the fact that a search of the DRC library holdings uncovered less than a half dozen publications on all these three topics together.

In a few previously unstudied areas, such as gender, a good and substantial start has been made just this last decade (see Enarson and Morrow 1998; Fordham 1998; Fothergill 1998). With respect to this it is perhaps a commentary of some kind also that the role of women seems to show up more, at least anecdotally, in studies of developing countries (see, e.g. Kelleher 1997). Related to this, and probably not coincidental, Western disaster researchers have paid very little attention to disasters in rural areas (but see such exceptions as Green 1984; Hammerton, Calixte and Pilgrim 1984; *Perspectives on Earthquakes in Rural Areas,* 1994; Mainville 2003). Apart from the people involved, it could be argued that agricultural losses in crops and animals, and damages to soils and topography cannot be rebuilt in the same way as buildings. Yet, if we are going to establish that there are human universals in the disaster area as has been argued for other aspects of human behavior (see Brown 1991), we clearly need systematic studies of rural populations and communities in disasters, because at least along some lines, there are clearly lifestyle differences between rural and urban areas.

Also, there are certain disaster-associated activities that have assumed almost the characteristic of fads, but have been very little studied. As examples we might cite, the Incident Command System especially being pushed in the fire community (for some minor questioning of the system see Stoffel 1994) and the supposed mental health effects of disasters on children (see Aptekar and Boore 1990;

Green 1994). Even the current emphasis on mitigation, begs the question. Do we really know, for instance, that mitigation is the strategy—where is the solid evidence that a focus on mitigation will have the greatest payoff (for a contrary point of view, see Douglas and Wildavsky 1992, who argue there is greater value in developing societal resilience to better cope with environmental adversities; see also Buckle 2003 who also has an earlier chapter in this volume).

Again, it would be worthwhile for someone to compile a master list of topics that have been only little if at all studied. Of course, such a listing requires at least some implicit theoretical notions about what is and is not important for research purposes. We personally, for example, think we need to start intensively looking at the international and national levels of disaster phenomena (about which Drabek 1986, reported we knew very little a decade and a half ago). From our perspective, a case could be made that it is important for a whole variety of reasons to start trying to understand, for example, the decision making involved in international disaster relief or the social norms and cultural values that come into being on giving priority to mitigation measures in a given social system. Others might pick different questions to study. Yet regardless of what criteria might be used, we have no doubt a substantial list of topics could be produced.

Examination Of "Deviant" Cases

We particularly think we need extensive studies of findings that are "deviant," that is, seeming exceptional results that do not fit in with generally accepted research findings. Examinations of such instances could force a major rethinking of accepted disaster generalizations. Of course, one has to encounter and recognize a "deviant" case in the first place, in order to be challenged.

For illustrative purposes, let us give a personal example. We have been one of many who during the years has contributed to the generalization that looting is very rare in disasters, at least in developed societies (this last qualification is not always made by everyone). It is also often said that such looting as does occur is, minor, done by individuals, covertly undertaken, socially disapproved, and opportunistic in nature. When Hurricane Hugo hit St. Croix in the U.S. Virgin Islands, there were immediate news reports about widespread looting on the island. Our initial reaction was to dismiss such accounts as typically incorrect reports (see a discussion of these kinds of reports in Wenger and Quarantelli 1989). However, something just did not seem "right" about the St. Croix situation. To cut a long story short, we ended up making three different trips to the island, doing both intensive interviewing of residents and officials, and a survey of all business in the four shopping centers on St. Croix.

Our field data proved very surprising. There had been massive looting after Hurricane Hugo, not to the extent news reports indicated, but nevertheless very extensive whether measured by places and/or amount of items looted. This conclusion was not in line with other consistent findings about looting in disasters in the United States (going as far back as Fritz 1961). However, that was not the most surprising finding. The looting that occurred in St. Croix was major, done by groups, overtly undertaken, socially approved, and situational in nature. Many will recognize that these features are not only the opposite of those typically found in disasters, but even more important, are the characteristics of looting behavior in riots and civil disturbances! (for looting in the latter situations, see Dynes and Quarantelli 1968; Quarantelli and Dynes 1969, 1970).

What we found was looting which is typical of riots appearing in a disaster occasion. As might be expected, we have pondered this finding and its implications considerably. It would be nice to be able to report that we have intellectually straightened everything out, but we are still considering "what it all means." But the idea of taking the larger social context into account, as we discussed earlier, might be a fruitful path to follow. Looting was far more extensive in the 1977 blackout in New York City than in the 2003 one. But crime statistics for the whole year show that in 1977 burglary occurred seven time as much as in 2003 and robberies occurred about two and a half time as much in 1977 than in 2003

(Traub 2003). To us, that is a significant indicator about the larger social context.

We think we need to examine all "deviant" cases intensively. It will force disaster researchers to at least reconsider what assumptions they are making and the validity of the data on which they base their conclusions. Although we will not have time to discuss the matter here, it is our belief that "deviant" cases are more likely to appear in cross-national, cross-societal and/or cross-cultural research, giving us another reason why we should do more and more such comparative work (for how few studies are actually of a truly comparative nature, see Dynes and Drabek 1994 or Perry and Hirose 1991).

So Far Neglected Institutional Areas

Researchers have very unevenly studied different institutional areas. For example, we have started to learn something about business recovery in the United States (see, French, Ewing and Isaacon 1984; Dahlhamer 1994; Tierney 1994; Dahlhamer and D'Souza 1995; Nigg 1995; for outside the United States, see Britton 1997). Yet we do not have even a descriptive picture, for instance, of the fast food outlets that provide much emergency assistance or how large corporate entities directly and indirectly respond to disasters. But newspaper stories about Hurricane Andrew reported that Exxon donated $300,000 to the Red Cross, Chevron gave $200,000, Home Depot sold plywood, shingles, roofing paper, and sheeting at cost; Beech-Nut Nutrition gave 1,000 cases of baby food, K mart donated 800 cartons of diapers, Campbell Soup sent 500,000 cans of food and General Motors created a matching contribution fund for its employees (Folk 1992: 6B). In some instances, preparedness actions are taken. For instance, Cellular One, the leading cellular telephone company in the Bay Area of San Francisco obtained a commitment from Motorola and AT & I, cellular phone manufacturers, for 4,000 cellular phones that would be distributed to Bay Area emergency response organizations for use in case of a major disaster in the region. Yet, the what, why and who about such activities are totally unknown territories to disaster researchers. Given this, it is not surprising too that there does not appear to be a single study about the role of labor unions in disasters. We think that this involvement of businesses and unions in disasters can as readily be found in societies besides the United States. If so, some interesting cross-societal studies on this topic could be done (for a start see Twigg 2002).

There are also other institutional areas barely touched by disaster scholars. For example, what do we know of religion and disasters? Extremely little we would say. Alexander in his chapter alludes in passing to the probable importance of religion in disasters. There can be no excuse here that religious behavior is unknown territory generally, since anthropologists and sociologists have done much work in the area outside of disasters and there has been a recent resurgence of the field (see, e.g., Leege and Kellstedt 1993; Hadden 1995; Christiano, Swatos and Kivisto 2001; Hunt 2002). It is also very probable that praying is almost certainly one of the most frequently used coping mechanisms for dealing with disastrous occasions. Why has it not been studied? Maybe it says something about the social scientists doing disaster research. Again, we find newspapers doing a better job of tapping such reactions. A New York Times article on a 1994 flood in Georgia with the subtitle; "People who have lost all find a message of solace in religion." (Applebone 1994:14) offered some very interesting observations.

How should we proceed? Taylor (1978) once wrote a chapter on future directions for study. In it, she examined and suggested research into seven institutional areas—political, economic, familial, religious, health, social welfare, mass communication (business is partly treated under economic institutions). Again, it might be worthwhile for someone to look at what she said, and to make some sort of systematic assessment of what is still lacking in the 25 years since that research agenda on institutional areas was set forth.

PROFESSIONAL IMPLEMENTATION

What can we generally conclude from the sweeping survey we have just made? If our observations are valid, we need to somehow or other to implement them. For that, we need cultures and organizations in the disaster area which would facilitate that. This matter will now be discussed although less extensively than the first three areas we have previously examined.

Since our graduate student days, we have always had an interest in the sociology of science and knowledge. Leaving aside technical definitions, these two areas study how social factors influence the development of scientific areas. The basic premise is that scientific behavior is social behavior and that scientists are social beings, and as such both are structured by all the social factors as any other kind of social activity. If so, what kind of cultures and organizations might be best for disaster studies?

Let us ask some relevant questions and issues that need to be addressed 1. How can we increase our funding base? 2. How can our professional infrastructure be strengthened? 3. In what way, can diversity be encouraged in the area? 4. What political considerations need to be addressed? 5. What are the pros and cons of interdisciplinary, multidisciplinary or interfiled activities?

How To Increase Our Funding Base?

A perennial complaint in the area is that there never is enough money to do the research that is necessary. We do not fully agree with this frequent statement—the need for more funding for disaster studies. Part of this stems from our years of reviewing and evaluating proposal submitted to funding agencies, including some outside of the United States. Let us leave aside that our rough estimate is that about half of the proposals should have never been submitted in the first place. More important is that in our judgment some of these as well as other marginal studied unfortunately ended up being funded. If many such studies of poor quality were never funded in the first place, there would be more than enough money to support good studies. at said, how can the current funding base be increased? Let us make two suggestions.

For one, instead of depending so much on governmental funding, a far greater effort should be made to get the support of private foundations and the private sector generally. A move in that direction should be facilitated by the following current conditions. As a market economy system has spread around the world, including in the former Soviet bloc, there is far more of a private sector in all societies than ever existed before. More important, many industries and businesses have very strong self interests for them to be interested and supportive of disaster planning and managing. Finally, for a variety of reasons, crisis management (broader than just the disaster area) has become important in many parts of the private sector. Thus, there is nothing to be lost and much to be gained by looking for more funding from the private sector.

The second idea is that social scientists ought to work much more with engineers and medical researchers. Why? At one level simply because they have much greater prestige and recognition in almost all societies and are more likely to get research funding. To the extent that social scientists can get the protective covering of other areas, they should take advantage of that possibility. This may seem rather cynical, but it is realistic.

Actually more important, the medical and engineering areas are going to be more and more involved in disaster research in the future. This of necessity will involve a multi-disciplinary approach (more of this in a later discussion). We recognize the inherent difficulties involved in social scientists trying to work with personnel from rather different scientific subcultures. We are sure that we could all relate anecdotes of trying to work in such situations but maybe discretion in telling such tales might be wise here!

How Can The Professional Infrastructure Be Strengthened?

Along some lines there has been a remarkable improvement with respect to that in the last decade or so. Among other things we now have a number of journals and newsletters primarily publishing disaster related material. There are professional associations in place particularly The International Research

Committee on Disasters (IRCD) with members in about three dozen countries around the world, and with recent increases in developing countries. The IRCD (www.udel.edu/DRC/IRCD.html) has just established its own publication series using an electronic on-line system as well as an electronic web site for reviewing disaster related material (see http://muweb.millersville.edu/~cdr). Also, the IRCD as well as other groups are having professional meetings and congresses; there seems to be at least one such meeting on the average every week. Finally, colleges and universities around the world have established regular degree programs for the training of disaster researchers and crisis managers. For example, just in the United States alone, there are programs in about 100 colleges and universities that offer 32 Associate Degrees, 39 Bachelor Degrees and 27 Graduate Degrees including the first Ph.D. in Emergency Management (personal communication from Wayne Blanchard).

So there is a partial professional infrastructure in place and it is increasing almost every day. However, far more needs to be done. We grant that the field will survive, but argue that it will not thrive without significant changes. For many reasons, social science studies of disasters will continue even if nothing is done to improve the quality of the studies undertaken. However, in our view, the research results will need to be producing, as we discussed earlier, theories, models, etc.

Where do we see the need for improvement or changes in the existing professional infrastructure? Stated very briefly, the following might be worthwhile. There are only about a half dozen professional journals focused exclusively on disasters. More are needed and should be established although, given the current status of journal subscriptions it might be difficult to get any new journal operative without being part of a professional association. As to the latter, there are probably enough professional associations in the disaster area. But all of them tend to draw only certain segments of the disaster research community. Something ought to be done about that problem. As to more publications, a major problem is that almost all commercial publishers seem to have decided that books on disaster topics written by researchers, are not likely to be profitable. One way to get around this problem is for professional associations to use electronic manuscript printers (such as the IRCD which uses Xlibris). Finally, information on disasters is embedded more and more in college and university courses (as well as courses focused only on disasters and hazards, etc.). So the trend is in the right direction, but there are some questions in our mind about the quality of some of the courses that are taught.

Encouraging Diversity of Scholars In The Area

For a variety of reasons attempts should be made to facilitate the bringing in of new perspectives on disaster research. There is always a need for new "blood" in the field who can see things differently (it was not until we visited Russia that we saw something we had not seen before, by the question a Russian colleague asked, namely, how valid are current research findings that assume a stable social environment for rather different settings such as the former Soviet Union where instability in the environment reigns and is part of everyday life. In retrospect this is an "obvious" question but had not occurred to us before). In fact, we think there is an urgent need to bring in the perspectives, social science as well as social-cultural ones, which are different from the Western ones that prevail. We suggest this because as we see it many older contemporary disaster researchers are not very open to approaches that deviate from what they learned in graduate school. This in no way should be taken as an attack on Western oriented scientific work, as some recent statements in the field seem to imply (see, for example, Hewitt 1995). But it is distressing that some social scientists in the disaster area are not adhering to the norm, even within Western social science, that what is studied and how it is studied should not be dogmatically treated as immutable principles, but as tentative and subject to change if something better appears on the scene.

Fortunately, there is one structural change that is occurring that will increase diversity of scholars in the area. This is that the field of science, including the social sciences, as said earlier is moving toward internationalization, and as Smelser (1991b), in a very insight article notes, there are both pluses and minuses to such a trend. However, one of the advantages are the new perspectives that can be brought to bear, something we do need in the disaster area.

We should try to recruit into the disaster research community, as many professionals and social scientists as possible from outside the discipline. This has nothing to do with simply getting greater number of disaster scholars. It has to do with the fact that there is considerable evidence from the sociology of knowledge area that the greatest innovations in a field are far more likely to be produced by recruited outsiders or peripheral-to-the-field scholars, rather than mainstream figures (Nowotony, Scott and Gibbons 2001). Put another way, intellectual orphans are more likely to have new and unorthodox worthwhile ideas since they are unlikely to know better! Joking aside, there is an important observation here supported by scientific research studies.

Addressing Political Considerations

Too often scientists in all disciplines assume that their research results are the most important factors in obtaining funding and in getting their findings accepted. According to studies in the sociology of science and knowledge, this is a naïve view at best and totally unrealistic at worst. For many reasons, political considerations in the broadest sense of the term "politics" enter into all major decisions in any society.

Given that, it would make sense for social science disaster researchers to get involved with legislative activities relevant to the disaster area. This involvement can range from interacting with key governmental bureaucrats, to testifying before congressional, parliamentary or local council committees, to forming "lobbying" or advocacy groups. This can work even in totalitarian societies and not just more democratically oriented political systems. It should never be forgotten, as political scientists have frequently pointed out, that the political arena is where competing interests in a social system are fought out and where decisions are eventually made. A failure to participate in that process means that either others make the decisions for disaster researchers, or other issues are given higher priority.

Researchers should serve, whenever possible, on multidisciplinary, advisory boards and committees that in some way are involved with the area of disasters. Sometime the presence of a disaster scholar does allow significant input into published reports or recommendations. For example, we think our past membership on the US National Academy of Sciences Board on Natural Disasters (BOND) allowed us to influence somewhat what was officially reported about the actual and possible roles of the social sciences in disaster studies, and to counterbalance the notions that most solutions to problems were to be sought primarily in engineering or the natural sciences.

Interdisciplinary, Multidisciplinary and Inter-field Linkages

At one level, everyone agrees that cooperating with other scientists is a good idea. However, at that level, such agreement is almost meaningless. In part, this is because the general idea obscures important distinctions that need to be made.

For one, a distinction ought to be made between interdisciplinary and multidisciplinary research. They are not the same. As to the former we do not see much of a future for it because there has not been much of a past. First proposed in ancient Greece, it has not fully come into being anywhere in any viable form for more than 2,000 years. Certainly it does not exist in the present spectrum of the sciences at the university levels. In the United States, post World War II failures of interdisciplinary departments at Harvard, Michigan, Columbia, Yale, etc. should tell us something. Why should one expect disaster studies to be in the lead on this when interdisciplinary research is not noticeable in contemporary social science?

Now, the issue of interdisciplinary application of research findings is a different matter, seldom noted, and which badly needs an exploration. The logic of this approach is that no one discipline can provide all the answers, solutions or whatever you want to call them, that would improve disaster planning and managing. This is the position that Britton explicitly advances in his chapter earlier in the volume. But personally we have no suggestions on how we might go beyond a single discipline. Hopefully other scholars might have some relevant ideas on how to proceed on this matter of integrating different and viable answers to common problems.

Then there is the matter of multidisciplinary studies. A stronger case can be made for multidisciplinary studies, although recent and current examples of such work in areas like the family and crime, are not notable for their scientific contributions. (Again, we are talking of research and not application). At least multi as over against interdisciplinary research does not completely forego the advantages of looking at phenomena from a particular disciplinary perspective. Overall, the issue is not a matter of maintaining territorial boundaries or making a claim for the supremacy of some disciplinary, explanatory approach. Rather it is that a disciplinary perspective allows one to see much and brings with it a depth of understanding that is otherwise not possible. The division of labor among the sciences, social ones included, exists because it is worthwhile and valid, and not because of the historical traditions of different disciplines or their intellectual conservatism. But that begs the question of how a meaningful integration can be brought about if the different disciplines are going to maintain their own valuable but different perspectives.

Perhaps if studies were made of actual team efforts of a multidisciplinary nature, we might get some clues on the better models that might be used. What are the pluses and minuses of different models? In addition, and this might have the biggest payoff, perhaps the integration might be sought in the application of research findings from multidisciplinary teams. Again we leave it to others more imaginative than our self to suggest the paths that might be explored. As an aside for those interested in linking different disciplines, there is something called interfield theories which deal with the problems of bridging two fields of science. There is a good discussion of this approach in Darden and Maull (1977).

Finally, we have not addressed at all the practical application of scientific research. This is a complex matter and deserves separate treatment. The only comment we will make here is that some sociologists have attempted to make a general case for the possible contributions of applied social research to more basic or theoretical issues. One of the better such statement is in the Presidential Address to the ASA by Peter Rossi. However, he grants that there is the counter argument that the: "bulk of applied social research is of poor quality and hardly likely to contribute even to the discipline, let alone to the solution of social problems. There is some truth to this argument: Much of applied social research is best left in the fugitive Xerox reports in which they were issued" (1980:891). But that may simply be saying that much applied research is not being done very well, not that it is inherently poor.

In conclusion, we should note that most of the changes advocated in this chapter, do not require new or additional funding. The argument that more money is needed is a perennial, but in our view, not always a valid excuse for failure to take new actions. Financial resources are indeed sometime crucial, but not always. Often more important is the willingness of a few scholars and researchers to take the lead and make some investment of time and effort in helping to improve an area. This would seem to be a minimum responsibility of a professional.

CONCLUSION

The authors of chapters earlier in this volume advanced a number of at least semi-new but also widely varying views on the theoretical issue of what a disaster is, might be addressed. Any advance on matters of disaster theory is worthwhile. However, if the major paradigmatic-related changes we are advocating for the field of disaster studies are to be brought about, it will be necessary to go beyond modifications just in theoretical ideas. The previous authors were not asked to discuss this larger intellectual thrust. But building on what was said, we have tried to suggest what additional theoretical questions ought to be asked, as well as what other changes are also needed in methodological and research activities in disaster studies. We also noted that the theoretical, methodological and research changes could not be brought about unless the field of disaster studies has a strong professional infrastructure to implement the suggested changes.

Our comments are undoubtedly not the last word on these matters. But we hope that they will help nudge the field along. Of course the readers of this volume will have the last words on that, hopefully of a positive nature.

BIBLIOGRAPHY

Abe, K. (1978) "Levels of trust and reactions to various sources of information in catastrophic situations," Pp. 147-158 in Quarantelli, E. L. (ed.), *Disasters: Theory and Research*: Beverly Hills, CA: Sage.

Adam, B. (1995) *Timewatch: The Social Analysis of Time*. Cambridge, MA: Blackwell.

Adam, B. (1998) *Timescapes of Modernity: The Environment and Invisible Hazards*. London: Routledge.

Adam, B., Beck, U. and Van Loon, J. (2000) *The Risk Society and Beyond*. London: Sage.

Agnew, N. and Pyke, S. (1994) *The Science Game*. Saddleback, NJ: Prentice-Hall.

Aguirre, B. (1994) "Cuban mass migration and the social construction of deviants," *Bulletin of Latin American Research* 13: 155-183.

Aguirre, B. (2002) "Can sustainable development help us?" *International Journal of Mass Emergencies and Disasters*. 20: 111-125.

Albala-Bertrand, J. (1993) *The Political Economy of Large Natural Disasters*. Oxford: Clarendon Press.

Alexander, D.E. (1982) "Leonardo da Vinci and fluvial geomorphology," *American Journal of Science* 282: 735-755.

Alexander, D.E. (1989) "Extraordinary and terrifying metamorphosis," Pp 127-150 in Tinkler, K. (ed.) *History of Geomorphology*. Winchester, MA: Unwin-Hyman.

Alexander, D.E. (1991) "Natural disasters: a framework for research and teaching," *Disasters* 15: 209-226.

Alexander, D.E. (1993) *Natural Disasters*. London: UCL Press.
Alexander, D.E. (2000) *Confronting Catastrophe: New Perspectives on Natural Disasters*. Harpenden, UK: Terra Publishing.
Alexander, D.E. (2002a) "Nature's impartiality, man's inhumanity: reflections on terrorism and world crisis in a context of historical disaster," *Disasters* 26(1): 1-9.
Alexander, D.E. (2002b) "From civil defence to civil protection—and back again," *Disaster Prevention and Management* 11(3): 209-213.
Alexander, D.E. (2002c) *Principles of Emergency Planning and Management*. NY: Oxford University Press.
Alexander, J. (1991) "Sociological theory and the claim to reason," *Sociological Theory* 9: 148-153.
Allen, P. (2003) Private communication.to Denis Smith. Liverpool, UK: Centre for Risk and Crisis Management University of Liverpool Management School
Almond, G.A., Flanagan, S.C. and Mundt, R.J. (1973) *Crisis, Choice, and Change: Historical Studies of Political Development*. Boston: Little, Brown and Company.
Amenta, E., Bonastia, C. and Caren, N. (2001) "Social policy in comparative and empirical perspective," *Annual Review of Sociology* 27: 213-234.
Amor, D. (2002) *The E-business E(revolution): Living and working in an interconnected society*. Uppers Saddle River, NJ: Prentice Hall.
Anderson, A. (1997) *Media, Culture and the Environment*. New Brunswick, NJ: Rutgers University Press.
Anderson, C. (2003) *Get Wireless Everything You Need to Know About the WI-F Revolution*. NY: Conde Nast Publications.
Anderson, M. (1995) "Vulnerability to disaster and sustainable development: A general framework for assessing vulnerability," Pp42-59 in M. Munasinghe and C. Clarke (eds.) *Disaster Prevention for Sustainable Development: Economic and Policy Issues*. Washington, DC: The World Bank.
Anderson, P. (1994) "Disaster mitigation in the age of distributed networking: The emergency preparedness information exchange project-EPIX," *STOP Disasters Newsletter* 22: 20-21.

Anderson, W.A. and Mattingly, S. (1991) "Future directions," Pp. 311-335, in T.E. Drabek and G.J.Hoetmer (eds.). *Emergency Management: Principles and Practice for Local Government.* Washington DC: International City Management Association.
Angell, M. (1996) *Science on Trial.* NY: Norton.
Applebome, P. (1994) "In a flooded Georgia city, care for living, and dead," *New York Times* July 10, P. 14.
Aptekar, L. and Boore, J. (1990) "The emotional effects of disaster on children: A review of the literature," *International Journal of Mental Health* 19: 77-90.
Atmor, M. (2001) "Politicisation of humanitarian aid and its consequences for Afghans," *Disasters* 25(4): 321-330.
Auge, M. (1995) *Non-places: Introduction to an Anthropology of Supermodernity.* London: Verso.
Austin, J. (2001) *Taking the Train: How Graffiti Art Became an Urban Crisis in New York City.* NY: Columbia University Press.
Austin, T. (1967) *Aberfan: The Story of a Disaster.* London: Hutchinson.
Baker, P. (1993) "Space, time, space-time and society (spacetime in the context of sociological and anthropological notions of space and time)," *Sociological Inquiry* 63: 406-424.
Baker, R. (2001) *Harold Shipman's Clinical Practice 1974-1998.* London: Department of Health.
Baldus, B. (1990) "Positivism's twilight," *Canadian Journal of Sociology* 15: 149-159.
Ball, M. and Smith, G. (1992) *Analyzing Visual Data.* Newbury Park, CA: Sage.
Banfield, E. C. (1958) *The Moral Basis of a Backward Society.* Glencoe, IL: Free Press.
Bankoff, G. (2001) "Rendering the world unsafe: 'vulnerability' as Western discourse," *Disasters* 25(1): 19-35.
Bankoff, G. (2003) *Cultures of Disaster: Society and Natural Hazard in the Philippines.* London: Routledge.
Barabasi, A. (2002) *Linked: The New Science of Networks.* London: Perseus.
Barkun, M. (1979) "Disaster in History," *International Journal on Mass Emergencies and Disasters* 2: 219-231.

Barnett, T. and Whiteside, A. (2002) *AIDS in the Twenty-first Century: Disease and Globalization*. Basingstoke: Palgrave Macmillan.

Barton, A. H. (1963) *Social Organization Under Stress: A Sociological Review of Disaster Studies*. Washington, DC: National Academy of Sciences-National Research Council.

Barton, A. H. (1969) Communities in Disaster. A Sociological Analysis of Collective Stress Situations. NY: Doubleday.

Barton, A. H. (1989) "Taxonomies of Disaster and Macrosocial Theory," Pp 346-351 in G. A. Kreps (ed.), *Social Structure and Disaster*. Newark, DE: University of Delaware Press.

Barton, A. H. (1995) "Asking why about social problems: ideology and causal models in the public mind," *International Journal of Public Opinion Research* 7(4): 299-327.

Barton, A. H. (2001) "The resurrection of Marxist economics in the age of globalization," Paper presented at the 5th Conference of the European Sociological Association, Helsinki, August, 2001.

Barton, A. H. (2003) Disaster and collective stress. Unpublished paper.

Barton, A. H. and Lazarsfeld, P. (1955) "Some functions of qualitative analysis in social research," (First published in the *Frankfurter Beitrare Zur Soziologie*. Republished as S-336 in Bobbs-Merrill Reprint Series in the Social Sciences).

Baxter, J. and Downing, M. (2001) *The Day that Shook the World: Understanding September 11th*. London: BBC Worldwide Ltd.

Beavers, J., Mileti, D. and Peek, L. (2000) "Dealing with natural hazards requires a new approach," *Natural Hazards Review* 1: 65-66.

Beck, U. (1992) *Risk Society: Towards a New Modernity*. London: Sage.

Becker, H. (1974) "Photography and sociology," *Studies in the Anthropology of Visual Communication* 5: 3-26.

Becker, J. (1996) *Hungry Ghosts: China's Secret Famine*. London: J. Murray.

Benthall, J. (1993) *Disasters, Relief and the Media*. London: I.B. Tauris.

Benton, M. J. (2003) *When Life Nearly Died*. London: Thames and Hudson.
Berger, P., Luckmann, T. (1966) *The Social Construction of Reality*. NY: Doubleday.
Bernstein, P.L. (1996) *Against the Gods: The Remarkable Story of Risk*. NY: John Wiley.
Berridge, V. (1996) *AIDS in the UK*. Oxford: Oxford University Press.
Berz, G. (2002) *The Future and Natural Disasters* Transcript Earthbeat Radio National (Australian Broadcasting Commission) 19 November 2002.
Best, J. (2001) "Review of: The culture of fear: why Americans are afraid of the wrong things," *Contemporary Sociology* 30: 113-115.
Bird, M. J. (1962) *The Town that Died*. NY: Putnam.
Blaikie, P., T. Cannon, I. Davis and B. Wisner (1994) *At Risk: Natural Hazards, People's Vulnerability and Disasters*. Routledge: London.
Blanchard, W. (2003) "Personal communication to E.L. Quarantelli." Newark, DE: University of Delaware Disaster Research Center.
Blanshan, S. A. (1978) "A time model: hospital organizational response to disaster," Pp. 35-49 in E. L. Quarantelli (ed.), *Disasters*: 173-198. Beverly Hills, CA: SAGE.
Bloch, E. (1977) *Das Materialismusproblem*. Frankfurt: Suhrkamp.
Blong, R. (1997) "The geography of perils," *Australian Geographer*. 28(1): 7-27.
Bluedora, A. (2002) *The Human Organization of Time*. Stanford, CA: Stanford Business Books.
Blumer, H. (1954) "What is wrong with social theory?" *American Sociological Review* 19: 3-10.
Boin, R.A. (2003) *Crisis Management in Europe: A Discussion of Key Factors in Improving Safety*. Unpublished paper.
Boin, R.A. and 't Hart, P. (2003) "Public leadership in times of crisis," *Public Administration Review* 63 (September): 544-552.

Boin, R.A. and Lagadec, P. (2000) "Preparing for the future: Critical challenges in crisis management," *Journal of Contingencies and Crisis Management*. 8:185-191.

Boin, R.A., Van Duin, M.J. and Heyse, L. (2001) "Toxic fear: The management of uncertainty in the wake of the Amsterdam air crash," *Journal of Hazardous Materials*. 88:213-234.

Bolt, B. A. (1999) *Earthquakes*. NY: W.H. Freeman.

Boorstin, D.J. (1992) *The Creators*. NY: Vintage Books.

Boulter, M. (2002) *Extinction. Evolution and the End of Man*. London: Fourth Estate.

Bourque, L., Kimberley, S. and L. Nguyen. (2002) "Survey research," Pp. 157-192 in R. Stallings (ed.) *Methods of Disaster Research*. Philadelphia, PA.: Xlibris Books.

Bovens, M. and 't Hart, P. (1996) *Understanding Policy Fiascoes*. New Brunswick, NJ: Transaction Books.

Bovens, M., 't Hart, P. and Peters, B.G. (eds.) (2001) *Success and Failure in Public Governance: A Comparative Perspective*. Cheltenham: Edgar Elgar.

Brecher, M. and Wilkenfeld, J. (1997) *A Study of Crisis*. Ann Arbor, MI: University of Michigan Press.

Britton, N.R. (1986) "Developing an understanding of disaster," *Australian and NewZealand Journal of Sociology*. 22(2):254-272.

Britton, N. R. (1997) "Making progress with business continuity planning for natural disaster management," Pp. 235-263 in N. Britton and J. Oliver (eds.) *Financial Risk Management for Natural Catastrophes*. Australia: Aon Group Australia Limited.

Britton, N.R. (1999) "Whither the emergency manager?" *International Journal of Mass Emergencies and Disasters*. 17(2): 223-235.

Britton, N.R. (2002) "A new emergency management for a new millennium?" *Australian Journal of Emergency Management*. 16(4): 44-54.

Brown, D. (1991) *Human Universals*. Philadelphia, PA: Temple University Press.

Brown, R. (1990) "Rhetoric, textuality, and postmodern turn in sociological theory," *Sociological Theory* 8:188-197.

Brown, T., & Duncan, C. (2002) "Placing geographies of public health," *Area*, 33(4): 361-369.
Buchanan, M. (2003) *Nexus: Small Worlds and the Groundbreaking Science of Networks.* NY: Norton.
Buckle, P. (2001) *Assessing resilience and vulnerability: A radical paradigm for disaster management.* Unpublished paper.
Buckle, P. *(2003) "Some contemporary issues in disaster management,"* International Journal of Mass Emergencies and Disasters *21: 109-122.*
Buckle, P., Marsh, G. and Smale, S. *(2001a)* Assessment of Personal and Community Resilience and Vulnerability. *Canberra: Report to Emergency Management Australia Project.*
Buckle, P., Marsh, G. and Smale, S. *(2001b)* Assessing Resilience and Vulnerability: Principles, Strategies and Actions. *Canberra: Report to Emergency Management Australia.*
Buckle, P., Marsh, G. and Smale, S. (2002) "Reframing risk, hazards, disasters and daily life," *International Journal of Mass Emergencies and Disasters* 20: 309-320.
Bull, P. (1983) *Body Movement and Interpersonal Communication.* N.Y.: Wiley.
Bunge, M. (1998) *Social Science under Debate: a philosophical perspective.* Toronto: University of Toronto Press.
Burby, R. (1998) *Cooperating with Nature: Confronting Natural Hazards With Land Use Planning for Sustainable Development.* Washington, DC: National Academy Press.
Burgess, R. (1984) *In the Field: An Introduction to Field Research.* London: Allen and Unwin.
Burns, J. (1985) "23 seconds in '76, and a Chinese city still aches," *New York Times,* February 13, P. 2.
Burstein, P. (1981) "The sociology of democratic politics and government," *Annual Review of Sociology* 7: 291-319.
Burstein, P. (1991) "Policy domains: Organization, culture and policy outcomes," *Annual Review of Sociology* 17: 327-350.
Burstein, P. (1998) "Bringing the public back in," *Social Forces* 77: 27-62.
Burton, I, Kates, R. and White, G. (1978) *The Environment as Hazard.* NY: Oxford University Press.

Burton, I, Kates, R. and White, G. (1993) *The Environment as Hazard*, second edition. NY: Guildford Press.

Buskens, V. (2002) *Social Networks and Trust*. Boston: Kluwer Academic Publishers.

Butler, D. (1994) "The information revolution and disaster management," *CUSEC Journal* 2: 4b.

Butler, D. (2002) "Selected internet resources on natural hazards and disasters," Pp. 389-464 in R. A. Stallings (ed.) *Methods of Disaster Research*. Philadelphia, PA: Xlibris Books.

Butler, D. (n.d.) *Information systems and knowledge transfer: Prospects for better understanding opportunities for increased hazard mitigation*. Unpublished paper.

Byrne, D. (1998) *Complexity Theory and the Social Sciences*. London: Routledge.

Byrne, D. (2002) *Interpreting Quantitative Data*. London: Sage Publications.

Calhoun, C., Price, P. and Timmer, A. (2002) *Understanding September 11*. NY: The New Press.

Calman, K., and Smith, D. (2001) "Works in theory but not in practice?" *Public Administration* 79(1): 185-204.

Cantor, N. F. (2001) *In the Wake of the Plague*. London: Pocket Books.

Carr, L. (1932) "Disaster and the Sequence-Pattern Concept of Social Change," *American Journal of Sociology* 38: 207-218.

Cassirer, E. (1956-1958). *Philosophie der symbolischen Formen*. Darmstadt: Wiss.Buchgesellschaft.

Chalmers, A. (1978) *What is this thing called Science?* Philadelphia, PA: Open University Press.

Charron, J. (2000) *Symbolic Interactionism: An Introduction, an Interpretation, an Integration*. NY: US Imports.

Checkland, P. B. (1981) *Systems Thinking, Systems Practice*. Chichester: Wiley.

Checkland, P. B., and Holwell, S. (1998) *Information, Systems and Information Systems*. Chicester: Wiley.

Checkland, P. B., and Scholes, J. (1990) *Soft Systems Methodology in Action*. Chichester: Wiley.

Chenault, W., Engler, R. and Nordlie, P. (1967) *Social and Behavioral Factors in the Implementation of Survival and Recovery Activities.* McLean, VA: Human Sciences Research Inc.
Chiles, J. (2001) *Inviting disaster.* NY: Harper.
Chowdbury. G. (2001) *Information Sources and Searching on the World Wide Web.* London: Library Association.
Christopher, B. (2002) *Postmodernism.* N.Y. Oxford.
Claessens, D. (1980) *Das Konkrete und das Abstrakte. Soziologische Skizzen zur Anthropologie.* Frankfurt: Suhrkamp
Clarke, L. (1999) *Mission Improbable: Using Fantasies to Tame Disaster.* Chicago: University of Chicago Press.
Clifford, N. (2001) "Physical geography: the naughty world revisited," *Transactions of the Institute of British Geographers, New Series,* 26(4): 387-389.
Cohen, S., Eimicke, W., and Horan, J. (2002) "Catastrophe and the public service," *Public Administration Review,* 62: 24-32.
Cohn, N. (1993) *Cosmos, Chaos, and the World to Come.* London: Yale University Press
Comfort, L. (1988) *Managing Disaster.* Durham,NC: Duke University Press.
Comfort, L., Wisner, B. Cutter, S., Pulwarty, R., Hewitt, K., Oliver-Smith, A., Wiener, J., Fordham, M., Peacock, W. and Krimgold,F. (1999) "Reframing disaster policy," *Environmental Hazards* 1:39-44.
Committee on Disaster Studies. (1956) *Disaster Study Number 1: Human Behavior in Extreme Situations.* Washington, DC: National Academy of Sciences-National Research Council.
Couch, S. (2000) "The cultural scene of disasters," *International Journal of Mass Emergencies and Disasters* 18(1): 21-38.
Coveney, P. and Highfield, R. (1995) *Frontiers of Complexity.* London: Faber and Faber.
Cross, J. (1990) "Longitudinal change in hurricane hazard perception," *International Journal of Mass Emergencies and Disasters* 8(1): 31-48.
Crow, G. and Heath, S. (2002) *Social Conceptions of Time.* NY: Palgrave MacMillian.

Crozier, M. (1964) *The Bureaucratic Phenomenon.* Chicago: University of Chicago Press.
CSIS (2000) *Defending American in the 21st Century.* Washington, DC: Center for Strategic and International Studies.
Cuny, F. (1983) *Disasters and Development.* NY: Oxford University Press.
Curtis, R. and Aguirre, B. (1993) *Collective Behavior and Social Movements.* Boston: Allyn and Bacon.
Cuthbertson, B. and Nigg, J. (1987) "Technological disaster and the nontherapeutic community," *Environment and Behavior* 19(4): 462-483.
Cutter, S. L. (1994) *Environmental Risks and Hazards.* Englewood Cliffs, N.J.: Prentice Hall.
Cutter, S. L. (2001a) *American Hazardscapes: The Regionalization of Hazards and Disasters.* Washington DC: The Joseph Henry Press.
Cutter, S. L. (2001b) "A research agenda for vulnerability science and environmental hazards," *IHDP Update, Newsletter of the International Human Dimensions Programme on Global Environmental Change* 2:8-9.
Cutter, S. L. (2003) "The vulnerability of science and the science of vulnerability," *Annals of the Association of American Geographers* 93 (1):1-12.
Cutter, S. L., Richardson, D. and Wilbanks, T. (2003) *The Geographical Dimensions of Terrorism.* NY: Routledge.
Dahlhamer, J. (1994) *Loan Request Outcomes in the U.S. Small Business Administration Loan Program.* Newark, DE.: Disaster Research Center, University of Delaware.
Dahlhamer, J. and D'Souza, M. (1995) *Determinants of Business Disaster Preparedness in two U.S. Metropolitan Areas.* Newark, DE: Disaster Research Center, University of Delaware.
Darden, L. and Maull, N. (1977) "Interfield Theories," *Philosophy of Science* 44: 43-64.
Dash, N. (2002) "The use of geographic information systems in disaster research," Pp. 320-333 in R. A. Stallings (ed.) *Methods of Disaster Research.* Philadelphia PA.: Xlibris.

Davies, G. (1989) "On the nature of geo-history, with reflections on the historiography of geomorphology," Pp. 1-10 in Tinkler, K. (ed.) *History of Geomorphology*. Boston: Unwin-Hyman.
Davis, D. (2002) *When smoke ran like water.* Oxford: Perseus Press.
Davis, M. (1998) *Ecology of Fear.* NY: Metropolitan Books.
Davis, M. (2001) *Late Victorian holocausts.* London: Verso.
Dearing, J. and Meyer, G. (1994) "An exploratory tool for predicting adoption decisions," *Science Communications.* 16: 43-57. de Boer, J. and Sanders, D. (2002) *Volcanoes in Human History.* Princeton: Princeton University Press.
Degg, M. (1993) "The 1992 Cairo Earthquake," *Disasters* 17: 226-238.
De Greene, K. (1996) "Field-Theoretic Framework for the Interpretation of the Evolution, Instability, Structural Change, and Management of Complex Systems," Pp. 273-323 in Elliott, E. and Kiel L. (eds.) *Chaos Theory in the Social Sciences* Ann Arbor: University of Michigan Press
Dembo, D., Morehouse, W. and Wykle, L. (1990) *Abuse of Power: Social Performance of Multinational Corporations.* NY: New Horizons Press.
Dempster, J. and Brammer, H. (1992) "Flood Action Plan: Bangladesh," *Outlook on Agriculture* 21(4): 301-305.
Denzin, N. (1986) "Postmodern Social Theory," *Sociological Theory* 4: 194-204.
Denzin, N. and Lincoln, Y. (2000) *Handbook of Qualitative Research. Second Edition.* Thousand Oaks, CA.: Sage.
Devereaux, S. (2000) *Famine in the Twentieth Century.* Sussex, UK: Institute of Development Studies.
Dilley, M. (2000) "Climate, change and disasters," Pp. 45-50 in Kreimer, A. and Arnold, M. (eds.) *Managing Risk in Emerging Economies.* Washington, DC: The World Bank.
Dilthey, W. (1972) Entwurf zu "Die Entstehung der Hermeneutik", Pp. 74-86 in: Pöggeler, O. (ed.) *Hermeneutische Philosophie*. München: Nymphenburger Verlagsgesellschaft.
Dombrowsky, W.R. (1989) *Katastrophe und Katastrophenschutz. Eine soziologische Analyse.* Wiesbaden: Deutscher Universitätsverlag.

Dombrowsky, W. R. (1995) "Again and again: Is a disaster what we call "disaster?" *International Journal of Mass Emergencies and Disasters* 13: 241-254.
Dombrowsky, W. R. (1998) "Again and again: Is a disaster what we call a disaster?" Pp. 19-30.in Quarantelli, E. L. (ed.) *What is a Disaster? Perspectives on the Question.* London. Routledge.
Douglas, M. and Wildavsky, A. (1982) *Risk and Culture.* Berkeley: University of California Press.
Downton, M. and Pielke Jr., R. (2001) "Discretion without accountability: Politics, flood damage, and climate," *Natural Hazards Review* 2(4):157-166.
Drabek, T.E. (1985) "Managing the emergency response," *Public Administration Review* 45: 85-92.
Drabek, T. E. (1986) *Human System Response to Disaster: an inventory of sociological findings.* NY: Springer Verlag.
Drabek, T.E. (1989) "Taxonomy and Disasters," Pp. 317-346 in Kreps, G. (ed.) *Social Structure and Disaster.* Newark, DE: University of Delaware Press.
Drabek, T.E. (1991) "The evolution of emergency management," Pp. 3-29. Drabek, T.E. and Hoetmer, G.J. (eds.) *Emergency Management: Principles and Practice for Local Government.* Washington DC: International City Management Association.
Dreze. J. and Sen, A. (1989) *Hunger and Public Action.* Oxford: Oxford University Press.
Dymond, D. (1981) *Writing Local History; A Practical Guide.* London: Bedford Square Press.
Dynes, R. (1978) "Interorganizational relations in communities under stress," Pp. 49-64 in Quarantelli, E.L. (ed.) *Disasters: theory and research*: Beverly Hills, CA: Sage.
Dynes, R. (1983) "Problems in emergency planning," *Energy*, 8(8-9): 653-660
Dynes, R. (1998) "Coming to terms with community disasters," Pp. 109-126 in Quarantelli, E.L. (ed.). *What is a Disaster? Perspectives on the Question.* London: Routledge.
Dynes, R. (2000a) "The Lisbon Earthquake in 1755: Contested Meanings in the First Modern Disaster," *TsuInfo Alert* 2: 10-18.

Dynes, R. (2000b) "The Dialogue between Voltaire and Rousseau on the Lisbon Earthquake: The Emergence of a Social Science View," *International Journal of Mass Emergencies and Disasters* 18: 97-115.

Dynes, R. and Drabek, T. E. (1994) "The structure of disaster research: Its policy and disciplinary implications," *International Journal of Mass Emergencies and Disasters* 12: 25-49.

Dynes, R. and Quarantelli, E. L. (1968) "Redefinition of property norms in community emergencies," *International Journal of Legal Research* 3:100-112.

Dynes, R. and Quarantelli, E. L. (1976) "The family and community context of individual reactions to disaster," Pp. 231-245 in Parad, H. Resnick, H. and Parad, L. (eds.) *Emergency and Disaster Management: A Mental Health Sourcebook*. Bowie, Maryland: Charles Press.

Dynes, R., Quarantelli, E. L. and Wenger, D. (1990) *Individual and Organizational Response to the 1985 earthquake in Mexico City, Mexico*. Newark, DE: University of Delaware Disaster Research Center.

Dynes, R. and Tierney, K. (eds.) (1994) *Disasters Collective Behavior and Social Organization*. Newark, DE: University of Delaware Press.

Dynes, R. and Yutzy, D. (1965) "The Religious Interpretation of Disasters," *Topic: A Journal of the Liberal Arts* 10 (Fall): 34-48.

Dynes, R., De Marchi, B. and Pelanda, C. (1987) *Sociology of Disasters: Contributions of Sociology to Disaster Research*. Milan, Italy: Franco Angeli.

Eakin, E. (2003) "Connect, they say, only connect" *New York Times* January 26, P. A5.

"Ecuadoreans wait uneasily on volcanoes: Threats of eruption leave life disrupted." *New York Times*, August 15, P. F5.

Edelman, M.J. (1971) *Politics as Symbolic Action: Mass Arousal and Quiescence*. Chicago: Markham.

Edelman, M.J. (1977) *Political Language: Words that Succeed and Policies that Fail*. NY: Academic Press.

Ehrlich, P. and Ehrlich, A. (1996) *Betrayal of Science and Reason*. Washington, DC: Shearwater.

Elias, N. (1981) Was ist Soziologie? München: Juventa
Ellemers, J.E. (2001) "Rampen in Nederland," *Sociologische Gids* 48:231-252.
Elliott, D., and Smith, D. (1993) "Football stadia disasters in the United Kingdom: Learning from tragedy," *Industrial and Environmental Crisis Quarterly*, 7(3): 205-229.
Elliott, D., Smith, D., and McGuinness, M. (2000) "Exploring the failure to learn: Crises and the barriers to learning," *Review of Business* 21(3): 17-24.
Ellis, C. and Ellingson, L. (2000) "Qualitative methods," Pp. 2287-2296 in Borgatta, B. and Montgomery, R. (eds.) *Encyclopedia of Sociology, Second edition*. N.Y.: Macmillan.
Ellis, P. (1998) "Chaos in the underground," *Journal of Contingencies and Crisis Management.* 6:137-151.
Emergency Management Australia. (1998) *Australian Emergency Manuals Series*. Canberra: Emergency Management Australia.
Emmison, M. (2000) *Researching the Visual: Image, Objects, Contexts and Interactions in Social and Cultural Inquiry*. London: Sage.
Enarson, E. and Morrow, B. (1998) *The Gendered Terrain of Disaster*. NY: Praeger.
Engstrom, D. (1997) *Presidential Decision Making Adrift: The Carter Administration and the Mariel Boatlift*. Lanham, MD: Rowan and Littlefield.
Epstein, S. (1996) *Impure Science*. Berkeley, CA: University of California Press.
Erikson, K.T. (1994) *A New Species of Trouble: Explorations in Disaster, Trauma and Community*. NY: Norton.
Esping-Anderson, G. (1985) *Politics Against Markets: The Social Democratic Road to Power*. Princeton, NJ: Princeton University Press.
Esser, J. K. and Lindoerfer, J. S. (1989) "Groupthink and the space shuttle Challenger accident," *Journal of Behavioral Decision Making* 2: 167-177.
Etkin, D. (1999) "Risk transference and related trends," *Environmental Hazards* 1: 69-75.
Fagan, B. (2000) *Floods, famines and emperors*. London: Pimlico.
Federal Emergency Management Agency (FEMA). (2003*) The*

Robert T. Stafford Disaster Relief and Emergency Assistance Act, (U.S.C. 5121, et seq.) Washington, DC: Federal Emergency Management Agency.
Feder, B. (1993) "Winners as well as losers in the Great Flood of '93," *New York Times,* August 15, P. F5.
Feyerabend, P. (1979) *Erkenntnis für freie Menschen.* Frankfurt: Suhrkamp.
Fielding, N. and Lee, R. (1991) *Using Computers in Qualitative Research.* Thousand Oaks, CA.: Sage.
Fischer, C. (1994) "In search of the plot," *Contemporary Sociology* 23: 31-44.
Fischer, H. (2003) "The *Sociology* of disaster: definitions, research questions and measurements," *International Journal of Mass Emergencies and Disasters* 21(1): 91-107.
Fisher, A. (1985) "Voluntary Labor, Utah, the L. D. S. Church, and the floods of 1983," *International Journal of Mass Emergencies and Disasters* 3(3): 53-74.
Fisher, R. V. (1999) *Out of the Crater: Chronicles of a Volcanologist.* Princeton, NJ: Princeton University Press.
Fisher, R. V., Heiken, G., and Hulen, J. B. (1997) *Volcanoes.* Princeton, NJ: Princeton University Press.
Flaherty, M. (1993) "Conceptualizing variation in the experience of time," *Sociological Inquiry* 63: 394-416.
Foerster, H. von. (1985) *Sicht und Einsicht. Versuche zu einer operativen Erkenntnistheorie.* Braunschweig: Friedrich Vieweg und Sohn
Folk, M. (1992) "Businesses rush to help," *USA Today,* September 1, P. 6B.
Fordham, M. (1998) "Making women visible in disasters," *Disasters* 22: 126-143.
Fothergill, A. (1996) "Gender, risk, and disaster," *International Journal of Mass Emergencies and Disasters* 14 (1): 33-56.
Forthergill, A. (1998) "The neglect of gender in disaster work: An overview of the literature," Pp. 11-25 in Enarson, E. and Morrow,B. (eds.) *The Gendered Terrain of Disaster.* Westport, CT.: Praeger.

Fothergill, A. (2000) "Knowledge transfer between researchers and practitioners," *Natural Hazards Review.* 1(2): 91-98.

Forrest, T. (1993) "Disaster anniversary: A social reconstruction of time," *Sociological Inquiry* 63:444-457.

Franke, R. and Chasin, B. (1994) *Kerala: Radical Reform as Development in an Indian State.* Oakland, CA: Institute for Food and Development Policy.

Frantz, D. (1994) "Reports describe widespread abuse in farm program," *New York Times* October 3, P. A1.

French, S., Ewing, C. and Isaacon,M. (1984) *Restoration and Recovery Following the Coalinqua Earthquake of May 1983.* Boulder, CO: Institute of Behavioral Science, University of Colorado.

Freudenburg, W. (1988) "Perceived Risk, Real Risk: Social Science and the Art of Probabilistic Risk Assessment," *Science* 242: 44-49.

Fritz, C. (1961) "Disaster," Pp. 651-694 in Merton, R. and Nisbet, R. (eds.) *Contemporary Social Problems.* NY: Harcourt.

Fritz, C. and Mathewson, J. (1957) *Convergence Behavior in Disasters.* Washington, DC: National Academy of Sciences.

Gabriel, P. (2002) "The development of municipal emergency management planning in Victoria, Australia," *International Journal of Mass Emergencies and Disasters* 20: 293-307.

Galtung, J. (1979) *Methodology and Development.* NY: Harper.

Gans, H. (1972) "The positive functions of poverty," *American Journal of Sociology* 78: 275-289.

Gans, H. (1992) "Sociological amnesia: The noncumulation of normal social science," *Sociological Forum* 7: 701-710.

Gatrell, A. and Vincent, P. (1990) *Managing Natural and Technological Hazards: The Role of GIS.* Lancaster, UK: Regional Research Laboratory, University of Lancaster.

Gherardi, S. (1998) "A cultural approach to disasters," *Journal of Contingencies and Crisis Management* 6(2): 80-83.

Giddens, A. (1990) *The Consequences of Modernity.* Cambridge: Polity Press.

Gigerenzer, G., Swijtink, Z., Porter, T., Daston, L., Beatty, J. and Krüger, L. (1989) *The Empire of Chance.* Cambridge: Cambridge University Press

Gilbert, C. (1995) "Studying disaster: A review of the main conceptual tools," *International Journal of Mass Emergencies and Disasters* 13: 231-240.

Gilbert, C. (1998) "Studying disaster: changes in the main conceptual tools," Pp. 11-18 in Quarantelli, E.L. (ed.) *What is a Disaster? Perspectives on the Question.* London: Routledge.

Glaser, B. and Strauss, A. (1967) *The Discovery of Grounded Theory: Strategies for Qualitative Research.* Chicago: Aldine.

Glassner, B. (1999) *The Culture of Fear: Why Americans Are Afraid of the Wrong Things.* NY: Basic Books.

Godschalk, R., Beatley, T., Berke, P., Brower, D. Kaiser, E. Bohl, C. and Goebel, R. (1999) *Natural Hazard Mitigation: Recasting Disaster Policy and Planning.* NY: Island Press.

Golec, J. (1983) "A contextual approach to the social psychological study of disaster recovery," *International Journal of Mass Emergencies and Disasters* 1(2) 255-276.

Goltz, J. (1984) "Are the news media responsible for the disaster myths?" *International Journal of Mass Emergencies and Disasters* 2(3): 345-368.

Gottlieb, M. (2003) "Campaign Starts to Help Iraq Rebuild Cultural Institutions," *New York Times,* April 30, P. A15.

Gould, S. J. (2000) "Deconstructing the "science wars" by reconstructing an old mold," *Science* 287:253-261.

Government of Victoria (2001) *Emergency Management Manual.* Melbourne: Government Printer.

Government of Victoria (1986) *Emergency Management Act.* Melbourne: Government Printer.

Grant, N., Hoover, D. Scarisbrick-Hauser, A. and Muffet, S. (2002) *Terrorism in Shanksville: A study in preparedness and response.* Boulder, CO: Natural Hazards Research and Applications Information Center, University of Colorado

Grass, G. (2002) *Crabwalk.* Orlando, FL: Harcourt.

Green, B. (1994) "Psychosocial research in traumatic stress: An update," *Journal of Traumatic Stress* 7: 341-441.

Green, K. (1984) *Implications of Rural-Urban Differentiation: A Study of Local Grass Roots Organizations in Disaster Situations.* Ph.D. Dissertation. Columbus, OH: Ohio State University.

Greenberg, J. W. (2002) "September 11, 2001 A CEO's story," *Harvard Business Review* 80(10): 58-64.

Griffin, L. (1992) "Temporality, events and explanation in historical sociology," *Sociological Methods and Research* 20: 403-427.

Gupta, D. (2003) *Three Types of Cultural Landscape*. Unpublished paper.

Habermas, J. (1973) *Positivismus, Pragmatismus, Historismus, in Erkenntnis und Interesse*. Frankfurt.: Suhrkamp.

Habermas, J. (1975 [1973]) *Legitimation Crisis*. Boston: Beacon Press.

Haggett, P. (2000) *The Geographical Structure of Epidemics*. Oxford: Oxford University Press.

Hadden, J. (1995) "Religion and the quest for meaning and order," *Sociological Focus* 28: 83-100.

Hammerton, J., Calixte, G. and Pilgrim, R. (1984) "Hurricanes and agriculture: Losses and remedial actions," *Disasters* 8: 279-286.

Hans, V. and Nigg, J. (1994) *Judgments of Responsibilities for Disaster Consequences*. Newark, DE: Disaster Research Center, University of Delaware.

Haque, C. and Blair, D. (1992) "Vulnerability to tropical cyclones; evidence from the April 1991 cyclone in coastal Bangladesh," *Disasters* 16: 217-229.

Harding, S. (1991) *Whose science, whose knowledge?* Ithaca, NY: Cornell University Press.

Harper, D. (1994) "On the authority of the image; Visual methods in the crossroads," Chapter 25 in Denzin, N. and Lincoln, Y. (eds.) *Handbook of qualitative Research*. Thousand Oaks, CA.: Sage.

't Hart, P. (1993) "Symbols, rituals and power: The lost dimensions of crisis management," *Journal of Contingencies and Crisis Management* 1:36-50.

't Hart, P. and Boin, R.A. (2001) "Between crisis and normalcy," Pp. 28-46 in Rosenthal, U., Boin, R.A. and Comfort, L. (eds). *Managing Crises: Threats, Dilemmas, Opportunities*. Springfield: Charles C. Thomas.

Heap, N., Thomas, R., Einon, G., Mason, R. and Mackay, H. (1995) *Information Technology and Society.* Beverly Hills, CA.: Sage.
Heidegger, M. (1972). Verstehen und Auslegung, Pp. 87-99 in Pöggeler, O. (ed.) *Hermeneutische Philosophie.* München: Nymphenburger Verlagsgesellschaft.
Heise, D. and Duric, A. (2000) "Qualitative models," Pp. 2296-2299 in Borgatta, E. and Montgomery, R. (eds.) *Encyclopedia of Sociology, Second edition.* N.Y.: Macmillan.
Heinz Center. (2002) *Human Links to Coastal Disasters.* Washington, DC: H. John Heinz Center for Science, Economics, and the Environment.
Hewitt, J. and Hall, P. (1973) "Social Problems, Problematic Situations, and Quasi-Theories," *American Sociological Review* 38: 367-374.
Hewitt, K. (1983) *Interpretations of Calamity from the Viewpoint of Human Ecology.* Boston: Allen and Unwin.
Hewitt, K. (1995) "Excluded perspectives in the social construction of disaster," *International Journal of Mass Emergencies and Disasters* 13: 317-339.
Hewitt, K. (1997) *Regions of Risk: A Geographical Introduction to Disasters.* Harlow, Essex: Longman.
Hewitt, K. (1998) "Excluded perspectives in the social construction of disaster," Pp. 75-91 in Quarantelli, E.L. (ed.). *What is a Disaster? Perspectives on the Question.* London: Routledge.
Hilgartner, S. and Bosk, C. (1988) "The Rise and Fall of Social Problems: A Public Arenas Model," *American Journal of Sociology* 94: 53-78.
Hillel, D. (1994) *Rivers of Eden: the Struggle for Water and the Quest for Peace in the Middle East. NY:* Oxford University Press.
Hills, A. (1998) "Seduced by recovery: The consequences of misunderstanding disaster," *Journal of Contingencies and Crisis Management.* 6: 161-169.
Hodder, I. (1994) "The interpretation of documents and material culture," Chapter 24 in Denzin, N. and Lincoln, Y. (eds.) *Handbook of Qualitative Research.* Thousand Oaks, CA. : Sage.

Hoffman, S. and Oliver-Smith, A. (2002) *Catastrophe and Culture: The Anthropology of Disaster.* NY: School of American Research Press.

Hohenemser, C., Kates, R. and Slovic, P. (1985) "A casual taxonomy," Pp. 69-87 in Kates, R., Hohenemser, C. and Kasperson, J. (eds.) *Perilous Progress: Managing the hazards of technology.* Boulder, CO: Westview Press.

Holt-Jensen, A. (1988) *Geography: History and Concepts.* Totowa, NJ: Barnes & Noble.

Holzer, R.,Borcherdt, R., Comartin, C., Hanson, R., Scawthorn, C., Tierney, K. and Youd, Y. (2003) *The Plan to Coordinate NEHRP Post-Earthquake Investigations.* Washington, DC: Government Printing Office.

Hooper, E. (2000) *The River.* Harmondsworth, UK: Penguin.

Hoover, K. and Donovan, T. (2001) *The Elements of Social Scientific Thinking.* Boston, MA: St. Martin's.

Horlick-Jones, T. (1995) "Agency and power in modern disasters," *International Journal of Mass Emergencies and Disasters* 13: 357-359.

Horgan, J. (1996) *The End of Science: Facing the Limits of Knowledge in the Twilight of the Scientific Age.* Reading, MA: Addison-Wesley.

Horwich, G. (1990) "Disasters and market response," *Cato Journal* 9: 531-541.

Houseknecht, S. and Pankhurst, J. (2000) *Family, Religion and Social Change in Diverse Societies.* NY: Oxford Press.

Hudson, R. (2001) *Producing Places.* NY: The Guilford Press.

Huff, T. (1973) "Theoretical innovation in science," *American Journal of Sociology* 79: 26 1-277.

Hunt, S. (2002) *Religion in Western Society.* N.Y.: Palgrave.

Huntington, S.P. (1996) *The Clash of Civilizations and the Remaking of World Order.* Carmel, CA: Touchstone Books.

Husserl, E. (1952) *Ideen zu einer reinen Phänomenologie und phänomenologischen Philosophie. Halle 1928*, reprinted in *Husserliana* Vol. 5, Den Haag.

Image-Based Research: A Source Book for Qualitative Researchers. (1998) London: Falmer Press.

International Federation of Red Cross and Red Crescent Societies. (2002) *World Disasters Report: Focus on Reducing Risk*. London: Eurospan.

Jackson, J. B. (1994) *A Sense of Place, a Sense of Time*. New Haven, CT: Yale University Press.

Jeffery, S.E. (1981) *Our Usual Landslide*. Boulder, CO: Natural Hazards Research and Applications Information Center.

Jigyasu, R. (2001) "From 'Natural' to 'Cultural' Disaster: Consequences of Post-earthquake Rehabilitation Process on Cultural Heritage in Marathwada Region," *Bulletin of the New Zealand Society for Earthquake Engineering* 33(3): 119-127.

Jigyasu, R. (2002) *Reducing Disaster Vulnerability through Local Knowledge and Capacity: The Case of Earthquake-prone Rural Communities in India and Nepal*. Trondheim: Department of Town and Regional Planning, Norwegian University of Science and Technology.

Johnston, D. and Johnson, N. (1989) "Role expansion in disaster: An investigation of employee behavior in a nightclub fire," *Sociological Focus* 22: 39-5 1.

Johnston, R.J. (1987) *Geography and Geographers: Anglo-American Human Geography since 1945*. London: Edward Arnold.

Johnson, N. (1987) "Panic and the breakdown of social order: Popular myth, social theory, empirical evidence," *Sociological Focus* 20: 171-183.

Johnson, N. (1988) "Fire in a crowded theater: A descriptive analysis of the emergence of panic," *International Journal of Mass Emergencies and Disasters* 6: 7-26.

Johnson, N., Feinberg, W. and Johnston, D. (1994) "MicroStructure and Panic," Pp. 168-189 in Dynes, R. and Tierney, K. (eds.) *Disasters, Collective Behavior and Social Organization*. Newark, DE: University of Delaware Press.

Jones, E.L. (1987) *The European Miracle: Environments, Economies and Geopolitics in the History of Europe and Asia*. Cambridge: Cambridge University Press.

Jones, S. (1995) *Cybersociety: Computer-Mediated Communication and Community*. Thousand Oaks, CA: Sage.

Jorgensen, D. (1989) *Participant Observation: A Methodology for Human Studies.* Newbury Park, CA.: Sage.
Journal of Contingencies and Crisis Management. (1994) "Systems, organizations and the limits of safety: A symposium," 2:205-240.
Kalton, O. and Anderson, D. (1986) "Sampling rare populations," *Journal of the Royal Statistical Society* 149: 65-82.
Kaplan, A. (1964) *The Conduct of Inquiry: Methodology for Behavioral Science.* San Francisco: Chandler.
Karlen, A. 1996. *Plague's Progress.* London: Indigo.
Karner, T. X. (2000) "Social capital," Pp. 2637-2641 in Borgatta, E. and Montgomery, R. (eds.) *Encyclopedia of Sociology, Second Edition.* NY: Macmillan.
Kartez, J.D. (1984) "Crisis response planning: toward a contingency analysis," *Journal of the American Planning Association,* 50(1): 9-21.
Kelleher, M. (1997) *The Feminization of Famine: Expressions of the Inexpressible?* Durham, NC. Duke University Press.
Kelly, C. (2000) "What is a disaster? Views from research and the field," Pp. 275-281 in Kowalski, K. and Trevits, M. (eds.) *TIEMS 2000 Proceedings of the Seventh Annual Conference of The International Emergency Management Society.* Pittsburg, PA.: The International Emergency Management Society.
Kelman, I. and Koukis, T. (2000) "Disaster diplomacy," *Cambridge Review of International Affairs* 14(1):21-33.
Kendra, J. and Wachtendorf, T. (2003) *Reconsidering convergence and converger legitimacy in response to the World Trade Center Disaster.* Unpublished paper.
Keys, D. (1999) *Catastrophe.* London: Arrow Books.
Killian, L. (1956) *An Introduction to Methodological Problems of Field Studies in Disasters.* Washington, D.C.: National Academy of Sciences.
King, D. (2002) "Post disaster surveys: Experience and methodology," *The Australian Journal of Emergency Management* 17: 39-47.
Kingdon, J.W. (1984) *Agendas, Alternatives and Public Policies.* Boston: Little, Brown and Company.

Klinenberg, E. (2002) *Heat Wave: A Social Autopsy of Disaster in Chicago*. Chicago: University of Chicago Press.
Korpi, W. (1983) *The Democratic Class Struggle*. London: Routledge and Kegan Paul.
Kouzmin, A. and Jarman, A. (1989) "Crisis decision making: Towards a contingent decision path perspective," Pp. 397-435 in Rosenthal, U., Charles, M. and 't Hart, P. (eds.). *Coping with Crises: The Management of Disasters, Riots and Terrorism*, Springfield: Charles C. Thomas.
Kreps, G. (1978) "The organization of disaster response: some fundamental theoretical issues," Pp. 65-85 in Quarantelli, E. L. (ed.) *Disasters: theory and research*: Beverly Hills, CA: Sage.
Kreps, G. (1989) "Disaster and the Social Order," Pp. 31-51 in Kreps, G. (ed.) *Social Structure and Disaster*. Newark, DE: University of Delaware Press.
Kreps, G. (1998) "Disaster as systemic event and social catalyst," Pp. 31-55 in Quarantelli, E.L. (ed.). *What is a Disaster? Perspectives on the Question*. London: Routledge.
Kroll-Smith, S. and Gunter, V.J. (1998) "Legislators, interpreters, and disasters: The importance of how as well as what is a disaster," Pp. 160-176 in Quarantelli, E.L. (ed.). *What is a Disaster? Perspectives on the Question*. London: Routledge.
Kroll-Smith, J. and Couch, S. (1991) "What is disaster? An ecological-symbolic approach to resolving the definitional debate," *International Journal of Mass Emergencies and Disasters* 9(3): 355-366.
Kuhn, T.S. (1962) *The Structure of Scientific Revolutions*. Chicago: University of Chicago Press.
Kunreuther, H. and Slovic, P. (1996) "Challenges in risk assessment and risk management, Special Issue," *Annals of the American Academy of Political and Social Science* 545:8-183.
Langlois, C. V. and Seignobos, C. (1898) *Introduction to the Study of History*. London: Duckworth.
Law, J. (1999) "After ANT: complexity, naming and topology," Pp. 1-14 in Law, J. and Hassard, J. (eds.), *Actor Network Theory and After*. Oxford: Blackwell.

Lazarsfeld, P. F. (1937) "Some remarks on typological procedures in social research," *Zeitschrift fur Sozialforschung* 6: 119-139.
Lazarsfeld, P. F. and Barton, A. H. (1962) "Qualitative measurement in the social sciences: Classification, typologies, and indices," Pp.155-192 in Lerner, D. and Lasswell, H. (eds.) *The Policy Sciences*. Stanford, CA.: Stanford University Press.
Leege, D. C. and Kellstedt, L. (1993) *Rediscovering the Religious Factor in American Politics*. Armonk, NY:M. E. Sharpe.
Le Poidevin, R. (2003) *Travels in four dimensions*. Oxford: Oxford University Press.
Levine, R. (1997) *A Geography of Time*. NY: Basic Books.
Lifton R.J. (1980) "The concept of the survivor," Pp 3-46 in Dimsdale, J. (ed.) *Survivors, Victims and Perpetrators: Essays on the Nazi Holocaust*. Hemisphere, NY.
Lincoln, Y. and Denzin, N. (2003) *Turning Points in Qualitative Research*. Walnut Creek, CA.: Alta Mira Press.
Lindell, M.K and Perry, R.W. (1992) *Behavioral Foundations of Community Emergency Planning*. Washington, DC: Hemisphere Publishing Corporation.
Lindell, M.K. and Perry, R. W. (2004) *Communicating Environmental Risk in Multiethnic Communities*. Thousand Oaks, CA: Sage.
Linz, J.J. and Stepan, A. (1978) *The Breakdown of Democratic Regimes*. Baltimore: Johns Hopkins University Press.
Lofland, J. and Lofland, L. (1984) *Analyzing Social Settings*. Belmont, CA.: Wadsworth.
Lombardi, M. (1997) "Media studies," *International Journal of Mass Emergencies and Disasters* 15(1): 103-116.
Lybrand, W. and Popper, R. (1960) *An Inventory of Selected Source Materials Relevant to Integration of Physical and Social Effects of Air Attack*. Arlington, VA.: Human Sciences Research.
Malcolm, B. (2001) *Approaches to Understanding Visual Culture*. NY: Palgrave.
Malik, S.C. (1990) *Modern Civilization: A Crisis of Fragmentation*. New Delhi: South Asia Books.

Malik, S.C. (1995) *Reconceptualising the sciences and the humanities: an integral approach.* New Delhi: Manohar Publishers.

Mann, C. and Stewart, F. (2000) *Internet Communication and Qualitative Research: A Handbook for Researching on Online.* Thousand Oaks, CA.: Sage.

Maravall, J.A. (1979) "La cultura de la crisis barocca," *Historia* 16: 80-90.

March, J. G. and Olson, J. (1986) "Garbage can models of decision making in organizations," Pp. 11-35 in March, J. G. and Weissinger-Baylon, R. (eds.) *Ambiguity and Command Organizational Perspectives on Military Decision Making.* Marshfield, MA: Pitman.

Marcuse, H. (1964) *The One-Dimensional Man. Studies in the Ideology of Advanced Industrial Society.* Boston: Beacon Press

Marks, E. and Fritz, C. (1954) *Human Reactions in Disaster Situations.* Chicago: National Opinion Research Center, University of Chicago.

Marx, G. and McAdams, D. (1994) *Collective Behavior and Social Movements: Process and Structure.* Englewood Cliffs, NJ.: Prentice Hall.

Maslin, M. (2002) *The Future and Natural Disasters.* Transcript Earthbeat Radio National (Australian Broadcasting Commission) 19 November.

Mauss, A. (1992) "Social Problems," Pp. 1916-1921 in Borgatta, E. and Borgatta, M. (eds.) *Encyclopedia of Sociology.* NY: Macmillan.

May, P. (1985) *Recovering from Catastrophes: Federal Disaster Relief Policy and Politics.* Westport, CT: Greenwood Press.

McCall, G. and Simmons, J. (1969) *Issues in Participant Observation.* Reading, MA: Addison-Wesley.

McCain, R. (2004) *Essential Principles of Economics: A Hypermedia Text (Second Revised Draft).* Philadelphia: Department of Economics, Drexel University.

McCann, J. (1987) *From Poverty to Famine in Northeast Ethiopia: A Rural History 1900-1935.* Philadelphia: University of Pennsylvania Press.

McCright, A. and Dunlap, R. (2000) "Challenging global warming as a social problem," *Social Problems* 47: 499-522.
McEntire, D. A., Fuller, C., Johnson, C., W., & Weber, R. (2002) "A comparison of disaster paradigms: the search for the holistic policy guide," *Public Administration Review* 62(3): 267-280.
McGrath, J. (1988) *The Social Psychology of Time: New Perspectives.* Newbury Park, CA.: Sage.
McGrath, J. and Kelley, J. (1986) *Time and Human Interaction: Toward a Social Psychology of Time.* NY: Guilford Press.
McKinney, J. (1969) "Typification, Typologies, and Sociological Theory," *Social Forces* 48: 1-12.
McPhail, C. (1991) *The Myth of the Madding Crowd.* NY: Aldine de Gruyter.
McPhail, C. (1995) Paper at the 1995 Annual Meetings of the American Sociological Association.
McPhail, C. and Wohlstein, R. (1983) "Individual and Collective Behavior," *Annual Review of Sociology* 9: 579-600.
Melucci, A. (1996) *Changing Codes: Collective Actions in the Information Age.* NY: Cambridge University Press.
Merton, R. K. (1945) "Sociological theory," *American Journal of Sociology* 50: 462-473.
Meyer-Abich, K.M. (1997) "Humans in nature: toward a physiocentric philosophy," Pp. 168-184 in Ausubel, J. and Langford, H. (eds.) *Technological Trajectories and the Human Environment.* Washington, DC: National Academy of Engineering.
Michaels, S. (2001) *Digital disaster assistance: How and why selected information technology firms contributed to recovery immediately after the September 11, 2001 terrorist attacks.* Boulder, CO: Natural Hazards Research and Applications Information Center, University of Colorado.
Miles, M. and Hubeman, A. (1994) *Qualitative Data Analysis.* Thousand Oaks, CA.: Sage.
Mileti, D. (1987) "Sociological methods and disaster research," Pp. 57-70 in Dynes, R., De Marchi, B. and Pelanda, C. (eds.) *Sociology of Disasters Contributions of Sociology to Disaster Research.* Milan, Italy: Franco Angeli.

Mileti, D. (1997) "Designing Disasters: Determining our Future Vulnerability," *Natural Hazards Observer.* 22(1): 1-3.
Mileti, D. (1999a) *Disasters By Design: A Reassessment of Natural Hazards in the United States.* Washington, DC: Joseph Henry Press.
Mileti, D. (1999b) "Disasters by design," Pp.1-16 in Britton, N. R. (ed.) *The Changing Risk Landscape: Implications for Insurance Risk Management.* Sydney: Southwood Press.
Mileti, D. (1999c) "The challenge for a safer 21st Century," Pp.290-292. in Ingleton, J (ed.). *Natural Disaster Management: A Presentation to Commemorate the International Decade for Natural Disaster Reduction 1990-2000.* Leicester: Tudor Rose.
Mileti, D. (2002) "Sustainability and hazards," *International Journal of Mass Emergencies and Disasters.* 20(2): 135-138.
Mill, J. (1872 [1843]) *A System of Logic: Ratiocinative and Inductive, Being a Connected View of the Principles of Evidence and the Methods of Scientific Investigation.* London: Longmans, Green, Reader, and Dyer.
Miller, D. (1998) *Network Exchange Theory.* Westport, CT: Praeger.
Mills, C.W. *(1963)* Power, Politics and People. *NY: Free Press.*
Mills, C.W. (1959) *The Sociological Imagination.* NY: Oxford University Press.
Mirzoeff, N. (1999) *An Introduction to Visual Culture.* London: Routledge.
Mitchell, J. K. (1994) "Recent developments in hazards research: A geographer's perspective," Pp. 43-62 in Quarantelli, E. L. and Popov, K. (eds.) *Proceedings of the United States-Former Soviet Union Seminar on Social Science Research on Mitigation For and Recovery From Disasters and Large Scale Hazards Volume I: The American Participation.* Newark,DE: Disaster Research Center, University of Delaware.
Mitchell, J.T., Thomas, D. Hill, A. and Cutter, S.L. (2000) "Catastrophe in reel life versus real life: perpetuating disaster myth through Hollywood films," *International Journal of Mass Emergencies and Disasters* 18(3): 383-402.

Mitroff, I. I., Pauchant, T. C., Finney, M., & Pearson, C. (1989) "Do (some) organizations cause their own crises?" *Industrial Crisis Quarterly* 3: 269-283.

Moore, H. (1958) *Tornadoes Over Texas*. Austin: University of Texas Press.

Moore, S., Eng, E. and Daniel, M. (2003) "International NGOs and the role of network centrality in humanitarian aid operations: A case study of coordination during the 2000 Mozambique floods," *Disasters* 27: 305-318.

Moran, R. (2003) *Doomsday. End of the World Scenarios*. Indianapolis: Alpha.

Munro, I. (1999) "Man-machine systems," *Systemic Practice and Action Research* 12(5): 513-532.

Mulwanda, M.P. (1992) "Active participants or passive observers?" *Urban Studies* 29(1): 89-97.

Mushtaque, A., Chowdhury, B. Bhyia, C. Choudhury, D. and Sen, E. (1993) "The Bangladesh cyclone of 1991: Why so many people died," *Disasters* 17: 291-306.

National Governors' Association. (1979) *Comprehensive Emergency Management: A Governor's Guide*. Washington DC: National Governors' Association, Center for Policy Research.

National Research Council. (2002) *Making the Nation Safer: The Role of Science and Technology in Countering Terrorism*. Washington DC: National Academy of Sciences.

Natsios, A. S. (1997) *U.S. Foreign Policy and the Four Horsemen of the Apocalypse*. Westport, CT: Praeger.

Natural Hazards Research and Applications Information Center. (2003) *Beyond September 11th: An Account of Post-Disaster Research*. Boulder, CO: National Hazards Research and Applications Information Center, University of Colorado.

Neal, D. (1997) "Reconsidering the phases of disasters," *International Journal of Mass Emergencies and Disasters* 15(2): 239-264.

Neal, D. and Phillips, B. (1990) "Female-dominated local social movement organizations in disaster threat situations," Pp. 277-301 in West, G. and Blumberg, R. (eds.) *Women and Social Protest*. NY: Oxford.

NEIC (2001) "Report," *BBC News* released 6 May.
New Zealand Government. (2002) *Civil Defence Emergency Management Act.* Wellington: Government of New Zealand.
Newman, K. S. (1988) *Falling From Grace: The Experience of Downward Mobility in the American Middle Class.* NY: Free Press.
Nigg, J. (1994) "Influence of symbolic interaction on disaster research," Pp. 33-50 in Pratt, G. and Gordon, C. (eds.) *Self: Collective Behavior and Society: Essays Honoring the Contributions for Ralph Turner.* Greenwich, CT: JAI Press.
Nigg, J. (1995) *Business Disruptions Due to Earthquake-Induced Lifeline Interruption.* Newark, DE: Disaster Research Center, University of Delaware.
Nigg, J. and Perry, R. W. (1988) "Influential first sources: Brief statements with long-term effects," *International Journal of Mass Emergencies and Disasters* 6: 311-344.
Nordlie, P. (1963) *An Approach to the Study of Social and Psychological Effects of Nuclear Attack.* McLean, VA: Human Sciences Research Inc.
Nowotny, H, Scott, P. and Gibbons, M. (2001) *Re-Thinking Science: Knowledge and the Public in an Age of Uncertainty.* Cambridge, UK: Polity Press.
Oliver-Smith, A. (1994) "Anthropological perspective in disaster research," Pp. 94-117 in Quarantelli, E. L. and Popov, K. (eds.) *Proceedings of the United States-Former Soviet Union Seminar on Social Science Research on Mitigation For and Recovery From Disasters and Large Scale Hazards. Volume I: The American Participation.* Newark, DE. Disaster Research Center, University of Delaware.
Oliver-Smith, A. (1998) "Global changes and the definition of disaster," Pp. 177-194 in Quarantelli, E.L. (ed.). *What is a Disaster? Perspectives on the Question.* London: Routledge.
Oliver-Smith, A. (1999) What is a disaster; Anthropological perspectives on a persistent question. Pp.18-34. in Oliver-Smith, A. and Hoffman, S. *The Angry Earth: Disaster in Anthropological Perspective.* NY. Routledge.
Oliver-Smith, A. (2002) "Theorizing disasters," Pp. 23-47. In Hoffman, S. and Oliver-Smith, A. (eds.) *Catastrophe and*

Culture: The Anthropology of Disaster. Sante Fe, NM: School of American Research Press.

Olson, R. A., Baird, A., Estrada, V., Gawronski, V. and Prieto, P. (1999) *Disaster and Institutional Response; Hurricane Georges in the Dominican Republic and Hurricane Mitch in Honduras and Nicaragua, September-October 1998.* Folsom, CA: Robert Olson Associates.

Olson, R.S. (2000) "Toward a politics of disaster: losses, values, agendas and blame," *International Journal of Mass Emergencies and Disasters* 18(2): 265-287.

Olson, R.S. and Drury, A. (1997) "Un-therapeutic communities: a cross-national analysis of post-disaster political unrest," *International Journal of Mass Emergencies and Disasters* 15(2): 221-238.

Oommen, T. K. (1995) "Contested boundaries and emerging pluralism," *International Sociology* 10: 251-268.

Parad, H.J., Resnick, H. and Parad, L. (1976) *Emergency and Disaster Management: A Mental Health Sourcebook.* Bowie, MD: Charles Press.

Parsons, T. (1949) *The Structure of Social Action.* Glencoe, IL: Free Press.

Pauchant, T. C., and Mitroff, I. I. (1992) *Transforming the Crisis-prone Organization.* San Fransisco: Jossey-Bass Publishers.

Peek, L. A. (2002) *Religious and ethnic issues after September 11, 2001: Examining Muslim university student experiences.* Boulder, CO: Natural Hazards Research and Applications Information Center, University of Colorado.

Peek, L. and Sutton, J. (2003) "An exploratory comparison of disasters, riots and terrorist acts," *Disasters* 27: 319-335.

Pelling, M. (2001) "Natural disaster," Pp. 170-188 in Castree, N. and Braun, B. (eds.) *Social Nature: Theory, practice, and politics.* Oxford: Blackwell Publishers.

Pelling, M. (2003a) *The Vulnerability of Cities: Natural Disasters and Social Resilience* London: Earthscan Publications.

Pelling, M. (2003b) "Paradigms of risk," Pp. 3-16 in Pelling, M. (ed.) *Natural Disasters and Development in a Globalizing World.* London: Routledge.

Perrow, C. (1984) *Normal Accidents*. NY: Basic Books.
Perrow, C. (1986) *Complex Organizations: A Critical Essay*. NY: McGraw-Hill.
Perrow, C. (1999) *Normal Accidents: Living with High-risk Technologies*. Princeton: Princeton University Press.
Perry, R.W. (1982) *The Social Psychology of Civil Defense*. Lexington, MA: D.C. Heath and Company.
Perry, R.W. (1998) "Definitions and the development of a theoretical superstructure for disaster research," Pp. 197-215. Quarantelli, E. L. (ed.) *What is a Disaster? Perspectives on the Question*. London. Routledge.
Perry, R.W. and Hirose, H. (1991) *Volcano Management in the United States and Japan*. Greenwich, CT: JAI Press.
Perry, R.W. and Lindell, M. K. (1997) "Earthquake Planning for Government Continuity," *Environmental Management* 21 (January): 89-96.
Perry, R. W. and Lindell, M. K. (2003) "Preparedness for emergency response: Guidelines for the emergency planning process," *Disasters* 27: 336-350.
Perez, Louis. (2003) *Winds of Change; Hurricanes and Transformation of Nineteenth-Century Cuba*. Chapel Hill, NC: University of North Carolina Press.
Pfaffenburger. B. (1988) *Microcomputer Applications in Qualitative Research*. Newbury Park, CA.: Sage.
Phillips, N. and Hardy, C. (2002) *Discourse Analysis: Investigating Processes of Social Construction*. Thousand Oaks, CA.: Sage.
Pidgeon, N. F. (1998) "Shaking the kaleidoscope of disasters research," *Journal of Contingencies and Crisis Management*, 6(2): 97-101.
Pink. S. (2001) *Doing Visual Ethnography: Images, Media and Representation in Research*. Thousand Oaks, CA.: Sage.
Pitt, C. (1972) *Using Historical Sources in Anthropology and Sociology*. NY: Holt, Rinehart and Winston.
Pittman, R. (1960) "Changes in concepts of sociology," *Sociology and Social Research* 45: 34-40.
Plate, E. and Merz, B. (2001) *Naturkatastrophen: Ursachen, Auswirkungen, Vorsorge*. Stuttgart: Schweizerbartsche Verlagsbuchhandlung.

Platt, R. (1999) *Disasters and Democracy: The Politics of Extreme Natural Events*. Washington, DC: Island Press.

Ploughman, P. (1995) "The American print media 'construction' of five natural disasters," *Disasters* 19(4): 308-326.

Plummer, K. (1983) *Documents of Life: An Introduction to the Problems and Literature of a Humanistic Method*. London: Allen and Unwin.

Popper, K. R. (1959) *The Logic of Scientific Discovery*. London: Hutchinson.

Porfiriev, B.N. (1998) "Issues in the definition and delineation of disasters and disaster areas," Pp. 56-72 in Quarantelli, E. L. (ed.) *What is a Disaster? Perspectives on the Question*. London: Routledge.

Prince, S.H (1920) *Catastrophe and Social Change*. London. Kind and Son.

Prior, L. (2003) *Using Documents in Social Research*. Thousand Oaks, CA.: Sage.

Pronovost-Giles, J. (1989) "The sociological study of time: Historical landmarks," *Current Sociology* 37: 4-19.

Pulido, L. (2000) "Rethinking environmental racism: White privilege and urban development in Southern California," *Annals of the Association of American Geographers* 90:12-40.

Putnam, H. (1975) *Mind, Language, and Reality*. NY: Cambridge University Press

Putnam, H. (1985) "The meaning of meaning," Pp. 288-298 in: *Philosophical Papers, Vol. 2: Mind, Language and Reality*. Cambridge: Cambridge University Press.

Quarantelli, E. L. (1954) "The nature and conditions of panic," *American Journal of Sociology* 60: 267-275.

Quarantelli, E. L. (1957) "The behavior of panic participants," *Sociology and Social Research* 41: 187-194.

Quarantelli, E. L. (1978a) *Disasters: Theory and Research*. Beverly Hills, CA: Sage.

Quarantelli, E. L. (1978b) "Some basic themes in Sociological studies of disaster," Pp. 1-14 in Quarantelli, E. L. (ed.), *Disasters: Theory and Research*: Beverly Hills, CA: Sage.

Quarantelli, E. L. (1979) "Some needed cross-cultural studies of emergency time disaster behavior: A first step," *Disasters* 3:307-314.
Quarantelli, E. L. (1984) *Emergent Behavior at the Emergency Time Period of Disasters.* Newark, DE: Disaster Research Center, University of Delaware.
Quarantelli, E.L. (1987a) "What should we study? Questions and suggestions for researchers about the concept of disasters," *International Journal of Mass Emergencies and Disasters.* 7(3): 243-251.
Quarantelli, E. L. (1987b) "Disaster studies: An analysis of the social historical factors affecting the development of research in the area," *International Journal of Mass Emergencies and Disasters* 5: 285-310.
Quarantelli, E. L. (1988a) "The NORC research on the Arkansas tornado," *International Journal of Mass Emergencies and Disasters* 6(3): 283-310.
Quarantelli, E.L. (1988b) Disaster studies: An analysis of the social historical factors affecting the development of research in the area. *International Journal of Mass Emergencies and Disasters* 5: 285-310.
Quarantelli, E. L. (l993a) "Community crises: An exploratory comparison of the characteristics and consequences of disasters and riots," *Journal of Contingencies and Crisis Management* 1: 67-78.
Quarantelli, E. L. (1993b) "Converting disaster scholarship into effective disaster planning and managing: Possibilities and limitations," *International Journal of Mass Emergencies and Disasters.* 11(1). Pp. 15-39.
Quarantelli, E. L. (1994a) *Future Disaster Trends and Policy Implications For Developing Countries.* Newark, DE: Disaster Research Center, University of Delaware.
Quarantelli, E. L. (1994b) *Looting and Antisocial Behavior in Disasters.* Newark, DE: Disaster Research Center, University of Delaware.
Quarantelli, E. L. (1995b) "Technological and natural disasters and ecological problems: Similarities and differences in planning

for and managing them," Pp. 87-112 in *Memoria del Coloquio Internacional: El Reto de Desastres Technologicos y Ecologicos*. Mexico City: Academia Mexicana de Ingenieria.

Quarantelli, E. L. (1998a) "Introduction. The basic question, its importance, and how it is addressed in this volume," Pp. 1-7 in Quarantelli, E. L. (ed.), *What is a disaster? Perspectives on the question*. London: Routledge

Quarantelli, E.L. (1998b) *What is a Disaster? Perspectives on the Question*. London: Routledge.

Quarantelli, E.L. (1998c) "Epilogue: Where we have been and where we might go," Pp. 234-273 in Quarantelli, E.L. (ed.) *What is a Disaster? Perspectives on the Question*. Routledge, London.

Quarantelli, E. L. (2001) "Statistical and conceptual problems in the study of disasters," *Disaster Prevention and Management* 10: 325-338.

Quarantelli, E. L. and Dynes, R. (1969) "Dissensus and consensus in community emergencies: Patterns of looting and property norms," *Il Politico* 34: 276-291.

Quarantelli, E. L. and Dynes, R. (1970) "Property norms and looting: Their pattern in community crises," *Phylon* 31:68-182.

Quarantelli, E.L. and Mozgovaya, A. (1994) *An Annotated Inventory of the Social Science Research literature on Disasters in the Former Soviet Union and Contemporary Russia*. Newark, DE.: Disaster Research Center, University of Delaware.

Queen, A. and Mann, D. (1925) *Social Pathology*. NY: Thomas Y. Crowell Company.

Raphael, B. (1986) *When Disaster Strikes: A Handbook for the Caring Professions*. London. Hutchinson Press.

Ratner, J. (2003) *Human Factors and Web Development*. Mahwah, N.J. : Lawrence Erlbaum.

Ravilious, K. (2001) "Songs before the storm," *New Scientist* 172: 30-34.

Reason, J. (1990) *Human Error*. Manchester: Manchester University Press.

Reason, J. (1997) *Managing the risks of organizational accidents*. Aldershot: Ashgate.

Reason, J. (2001) "Understanding adverse events: the human factor," Pp. 9-30 in Vincent, C. (ed.), *Clinical risk management. Enhancing patient safety*. London: BMJ Books.

Reed-Danahay, D. (1997) *Auto-Ethnography. Rewriting the Self and the Social*. Oxford: Berg.

Redfern, M., Keeling, J., and Powell, E. (2000) *The Royal Liverpool Children's Inquiry Report*. London: The Stationary Office.

Reiss, A.J. (1972). "Sociology (The Field)," in *Encyclopedia of the Social Sciences*, Sills, D. (ed.) London: Macmillan.

Repcheck, J. (2003) *The Man Who Found Time*. London: Simon and Schuster.

Reshaur, L. (1998) *Collective Violence and Theories of Collective Behavior: An Analysis of the 1992 Los Angles Unrest*. Ph. D. dissertation. Newark, DE: University of Delaware.

Rhodes, R. R. (1997) *Deady Feasts*. NY: Touchstone.

Rihani, S. (2002) *Complex Systems Theory and Development Practice*. London: Zed Books.

Rivera, A. (1991) *Decision and Structure*. Lanham, MD: University Press of America.

Roberts, V. (1994) "Flood management," *Disaster Prevention and Management* 3: 44-60.

Rochlin, G.I. (1996) "Reliable organizations: Present research and future directions," *Journal of Contingencies and Crisis Management*. 4:55-59.

Rogers, G.O. and Nehnevajsa, J. (1984) *Behavior and Attitudes Under Crisis Conditions*. Pittsburgh, PA: University Center for Social and Urban Research, University of Pittsburgh.

Rose, G. (2001) *Visual Methodologies: An Introduction to the Interpretation of Visual Materials*. Thousand Oaks, CA.: Sage.

Rosenau, J. and Singh, J. (2002) *Information Technologies and Global Politics*. Albany, NY: SUNY Press.

Rosenberg, T. (2001) "Look at Brazil," *New York Times Magazine*, January 28, P. 26-31.

Rosenthal, U. (1998) "Future disasters, future definitions," Pp. 146-159 in Quarantelli, E.L. (ed.) *What is a Disaster? Perspectives on the Question*. London: Routledge.

Rosenthal, U., Boin, R.A. and Bos, C.J. (2001) "Shifting identities: The reconstructive mode of the Bijlmer air crash." Pp. 200-215 in Rosenthal, U., Boin, R.A. and Comfort, L. (eds.). *Managing Crises: Threats, Dilemmas, Opportunities*. Springfield, MA: Charles C. Thomas.

Rosenthal, U., Boin, R.A. and Comfort, L. (2001) *Managing Crises: Threats, Dilemmas, Opportunities*. Springfield, MA: Charles C. Thomas.

Rosenthal, U., Boin, R.A. and Comfort, L. (2002) *From Crises to Contingencies: A Global Perspective*. Springfield, IL: Charles C. Thomas.

Rosenthal, U., Charles, M. and 't Hart, P. (1989) *Coping with Crises: The Management of Disasters, Riots and Terrorism*, Springfield, MA: Charles C. Thomas.

Rossi, P. (1980) "The Presidential address: The challenge and opportunities of applied social research," *American Sociological Review* 45: 889-904.

Rubin, C. B. and Renda-Tanali, L. (2001) *The Terrorist Attacks on September 11, 2001*. Boulder, CO: Natural Hazards Research and Applications Information Center, University of Colorado.

Rubonis, A.V. and Bickman, L. (1991) "A test of the consensus and distinctiveness attribution principles in victims of disaster," *Journal of Applied Social Psychology* 21(10): 791-818.

Saarinen, T.F., Seamon, D. and Sell, J. (1984) *Environmental Perceptions and Behavior: An Inventory and Prospect*. Chicago: University of Chicago.

Sachs, W. (1999) "Introduction," Pp. 1-5. in Sachs, W. (ed.), *The Development Dictionary: A Guide to Knowledge as Power*. Johannesburg: Development Press.

Sagan, S. (1993) *The Limits of Safety: Organizations, Accidents and Nuclear Weapons*. Princeton: Princeton University Press.

Sassower, R. (1991) "Postmodernism and philosophy of science: A critical engagement," *Philosophy of the Social Sciences* 23: 426-445.

Sattler, D. N. (2002) *The September 11th attacks on America*. Boulder, CO: Natural Hazards Research and Applications Information Center, University of Colorado.

Saylor, C. (1993) *Children and Disasters*. NY: Plenum.
Scanlon, J. (1988) "Winners and losers: Some thoughts about the political economy of disaster," *International Journal of Mass Emergencies and Disasters* 6: 47-63.
Scanlon, J. (1992) *Convergence Revisited: A New Perspective on a Little Studied Topic*. Boulder, CO.: Institute of Behavior Science, University of Colorado.
Scanlon, J. (1994) "The Occasion Instant," Pp.96-117 in Ruffman, A. and Howell, C. (eds.) *Ground Zero—A Reassessment of the 1917 Explosion in Halifax Harbour*. Halifax, Canada: Nimbus Publishing.
Scanlon, J. (2002) "Researching the 1917 Halifax explosion," Pp. 266-302 in Stallings, R. (ed.) *Methods of Disaster Research*. Philadelphia, PA: Xlibris Books.
Scarth, A. (2002) *La catastrophe. The eruption of Mount Pelee, the worst volcanic disaster of the 20th Century*. Oxford: Oxford University Press.
Schmuck, H. (2000) "'An Act of Allah': Religious Explanations for Floods in Bangladesh as Survival Strategy," *International Journal of Mass Emergencies and Disasters* 18: 85-96.
Schneider, J. (1985) "Social problems theory: The constructionist view," *Annual Review of Sociology* 11: 209-229.
Schutz, A. (1967) *Collected Papers, Volume 1, The Problem of Social Reality*. Natanson, M. (ed.). The Hague: Martinus Nijhoff.
Schütz, A. (1974) *Der sinnhafte Aufbau der sozialen Welt. Eine Einleitung in die verstehende Soziologie*. Frankfurt: Suhrkamp
Schware, R. (1982) "Official and folk flood warning systems: an assessment," *Environmental Management* 6(3): 209-216.
Schwartz, H. S. (1990) "Organizational disaster and organizational decay: The case of the National Aeronautics and Space Administration," *Industrial Crisis Quarterly* 3: 319-334.
Scott, J. (2001) "A nation by the numbers, smudged," *New York Times* July 1: P. 21-22.
Sebald, W. (2003) *On the Natural History of Destruction*. NY: Random House.
Selznick, P. (1957) *Leadership in Administration: A Sociological Interpretation*. NY: Row-Peterson.

Sen, A. (1993) "The economics of life and death," *Scientific American*, May: 40-47.
Sennet, R. (1998) *The Corrosion of Character*. NY: W.W. Norton.
Sex Workers' Forum Kerala. (2002) "Kerala sex workers forum plan an agitation," http:archives.healthdev.net/sex-work/msg00047.html.
Shilts, R. (2000) *And the Band Played On*. NY: St Martins Press.
Shreve, R.L. (1966) "Sherman landslide, Alaska," *Science* 154: 1639-1643.
Shrivastava, P. (1987) *Bhopal. Anatomy of a crisis*. Cambridge, MA: Ballinger Publishing.
Simon, Richard. (1994) "Aftershock: Post-quake burial costs," *Wilmington News Journal*, July 4, P. A3.
Sims, J.H. and Baumann, D. (1972) "The tornado threat: coping styles of North and South," *Science* 176(4042): 1386-1392.
Sipika, C., and Smith, D. (1993) "From disaster to crisis: The failed turnaround of Pan American Airlines," *Journal of Contingencies and Crisis Management*, 1(3): 138-151.
Sirken, M. (1970) "Household surveys with multiplicity," *Journal of the American Statistical Association* 65: 202-209.
Sjoberg, G. and Nett, R. (1968) *A Methodology for Social Research*. New York: Harper.
Skocpal, T. (1992) *Protecting Soldiers and Mothers—The Political Origins of Social Policy in the United States*. Cambridge, MA: Harvard University Press.
Smelser, N. (1991a) "The social sciences in a changing world society," *American Behavioral Scientist* 34: 518-529.
Smelser, N. (1991b) "Internationalization of social science knowledge," *American Behavioral Scientist* 35: 65-91.
Smelser, Neil. (2003) "On comparative analysis, interdisciplinarity and internationalization in sociology," *International Sociology* 18: 643-657.
Smith, D. (1990a) "Beyond contingency planning: Towards a model of crisis management," *Industrial Crisis Quarterly* 4(4): 263-275.
Smith, D. (1990b) "Corporate power and the politics of uncertainty: Risk management at the Canvey Island complex," *Industrial Crisis Quarterly*, 4(1): 1-26.

Smith, D. (1995) "The dark side of excellence: managing strategic failures," Pp. 161-191 in Thompson, J. (ed.), *Handbook of Strategic Management*: London: Butterworth-Heinemann.

Smith, D. (2000a) "Crisis Management Teams: Issues in the management of operational crises," *Risk Management: An International Journal*, 2(3): 61-78.

Smith, D. (2000b) "On a wing and a prayer? Exploring the human components of technological failure," *Systems Research and Behavioural Science*, 17: 543-559.

Smith, D. (2002) "Not by error, but by design: Harold Shipman and the regulatory crisis for health care," *Public Policy and Administration*, 17(4): 55-74.

Smith, D., and McCloskey, J. (1998) "Risk communication and the social amplification of public sector risk," *Public Money and Management* 18(4): 41-50.

Smith, D., and McCloskey, J. (2000) "History repeating itself? Expertise, barriers to learning and the precautionary principle," Pp. 101-124 in Coles, E. Smith, D. and Tombs, S. (eds.), *Risk Management and Society*: Dordrecht: Kluwer.

Smith, D., and Sipika, C. (1993) Back from the brink: post crisis management," *Long Range Planning*, 26(1): 28-38.

Smith, M. and others. (2002) *Internet: An Overview of Key Technology Policy Issues*. NY: Novinka Books.

Snow, C.P. (1969) *The Two Cultures: And A Second Look*. Cambridge: Cambridge University Press.

Spector, M. and Kitsuse, J. (1977) *Constructing Social Problems*. Menlo Park, CA: Cummings.

Stallings, R. (1978) "The structural patterns of four types of organizations in disaster," Pp. 87-103 in Quarantelli, E. L. (ed.) *Disasters: Theory and Research*. Beverly Hills, CA: Sage.

Stallings, R. (1988) "Conflict in natural disasters: A codification of consensus and conflict theories," *Social Science Quarterly* 69: 569-586.

Stallings, R. (1995) *Promoting Risk: Constructing the Earthquake Threat*. NY: Aldine de Gruyter.

Stallings, R. (1997) "Social System Causes of Aviation Disasters: The Crash of a Birgenair Boeing 757," Paper presented at the Annual Meeting of the American Sociological Association, Toronto.

Stallings, R. (1998a) "What is a Disaster? A Weberian Answer," Paper presented at the XIVth World Congress of Sociology, Montréal.

Stallings, R. (1998b) "Switzerland's 'Holocaust Assets' Crisis: Its Relevance for a Theory of the Social Order and Disasters," Paper presented at the XIVth World Congress of Sociology, Montréal.

Stallings, R. (1998c) "Disaster and the Theory of Social Order," Pp. 127-145 in Quarantelli, E. L. (ed.), *What Is a Disaster? Perspectives on the Question*. London: Routledge.

Stallings, R. (2001) "Disasters, Epidemics, Terrorism, and Other Calamities: Resurrecting Simmel's Form and Content," Paper presented at the 5th European Congress of Sociology, Helsinki.

Stallings, R. (2002) *Methods of Disaster Research*. Philadelphia, PA: Xlibris.

Standards Australia (1999) *Risk Management 2nd Edition*. Sydney: Australia and New Zealand Standards.

Standards New Zealand (2000) *Risk Management Handbook for Local Government*. Wellington: Standards New Zealand.

Stasz, C. (1979) "Texts, images and display conventions in sociology," *Qualitative Sociology* 2: 29-44.

Steinberg, T. (2000) *Acts of God. The unnatural history of natural disasters in America*. NY: Oxford University Press.

Stephens, T., and Brynner, R. (2001) *Dark Remedy: The Impact of Thalidomide and its Revival as a Vital Medicine*. Cambridge, MA: Perseus Publishing.

Stern, E. and Sundelius, B. (2002) "Crisis management Europe: An integrated regional research and training program," *International Studies Perspectives*, 3: 71-88.

Stigler, J. E. (2002) *Globalization and Its Discontents*. NY: W.W. Norton.

Stinchcombe, A.L. (1997) "Tilly on the past as a sequence of futures," Pp. 387-409 in Tilly, C. (ed.). *Roads from Past to Future*. Lanham: Rowman and Littlefield Publishers.

Stocking, S. H. and Holstein, L. (1993) "Constructing and reconstructing scientific ignorance," *Knowledge Creation Diffusion and Utilization* 5: 186-2 10.
Stoffel, R. (1994) "The EOC/ICS connection," *NCCEM Bulletin* 28:1-3.
Stokes, D. E. (1997) *Pasteur's Quadrant: Basic Science and Technological Innovation*. Washington DC: Brookings Institution.
Stone, A. and Castaneda, C. (1990) "The earthquake by the numbers." *USA Today* October 12, P. 6A
Sturken, M. (2001) *Practices of Looking: An Introduction to Visual Culture*. NY: Oxford University Press.
Sylves, R.T. and Waugh Jr., W. (1996) *Disaster Management in the U.S. and Canada: the Politics, Policymaking, Administration and Analysis of Emergency Management*. Springfield, IL: Charles C. Thomas.
Taylor, T. (2003) "Bringing 'complex terrorism' and 'corporate malfeasance' into a classification schema for disasters," *Australian Journal of Emergency Management* 18:7-9.
Taylor, V. (1978) "Future directions for study," Pp. 251-281 in Quarantelli, E. L. (ed.) *Disasters: Theory and Research*. Beverly Hills, CA.: Sage.
Tenner, E. (1997) *When Things Bite Back: Technology and the Revenge of Unintended Consequences*. NY: Knopf.
Thomas, D., Cutter, S. L., Hodgson, M., Gutekunst, M. and Jones, S. (2002) *Use of spatial data and geographic technologies in response to the September 11 terrorist attack*. Boulder, CO: Natural Hazards Research and Applications Information Center, University of Colorado.
Thomas, W. I. (1909) *Source Book for Social Origins: Ethnological Materials, Psychological Standpoint, Classified and Annotated Bibliographies for the Interpretation of Savage Culture*. Boston: Gorham Press.
Thomas, W.I.and Znaniecki, F. (1918) *The Polish peasant in Europe and America*. Chicago: University of Chicago Press.
Tierney, K. (1992) "Organizational features of U.S. lifeline systems and their relevance for disaster management," Pp. 423-436 in

Proceedings of the 4th US-Japan Workshop on Earthquake Disaster Prevention for Lifeline Systems. Washington, DC: Government Printing Office.

Tierney, K. (1994) *Business vulnerability and disruption: Data from the 1993 Midwest flood.* Newark, DE: Disaster Research Center, University of Delaware.

Tierney, K. (2002a) "The field turns fifty: Social change and the practice of disaster fieldwork," Pp. 349-375 in Stallings, R. (ed.) *Methods of Disaster Research.* Philadelphia, PA.: Xlibris Books.

Tierney, K. (2002b) *Strength of a city: A disaster research perspective on the World Trade Center.* NY: Social Science Research Council.

Tierney, K., Lindell, M., and Perry, R.W. (2001) *Facing the Unexpected: Disaster preparedness and Response in the United States.* Washington, DC: Joseph Henry Press.

Tiryakian, E. (1994) "The new worlds and sociology: An overview," *International Sociology* 9:131-148.

Toulmin, S. (1981) "The emergence of postmodern society," Pp. 68-114 in *Encyclopedia Britannica.* Chicago: University of Chicago Press.

Tourraine, A. (1994) *The Future of Social Movements.* Unpublished paper.

Turner, B. A. (1976) "The organizational and interorganizational development of disasters," *Administrative Science Quarterly*, 21: 378-397.

Turner, B.A. (1978) *Man-made Disasters.* London: Wykeham

Turner, B.A. and Pidgeon, N.F. (1997) *Manmade Disasters.* Oxford: Butterworth-Heinemann.

Turner, R., Nigg, J. and Heller-Paz, D. (1986) *Waiting for Disaster: Earthquake Watch in California.* Berkeley: University of California Press.

Twigg, J. (2002) *Corporate Social Responsibility and Disaster Reduction: Conclusions and Recommendations.* Unpublished paper.

Urry, J. (2003) *Global Complexity.* Cambridge: Polity Press.

U.S. Agency for International Development. (2002) "Status of HIV

epidemic in India, 1998, by state." http://www.usaid.gov/in/programareas/hiv_epidemic_in_india.htm.
U.S. Strategic Bombing Survey. (1947a) *The Effects of Strategic Bombing on German Morale*. Washington, DC: Government Printing Office.
U.S. Strategic Bombing Survey. (1947b) *The Effects of Strategic Bombing on Japanese Morale*. Washington, DC: Government Printing Office.
Valente, T. (1993a) "Diffusion of innovations and policy decision-making," *Journal of Communication* 43:30-45.
Valente, T. (1993b) *Network Models of the Diffusion of Innovation*. Cresskill, N.J.: Hampton Press.
Van Belle, D. (1999) "Race and U.S. foreign disaster aid," *International Journal of Mass Emergencies and Disasters* 17(3) 339-365.
Van Leeuwen, L. and Jewitt, C. (2001) *The Handbook of Visual Analysis*. Thousand Oaks, CA.: Sage.
Vatsayan, K. (1994) *Concepts of Space: Ancient and Modern*. Delhi: South Asia Books.
Vass, A. (2001) "AIDS now fourth biggest killer worldwide," *British Medical Journal*, 323: 1271.
Vidal, G. (2002) *Perpetual War for Perpetual Peace. How We Got To Be So Hated*. NY: Thunder's Press Books.
Vitaliano, D. B. (1973) *Legends of the Earth: Their Geologic Origins*. Bloomington: Indiana University Press.
Vogt, E. and O'Dea, T. (1953) "A comparative study of the role of values in social action in two southwestern communities," *American Sociological Review* 18: 645-654. von Bretzel, P. and Nagasawa, R. (1977) *Logic, Theory and Confirmation in Sociology*. Washington DC: University Press of America.
Vonnegut, K. (1968) *Slaughter-House Five or the Children's Crusade: A Duty-Dance with Death*. New York: Dell Publishing Company.
Walker, D. M. (2002) "9/11: the implications for public-sector management," *Public Administration Review*, 62: 94-97.
Walker, G. (2003) *Snowball Earth*. London: Bloomsbury.

Wallace, A. F. C. (1970) *The Death and Rebirth of the Seneca.* NY: Knopf.
Wallerstein, I. (1995) "Letter from the President, No.2," *International Sociological Association Newsletter.*
Warner, J. (2003) "Risk regime change and political entrepreneurship: river management in the Netherlands and Bangladesh," Pp. 185-198 in Pelling, M. (ed.) *Natural Disasters and Development in a Globalizing World.* London: Routledge.
Watzlawick, P. (1976) *Wie wirklich ist die Wirklichkeit?* München: Piper
Watts. D. (2003) *Six Degrees: The Science of a Connected Age.* NY: Norton.
Waugh, W.L. (2000) *Living with Hazards Dealing with Disasters: Introduction to Emergency Management.* NY: M E Sharpe.
Webb, E., Campbell, D. Schwartz, R. Sechrest, L. and Grove, J. (1981) *Nonreactive Measures in the Social Sciences.* Boston: Houghton Muffin.
Webb, G. and Quarantelli, E. L. (2004) *The Popular Culture of Disasters: Views from the Social Sciences and the Humanities and Histories.* Philadelphia, PA: Xlibris.
Webb, G., Wachtendorf, T. and Eyre, A. (2000) "Bringing culture back in: Exploring the cultural dimensions of disasters," *International Journal of Mass Emergencies and Disasters* 18: 5-19.
Weber, M. (1949) *The Methodology of the Social Sciences.* NY: The Free Press.
Weber, M. (1958) *The Protestant Ethic and the Spirit of Capitalism.* NY: Charles Scribner's Sons.
Weber, M. (1978) *Economy and Society: An Outline of Interpretative Sociology.* Berkeley: University of California Press.
Weick, K. E. (1988) "Enacted sensemaking in crisis situations," *Journal of Management Studies* 25: 305-317.
Weick, K. E. (1990) "The vulnerable system: An analysis of the Tenerife air disaster," *Journal of Management,* 16: 571-593.
Weick, K. E. (1993) "The collapse of sensemaking in organizations," *Administrative Science Quarterly,* 38: 628-652.

Weick, K. E. (1995) *Sensemaking in organizations.* Thousand Oaks: Sage.
Weick, K. E. (1998) "Foresights of failure: An appreciation of Barry Turner," *Journal of Contingencies and Crisis Management,* 6(2): 72-75.
Weick, K. E., and Sutcliffe, K. M. (2001) *Managing the unexpected. Assuring high performance in an age of complexity.* San Francisco, CA: Jossey-Bass.
Weiss, T. G. and Collins,C. (2000) *Humanitarian Challenges and Interventions.* Boulder, CO: Westview Press.
Wenger, D. and Quarantelli, E. L. (1989) *Local Mass Media Operations, Problems and Products in Disasters.* Newark, DE: University of Delaware Disaster Research Center.
Wengraf, T. (2001) *Qualitative Research Interviewing.* Thousand Oaks, CA.: Sage.
Westcoat, J., Chowdhury, J., Parker, D.H Khondker, H. James, L. and Pitman, K. (1992) "Five comments on the Bangladesh flood action plan," *Natural Hazards Observer* 16(4): 1-7.
White, G.F. (1974) *Natural Hazards: Local, National, Global.* NY. Oxford University Press.
White, G. F. (1988) "Paths to risk analysis," *Risk Analysis* 8: 171-175.
White, G. F., Kates, R. and Burton, I. (2001) "Knowing better and losing even more: The use of knowledge in hazards management," *Environmental Hazards* 3: 81-92.
Wildavsky, A. (1988) *Searching for Safety.* New Brunswick, NJ: Transaction Books.
Wisner, B. (2001) "Capitalism and the shifting spatial and social distribution of hazard and vulnerability," *Australian Journal of Emergency Management* Winter, Pp. 44-50.
Wisner, B. (2003) "Changes in capitalism and global shifts in the distribution of hazard and vulnerability," Pp. 43-56 in Pelling, M. (ed.) *Natural Disasters and Development in a Globalizing World.* London: Routledge.
Wohlstein, R. and McPhail, C. (1979) "Judging the presence and extent of collective behavior from film records," *Social Psychology Quarterly* 42: 76-81.

Wolfenstein, M. (1957) *Disaster: A Psychological Essay* Glencoe, IL: Free Press.

Yammarino, F. J., and Dansereau, F. (2002) *The Many Faces of Multi-level Issues.* Oxford: JAI (Elsevier Science Ltd).

Yukl, G. (2002) *Leadership in Organizations.* Upper Saddle River, NJ: Prentice-Hall.

Zebrowski E. (1997) *Perils of a Restless Planet: Scientific Perspectives on Natural Disasters.* Cambridge: Cambridge University Press.

Zerubavel, E. (1981) *Hidden Rhythms: Schedules and Calendars in Social Life.* Chicago: University of Chicago Press.

Zerubavel, E. (2003) *Time Maps: Collective Memory and the Social Shape of the Future.* Chicago: University of Chicago Press.

CPSIA information can be obtained
at www.ICGtesting.com
Printed in the USA
LVHW102226250123
737977LV00004B/53